O9-ABF-161

How the *Scots* Invented the Modern World

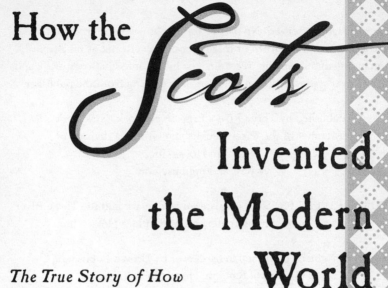

How the *Scots* Invented the Modern World

*The True Story of How
Western Europe's Poorest Nation
Created Our World & Everything in It*

Arthur Herman

 THREE RIVERS PRESS · NEW YORK

Copyright © 2001 by Arthur Herman

All rights reserved. No part of this book may be reproduced or
transmitted in any form or by any means, electronic or mechanical,
including photocopying, recording, or by any information storage and
retrieval system, without permission in writing from the publisher.

Published by Three Rivers Press, New York, New York.
Member of the Crown Publishing Group, a division of
Random House, Inc.
www.randomhouse.com

THREE RIVERS PRESS is a registered trademark and the Three Rivers
Press colophon is a trademark of Random House, Inc.

Originally published in hardcover by Crown Publishers,
a division of Random House, Inc., in 2001.

Printed in the United States of America

Design by Fearn Cutler de Vicq

Library of Congress Cataloging-in-Publication Data
Herman, Arthur, 1956–
How the Scots invented the Modern World: the true story of how
western Europe's poorest nation created our world and everything
in it / Arthur Herman.
1. Civilization, Modern—Scottish influences.   2. National
characteristics, Scottish.   3. Scotland—Civilization.   4. Scots. I. Title.
DA772.H53 2001
941.1—dc21 2001028951

ISBN 0-609-80999-7

1 0 9 8 7 6 5

FIRST PAPERBACK EDITION

Contents

Preface

People of Scottish descent are usually proud about their history and achievements. Yet even they know only the half of it.

They can recite many names and details in the familiar story of their people. "Braveheart" William Wallace and Robert the Bruce; the Arbroath Declaration and Mary Queen of Scots; Robert Burns and Bonnie Prince Charlie. They point out how James Watt invented the steam engine, John Boyd Dunlop the bicycle tire, and Alexander Fleming penicillin. Yet no one else seems to pay much attention. Scots often complain that Scotland's place among nations deserves more exposure than it gets. But their complaints have an ironic, rather than a beseeching, tone. They seem to take a perverse pride in being so consistently underestimated.

The point of this book is that being Scottish is more than just a matter of nationality or place of origin or clan or even culture. It is also a state of mind, a way of viewing the world and our place in it. This Scottish mentality was a deliberate creation, athough it was conceived by many minds and carried out by many hands. It is a self-consciously modern view, so deeply rooted in the assumptions and institutions that govern our lives today that we often miss its significance, not to mention its origin. From this point of view, a large part of the world turns out to be "Scottish" without realizing it. It is time to let them in on the secret.

This is the story of how the Scots created the basic ideals of modernity. It will show how those ideals transformed their own culture and society in the eighteenth century, and how Scots carried them with them wherever they went. Obviously, the Scots did not do everything by themselves; other nations—Germans, French, English, Italians, Russians, many others—supplied bricks and mortar for building the modern world. But it is the Scots who drew up the blueprints and taught us how to judge the final product. When we gaze out on a contemporary world shaped by technology, capitalism, and modern democracy, and struggle to find our own place in it, we are in effect viewing the world through the same lens as the Scots did.

Such an understanding did not come easily. Sir Walter Scott said, "I am a Scotsman; therefore I had to fight my way into the world." The history of Scotland in the eighteenth and nineteenth centuries is one of hard-earned triumph and heartrending tragedy, spilled blood and ruined lives as well as great achievements. In 1700 Scotland was Europe's poorest independent country (Ireland, after all, was governed by Englishmen, and Portugal still owned Brazil). Yet the story of how this small, underpopulated (fewer than two million people as late as 1800), and culturally backward nation rose to become the driving wheel of modern progress is not only largely unknown, it may even be inspiring.

For if you want a monument to the Scots, look around you.

Prologue

The Tron Church stands on Edinburgh's High Street, almost at the midpoint of the Royal Mile, which rises to Edinburgh Castle at one end and slopes down to Holyrood Palace at the other. In 1696 the Tron Church was in many ways a monument to the strength and success of Scottish Presbyterianism, or as the Scots themselves call it, the Kirk. In 1633 the Edinburgh Town Council had decided they needed a new place of worship near the "tron," or public scales, where merchants and officials established the true weight and measure of commodities sold in the city markets. It would be designed as a specifically Presbyterian church. Unlike the larger St. Giles Cathedral, or the former monastery site of Greyfriars Church off Candlemakers Row, it carried no taint of association with Scotland's Roman Catholic past. Nor would it be under the sway of the new Bishop of Edinburgh, appointed by King Charles I to thrust a foreign Anglican creed down the people's throats.

Construction got under way in 1637. Then, the next winter, High Street was filled with the sound of drums and psalm-singing crowds, as citizens flocked to sign a National Covenant to take up arms against King Charles. The Covenanters took over the city in defiance of their English oppressors. The Tron Church sat unfinished while the Scots routed Charles's army in the Bishops' War. It withstood the siege of Edinburgh by Oliver Cromwell's troops in 1652. It was still unfinished when Charles I's son, Charles II, sailed across the English Channel to be restored to his throne in 1660. Not until 1678 did builders finally complete its unpretentious steeple, "an old Dutch thing composed of

❖ 1

wood and iron and lead edged all the way up with bits of ornament,"
and set Edinburgh's coat of arms above the doorway, with this inscrip-
tion in Latin:

THE CITIZENS OF EDINBURGH DEDICATE
THIS BUILDING TO CHRIST AND HIS CHURCH.

Edinburgh's tron served the community in another way, as the town
pillory, where the courts sentenced transgressors to be bound and punished. "Much falset and cheiting was daillie deteckit at this time by the
Lords of Session," wrote one diarist in 1679. He continued with relish,
"there was daillie nailing of lugs and binding of people to the Tron, and
boring of tongues; so that it was a fatal year for false notaries and witnesses, as daillie experience did witness."

Sixteen hundred ninety-six would be a fatal year for another kind of
transgressor. August had been a cold month, in fact it had been raining
and freezing all summer. As the Tron Church struck eight o'clock, four
young men were hurrying past, huddled against the cold. One was John
Neilson, law clerk in the Court of Session, aged nineteen; the next
Patrick Midletoyne or Middleton, aged twenty, a student at the College
of Edinburgh. With them were Thomas Aikenhead, almost nineteen, a
theology student, and John Potter, also a university student at the tender age of thirteen. We do not know for certain, but they may have been
coming from Cleriheugh's Tavern, a favorite neighborhood haunt for
students, law clerks, and members of the legal profession.

As they passed the church, Aikenhead shivered from the cold wind
blustering around them. He turned and remarked to the others, "I wish
right now I were in the place Ezra called hell, to warm myself there."
Again, it is not known whether any of the other lads laughed at his little joke. But the next day one of them, or another of their circle,
informed the kirk authorities of what Aikenhead had said.

Aikenhead's joke turned out to be no laughing matter. Other students revealed that, in between theology classes, Thomas Aikenhead had
been systematically ridiculing the Christian faith. He had told astonished listeners that the Bible was not in fact the literal Word of God but

the invention of the prophet Ezra—"Ezra's romances," as he called it. He asserted that Jesus had performed no actual miracles, that the raising of Lazarus and curing the blind had all been cheap magic tricks to hoodwink the Apostles, whom he called "a company of silly witless fishermen." He said the story of Christ's Resurrection was a myth, as was the doctrine of Redemption. As for the Old Testament, Aikenhead had said that if Moses had actually existed at all, he had been a better politician and better magician than Jesus (all those plagues of frogs and burning staffs and bushes and so forth), while the founder of Islam, Mohammed, had been better than either.

All this would have been horrifying and insulting for a believing Presbyterian to listen to, but Aikenhead had expounded larger issues as well. He claimed that God, nature, and the world were one, and had existed since eternity. Aikenhead had opened the door to a kind of pantheism; in other words, the Genesis notion of a divine Creator, who stood outside nature and time, was a myth.

Maybe Aikenhead had been bored. Maybe the theology student was merely showing off his ability to play fast and loose with issues that others treated with reverential care. The stunned silence and dumbfounded looks of his listeners must have been very gratifying to a young man who, at the ripe old age of eighteen, believed he knew it all. But the authorities were not amused. The truly damning evidence against Aikenhead came from his friend Mungo Craig, aged twenty-one, who said that he had heard Aikenhead say that Jesus Christ Himself was an impostor. When the Lord Advocate, the Scottish equivalent of attorney general, heard this, he decided that Aikenhead's remarks constituted blasphemy as defined by an act of Parliament in 1695, which decreed that a person "not distracted in his wits" who railed or cursed against God or persons of the Trinity was to be punished with death.

Scotland's legal system operated very differently from the system in England. All power of criminal prosecution rested in the hands of one man, the Lord Advocate. He had full powers to prosecute any case he chose. He could imprison anyone without issuing cause, or decide to drop a case even in the teeth of the evidence, or pursue it even when the local magistrate deemed it not worth the effort. Lord Advocate

James Stewart was learned in the law, heir to a landed fortune, and a keen member of the Scottish Presbyterian Church. He also knew that the Kirk was deeply concerned about the wave of new religious thinking coming up from the south, from England, which its enemies called "latitudinarianism."

Latitudinarians were "big-tent" Anglicans. The name came from the supposedly wide latitude they were willing to give to unorthodox religious opinions that a more tradition-bound Protestant might see as lax or even blasphemous. They believed Christianity should be a religion of tolerance and "reasonableness" rather than rigid dogma. Although they were deeply despised in Scotland, the Latitudinarians had become quite powerful in the Church of England. Several were now bishops; one, John Tillotson, was even Archbishop of Canterbury. Tillotson and the other "Latitude men" were also closely wired into the new scientific ideas sweeping across seventeenth-century Europe. They were keen admirers of England's two most famous scientists, the chemist Robert Boyle and the mathematician Isaac Newton, and saw no conflict between religious belief and rational scientific inquiry into the nature of man and the world. To a Scottish Presbyterian of the old school, Latitudinarianism was little different from atheism. And in Aikenhead's jocose remarks, Lord Advocate Stewart sensed more than a whiff of both.

Stewart had a formidable battery of laws with which to prosecute the case. In 1695 the General Assembly of the Reformed Church had recommended that ministers apply directly to civil magistrates for punishing cases of blasphemy and profanity. Scotland's Parliament had then obliged by stiffening the old blasphemy statute with a "three strikes and you're out" provision, in which after the third offense the unrepentant sinner could be put to death "as an obstinate blasphemer."

Now, Aikenhead was no third-time offender. This was the first time he had been up before the magistrate, and by law that was punishable only by imprisonment and public penance. But if it could be proved that he had "railed and cursed" against God and the Trinity, then he came under the special death-penalty provision. This is what Lord Advocate James Stewart decided Craig's testimony established, and so when he ordered Aikenhead's arrest on November 10, 1696, he fully intended to see him on the gallows.

Aikenhead was taken to a cell in Edinburgh's municipal prison, the Tollbooth. He realized at once that he was in a very serious position. At first he strenuously denied he had ever said such things. But when presented with the depositions, he claimed that if he did say them, he was just repeating doctrines he had read in some books (he did not specify which) that he had been given by another student—ironically, the chief witness against him, Mungo Craig. He instantly regretted everything. He did not only "from my very heart abhorre and detest" the words he had uttered, he wrote to the court, "but I do tremble" at the very sound of hearing them read aloud again. He stressed his sincere belief in the Trinity, in Jesus Christ as Savior, and in the truth of Scripture. As a native of Edinburgh, it was "my greatest happiness that I was born and educated in a place where the gospel was professed, and so powerfully and plentifully preached." Thomas asked that his case be set aside, pleading his repentance and his extreme youth. But he was now in the grip of larger forces.

The trial got under way, with Lord Advocate Stewart himself conducting the prosecution. There was no defense counsel.

A Scottish jury had three options, not two, in offering a verdict, just as it does today. They are "guilty," "not guilty," and "not proven," which jurors invoke when they decide the prosecution has failed to make a compelling case even when the prisoner is obviously guilty. Such a verdict might have enabled Aikenhead to escape the extreme penalty Stewart was demanding. But, confronted with the evidence absent a formal rebuttal, and with a prosecutor determined to make a public example of the boy, the jury found Aikenhead guilty of blasphemy.

On December 23, Stewart asked for the death penalty. "It is of verity, that you Thomas Aikenhead, shaking off all fear of God and regard to his majesties laws, have now for more than a twelvemonth . . . made it as it were your endeavor and work to vent your wicked blasphemies against God and our Savior Jesus Christ." Having been found guilty, Stewart added, "you ought to be punished with death, and the confiscation of your movables, to the example and terror of others." The sentence was duly pronounced, and Aikenhead was condemned to hang on January 8 of the new year.

By now the case was acquiring some notoriety. Two of Scotland's leading jurists, Lord Anstruther and Lord Fountainhall, visited the boy in prison. They were disturbed by what they heard and saw. They found Aikenhead in tears and near despair. He told them he repented that he had ever held such beliefs, and asked for a stay of execution, "for his eternal state depended on it." Anstruther in particular had his doubts about using a secular court to prosecute a case of blasphemy. "I am not for consulting the church in state affairs," he wrote to a friend. The purpose of the courts, and of capital punishment, Anstruther said, was to punish crimes that disturb society and government, rather than sins against God. The law normally paid no attention to questions of cursing, lying, and drunkenness, and correctly so. "But," he confessed, "our ministers generally are of a narrow set of thoughts and confined principles and not able to bear things of this nature."

One of those who certainly could not was Thomas Hallyburton, later Professor of Divinity at the University of St. Andrews. His argument against Aikenhead was straightforward and brooked no opposition. God makes the laws, not man, and they must be obeyed. "We by our very beings," he argued, "are bound to obey, submit, and subject ourselves to his will and pleasure who made us . . . and therefore his will, if he make it known," as in scripture and the Gospels, "is a law, and the highest law to us." Aikenhead, "this inconsiderable trifler," had broken that law and so he had to be punished. Hallyburton's attitude was, let him serve as an example to anyone who tries the same thing.

A battle was shaping up between two different views of the proper relations between the civil and the religious law, with hard-liners like Hallyburton on one side and more secular-minded lawyers like Anstruther on the other. Someone who took an obvious interest in this, and in the Aikenhead case generally, was the Englishman John Locke. Locke was nearing the end of his career as a political writer and theorist, but his most recent work touched directly on these issues. This was *A Letter Concerning Toleration,* published in October 1689, which took the exact opposite approach to Hallyburton's. "The care of Souls cannot belong to the Civil Magistrate," Locke had written, "because his Power consists only in outward force; but true and saving Religion consists in the inward persuasion of the Mind, without which nothing can be acceptable to God."

Locke's point was that it did not matter whether Aikenhead had broken God's laws by saying that the Apostles were "witless fisherman" or Jesus was an impostor, or not. Religious belief was a matter of private conscience, and no public authority has the right to interfere in how it is exercised. It was a view closely allied with that of the Latitudinarians: "I esteem Toleration to be the chief Characteristical Mark of the True Church," Locke said. It also overlapped with Anstruther's. Civil power was limited to "Civil Concernments," as Locke put it, which by their nature excluded religious matters. Locke's arguments, which form the basis of our modern idea of the separation of church and state, were beginning to have an impact in England, as the Act of Toleration of 1689 showed. But in Scotland, where witches were still being prosecuted in the courts and hanged (two would be executed that next year), as in Massachusetts (the infamous Salem witch trial had taken place in 1692), a different attitude prevailed.

Another Scottish lawyer who was sympathetic to Aikenhead's cause, James Johnstone, kept Locke informed of the trial, including copies of the indictment, the student depositions, and Aikenhead's appeal. Johnstone pointed out that all the witnesses against Aikenhead were barely out of their teens, and that "none of them pretend, nor is it laid in the Indictment, that Aikenhead made it his business to seduce any man." He noted, "Laws long in desuetude should be gently put in Execution, and the first example made of one in circumstances that deserve no compassion, whereas here there is youth, levity, docility, and no design upon others."

Meanwhile, Aikenhead had petitioned Scotland's leading judicial officer, the Lord Chancellor, and its governing body of royal officials, the Scottish Privy Council, for mercy. He restated his regrets and his desire to repent. "May it therefore please your Lordships," he wrote, "for God's sake, to consider and compassionate my deplorable circumstances." Anstruther also stepped forward as the boy's advocate, pleading mercy and saying that in his opinion Aikenhead would grow up to be an eminent Christian if his life was spared. But the Privy Council told him there was no chance of mercy unless the Kirk interceded for him. This it would not do. Instead, as Anstruther wrote, "the ministers out of a pious and ignorant zeal spoke and preached for cutting him off."

When the final vote came in the Privy Council on Aikenhead's appeal, it was a tie. Then Lord Chancellor Polwarth cast the deciding vote for death.

Only one possible source of rescue remained, and that was in London. The English Parliament and the Privy Council were of course powerless to do anything; this was Scotland and out of their jurisdiction. If, however, King William and Queen Mary, who resided at Whitehall Palace but who were also rulers of Scotland, got wind of the case, they could use their power to issue a pardon or at least a reprieve. This is what the Kirk now had to forestall. They sent a petition to William and Mary: "We cannot but lament the abounding impiety and profanity in this land, so we must acknowledge your Majesty's Christian care in enacting good laws for suppressing the same, the rigorous execution of which we humbly beg."

Execution was right. On January 8, the Year of Our Lord 1697, at two o'clock in the afternoon, Thomas Aikenhead was taken to the gallows on the road between Edinburgh and Leith. Shivering in the cold wind, he delivered a final speech, the condemned man's right by custom. "I can charge the world, if they can stain me, or lay any such thing on my charge, so that it was out of a pure love of truth, and my own happiness, that I acted," he declared in a wavering voice. "It is a principle innate and co-natural to every man to have an insatiable inclination to truth," he added, and to follow reason where it leads. This he had done, and now it would cost him his life.

He then blasted the chief witness against him, Mungo Craig, "whom I have to reckon with God and his own conscience, if he was not as deeply concerned in those hellish notions (for which I am sentenced) as ever I was." But then he forgave Craig, as he forgave all concerned in the trial, and wished that the Lord might forgive Craig likewise.

He then uttered his last wish: "It is my earnest desire that my blood may give a stop to that raging spirit of Atheism which hath taken such footing in Britain. . . . And now, O Lord, Father, Son, and Holy Ghost, in thy hands I recommend my spirit." The hangman pulled away the ladder, the body swung, and Thomas Aikenhead, not quite nineteen, was dead.

Such was Scotland as it stood at the end of the seventeenth century. A nation governed by a harshly repressive Kirk; a nation of an unforgiving and sometimes cruel Calvinist religious faith; of trials for blasphemy and witchcraft; of a cranky, even perverse contrariness in the face of an appeal to mercy or reason or even the facts.

This was Scotland on the threshold of the modern world. Yet it would be misleading to call it "traditional Scotland." It was in fact of relatively recent vintage. The men who persecuted Thomas Aikenhead belonged to a cultural world that had come into being a little more than one hundred years before, with the Scottish Reformation.

To men such as the Reverend Thomas Hallyburton or Lord Advocate Stewart, the religious revolution John Knox had brought to Scotland in the sixteenth century had left a legacy of glory, but also of great bitterness. The True Faith had triumphed over Popery and corruption. But it had cost a century of almost uninterrupted violence and bloodshed, with Scotland torn apart by anarchy, civil war, foreign invasions, religious persecution, and repression. Throughout it all, the Scottish Kirk had had to fight a relentless battle against established political power. Securing the Presbyterian faith had led to the overthrow of one monarch (Mary Queen of Scots), rebellion against and then execution of another (Charles I), and the forcible removal of a third (James II).

In 1696, memories of the struggle were still fresh. Scots gave the years of the Restoration, the 1660s and 1670s, a sardonic nickname: "the Killing Time." In England, King Charles II is remembered as an easygoing, amiable rogue. In Scotland, however, his government used brutal armed force to stamp out the remnants of the National Covenant movement, which had rebelled against his father. Many of the

Presbyterian ministers who asked William and Mary not to save Thomas Aikenhead could tell of having to go into hiding for their faith, pursued like animals across mountains and glens, and watching friends and neighbors murdered or transported into servitude across the Atlantic.

Aikenhead's prosecutor, James Stewart, had been forced to flee for his life abroad. Patrick Hume, Baron of Polwarth, who had cast the decisive vote for death, was no decadent bewigged Restoration aristocrat. He knew what it was to be a hunted man. When several prominent opponents of Charles II were arrested for plotting against his life (the so-called Rye House Plot of 1683), Hume, although not directly implicated, had been forced to hide in the family burial vault in the parish church in Polwarth. For one month he had remained there, surviving on food smuggled in by loyal servants, with no light except through a narrow slit in the stone. By that tiny beam he had read and reread a Latin translation of the Psalms to keep his spirits up, so that, at age eighty, he could still recite them by heart.

Having received no mercy themselves, how likely was it that they would extend it to the likes of young Aikenhead the blasphemer?

Yet in 1696 this old order was already on its last legs. The execution of Aikenhead was the last hurrah of Scotland's Calvinist ayatollahs. There was already a new generation on the rise of ministers and university professors and lawyers like Anstruther and Johnstone, who were not immune to the more progressive attitudes percolating up from the south. Then in 1701 James Stewart himself pushed through Parliament an important legal reform, an act of habeas corpus that limited the Lord Advocate's power of arbitrary arrest and imprisonment.

There were other, more ominous changes in the offing. On the same day Aikenhead was executed, January 8, the Edinburgh city fathers asked the Scottish Privy Council to make provision for the multitudes of poor and indigent people begging in the streets "in this great dearth and time of scarcity." The traditional economy of Scotland was dying, under the hammer blows of harvest failures and famine. Beginning in 1695, Scots suffered three failed harvests in a row. Two hundred years later a historian described what happened:

The crops were blighted by easterly "haars" or mists, by sunless, drenching summers, by storms, and by early bitter frosts and late snow in autumn. For seven years this calamitous weather continued—the corn rarely ripening, and the green, withered grain being shorn in December amidst pouring rain or pelting snow-storms . . . The sheep and oxen died in the thousands, the prices of everything among a peasantry that had nothing went up to famine pitch, and a large proportion of the population in rural districts was destroyed by disease and want.

No one knows how many died during the famine of the Lean Years of 1697–1703, but they probably numbered in the tens of thousands. Wrote Sir Robert Sibbald at the time, "Everyone may see Death in the Face of the poor." For an already impoverished and sparsely populated country of fewer than two million souls, the 1690s set a benchmark of collective misery and misfortune Scots never approached again, not even in the worst years of the Highland Clearances.

The new century, then, marked the end of one way of life for Scotland and the beginning of another, simply because there was nowhere else to go. For the next generation of Lowlands Scots, the world of their fathers—of Covenanters, of the Killing Time, of famine and starvation, of pillories at the Tron, of the execution of witches and of Thomas Aikenhead—would become more and more a remote memory.

For this was the culturally and materially backward nation that forward-thinking Scotsmen worked to change. In doing so, they would also change the world. Before the eighteenth century was over, Scotland would generate the basic institutions, ideas, attitudes, and habits of mind that characterize the modern age. Scotland and the Scots would go on to blaze a trail across the global landscape in both a literal and a figurative sense, and open a new era in human history. In fact, the very notion of "human history" is itself, as we shall see, a largely Scottish invention.

Fundamental to the Scottish notion of history is the idea of progress. The Scots argued that societies, like individuals, grow and improve over time. They acquire new skills, new attitudes, and a new understanding of what individuals can do and what they should be free to do. The Scots would teach the world that one of the crucial ways we measure progress is by how far we have come from what we were before. The present judges the past, not the other way around. And for the modern Scot, for Adam Smith or David Hume or Henry Brougham or Sir Walter Scott or any of the other heroes of this book, that past was the Scotland that had tried and executed Thomas Aikenhead.

Yet that same fundamentalist Calvinist Kirk had actually laid the foundations for modern Scotland, in surprising and striking ways. In fact, without an appreciation of Scotland's Presbyterian legacy, the story of the Scots' place in modern civilization would be incomplete.

PART ONE

Epiphany

Is it not strange that at a time when we have lost our Princes, our Parliaments, our independent government, even the Presence of our chief Nobility, are unhappy in our accent and pronunciation, speak a very corrupt Dialect of the Tongue which we make use of, is it not strange, I say, that in these Circumstances, we shou'd really be the People most distinguished for Literature in Europe?

—*David Hume, 1757*

The constant influx of information and of liberality from abroad, which was thus kept up in Scotland in consequence of the ancient habits and manners of the people, may help to account for the sudden burst of genius, which to a foreigner must seem have sprung up in this country by a sort of enchantment, soon after the Rebellion of 1745.

—*Dugald Stewart*

CHAPTER ONE

The New Jerusalem

I

 Just as the German Reformation was largely the work of a single individual, Martin Luther, so the Scottish Reformation was the achievement of one man of heroic will and tireless energy: John Knox.

Like Luther, Knox left an indelible mark on his national culture. Uncompromising, dogmatic, and driven, John Knox was a prolific writer and a preacher of truly terrifying power. His early years as a Protestant firebrand had been spent in exile, imprisonment, and even penal servitude chained to a rowing bench in the king's galleys. The harsh trials toughened him physically and spiritually for what was to come. He became John Knox, "he who feared the face of no man." Beginning in 1559, Knox single-handedly inspired, intimidated, and bullied Scotland's nobility and urban classes into overthrowing the Catholic Church of their forebears and adopting the religious creed of Geneva's John Calvin. Its austere and harsh dogmas—that the Bible was the literal Word of God, that the God of that Bible was a stern and jealous God, filled with wrath at all sinners and blasphemers, and that the individual soul was by God's grace predestined to heaven or hell regardless of any good works or charitable intentions—were themselves natural extensions of Knox's own personality. Calvinism seemed as natural to him as breathing, and he taught a generation of Scotsmen to believe the same thing themselves.

Above all, John Knox wanted to turn the Scots into God's chosen people, and Scotland into the New Jerusalem. To do this, Knox was willing to sweep away everything about Scotland's past that linked it to the Catholic Church. As one admirer said, "Others snipped at the branches of Popery; but he strikes at the roots, to destroy the whole." He and his followers scoured away not only Scottish Catholicism but all its physical manifestations, from monasteries and bishops and clerical vestments to holy relics and market-square crosses. They smashed stained-glass windows and saints' statues, ripped out choir stalls and roodscreens, and overturned altars. All these symbols of a centuries-old tradition of religious culture, which we would call great works of art, were for Knox marks of "idolatry" and "the synagogue of Satan," as he called the Roman Catholic Church. In any case, the idols disappeared from southern Scotland, and the Scottish Kirk rose up to take their place.

Knox and his lieutenants also imposed the new rules of the Calvinist Sabbath on Scottish society: no working (people could be arrested for plucking a chicken on Sunday), no dancing, and no playing of the pipes. Gambling, cardplaying, and the theater were banned. No one could move out of a parish without written permission of the minister. The Kirk wiped out all traditional forms of collective fun, such as Carnival, Maytime celebrations, mumming, and Passion plays. Fornication brought punishment and exile; adultery meant death. The church courts, or kirk-sessions, enforced the law with scourges, pillories, branks (a padlocked iron helmet that forced an iron plate into the mouth of a convicted liar or blasphemer), ducking-stools, banishment, and, in the case of witches or those possessed by the devil, burning at the stake.

The faithful received one single compensation for this harsh author-itarian regime, and it was a powerful one: direct access to God. The right of communion, receiving the body and blood of Christ in the form of wine and bread, now belonged to everyone, rich and poor, young and old, men and women. In the Catholic Church, the Bible had been liter-ally a closed book. Now anyone who could read, or listen to someone else read, could absorb the Word of God. On Sundays the church rafters rang with the singing of psalms and recitations from the Gospel. The Lord's Supper became a community festival, with quantities, sometimes plentiful, of red wine and shortcake (John Knox presided over one

Sunday communion where the congregation consumed eight and a half gallons of claret).

The congregation was the center of everything. It elected its own board of elders or presbyters; it even chose its minister. The congregation's board of elders, the consistory, cared for the poor and the sick; it fed and clothed the community's orphans. Girls who were too poor to have a dowry to tempt a prospective husband got one from the consistory. It was more than just fear of the ducking-stool or the stake that bound the Kirk together. It was a community united by its commitment to God and its sense of chosenness. "God loveth us," John Knox had written, "because we are His own handiwork."

To a large extent Knox's mission to create the New Jerusalem in Scotland succeeded. The Reformation laid down strong roots in the Scottish Lowlands, that belt of fertile land and river valleys running from the Firth of Clyde and Glasgow in the extreme west to just north of Carlisle and Hadrian's Wall across to Edinburgh and Berwick-on-Tweed in the east. North of this in the beautiful but barren and sparsely populated Highlands, its record was more spotty. But in all the areas that came under his influence, the Kirk created a new society in the image of Knox's utopian ideal. It had turned its back not only on Scotland's past, but on all purely secular values, no matter what the source. Knox made his view clear in one of his last letters before he died in November 1572. "All worldlie strength, yea even in things spiritual, decays, and yet shall never the work of God decay."

One of those pillars of "worldlie strength" that Knox despised was political authority, or more precisely the power of monarchs. Perhaps because Knox's closest allies were Scottish nobles who wanted to see the Scottish monarchy tamed, or because nearly every monarch he dealt with was either a child or a woman (the boy king Edward VI of England, Mary Queen of Scots, the Scottish Regent Mary of Guise, and English queens Mary Tudor and Elizabeth I), he treated them all with impatience and contempt. Yet neither Mary of Guise nor Mary Queen of Scots could do without him. Even though they were Catholics, Knox represented a spiritual authority they needed to legitimize their own. When Queen Mary announced her plans to marry her worthless cousin

Lord Darnley, Knox gave her such a fierce public scolding that she burst into tears in full view of her court. She made the mistake of marrying Darnley anyway, and set in motion the series of scandals that would finally push her off the throne. By 1570, Knox recognized that Mary no longer had any part to play in making the New Jerusalem and he swept her aside, like a useless piece from the game board. Her infant son James VI was installed in her place, with George Buchanan, Scotland's leading humanist, as his tutor, so that the boy could be raised in the Presbyterian faith.

Knox and Buchanan believed that political power was ordained by God, but that that power was vested not in kings or in nobles or even in the clergy, but in the people. The Presbyterian covenant with God required them to defend that power against any interloper. Punishing idolatry and destroying tyranny was a sacred duty laid by God on "the whole body of the people," Knox wrote, "and of every man in his vocation."

Here was a vision of politics unlike any other at the time. George Buchanan turned it into a full-fledged doctrine of popular sovereignty, the first in Europe. Buchanan came from Stirlingshire in central Scotland, at a time when it was still much like the Highlands in its culture and character—in fact, Buchanan grew up speaking both Gaelic and Scots. He studied at the University of St. Andrews and then at the University of Paris alongside other future giants of the Reformation such as John Calvin and Ignatius Loyola, the later founder of the Jesuits. As a Greek and Latin scholar, Buchanan had few peers. But he was also a founding father of Scottish Presbyterianism: he served as Moderator of the Kirk's General Assembly—the only layman ever to do so—and helped write the Kirk's First Book of Discipline. His greatest achievement, however, was his book on the nature of political authority, titled *The Law of Government Among the Scots,* published in 1579.

In it Buchanan asserted that all political authority ultimately belonged to the people, who came together to elect someone, whether a king or a body of magistrates, to manage their affairs. The people were always more powerful than the rulers they created; they were free to remove them at will. "The people," he explained, "have the right to confer the royal authority upon whomever they wish." This is the sort of view we are used to ascribing to John Locke; in fact, it belongs to a Presbyterian Scot from Stirlingshire writing more than a hundred years earlier. And Buchanan went further. When the ruler or rulers failed to act in the people's interest, Buchanan wrote, then each and every citizen, even "the lowest and meanest of men," had the sacred right and duty to resist that tyrant, even to the point of killing him.

Here was a powerful formula for democracy: government of the people and for the people. In the crude circumstances of the late sixteenth century, however, it was also an invitation to anarchy. That was what Scotland got for nearly two decades after Knox's death, until Mary's son, James VI, overturned his old tutor's theories and reasserted the power of the monarchy. The dream of the people as sovereign died. But it would leave its trace within the church itself, in the system of synods peculiar to every parish and province in Scotland. It was the single most democratic system of church government in Europe. Even the minister was chosen by the congregation's consistory of elected elders, instead of by some powerful aristocrat or laird. The elders also sent deputations to their local synod, who in turn sent representatives to the Kirk's General Assembly. This meant that the members of the Kirk's governing body really were representatives of the people, in addition to being enforcers of godly discipline and propagators of the Word of God.

Not surprisingly, a self-governing Kirk coexisted uneasily with monarchs such as the Stuarts, who claimed to rule by divine right. To the Presbyterian, it was still God and His people, not kings, who ruled. Preacher Andrew Melville once even told James VI that Scotland was two realms, not one, and that James as king of the first was also a subject of the second, which belonged to Jesus Christ. During his almost fifty-year reign, James VI (who after the death of Elizabeth Tudor in 1603 also became King James I of England) had the good sense not to force the issue. His son Charles I did not. When Charles finally did try to break the Presbyterian Church to his will, including forcing it to accept the Anglican Book of Common Prayer in its church services, he set off this explosive democratic mixture.

On Sunday, July 23, 1637, the dean of St. Giles in Edinburgh opened his morning service with the new royal prayer book, as King Charles had ordered. As soon as he started, women in the congregation began to shout insults; others threw stools and with loud protests stormed out of the church. The riots that followed over the next several months forced the Bishop of Edinburgh to flee for his life. Inspired by the resistance, ministers, nobles, and ordinary citizens gathered on the last week of February of 1638 to sign a National Convenant.

The National Covenant was more than just a petition or a declaration of faith. It was the Presbyterian version of democracy in action. In the name of true religion, it challenged the king's prerogative to make law without consent, and affirmed that the Scottish people would oppose any change not approved by a free General Assembly and Parliament. Those who signed swore to uphold the faith John Knox had founded, and that "we shall defend the same . . . to the utmost of that power that God hath put into our hands, all the days of our lives."

Bands of signatories carried copies from Edinburgh to neighboring towns and then the rest of the country. Thousands flocked to sign, both men and women, young and old, rich and poor. Ministers led their congregations to sign en masse. "I have seen more than a thousand all at once lifting up their hands," wrote one, "and the tears falling down from their eyes." In the southwest, some were said to have signed the Covenant in their own blood.

By the end of May, the only parts of Scotland that had not signed were the remote western Highlands, the islands north of Argyll, and the shires of Aberdeen and Banff, where the king's most resolute aristocratic supporters, the Gordons, held the balance of political power. The covenanting drive even spread to the Scottish settlements in Ulster, where hundreds signed despite the desperate efforts of royal officials to stop them.

In November the General Assembly in Glasgow declared war on "the kingdom of Satan and Antichrist," meaning Charles and his bishops. The Scots had forced on Charles a war he neither wanted nor could afford. Thousands of volunteers flocked into the Covenanters' army, armed in many cases with little more than hoes and scythes. Yet they managed to best Charles's invading mercenaries and compelled him to sue for peace. The Bishops' War (there were actually two, the second following a brief truce that ended the first) revealed the flimsiness of Stuart rule, and encouraged the Parliament in London to defy Charles in turn. A civil war ensued, which culminated in the king's execution in 1649 and the emergence of Oliver Cromwell as Lord Protector. The English Civil War would destroy forever the façade of absolute monarchy in Britain. A new political ideal, that of government with the consent of the governed, had arrived. But it took its original impulse from the Scottish Covenanters.

Yet we should remember that the Covenanters were inspired less by their love of democracy than by their hatred of Satan. As with the rules of the Kirk, choice never entered into the matter. Those who failed to sign were often thrown into the public pillory or forced to leave town. The men and women who drove the Covenant forward were religious zealots, prepared to destroy anyone—king, bishop, or halfhearted neighbor—who stood in their way. The things we associate with a democratic society today—the free exchange of ideas, freedom to express one's own thoughts and opinions, a belief in tolerance and rational restraint—meant nothing to them.

Yet that same fanaticism had two faces. On one side, as the Aikenhead case would later show, it was the enemy of individual liberty and thought. For that reason, later Scots of the Enlightenment despised it, and singled it out as the single greatest threat to a free society— much as intellectuals despise and fear the so-called religious right today. But on the other side, it was also the enemy of public tyranny. It empowered individuals to defy authority when it crossed a certain line. David Hume, who himself suffered from persecution by the Kirk, saw this quality in the Covenanters of 1638. The religion of John Knox "consecrated . . . every individual," he explained to readers in 1757, "and, in his own eyes, bestowed a character on him much superior to what forms and ceremonious institutions could alone confer."

The effect of this egalitarian democratic spirit on Scottish culture would be profound and long-lasting. When Englishman Gilbert Burnet visited western Scotland in the 1660s, he had never seen anything like it. "We were indeed amazed to see a poor commonalty so capable to argue upon points of government, and on the bounds to be set to the power of princes," he wrote afterwards. "Upon all these topics they had texts of scripture at hand; and were ready with their answers to anything that was said to them." Burnet also added, "This measure of knowledge was spread even amongst the meanest of them, their cottagers and servants."

Robert Burns framed it more memorably: "a man's a man for a' that." To the Scot, appearance and outward form mean little. Instead, it is the quality of one's inner self—one's religious zeal, as in the case of the Covenanters, or one's moral and intellectual integrity—that separates the extraordinary man from the ordinary one. Even in Burns, the religious skeptic and radical, we can still hear the Covenanters speaking across the centuries.

> *What though on hamely fare we dine,*
> *Wear hodden-gray, an' a' that;*
> *Gie fools their silks, and knaves their wine,*
> *A man's a man for a' that.*
> *For a' that, an a' that,*
> *Their tinsel show, an' a' that;*
> *The honest man, though e'er sae poor,*
> *Is king o' men for a' that.*

Burns also understood how important education can be in shaping the character of the inner self. And here, too, Scottish Presbyterianism managed to achieve something that had profound consequences for the future.

In 1696, ironically the same year Thomas Aikenhead was arrested, Scotland's Parliament passed its "Act for Setting Schools," establishing a school in every parish in Scotland not already equipped with one. Each parish was now to supply a "commodious house for a school" and a salary for a teacher of not less than a hundred marks (or about sixty Scottish pounds or five pounds in English money) and no more than two hundred.

The reason behind all this was obvious to any Presbyterian: boys and girls must know how to read Holy Scripture. Knox's original 1560 Book of Discipline had called for a national system of education. Eighty years later Parliament passed the first statute to this effect. The 1696 act renewed and enforced it. The result was that within a generation nearly every parish in Scotland had some sort of school and a regular teacher. The education must have been fairly rudimentary in some places: the fundamentals of reading and grammar and nothing more. But it was available, and it was, at least in theory if not always in practice, free.

Historians are still arguing about how many Scots really learned to read and write as a result of the School Act. In this, as in so many things, the Highlands lagged far behind. But one thing is certain: Scotland's literacy rate would be higher than that of any other country by the end of the eighteenth century. An English observer noted with astonishment that "in the low country of Scotland . . . the poorest are, in general, taught to read." In 1790 nearly every eight-year-old in Cleish, in Kinross-shire, could read, and read well. By one estimate male literacy stood at around 55 percent by 1720; by 1750 it may have stood as high as 75 percent, compared with only 53 percent in England. It would not be until the 1880s that the English would finally catch up with their northern neighbors.

Scotland became Europe's first modern literate society. This meant that there was an audience not only for the Bible but for other books as well. As the barriers of religious censorship eventually came down in the eighteenth century, the result was a literary explosion. Intellectuals such as Adam Smith and David Hume wrote not just for other intellectuals but for a genuine reading public. Even a person of relatively modest means had his own collection of books, and what he couldn't afford he could get at the local lending library, which by 1750 virtually every town of any size enjoyed.

A good example is Innerpeffray, near Crieff in Perthshire. Its library's records of book borrowing run from 1747 to 1800. They show books loaned out to the local baker, the blacksmith, the cooper, the dyer and the dyer's apprentice and to farmers, stonemasons, quarriers, tailors, and household servants. Religious books predominated; but more than half of the books borrowed were on secular themes, and included works by John Locke, the French Enlightenment naturalist George-Louis Leclerc de Buffon, and Scotland's own Enlightenment historian, William Robertson.* Literacy opened up new cultural choices, and reinforced others: a specifically Scottish reading public developed, with an appetite for the new as well as the familiar and well-worn.

Robert Burns's father was a poor farmer from Alloway in south-western Scotland, who taught his son to make a living by handling a plow. But he also saw to it that young Robert received an education worthy of any English gentleman, including studying Latin and French. For the future poet, it opened up an incredible new world. "Though I cost the schoolmaster some thrashings," Burns remembered later, "I made an excellent scholar." The first books he read were a biography of Hannibal and *The Life of Sir William Wallace,* lent to him by the local blacksmith. "The story of Wallace poured a Scottish prejudice in my veins," Burns recalled, "which will boil along there till the flood gates of life shut in eternal rest." By the time he was sixteen, Burns the budding Ayrshire plowman had made his way through generous portions of Shakespeare, Alexander Pope, Addison's *Spectator* essays, and the Scottish poet Allan Ramsay, along with Jeremy Taylor on theology, Jethro Tull on agriculture, Robert Boyle's lectures on chemistry, John Locke's *Essay Concerning Human Understanding,* several volumes on geography and history, and the French Enlightenment philosopher Fénélon's *Télémaque* in the original.

Do we treat Burns's case as typical? Of course not. But his story does illustrate how early on reading and writing became embedded in Scottish society, even in rural areas. In Edinburgh the book trade was an important part of the local economy. There were six publishing houses in 1763, for a city with a population of only sixty thousand. By 1790 there were sixteen. Papermaking become a mainstay of the national economy; in fact, as the historian Anand Chitnis notes, "of Scottish domestic manufactures, only woolens, linen, and hemp, iron and liquors employed more people than the paper industry." The paper mill was often the only industry in rural villages and hamlets in the Lowlands

*For more on Robertson, see chapter 4.

agricultural belt. The one at Currie brought two hundred new inhabitants into the village when it opened.

Bookselling, printing, the paper and ink industries—a whole range of businesses to service a large literate public. An official national survey in 1795 showed that out of a total population of 1.5 million, nearly twenty thousand Scots depended for their livelihood on writing and publishing—and 10,500 on teaching. All this meant that despite its relative poverty and small population, Scottish culture had a built-in bias toward reading, learning, and education in general. In no other European country did education count for so much, or enjoy so broad a base.

This attitude also decisively shaped the character of Scotland's universities. As we shall see later, they would play a key role in creating modern Scotland. But their roots ran solid and deep. Glasgow and St. Andrews, in particular, enjoyed a long tradition that reached back to the Middle Ages. The greatest figure of later medieval thought, John Duns Scotus, had been a Scot, while John Mair, dubbed "the prince of philosophers and theologians" at the University of Paris, finished his career teaching at both Glasgow and St. Andrews (his students there included George Buchanan and John Knox). In 1574 an observer wrote that "there is no place in Europe comparable to Glasgow for a plentifull and gude chepe mercat of all kind of langages artes and sciences."

The University of Edinburgh and Aberdeen's Marischal College and King's College had been founded more recently, but, like Glasgow and St. Andrews, they never became remote ivory towers or intellectual backwaters, as eighteenth-century Oxford and Cambridge did. Despite their small size, Scottish universities were international centers of learning, and drew students from across Protestant Europe as well as England and Ulster (since only Episcopalians could attend Oxford or Cambridge or Trinity College in Dublin).

Thanks to the swelling tide of literacy, these universities became in effect centers of popular education as well as more academic learning. Between 1720 and 1840 the college student population of Scotland *trebled*. Knowledge of Latin was usually enough to get you in, and many students learned this at their parish schools. A university education was also relatively cheap.

At Glasgow the tuition fee of five pounds a year was one-tenth the cost of going to Cambridge or Oxford. This meant that students like the Edinburgh apothecary's son Thomas Aikenhead were more the rule rather than the exception. A father in trade, commerce, or the professions was more typical than a working- or laboring-class one; but even this contrasted with the socially top-heavy landed gentry and aristocratic student bodies in the English universities. More than half of the students at the University of Glasgow between 1740 and 1830 came from middle-class backgrounds. Many, although probably not very many, of the rest came from lower down the social ladder.

In the eighteenth century, sons of artisans and shopkeepers and farmers, some as young as thirteen or fourteen, would scrape together enough money to pay their university fees, attending lectures alongside Frasers and Maxwells and Erskines, the sons of Scotland's most aristocratic families. Robert Foulis, who was an apprentice barber and the son of a maltman, spent his spare time in the 1730s taking classes with the University of Glasgow's most distinguished philosopher, Francis Hutcheson, as well as the mathematician Robert Simson. Hutcheson was so impressed by Foulis that he hired him as his classroom assistant. It was the sort of scene unimaginable at Oxford or Cambridge until very late in the Victorian era.

Nor were boys the only ones who benefited from this. Auditing university classes became a favorite hobby among Edinburgh and Aberdeen townspeople, just as professors regularly engaged in a "community outreach" to offer classes to students outside the academic setting.

Robert Dick, at the University of Glasgow, taught natural philosophy to a lecture hall of townspeople, men and women, in the 1750s. In the early nineteenth century, University of Edinburgh chemistry professor Thomas Hope's public lectures drew more than three hundred serious-minded ladies from the town. For middle-class Scots, education was more than just a means to professional credentials or social advancement. It became a way of life.

The Schools Act of 1696 had set off far-reaching changes the Kirk could never have foreseen—a good example of how social actions have unintended consequences, as Adam Smith and a later generation of

Scottish thinkers so well understood. Smith observed, in his *Wealth of Nations,* how Scotland's parish school system taught "almost the whole common people to read, and a very great proportion of them to write and account." Today we recognize that literacy and its mathematical counterpart, numeracy, are fundamental skills for living in a complex modern society. In that sense, no other society in Europe was as broadly prepared for "takeoff" into the modern age as was eighteenth-century Scotland.

II

This seems odd, because the obvious candidate for that lead position had always been England. The Scots themselves certainly thought so. Already by the 1690s, Scots were beginning to suffer from an inferiority complex regarding the kingdom to their south. They were taking several significant steps to remedy that problem—including, in a bizarre way, prosecuting the Aikenhead case, which Kirk hard-liners saw as a kind of preemptive strike against an encroaching English religious culture. But if the relationship between the two nations had never been easy, it had also not been so unbalanced until very recently.

England and Scotland had been joined together by history and geography since the fall of the Roman Empire. They were in effect twin kingdoms, born in the same era and from the same forces. Both were remote from the older traditional centers of European culture. Both had fought off the same foreign invaders—the Viking Norsemen—in the tenth and eleventh centuries.

Both had taken shape through the consolidation of power in the hands of feudal kings, who gave land to their powerful followers—in the case of Scotland, the heads of the clans—in exchange for obedience. Both spoke the same language, since the Scottish royal court had adopted English (or a dialect related to Middle English called Scots) back in the eleventh century, relegating Gaelic to the cultural backwater.

English and Scottish kings alike had not hesitated to take advantage of the other's weakness to wage war, in order to grab territory and wealth. The result was a long and bitter enmity between the two peoples, each of whom viewed the other with suspicion and loathing. Scots are taught, of course, to see a figure such as William Wallace as the great Braveheart, who saved Scotland from English domination. But to the English, Wallace was a heartless murderer, who burned and ethnically cleansed entire regions of the north Border country in order to expand Scottish settlements. The Lanercost Chronicles celebrated Wallace's gruesome execution in 1305:

> *Butcher of thousands, threefold death be thine:*
> *So shall the English from thee gain relief.*
> *Scotland, be wise, and choose a nobler chief.*

Likewise, English history views King Edward I (1277–1307) as one of the Middle Ages' most effective monarchs, who consolidated control over Wales and the north, creating the core of what would become the Kingdom of Great Britain. Scots, on the other hand, see him as a villain of the first rank, a treacherous tyrant who ravaged Edinburgh and stole Scotland's holy Stone of Scone, on which her kings had been crowned for centuries.

Even the Reformation, when both kingdoms abandoned the Catholic Church for slightly differing versions of Calvinist Protestantism, failed to heal the hatred between Scottish Presbyterian and English Episcopalian. Each persecuted the other whenever he could. But then, in 1603, dynastic accident intervened. Elizabeth, the last Tudor, died unwed and childless, and the throne of England passed to her cousin, the son of her hated rival Mary Queen of Scots, James VI of Scotland, and now James I of England. For the next hundred years both kingdoms would be ruled by a single royal family, the Stuarts.

It was not a pleasant experience. Control of Scottish affairs was turned over to royal appointees who ran things according to the demands of the king's advisers at Court. "With my pen I govern Scotland," said King James with complacent self-satisfaction from his palace at Whitehall. He kept Scotland's aristocratic families on a short leash, schooling them in the advantages of subservience to royal will and favor, and in the disadvantages of self-assertion.

He forced her ministers to accept the rule of bishops and to teach their congregations to kneel at the Holy Sacrament. Scottish noblemen who flocked to James's court in London earned a reputation as needy and greedy spongers and parasites. It left a negative impression about Scots that lasted all the way down to the era of the American Revolution—the distant origin of the stereotype of the grasping, tight-fisted Scot that still persists today.

Meanwhile, the high-handed policies of James I and then his son Charles I managed to offend both kingdoms so thoroughly that they rose up in arms. The English Civil War was as much a Scottish war as an English one; and when Charles I lost his fight against his English subjects in 1647, he offered the Scots religious freedom and state support of their Kirk if they would help him retake his southern crown. With astonishing shortsightedness and ineptitude, they accepted, only to be defeated at the battle of Preston by Oliver Cromwell. The result was that Charles lost not only his northern kingdom but his head as well, and the Scots their independence. Scotland underwent the full rigors of English military occupation and martial law over the Lowlands and Highlands for nearly a decade.

In fact, Oliver Cromwell managed to do what no monarch had done in over a thousand years of trying. He had unified not only England and Scotland under a single regime, but Ireland as well, after his brutal, cold-blooded massacre of the inhabitants of Drogheda in 1652 terrified that island into submission. The only thing this remarkable achievement earned him, however, was the undying enmity of posterity in all three nations. If there is one historical figure whom Irishmen, Englishmen, and Scotsmen can all agree to hate even today, it is Oliver Cromwell.

It was Scotland, not England, that first recognized Charles II as its king. His return to London in May 1660 ought to have signaled a new era of reconciliation between the northern and southern kingdoms. But Charles was determined to bend the Scots to his will, and on the one issue guaranteed to arouse the most intense opposition: that of religion.

He was as committed to impose an Episcopalian establishment on Scotland as his father had been. His chosen instrument was his Secretary for Scotland, the Duke of Lauderdale, who ruled Scotland as virtual dictator from 1667 to 1680. These were the years of the Killing Time. In the words of John Hill Burton, "never was Eastern despot blessed with the minister of his will more obedient, docile, and sedulous." Lauderdale used military occupation, torture, execution, and penal servitude in the West Indies to pound opponents into obedience. The Killing Time taught Scottish Calvinists to hate governance from London, the Episcopal Church, and Englishmen in general—and Highlanders as well, since Lauderdale liked to deploy regiments drawn from the pro-Stuart Highland clans (dubbed the "Highland Host") for his military forays into the Covenant-ing southwest Lowlands.

The dismal sequence of religious persecution and popular resistance persisted after Lauderdale's recall in 1680, and reached a crescendo when Charles's Catholic brother James became James II. Scottish nobles such as the Earl of Argyll joined conspiracies with English anti-Catholics to overthrow James, and, like Argyll, paid for their failure with their lives.

So in the end the Scottish political nation greeted the events of 1688 with relief, when James II was driven from his throne and his Protestant daughter Mary, with her husband, William of Orange, took his place. As in England, the Glorious Revolution brought a loosening of old tensions and conflicts. The Kirk regained its independence. William and Mary abolished the hated Lords of the Articles, whom the Stuarts had used to dominate Scotland's Parliament. But elsewhere a new split began to show. Some Highland clans, such as the Camerons, the Appin Stewarts, the MacLeods, and the MacDonalds of Glencoe, had prospered under the old regime. They were more than willing to see James II back on the throne. They resented the new regime's focus on events on the Continent, where William was fighting a war with Louis XIV and the French. These were the first stirrings of Jacobitism, inspired perhaps less by loyalty to the fickle Stuarts than by resistance to the shift of the center of power from Edinburgh to London.

By 1689, little had changed, at least on the surface. The two king-

doms were still ruled by a single crown, with separate capitals and separate parliaments. But the balance between the two kingdoms had
shifted. Economics, rather than religion, was becoming the new issue of
contention. England had acquired an empire, reaching across the
Atlantic to the New World, and extending south and east to Asia. From
1660 to 1688 the total tonnage of goods carried in English ships doubled. London and Bristol merchants had learned to shift their activities
from woolen cloth exports, the staple of English trade since the Middle
Ages, to re-exporting goods from America and Asia to the rest of
Europe: sugar, tobacco, pepper, molasses, and cotton. Costs fell,
demand grew, London boomed, and Parliament passed laws called the
Navigation Acts, securing English merchants' control over their Atlantic
and Asian markets. The navy expanded into the largest in the world to
protect the trade links with America and Asia, which would soon
include India, and the slave trade with Africa. A new cluster of institutions—the Bank of England, the Royal Exchange, and the Board of
Trade—turned the growing wealth of English business into the wealth
of the nation at large, and of government. Richer, more populous, and
more politically stable than Scotland, England was emerging as Europe's
new superpower.

Scotland's traditional economy, by contrast, had reached its limits.
Both Lowlands and Highlands still depended on the ancient ties
between laird and tenant to work the land and produce enough food to
feed her one million people. Her diet was monotonous even in the best
of times. Ordinary Scots relied heavily on whole grains such as oatmeal
and barley, with very little meat beyond the occasional piece of fish or
a bit of lean pork. Probably nutritionists today would consider it a
healthier diet than the typical fat-laden, sugar-sweetened, alcohol- and
tobacco-ridden meals of the English and Scottish ruling classes. But it
was not a meal anyone sat down to with relish. And that was when there
was enough to eat. After 1695, when the first of a series of bad harvests
hit, there would not be.

The English, like the Dutch before them, had learned how to import
food when they needed it, in exchange for profitable manufactured
goods. Scotland did have her overseas trade, but it rested on shipping

unprocessed primary goods such as grain, cattle, wool, fish, coal, and lead ore: the sort of low-value exports of today's poorest Third World countries. To make matters worse, the wars of King William and then Queen Anne on the Continent disrupted relations with her principal trading partner, France, while the Navigation Acts denied her access to the booming English markets and colonies. Scotland and the Scots were stuck in the mean and unproductive patterns of the past, and they knew it.

By 1695 the Scottish ruling class assembled in Parliament in Edinburgh decided to do something about it. Their plan was simple and straightforward. Scotland would compete at the English level by doing as the English had done: creating a new economy by legislation. The same Parliament that passed the Blasphemy Act and the School Act also established a Bank of Scotland, closely modeled on the highly successful Bank of England, founded the year before (although it was much smaller, with a starting capital of only 100,000 pounds sterling, compared to the Bank of England's almost 600,000 pounds). Then, the next year, Parliament authorized a public chartered corporation, modeled on the British East India Company, to create a seaborne Scottish trading empire flowing both east and west. The resulting Darien Company occupies one of the bitterest and saddest chapters in Scottish history.

It was the brainchild of William Paterson, a Dumfriesshire Scot living in London who was also the man who had drawn up the original proposal for the Bank of England. Like another fast-talking Scot, John Law, who would convince the French crown to set up the Bank Royale in 1718, Paterson had a keen grasp of the realities of the new overseas trading economies emerging in seventeenth-century Europe. And like Law, whose ambitions would eventually push the French financial system into ruin, Paterson was something of a dreamer who never let details stand in the way of a good plan. With the help of an East Lothian landowner and member of Parliament named Andrew Fletcher, who will become a key figure in our story later on, Paterson urged his fellow Scots to get in on the public joint stock company sweepstakes that was bringing in such wealth for England, such as the East India Company and Royal Africa Company, the latter of which dominated the slave trade. Parliament agreed and, on May 26, 1695, duly granted Paterson's company a permanent monopoly for Scottish trade with Asia and Africa, and a thirty-one-year monopoly with America.

English merchants reacted with predictable dismay and hostility. They lobbied Parliament, which petitioned King William not to sign the bill. Although he did sign it, the business and political climate in London and Westminster became so antagonistic that the Scottish company's original hopes of cashing in on the existing English trade links had to be scaled back. Paterson had another plan up his sleeve, however. On July 23, 1696, the Scottish Parliament's Committee on Foreign Trade agreed to his proposal to use the company to found a Scottish colony in Panama, on the Isthmus of Darien. Paterson had an almost mystical belief in the importance of this uninhabited strip of beach and jungle to the future of world trade. Darien would be the perfect entrepôt for the flow of goods between the Atlantic and the Pacific, he believed, between East and West; he called Panama "the door of the seas, and the key of the Universe." And now it could belong to Scotland rather than to England or Spain (who had laid claim to it since the time of Balboa). The company's original mission had changed from encouraging trade to creating colonies. All Paterson needed were volunteers willing to go to Panama as colonists—which did not seem too difficult, since rural Scotland was slowly sinking into a prolonged famine—and money.

The English did everything they could to prevent the money from being raised. English subscribers withdrew; bankers in Amsterdam and Hamburg were told in no uncertain terms what would happen to their favorable dealings with London if they contributed funds to the Darien scheme. Instead, the Scots themselves raised the necessary cash, in a huge outpouring of patriotic sentiment—and anti-English resentment—not seen since the National Covenant. Hundreds of landowners and merchants emptied their pockets to buy Darien stock. Many of Scotland's leading aristocratic families mortgaged their fortunes. The company raised the entire amount of 400,000 pounds in a matter of months, although it amounted to almost half of the total money in circulation in Scotland.

It was a magnificent gesture, yet what motivated the vast majority of subscribers was not a sense of a good investment opportunity, but rather a point of honor. The English had tried to sabotage the project, or so everyone believed; therefore they had to show the English what Scots were made of. London's political point man in Edinburgh, the Marquis of Queensberry, had strong misgivings about the whole enterprise. However, he ended up subscribing three thousand pounds when he learned that the Duchess of Hamilton had done the same.

Ships, stores, and settlers, among them William Paterson and his family, soon gathered at Leith harbor near Edinburgh. The goods they would carry to Panama to trade with the natives included five thousand English-language Bibles and four thousand powdered wigs. On July 17, 1698, "amidst the tears and prayers and praises" of the entire city of Edinburgh, five ships set sail for the New World. On November 3 they dropped anchor at the Bay of Darien.

From start to finish, their stay was a disaster. On arriving, Paterson and his fellow colonists realized they had taken on provisions for only six months, instead of nine as originally intended. The English, from their bases in Jamaica and Havana, made sure that no more were to be had. As anyone could have predicted who knew that mosquito-infested coast, fever broke out, eventually killing settlers at a rate of twelve a day. Drunkenness spread, and discipline, godly or otherwise, collapsed. Then the Spanish reasserted their claims to Darien as part of Panama. They seized one of the company ships and threatened to attack. Beaten, exhausted, and decimated by disease, the survivors set sail again in July 1699, only one year after they had left Leith harbor to the clamor and acclaim of their countrymen.

Of the 1,200 who originally set out, very few returned home. Among the dead was William Paterson's own wife, buried, along with her husband's dazzling dream, on the surf-swept beach at Darien.

Characteristically, the Scots still refused to quit. Two more expeditions set out, but neither one did any better. The last one, better armed and provisioned and with more men, fought the Spanish and the jungle almost incessantly from the day they landed. Finally, in April 1700, they too gave up. The four ships, crowded with men, according to one eyewitness, "like hogs in a sty," set out for home but ran into terrible storms. The ships scattered, and two foundered. The other two found refuge in nearby English and Spanish ports, but were seized by authorities. Not one ship returned to Scotland.

The Darien venture cost more than two thousand lives and over 200,000 pounds. It also broke the bank, literally. The loss of so much hard currency, and the ruin of so many families and business concerns that had been tied up with the Darien scheme, pushed the still-struggling Bank of Scotland over the edge. In December 1704 it suspended payments to creditors. With the kingdom's finances in tatters, and its agriculture in the grip of famine and starvation, Scotland's ruin was complete.

Darien also further poisoned relations between the two kingdoms. "I have been ill served in Scotland," was King William's remark, and when he died in 1702 and his wife's sister Anne, the last of the Protestant Stuarts, took over as queen, the bitterness over Darien deepened. The English had been by turns amused, scared, and relieved by the debacle. They now saw the Scots as upstart economic rivals, pure and simple, and decided that their empire and its wealth must be permanently walled off from any Scottish interlopers. In 1704 Parliament passed an Aliens Act, which ruled that all Scottish nationals living in England were now officially foreign aliens, and incapable of passing their English property on to their heirs. It also banned all major import trade with Scotland. The law was revoked two years later, but it reveals a good deal about the depth of anti-Scottish feeling in the southern kingdom.

The Scots, too, were furious. Any sensible person would have realized that the Darien venture was doomed from the start. As a modern historian, Patrick Riley, explains, "No one can really defend an attempt to establish a colony in a fever-ridden territory belonging to someone else." Although Paterson and the other directors knew the enterprise would generate huge English resistance, they did nothing to try to head it off. Instead of seeking English cooperation and making concessions to get it, Paterson and Fletcher had started with an aggressive arrogance, determined to beat Parliament and the City of London at its own game. Now that it did fail, however, everyone knew whom to blame: the English.

In late April 1705, an English ship that was rumored to have sunk one of the last Darien vessels put into Leith from the Firth of Forth. Scottish authorities ordered it seized and the captain and crew arrested for murder and piracy. A trial of sorts took place, in a lynch-mob atmosphere. The English captain and fourteen crewmen were found guilty and sentenced to death. This time, unlike the earlier Aikenhead case, the Crown intervened and pardoned the condemned men. However, the Scottish Privy Council, terrified by the howls of protest from the Edinburgh crowd, allowed the captain and two officers to be hanged. Vengeful Scots celebrated; indignant Englishmen raged; relations between the two countries sank to a new low.

To wiser observers in Scotland, including many newly sobered former Darien investors, all this proved one thing: that Scotland could not succeed in getting into the new Atlantic trading economy without English help. Under current arrangements, as two separate sovereignties governed by a single monarch, that would not happen. Darien proved that if the king or queen had to choose between English and Scottish interests, he or she would always gravitate toward the richer, more populous southern kingdom. Scotland would always come in second, unless some new, larger interest could be created, which would look to satisfy both.

Here the solution seemed to be the word more and more on the lips of the political classes of both nations: *union*. It had come up before in parliamentary debates and pamphlets; now, paradoxically, the bitterness over the Darien debacle turned it into a tangible issue. English political opinion was largely in favor of it. In fact, the Aliens Act of 1704 carried a provision calling for the naming of Scottish and English commissioners to negotiate "concerning the Union of the Two Kingdoms." Whigs and Tories both saw it as a means of keeping the reins on any future Scottish enterprise like Darien, and of making sure Scotland remained in the English economic and political orbit.

And from the English standpoint, there were now strong geopolitical reasons for union, as well. After James II had been stripped of his throne and his title in 1688, he had found a ready ally in England's chief enemy, France's Louis XIV. With French help, James had landed in Ireland and raised a Catholic army against English rule. At the Battle of the Boyne, in June 1690, William and his Irish Protestant allies had managed to crush the revolt. But pro-James or "Jacobite" sentiment was also strong in Scotland. Through union, English politicians believed, they could prevent Scotland from being used as a strategic base for any future Stuart countercoup.

Scottish opinion was more mixed. Some, such as Andrew Fletcher, believed that the Darien venture proved that Scotland could never rely on any English help or cooperation. "There is no way left to make the Scots a happy people, but by separating from England and setting up a King of their own," he told members of the Scottish Parliament in 1705. Pro-Jacobite Scots, such as George Lockhart of Carnwath, agreed with him. Of course the English were in favor of union, Lockhart wrote, "because it rivetted the Scots in perpetual slavery, depriving them of any legal method to redress themselves of the injuries they might receive from them." He could have added that it also deprived James Stuart and his son of any claim to the crown, since by act of Parliament no Roman Catholic could sit on the throne of England—or, by extension, on the throne of an England-Scotland merger.

So, improbably enough, within five years of the Darien debacle, union had become the hot new political issue in both England and Scotland. The Scottish Parliament even agreed in principle to formation of a commission to discuss and negotiate a possible treaty. Everyone understood that the current relationship between the two kingdoms was no longer working, and that a new one was needed. The key question was what kind.

CHAPTER TWO

A Trap of Their Own Making

I

In the autumn of 1707, all eyes turned to Edinburgh. There Scotland's Parliament would assemble on October 3 to vote on a treaty of union between England and Scotland. Daniel Defoe, the author of *Robinson Crusoe,* was also a sometime government propagandist and spy for Queen Anne's minister Lord Harley. He had come to Scotland to watch events and report back to his masters. He found the atmosphere tense, to say the least. As Defoe wandered through the dark, narrow streets and wynds (or alleys) of Edinburgh, all the talk was about "slavery to the English, running away with the Crown, taking away the Nation, and the like." It was fortunate, Defoe figured, that London had not published the terms of the draft treaty before now. If the Scottish negotiators had then tried to return to Scotland, he said, "there was not many of them would dared to have gone home, without a guard to protect them."

The treaty had been negotiated and signed that previous spring in London by two teams of commissioners, one for Scotland, the other for England. *Negotiated* might not be the best word. Scotland's Parliament had authorized a slate of treaty commissioners in 1705, but played no part in choosing them. In fact, both teams, English and Scottish, had been handpicked by the Crown. They had all been chosen for their willingness to endorse what was called "an incorporating union," a merger that fully absorbed Scotland into the kingdom of England. That was what Queen Anne and her English advisers wanted, and it was what the Scottish commissioners were expected to provide. "You see that what we are to treat of is not in our choice," wrote one of them to a friend. Perhaps for that reason, despite the document's twenty-eight separate clauses and momentous significance, negotiations had taken only eighteen days. Now it only required ratification by the Scottish Parliament to become law. But no one supposed that was going to be easy.

The terms were indeed drastic, especially for Scots who had hoped that union would mean a federation of the two kingdoms. As one supporter explained, this would have allowed two "Distinct, Free and Independent Kingdoms [to] unite their separate interests into one common interest, for the mutual benefit of both." Instead, the treaty created a single new entity, Great Britain, governed by a single monarch and by a single British Parliament. The fine print, though, showed that the new government would be far more English than Scottish. The seat of government would be in London, nearly four hundred miles to the south. The Scottish Privy Council would lose all its power, while England's would now assume direct control over everything that affected both nations, including taxes, custom and excise duties, and military and foreign affairs.

The treaty did leave some concessions to Scottish pride. Scotland's separate legal system and courts would remain, as would the independence of her towns or burghs. Even more important, Scottish merchants would now have access to England's overseas markets, from America and the Caribbean to Africa and India. But nothing was said about the independence of the Kirk, or the powers of its General Assembly, under the new arrangement. This uncertainty disturbed every self-respecting Presbyterian, and seriously weakened pro-union sentiment in the Scottish heartland.

One issue above all others, however, made passage of the treaty look very doubtful. The terms of union required the end of a separate Scottish Parliament. Scots would have 45 seats in the new British House of Commons—out of 558. Scottish nobles would have even less representation; only sixteen would be able to take seats in the new House of Peers. In effect, by signing the treaty of union, Scotland's political class was committing suicide. Yet this was exactly what London, and the Scottish commissioners, expected them to do.

The leader of the pro-union forces in Parliament was James Douglas, Marquis of Queensberry. His orders were simple: secure ratification of the treaty by any means necessary, up to and including buying the votes to do it. London had even provided him with a secret slush fund of twenty thousand pounds to help make its arguments persuasive. Contemporaries, and later historians, would make a great deal about how this secret money "bought" the Scottish Parliament. In the end, however, it was probably more than Queensberry and the Crown needed (Queensberry himself ended up pocketing more than twelve thousand pounds of it for his own expenses). Whatever their principles, Scotland's nobles and lairds had fallen on hard times, especially after the Darien disaster. John Locke's friend James Johnstone, for example, found himself pro-union out of necessity. He was desperate for money—"which I need more than I thought I should do," he confessed, because without it, "my house should fall." As Defoe remarked to Harley: "In short, money will do anything here."

The Court party was united by long subservience to royal command, and the need for royal favor. The opposition, on the other hand, was a hodgepodge of discontented groups and factions who all had something to lose from union, or thought they did. Lowland lairds allied themselves with Highland chiefs, along with Edinburgh and Glasgow burghers who worried about having to compete for markets with English merchants. Presbyterian hard-liners who feared a weakened Kirk found themselves joining hands with crypto-Catholic Jacobites, who believed (correctly) that a Scottish-English union would finish off any chance of a restoration of the Stuarts to their ancestral throne. The ostensible leader of opposition to the treaty was the fifth Duke of Hamilton, but its real spokesman was the former cofounder with William Paterson of the Darien Company, the wild and unpredictable Andrew Fletcher of Saltoun.

Fletcher despised any and all authority, but particularly that of the Stuarts. He was born into an old East Lothian landowning family in Saltoun. His mother claimed to be a descendant of Robert the Bruce. Andrew had proved himself to be a political firebrand from his early twenties, and the bane of successive governments in Edinburgh. Someone described him as "a low, thin man, brown complexion, full of fire, with a stern, sour look." The Earl of Darmouth knew him well: "He was very brave, and a man of great integrity, [but] he had strange chimerical notions of government, which were so unsettled, that he would be very angry next day for any body's being of an opinion that he was himself the night before. . . ."

Fletcher's involvement in the Darien scheme was only one of a number of similar quixotic ventures. In 1685 he had thrown in his lot with the Earl of Argyll and the circle of hard-core anti-Catholic revolutionaries who had tried to preempt James II's succession and to put Charles II's bastard son, the Duke of Monmouth, in his place. Fletcher's explosive temper helped to ruin the expedition but probably saved his life. He quarreled with the expedition's chief guide over a horse, and shot him dead. Monmouth had wanted Fletcher to command his cavalry, but had to send him abroad instead. Monmouth proceeded to lose the battle of Sedgemoor, and was executed for treason along with Argyll. Fletcher, without wanting to be, was safe back in Holland. Instead, his punishment was limited to being sentenced to death in absentia and the confiscation of his Saltoun estates.

It was during his exile in Holland that Fletcher met William of Orange, the future William III. They became friends, and Fletcher joined him on his expedition to England in 1688. But after the Glorious Revolution, Fletcher turned against William, as well, when he realized the new king was chiefly interested in using the Scots as allies in his wars in Europe, and not in setting Scotland free.

Andrew Fletcher cared passionately about freedom, but it was a peculiar kind of freedom. In 1697 he had called for a compulsory universal militia, creating four camps, one in Scotland and three in England, where every young man, on beginning his twenty-second birthday, would receive military training of the most rigorous kind. "No woman should be suffered to come within the camp, and the crimes of abusing their own bodies any manner of way, punished with death." The next year he proposed solving Scotland's economic depression by in effect turning the Scottish peasantry into slaves, dividing up the indigent poor among the local landlords (such as himself), and giving the latter the power of life and death over their human herds.

By instinct and temperment, Fletcher was an authoritarian anarchist. He liked to think of himself as a Scottish laird of the old school. In fact, he had lived abroad almost as long as he had lived in Scotland. Fletcher was a genuine intellectual and amazingly well read: he had what was reputed to be the best private library in Scotland. Treaty supporters such as the Earl of Mar dismissed Fletcher as a "violent, ingenious fanatic." But he was also a hero to many, because in the Parliament of 1703 he had pushed through a bill guaranteeing a Protestant succession in Scotland (although Fletcher was no admirer of the Kirk or its ministers) and establishing the principle that any change in the royal succession required the consent of the Scottish Parliament.

"I regard not names," he wrote, "but things." And for Fletcher, the thing that counted was land, as a place of employment for those who worked it and as a source of wealth for those who owned it. "For what end, then," he wrote in 1703, "did God create such vast tracts of land, capable of producing so great variety and abundance?" He knew the value of commerce, as his involvement in the Darien Company showed: but he despised those who lived by it. "Can there be a greater disorder in human affairs," he wrote, than having human beings jammed together in cities, earning their living by "the exercise of a sedentary and unmanly trade, to foment the luxury of a few"?

Fletcher despised merchants as much as he despised human weakness and big government. In his mind, they were natural allies. And he saw all of them in a treaty of union. Fletcher saw the proposed treaty as a devil's bargain: trading away Scotland's independence in exchange for a share in England's seaborne empire. But he also saw in it the specter of change, the rise of a new society organized around money and commercial enterprise, which he saw as profoundly unnatural and "unmanly." If this was the future, Andrew Fletcher was determined not to give in to it without a fight.

II

The Scottish Parliament traditionally opened with a stunning if anachronistic display of medieval pageantry.* The Lord High Constable would take his ritual place in an armchair at the door of Parliament House. Officers of state, in their magnificent robes of office, stood on each side. Then, at the appointed hour, the members of Parliament began their parade from Holyrood Palace up High Street to St. Giles Church and Parliament House, with two mounted trumpeters leading the cavalcade. First came the Estate of the Burghs or towns, also on horseback, arranged two by two. Then came the Estate of the Shires, representatives from the rural counties of Scotland, similarly mounted and in twos.

The Lords Baron followed, gorgeously decked out in colorful robes and velvet surcoats bearing their coats of arms, each accompanied by a gentleman leading his horse and three servants wearing his lord's heraldic badges. Then the earls, each with four servants; more trumpeters; then the Lord Lyon, King of Arms, followed by the royal regalia: the Sword of State, the Sceptre, the Purse, and the Crown. The Lord High Commissioner, Queensberry himself, rode along surrounded by servants, pages, and footmen; then dukes, marquises, and finally John Campbell, Duke of Argyll, with the Captain of the Horse Guards and the Royal Horse Guards bringing up the rear. "The Riding of Parliament" was a powerful visual reminder that Parliament was really the gathering of the kingdom's traditional feudal order, a living tableau of the "bodie politicke" as it had been envisioned since the days of John Balliol and Robert the Bruce.

This time the crowd of Edinburgh citizens gathered to cheer their heroes, the Duke of Hamilton and his ally Atholl, and heckle Queensberry, Mar, and the other commissioners. Mutters and curses of "no union" and "treaters-traitors" greeted them as they entered

---

*The last of these took place in 1703, when the Parliament that voted the treaty of union first took their seats.

Parliament House. Daniel Defoe stood nearby and watched with amazement. "To find a nation but a few months before, were earnestly crying out for a Union, and the nearer the better . . . now fly in the face of their masters, and upbraid the gentlemen, who managed it, with selling and betraying their country . . ."

But pro-union forces had a strategy to circumvent their furious opponents. This was the treaty's tantalizing promise of economic prosperity for Scotland, as trade barriers would come down and Scottish merchants would be able to enter English overseas markets. The Earl of Stair, Queensberry's right-hand man, had from the beginning stressed the need to present the trade issue to Parliament first. Then, he told the queen and her advisers, questions about the loss of power to London, the abolition of Parliament, the succession, and the rest would take care of themselves.

Here, Fletcher and Stair were in agreement. Union was indeed a devil's bargain. Scots were being asked to exchange their political autonomy for economic growth, or, to put it more crudely, for money. But this raised a question. What was the real value of that much-vaunted autonomy, and independent legislation by Parliament, which they were being asked to give up?

In that sense, all the solemn procession and pageantry was a sham. London had actually been running Scottish affairs for more than a century, since the reign of James I. Scotland's greatest families had long since been brought to heel. As for Parliament, no one had any illusions about its claims to be a body representative of the Scottish nation. The current Parliament had been elected in 1703; the last election before that had been in 1689.

Unlike its English counterpart, Scotland's Parliament did not enjoy a long-established reputation as a forum for public debate or as the defender of the rights of freeborn citizens. On the contrary, it had a long and shameless history of supine subservience to royal authority. Most Scots barely noted its existence. If it disappeared, very few beyond its actual members would notice or care. James Johnstone, the needy pro-union Lord Clerk Register, pointed this out to friends even before the Parliament began. "As for the giving up the legislative [power], we had none to give up." He went on, "For the true state of the matter was, whether Scotland should continue subject to an English ministry without [the privilege of trade] or be subject to an English Parliament with trade."

Others, however, were determined not to be so clearheaded or realistic. Here they had one trump card to play: religion. Once Parliament had opened and the Queen's letter was read, urging them to ratify the treaty, the member for Pardivan rose to propose a public fast day before proceeding any further. His intention was clear: to stir up resentment against the treaty within the Kirk and among the Presbyterian clergy. The treaty had said nothing about the Kirk. Unlike independence of Parliament, the independence of the Presbyterian Church and its General Assembly was an issue that could stir deep emotion in Scotland. Many ministers were already fiercely opposed to union; a public fast day would certainly turn into a series of massive public demonstrations against the treaty and the hated English.

And Queensberry and the pro-union forces knew it. As one member put it, the fast-day proposal "occasioned a long jangle" but was finally defeated. But the question of the Kirk still remained unresolved. The first serious vote took place on October 15, on whether to proceed to consider the treaty article by article. Fletcher, Hamilton, and the others fought hard to delay, but the motion was carried by sixty-six votes.

The next day the opposition received a body blow they had not expected. The General Assembly of the Kirk of Scotland, meeting in Edinburgh at the same time, gave its tacit consent to the union treaty.

———

This coup can be credited to the efforts of one man: William Carstares, Principal of the University of Edinburgh and current Moderator of the General Assembly. Alert, intelligent, and close-mouthed, Carstares, like so many prominent men in pre-Union Scotland, had suffered heavily for his faith. He was the eldest of nine children of a prominent Covenanting minister who had been driven into hiding by Lauderdale's dragoons. Carstares was then jailed in Edinburgh Castle for distributing anti-Lauderdale broadsides. He had fled to Holland after his release, where he joined a plot against James II, and was arrested again. Under torture, Carstares had provided evidence that sent an innocent man to the gallows at Grassmarket. Perhaps for that reason he had acquired an inner taciturnity, a guardedness in dealing with both friends and foes, as well as a studied hatred of the Stuarts and their supporters.

When he returned to Holland, he had met William of Orange. The future king was immediately attracted by Carstares's honesty, dedication, and pious eloquence, and made him his chaplain. Unlike Andrew Fletcher, he had remained loyal to William after 1688, and proved a rock of support for the government in Edinburgh and in the Kirk. In 1703 he became Principal of Edinburgh's university. With his brother-in-law William Donlop serving as Principal of the University of Glasgow, he dominated Scottish education with a Colossus-like presence. Thanks to Carstares, university life in Scotland would from that time on be resolutely "Whig"*: pro-Revolution, pro–Protestant succession, pro–House of Hanover—and pro-union.

Carstares's Presbyterian credentials and support for a strong independent Kirk were a byword in Edinburgh (before his death in 1715, he would even pen a forthright if qualified defense of the hanging of Thomas Aikenhead). But his fear of a Stuart restoration ran deeper. Almost to a man, the Kirk was opposed to the treaty. But Carstares warned his colleagues in the General Assembly that if the treaty of union failed, they might well find themselves with a Roman Catholic king. They faced a trade-off. If they insisted on getting everything they wanted, they could end up losing it all. But if they could accept an

---

*Whig is one of the most famous words in English politics; its origin, however, is Scottish (just as its counterpart, Tory, is an Irish word). Whigg is Scots for a kind of sour milk or whey. In hard times it was the main diet of the poor and indigent; since many of the Covenanters were thought to be lower-class trash, opponents taunted them with the word. When a group of Covenanters marched on Edinburgh to prevent the Engagement with Charles I in 1648, it became known as the "march of the whiggamores" or "sour milk men." Whiggamore soon shortened to Whig; in John Locke's day, it referred to anyone bound and determined to have a Protestant succession, whether in Scotland or England.

Episcopalian king and the merger with England, they would win concessions on the final draft, and preserve the Kirk's control over its doctrine and discipline. His arguments worked, and the General Assembly agreed to the treaty. It was a monumental act of statesmanship on Carstares's part—and done, in defiance of critics of union, without recourse to a single bribe. It also deprived treaty opponents of their most potent resource, the religious card. Years later someone would find an unsigned letter addressed to Carstares preserved in his private papers. It read simply, "The union could never have had the consent of the Scottish Parliament if you had not acted the worthy part you did."

Now the Earl of Mar, writing to Harley in London, was more confident than ever that the treaty would pass. But he believed that the opposition would still try "some foolish extravagant thing" to postpone the final day.

That "foolish extravagant thing" came on October 23. A mob stormed the house of Patrick Johnson, Lord Provost (or mayor) of Edinburgh and a treaty commissioner. The municipal guard had to be called out, and they arrested six rioters. The rest roamed the streets unchecked, smashing windows and threatening passersby. By nine o'clock they had intimidated any and all law-enforcement authorities and marauded at will. Queensberry sent a party of soldiers from Holyrood to the Netherbow Port to keep at least one gate out of the city open.

The next day three regiments of royal troops marched in at Queensberry's orders. Edinburgh was placed under martial law, and the city streets again became clear. But from this point on, no supporter of union dared go outside without armed bodyguards. Queensberry himself took the precaution of leaving Parliament House every day in a closed carriage at full gallop, while the crowd flung curses and excrement at the scrambling vehicle.

On November 7 the unrest spread to Glasgow, whose Provost fled to Edinburgh to escape the enraged throng. Anti-union protesters tried to stir many of the same emotions as the National Covenant had done seventy years earlier. On November 20 an armed mob marched into

Dumfries, burned a copy of the treaty, and tacked up a crudely written proclamation that said ratification of union would be "contrary to our fundamental liberties and privileges . . . as men and christians."

But this was 1707, not 1637. And day by day, ratification of the treaty went ahead as planned.

On November 4 the first article, providing that England and Scotland "for ever after be united in one kingdom by the name of Great Britain," was presented to the assembled Parliament (unlike the English division into Lords and Commons, all the members of the Scottish Parliament met as a single body). The most emotional outburst from the opposition came not from Andrew Fletcher, but from another diehard member of the opposition, Lord Belhaven. In a long, almost hysterical speech, he compared the proposed treaty to an act of murder, with Scotland's ancient mythic mother, Caledonia, expiring under the dagger blows of her treacherous sons, as her dying breath paraphrased Shakespeare's Julius Caesar: "And you too, my children!"

Belhaven saw a powerful and prosperous England, its navy "the terror of Europe," devouring a defenseless Scotland. "We are an obscure, poor people, though formerly of better account, removed to a remote corner of the world, without name and without alliance. . . . Now we are slaves forever." Then he employed a different classical allusion: "Hannibal, My Lord, is at our gates; Hannibal is at our gates; Hannibal is come the length of this table, he is at the foot of the throne: he will demolish this throne if we take not notice; he would seize upon this regalia," Belhaven bellowed, pointing to the Crown and Sceptre of State, "and whip us out of this house never to return."

Then he turned to the other members. "We want neither men nor sufficiency of all manner of things to make a nation happy," he cried, and then in a mighty wail, "Good God, what is this! An entire surrender." Overcome with emotion, Belhaven broke off his speech, pleading that he was unable to finish.

The house sat, stunned. Then another figure, leaner and much older, rose to speak. It was Lord Chancellor Polwarth, newly honored by the Queen with the earldom of Marchmont, the same man who had cast the final vote sentencing Thomas Aikenhead to death eleven years earlier.

Now he had a slight smile on his lips. "Behold, he dreamed," Lord Marchmont sneered, with a glance at Belhaven, "but lo: when he awoke, behold it was a dream." The remark broke the spell. The house voted, and Article One passed by thirty-two votes. "A good plurality," wrote the Earl of Mar, and added, "but fewer than we expected."

The next two articles also passed, after bitter wrangling. Then debate began on Article Four, providing for "full freedom and intercourse of Trade and navigation." Andrew Fletcher had largely held his fire until now. He had moved to protest the use of royal troops to suppress the disturbances on October 23, saying that the rioters had been the true voice of the Scottish people. He had quarreled with his ostensible leader, the Duke of Hamilton, who had turned out to be a huge disappointment and a weak reed in organizing opposition—but then Fletcher was always quarreling with the Duke of Hamilton.

Now Fletcher came into his own. The treaty's economic provisions, the heart of the union, raised Fletcher, as one friend put it, to "a vast heat." The prospects for Scotland of access to English markets seemed to him dim. "For my part, I cannot see what advantage a free trade to the English plantations [in America] would bring us, except a further exhausting of our people, and the utter ruin of all our merchants. . . ." The union, he thundered, "would certainly destroy even those manufactures we now have."

Nor was it clear to him how foreign trade, which he contemptuously described as "the golden ball for which all nations of the world are contending," would benefit Scotland as a whole. "Our trade cannot increase on a sudden," Fletcher argued, and there would be no money left after the rich and well-born had taken their share to spend on extravagant houses and clothes in London. Scotland's own geographic advantages would play against her. "The wholesomeness of our air, and the healthfulness of our climate," he had written, "afford us great numbers of people, which in so poor a country can never be all maintained by manufactures, or public workhouses, or any other way" than the one Fletcher had proposed fourteen years earlier: slavery. "Besides," he added, "the natural pride of our commonalty, and their indisposition to labor, are insuperable difficulties, which the English have not to contend with in their people." In short, the English might find a way to make commerce pay as a source of national wealth; the Scots, Fletcher believed, never could. Hence, growth through union was an illusion.

With or without the help of bribes, the vast majority in the Parliament understood that the real illusion was Fletcher's: that formal independence could be maintained without economic strength. Treaty supporters understood that Scotland's material poverty and failing economy were powerful reasons to *support* union. The future for Scotland, and the world, lay in the sea lanes of trade and empire. "This nation being poor," said William Seton of Pitmedden, a former treaty commissioner, "and without force to protect its commerce, cannot reap great advantage by it, till it partake of the trade and protection of some powerful neighbor nation, that can communicate both these." Article Four passed overwhelmingly, 156 to 19. Fletcher himself was so disappointed and furious at the final vote that he stormed out of the house.

The next two months were anticlimax, as Parliament made its way through the rest of the twenty-five articles, approving each after wearying and inconsequential debate with the symbolic touch of the Sceptre of State. By the first of the year of 1707, the Crown's ministers began to talk of being "in sight of land." Then, in January, they came to the last great barrier to final approval. This was Article 22, which abolished the Scottish Parliament and fixed representation in the new British Parliament at sixteen Lords and forty-five Commons, a ten-to-one advantage for the English members. To opponents, no provision of the treaty seemed to symbolize Scotland's reduced status in the new union as much as did Article 22. "The Scots deserve no pity," Fletcher had warned, "if they voluntarily surrender their united and separate interests to the Mercy of an united Parliament," where the Scots would have only forty-five elected members. The very principle of representative government for which both Scots and English had fought and died, first in the Civil War and then in 1688, seemed under attack.

It was going to be a fierce debate, and to lead it Queensberry had chosen his right-hand counsel, John Dalrymple, Earl of Stair. Stair was, as John Prebble has put it, "witty, wise, and ambitious." The son of Scotland's most distinguished jurist, both he and his father had been savagely persecuted by the Stuarts. Then the son, realizing there were advantages to going with the flow, switched sides. He became Lord Advocate, and finally Secretary of State for Scotland.

A man constrained by few principles or much sense of humanity, Stair, more than anyone else, was responsible for the hideous events in Glencoe on February 13, 1692, when the pro-Orange Campbells had slaughtered thirty-seven of their pro-Jacobite neighbors, the MacDonalds of Glencoe, including women and children ("'tis strange to me," he wrote callously when the news of the massacre set off shockwaves in the Scottish Parliament, "that means so much regret for such a sept of thieves").* The ensuing scandal had forced his resignation from the secretaryship, but his loyalty to William and Mary earned him the title Earl of Stair in 1700.

As a public figure, Stair was viewed by ordinary Scots with alarm, even fear. Rumors had it that he and his family were possessed by the devil. His sister Sarah was said to be able to levitate over walls at will. His mother was popularly believed to be a witch, and when her daughter Janet married against her will, her mother had (according to scandalmongers) cursed her: "Ye may marry him, but sair ye shall repent it!" On the wedding night, terrible screams were heard from the bridal chamber. When the door was opened the next morning, the daughter was found dead, bathed in blood, with the groom raving in the chimney corner, hopelessly insane.

The sensational story of "the Dalrymple curse" became the original for a novel by Sir Walter Scott and memorable to generations of operagoers as the Mad Scene in Donizetti's *Lucia di Lammermoor*. Although the story is false (in fact, Janet Dalrymple died of a natural illness two weeks after her marriage), the myth of a curse gave Stair a certain intimidating presence among his colleagues—all except, of course, Andrew Fletcher, who at one point in the debate offered to tie Stair to his horse's tail and drag him through the streets of Edinburgh (he was forced to apologize for the remark the next day).

---

*Sept refers to a subclan of Highlanders commanded by a minor chieftain. For more about this, see chapter 5.

It was Stair who helped Queensberry draw up his list of pliant Scottish commissioners for the original signing of the treaty. It was Stair who proposed the original strategy for getting the treaty past the Parliament, by offering up the molasses first, especially freedom of trade, before getting down to the sulfur, which meant Article 22. Now it was this extraordinary and amoral man, the very opposite of William Carstares in public reputation and integrity, who rose to carry the treaty over its final hurdle.

His argument was characterstically direct and unsentimental. All this talk of principle would get Scotland nowhere. The real issue was who paid the bills. The only way to draw any sensible comparison between the two kingdoms in representative terms, Stair explained, was not how many members each Parliament had before union, but how much each was willing to pay in taxes. The English would begin by paying into the new British Treasury thirty-five times the amount of revenue the Scots would pay. From that perspective, he concluded for his colleagues, the English were entitled to a thirty-five-to-one advantage in members. Take ten-to-one, he told them; at that rate, union comes cheap.

The debate was furious and emotional. Stair stood like a rock, however, answering every objection and insult and in the end, on January 7, Article 22 passed by forty votes. Stair left Parliament House exhausted but exultant, and threaded his way past the usual hostile crowds to his Edinburgh lodging. He retired early and never woke up. When his servant opened the door to his room early the next morning, he found his master dead in bed, a victim of a stroke. He was fifty-eight years old.

The treaty of union had claimed its first martyr. Supporters and his family printed up a broadside in his memory, decorated with black borders and skulls, declaring that "The Union shall perpetuate his name, as long as there's an ear or mouth in fame!" Opponents pointed to the Dalrymple curse, and suggested a different epitaph:

Stay, passenger, but shed no tear.
A Pontius Pilate lieth here.

On January 14 the final article of the treaty was passed. The opposition had played every card they had, including threatening to walk out, all to no avail. On the sixteenth, the members entered Parliament House to approve the treaty as a whole. The final vote was 110 to 69. Queensberry touched it with the Sceptre of State, and the kingdom of Scotland ceased to exist. "Now there's an end of an old song," said Lord Seafield, with a singular lack of appropriate solemnity for an event that marked the end of a kingdom and an epoch. But he and the rest of the treaty supporters were thinking not of the past, of Belhaven and Fletcher's "dream" of a free and independent Scotland that had never existed. They were thinking of themselves, and the future.

There was, however, one final bit of comedy to be played out. When the members reassembled at Parliament House to sign the final treaty, the furious crowd outside immediately turned on them and the members were forced to flee. They tried to meet again at a nearby tavern, and then at a small summer house behind Moray House in the Canongate. Each time, someone spotted them and raised the hue and cry to other townspeople, and the terrified members had to run for their lives. Finally they pretended to give up and go home; then, one by one, they found their separate ways to a cellar in High Street directly opposite the Tron Church. There, with hushed tones and frequent glances out the window, they signed the documents and slipped out the door. Everyone took Queensberry's cue and left for London that night. Rumors said the Edinburgh mob was planning to meet Queensberry's carriage as it left the city in the morning. No one was in the mood to take any chances.

As they made their way to London, the wrangling began about money. Some treaty supporters found themselves richly recompensed. The Marquis of Queensberry walked away with 12,000 pounds. Lord Marchmont received 1,100 pounds. Campbell of Cessnock received 50 pounds, which seems paltry until one realizes that one English pound was equal to twelve Scottish, so that he was actually pocketing the equivalent of 600 Scottish pounds. The Earl of Glasgow secured the Register's Office for life and an annual grant of 1,200 pounds sterling.

Many Darien investors received compensation for what they had lost, under a special provision (Article 15) of the treaty. But others received little or nothing of what had been promised. Inevitably there was bad blood and jealousy afterwards, and no one, except perhaps Queensberry, could say he had been rewarded above and beyond what his vote had cost him in honor and integrity in the eyes of posterity.

Things looked a little brighter from London. On March 4 the treaty passed both houses of Parliament at Westminster. If public opinion despised the treaty in Scotland, it found more supporters south of the Tweed, especially in London. Scotland was now secure from a Stuart takeover, it was assumed; the Protestant succession was safe, and Scotland's subordinate role to English political and mercantile interests was now a matter of law.

But in Scotland even treaty supporters had little cause for celebration. They had taken a huge plunge into the unknown, and a great gamble; no one knew what would actually happen. On May 1, 1707, the day the treaty came into force, the Earl of Mar received a letter from a friend in Edinburgh. "The tune of our musick bells this day was," he wrote, "'Why should I be sad on my wedding day?'"

Andrew Fletcher was, as usual, more caustic. "They may dance around to all Eternity," he said of the treaty's supporters, "in this Trap of their own making."

But Fletcher and the other doomsayers were wrong. Instead of becoming a trap, the Act of Union launched an economic boom. In the span of a single generation it would transform Scotland from a Third World country into a modern society, and open up a cultural and social revolution. Far from finding themselves slaves to the English, as opponents had prophesied, Scots experienced an unprecedented freedom and mobility. For the first time, the term *growth* began to apply to Scottish society, in every sense of the word. "What the Revolution had begun," declared the first number of the *Edinburgh Review,* referring to Scotland's first initial burst of creativity and energy after 1688, "the Union rendered compleat."

It is a judgment that, for almost two decades after the treaty signing, would have seemed ridiculous. Supporters of union had been gambling on the future. In a very short time, that future looked pretty bleak.

The first blow came in 1708, when London's Parliament abolished the Scottish Privy Council. This made even William Carstares, the man who had saved the treaty in the General Assembly, blink. By taking away the Privy Council, Parliament had deprived Scots of the one remaining intermediary body between them and the government in London. From that moment, the notion of a separate Scottish political interest had ceased to exist.

Then in 1709 came the introduction of the English liturgy for use in Anglican church services in Edinburgh. The very use of the word liturgy conjured up visions of Catholic Mass, Popery, and the Scarlet Woman of Rome for devout Scots. The Edinburgh Town Council and the Court of Session both issued bans against the practice, but the House of Lords—in London—overturned them. Anglicanism was now here to stay, and in 1712 another blow fell when Parliament—again, operating from London—passed an Act of Toleration for all Episcopalians in Scotland, ending the Kirk's claim to a monopoly over official religious life.

Even in London, some began to turn against the treaty, especially when opposition English Tories realized it was Scottish MPs' support that had kept successive Whig governments in power. In 1713 a bill was introduced in Parliament to dissolve the union. Ironically, it was Lord Seafield, who had declared the treaty "an end of an old song" as it was touched with the scepter, who now moved to undo the treaty in the House of Peers. In the end, supporters rallied and the dissolution bill was defeated by four votes—so slender was the thread that finally held the two kingdoms together!

Nor were the hopes that union would secure a Protestant succession borne out.

Queen Anne, the last Stuart, had no children or heirs. To keep a Protestant on the throne, Parliament had arranged for the crown to pass to her taciturn German cousin the Elector George of Hanover. After a long illness, Anne died on August 1, 1714. Her physician was John Arbuthnot, a Scot from Kincardineshire with a medical degree from

St. Andrews. He now watched with disgust as courtiers, politicians, and civil servants scrambled to find themselves places in the government of the new king, George I. "I have an opportunity calmly and philosophically to consider that treasure of vileness and baseness that I always believed to be in the heart of man," he wrote to his friend Alexander Pope.

One of the big losers in the scramble was the Earl of Mar, who was forced to surrender his powerful and lucrative post as Secretary of State for Scotland. Like most aristocrats, English or Scottish, he was helpless without his pensions or royal favor. Desperate for money, he stayed at Court for an entire year waiting for a chance to ingratiate himself with George I, but without success. Finally, when they met at a royal function in August of 1715, the king ostentatiously turned his back on Mar and refused to speak to him. Mar left England in a fury. He called on his friends and dependents to join him in his traditional annual stag hunt in the glens and forests around Braemar, overlooking the river Dee. After the hunt, Mar and the others drank a hot punch of whisky, honey, and boiling water, which their servants had brewed up in a rock outcropping. As they drained their cups, Mar spoke.

He told them, "That tho' he had been instrumental in forwarding the Union of the Two Kingdoms in the reign of Queen Anne, yet now his eyes were opened and he could see his error . . ." He swore to his amazed friends that he now would work to undo that "*cursed* Union" and make the Scots "again a free People, and that they should enjoy their ancient liberties." A few days later he raised the banner of the exiled James Stuart as rightful ruler of Scotland and England.

At one fell swoop, John Erskine, sixth Earl of Mar, had united two political causes, opposition to the Union and support for the Catholic James Stuart, or James the Pretender. Mar was not in contact with James, who was living in France; news of the rising came as much a surprise to James as to everyone else. But the rash gesture worked. Although Mar was a Lowland lord and had no clan to command, Highlanders from the west and east rose up to meet him. Gordons, Frasers, Campbells of Breadalbane and Glenlyon, Mackenzies, Macleans, and MacDonalds of Clanranald offered their swords and lives to Mar and the Stuart cause.

By October the Earl of Mar had an army of ten thousand infantry and cavalry, far larger than the ragtag bunch Prince Charles would assemble during the more famous Jacobite revolt in 1745. Virtually all of Scotland north of the Firth of Forth was in open support for James, along with large sections of the Presbyterian Lowlands and even northwest England. Gentlemen from Renfrewshire armed with pistols and breastplate rode side by side with Highland chiefs with broadsword and tartan. James became so confident the revolt would succeed that he landed with his entourage at Peterhead on December 22 and made plans for his coronation at Scone.

However, by then Mar had blown his chance. At Sheriffmuir on November 13 he met the much smaller loyalist forces commanded by the Duke of Argyll. By strange coincidence, each army managed to rout a large part of the other.

> *There's some that say that we wan,*
> *And some that they wan,*
> *And some say that nane wan at a' man;*
> *But one thing I'm sure,*
> *That at Sheriff-muir,*
> *A battle there was which I saw, man.*

In fact, the old song was wrong. Argyll won the battle by keeping his head and holding his ground with his remaining soldiers. Mar did not. He pulled back to his base at Perth and waited for French reinforcements that never came. As Argyll's forces grew in strength, Mar and James were forced to evacuate Perth. On February 3, 1716, James Stuart went sadly back into exile in France with the humiliated Mar.

The Jacobite revolt of 1745, "the Forty-five," is more famous than the one in 1715. However, "the Fifteen" was far more serious, in that it delivered a severe shock to the political class of both England and Scotland. Only the Earl of Mar's hesitations and incompetence had saved the situation. The Fifteen added a new and bitter division within Scotland, between Jacobites and "Whigs," or those who supported the House of Hanover. It also left an air of tension and uncertainty. No one knew just when James the Pretender might come back, and whether the whole political edifice of Great Britain might someday come crashing to the ground.

Even the new economic arrangements, the centerpiece of the pro-union public relations campaign, still looked bad a decade after the treaty. As Fletcher and others had predicted, it killed off domestic industries that had previously relied on tariffs and restrictions for their survival. One was the Scottish wool industry, which could not compete with its cheaper and more efficient English counterpart. Linen, once Scotland's most important manufacture, took a severe beating, as did brewing and papermaking.

Even more ominously, Scots were also paying more, a lot more, in taxes. The English were used to paying high customs and duties even on domestic products, and excise taxes on the basic necessities of life. The Scots were not. Taxes on linen, on paper, and on salt all warmed Scottish resentment against the union, and led many, even in the Presbyterian Lowlands, to look favorably on the rebels of the Fifteen. The last straw came in 1725, when Parliament imposed a heavy duty on malt, a crucial ingredient in brewing beer—and in making *uisge beatha,* or whisky. Glasgow exploded in revolt, the most serious popular violence to occur in Scotland in the entire century.

Yet even then a fundamental truth was beginning to dawn on the more farsighted Scottish merchants and members of the landowning class. The reason the English willingly paid more taxes was they got better government for their money. Since the mid–seventeenth century the English state had evolved into a powerful, purposeful bureaucracy, generating stability and efficiency across the political landscape. It kept public order and enforced the law; it provided usable roads for transport and communication between the capital, London, and the outlying counties; it supplied patronage jobs for local landowners and town patricians; it fed and equipped a standing army of nearly 100,000 men to protect British interests on the Continent and abroad; it maintained a navy that defended the lanes of sea traffic and trade from Newfoundland to Calcutta.

By the Act of Union, Scotland found itself yoked to this powerful engine for change, which expanded men's opportunities at the same time as it protected what they held dear: life, liberty, and property. It was a revelation. One result was that in the eighteenth century, enlightened Scots never worried about too much government. On the contrary, they had learned to see the benefits of strong state power and to see how too little of it, as before the Union, could hold back social and economic change.

And here, the fact that Scotland was very much the junior partner in this union also turned out to be an advantage. The new Parliament largely ignored Scotland; outbursts such as the malt riots and the threat of Jacobitism apart, the government in London paid little attention to what was happening north of the border. Scots ended up with the best of both worlds: peace and order from a strong administrative state, but freedom to develop and innovate without undue interference from those who controlled it. Over the next century, Scots would learn to rely on their own resources and ingenuity far more than their southern neighbors would. Scottish merchants and capitalists, like their American counterparts, recognized the advantages of a laissez-faire private sector far earlier than did the English or other Europeans.

A strong government that leaves well enough alone: this was the dual, seemingly contradictory, nature of the British state as it became part of life in post-union Scotland. Scots became used to these dualities, and learned to accept them as basic reality, just as the Union itself involved a fundamental duality: "a ship of state with a double-bottomed hull," as Jonathan Swift put it. They also learned to think in a new way as a result of the Union: in terms of the long term.

"In the long term," wrote the English economist John Maynard Keynes, "we are all dead." The Scottish Enlightenment learned a different lesson from the changes brought by union with England. Its greatest thinkers, such as Adam Smith and David Hume, understood that change constantly involves trade-offs, and that short-term costs are often compensated by long-term benefits. "Over time," "on balance," "on the whole"—these are favorite sentiments, if not expressions, of the

eighteenth-century enlightened Scot. More than any other, they capture the complex nature of modern society. And the proof came with
the Act of Union.

Here was a treaty, a legislative act inspired not by some great political vision or careful calculation of the needs of the future, or even by
patriotism. Most if not all of those who signed it were thinking about
urgent and immediate circumstances; they were in fact thinking largely
about themselves, often in the most venal terms. Yet this act—which in
the short term destroyed an independent kingdom, created huge political uncertainties both north and south, and sent Scotland's economy
into a tailspin—turned out, *in the long term,* to be the making of modern Scotland

Nor did Scots have to wait that long. Already by the 1720s, as the
smoke and tumult of the Fifteen was clearing, there were signs of
momentous changes in the economy. Grain exports more than doubled,
as Scottish agriculture recovered from the horrors of the Lean Years and
learned to become more commercial in its outlook. Lowland farmers
would be faced now not with starvation, but with falling prices due to
grain surpluses. Glasgow merchants entered the Atlantic trade with
English colonies in America, which had always been closed to them
before. By 1725 they were taking more than 15 percent of the tobacco
trade. Inside of two decades, they would be running it.

A wide range of goods, not just tobacco but also molasses, sugar,
cotton, and tea, flooded into Scotland. Finished goods, particularly
linen textiles and cotton products, began to flood out, despite the
excise tax. William Mackintosh of Borlum saw even in 1729 that
Scotland's landed gentry were living better than they ever had, "more
handsomely now in dress, table, and house furniture." Glasgow, the first
hub of Scotland's transatlantic trade, would soon be joined by Ayr,
Greenock, Paisley, Aberdeen, and Edinburgh. By the 1730s the Scottish
economy had turned the corner. By 1755 the value of Scottish exports
had more than doubled. And it was due almost entirely to the effect of
overseas trade, "the golden ball" as Andrew Fletcher had contemptuously called it, which the Union of 1707 had opened.

Fletcher himself had died in 1716. He played no part in the Fifteen.

His attitude toward Jacobite and Whig was "a plague on both their houses." Almost his last words were, "Lord have mercy on my poor Country that is so barbarously oppressed." Ironically enough, he died in the oppressor's capital, in London—on his way home from Europe, where he spent most of the years after the Union treaty. Someone had asked him when he left Scotland, "Will you forsake your country?" He answered, "It is only fit for the slaves who sold it." How strange that the laird of Saltoun, who had once been prepared to turn a large portion of his fellow countrymen into slaves, should use that word to describe the Scots who had repudiated his retrograde vision for the kingdom. How strange, too, that a man who claimed to despise trade and traders should choose to spend so much of his life in large, cosmopolitan cities— London, Paris, Amsterdam—that were built by mercantile wealth. It was precisely that wealth which he had hoped to deny Scotland, for the sake of an abstract and austere ideal of liberty. It was that wealth which Scotland's urban centers now enjoyed by being part of Britain, and which promised to create a new and very different Scotland.

Yet the Act of Union could not by itself force that change to come about. Instead, the next crucial stage of Scotland's emergence into the modern world did not come from outside influences, but from deep within two of its own institutions: its universities and its law courts.

CHAPTER THREE

The Proper Study of Mankind I

The proper Study of Mankind is Man.
—*Alexander Pope*

t was an eighteenth-century Englishman, Alexander Pope, who said it. But it was a pair of Scots, Francis Hutcheson and Lord Kames, who proved it.

As the founding fathers of the Scottish Enlightenment, they are a study in contrasts. One was a clergyman and teacher, considerate of his students, diffident and soft-spoken, who nonetheless inspired a generation of Scottish intellectuals—"the never to be forgotten Hutcheson," as his most famous pupil, Adam Smith, called him. Kames was a lawyer and a judge. Tough and outspoken, he was a formidable presence in the rough-and-tumble world of the Scottish legal system who rose to the Scottish equivalent of the Supreme Court. Kames had to write his influential books on the origins of law and society—there were more than twenty of them—in between court sessions. His view of the world was pragmatic, worldly, even cynical, compared with that of the high-minded Hutcheson. But together they revolutionized the Scottish intellect, and created a new understanding of human nature and society that has lasted down to today.

What makes the Scottish Enlightenment so important? When you mention the Enlightenment to most people, it conjures up images of glittering aristocratic salons lit by scores of candles, of scandalous wit and cultivated laughter, of bewigged philosophers and critics pressing their progressive ideas on various European autocrats. Voltaire visiting Frederick the Great at Sans Souci; Denis Diderot editing the *Encyclopédie* and urging Catherine the Great of Russia to outlaw the use of torture and the knout; Jean-Jacques Rousseau scandalizing polite society in the years leading to the French Revolution. Indeed, the famous names of the French Enlightenment seem to dominate almost every discussion of culture in the eighteenth century.

This is a mistake. The Scottish Enlightenment may have been less glamorous, but it was in many ways more robust and original. More important, it was at least as influential. In fact, if one were to draw up a list of the books that dominated the thinking of Europeans in the last quarter of the eighteenth century, the Scottish names stand out. Adam Smith's *A Theory of Moral Sentiments* and *Wealth of Nations.* David Hume's *Treatise of Human Nature* and *Essays Political, Literary, and Moral.* William Robertson's *History of Scotland* and *History of the Reign of Charles V.* Adam Ferguson's *Essay on the History of Civil Society.* John Millar's *The Origin of the Distinction of Ranks.* Thomas Reid's *Inquiry into the Human Mind.* And at the top of the page, Francis Hutcheson's *System of Moral Philosophy* and Lord Kames's *Sketches of the History of Man.*

It is an impressive list. If one had to identify two themes that most of these works share, they would be "history" and "human nature." Indeed, it is the Scots who first linked them together. The Scottish Enlightenment presented man as the product of history. Our most fundamental character as human beings, they argued, even our moral character, is constantly evolving and developing, shaped by a variety of forces over which we as individuals have little or no control. We are ultimately creatures of our environment: that was the great discovery that the "Scottish school," as it came to be known, brought to the modern world.

At the same time, they also insisted that these changes are not arbitrary or chaotic. They rest on certain fundamental principles and discernible patterns. The study of man is ultimately a *scientific* study. The Scots are the true inventors of what we today call the social sciences: anthropology, ethnography, sociology, psychology, history, and, as mention of the name Adam Smith makes us realize, economics. But their interests went beyond that.

The Scottish Enlightenment embarked on nothing less than a massive reordering of human knowledge. It sought to transform every branch of learning—literature and the arts; the social sciences; biology, chemistry, geology, and the other physical and natural sciences—into a series of organized disciplines that could be taught and passed on to posterity. The great figures of the Scottish Enlightenment never lost sight of their educational mission. Most were teachers or university professors; others were clergymen, who used their pulpits and sermons for the same purpose. Some, like Hutcheson, Ferguson, and Thomas Reid, were both. In every case, the goal of intellectual life was to understand in order to teach others, to enable the next generation to learn what you yourself have mastered and build on it. From the Scots' point of view, the advancement of human understanding was an essential part of the ascent of man in history.

This attitude produced one great achievement that would live on long after the Scottish Enlightenment itself had all but departed from the scene. In fact, to this day most of us have it on our bookshelves or on our computer disks. We and our children use it almost daily. It is called the *Encyclopaedia Britannica,* the first volume of which appeared in Edinburgh in 1768. Its editors intended it to be a complete summary of scientific and human knowledge, incorporating the latest discoveries as part of a coherent and graspable whole. It worked. While the French Enlightenment's version, Diderot's *Encyclopédie,* is today merely a historical curiosity, the *Encyclopaedia Britannica* has continued to grow, develop, and change over two centuries—just as its first editors had intended.

The editors of the *Encyclopaedia Britannica* also regarded their handiwork as a *British* encyclopedia—not an English encyclopedia, or even an Scottish one. They, like all the leading figures of the Scottish Enlightenment, saw themselves as Britons, members of a new, modern community created by the Act of Union. Some even dropped the term "Scots" altogether, and began referring to themselves as "North Britons." It was not as strange a locution as it sounds. In their minds, the Act of Union of 1707 had closed a door on an earlier era, on Scotland's cramped, crabbed, and violent past. The key question for Scots now had to be, where do we go from here?

It was Hutcheson and Kames who first laid out the contours of this new cultural landscape. Their disciples and followers—Smith, Hume, Robertson, and the rest—would fill in and embellish the areas they initially staked out. A new mental world was taking shape in Scotland's cities and universities, very different from that of medieval Scotland or the austere fundamentalism of the Reformation Kirk. At its center lay not God any longer, but human beings. Human beings considered as individuals but also as the products, even the playthings, of historical and social change: in other words, human beings as we understand them today.

I

Francis Hutcheson was the son of a Presbyterian clergyman, but in the "other" Scotland, the Ulster settlements of northern Ireland. In 1606 two Scottish noblemen, Hugh Montgomery and James Hamilton, arranged an amnesty for the Irish rebel Con O'Neill in exchange for a third of his vast property holdings in counties Down and Antrim. They then encouraged tenants from other parts of Scotland to settle there and establish farms. James I realized this could be a useful way to pacify the Catholic Irish in the neighboring territory. In 1610 he set aside nearly half a million acres across six counties, promising land to any settler willing to take the Oath of Supremacy (meaning they recognized James as the head of the English Church, which automatically excluded any Catholics). The settlers came in two great waves: first Highlanders from the Western Isles, then Lowlanders and some English emigrants financed by merchants in London (hence the name of the town where many made their homes, Londonderry). However, it was the Scots who predominated, and who left their stamp on the six counties of Protestant Ulster. Today Americans call their descendants "Scotch-Irish," but we must consider them Scots in every significant respect. In truth, they are the first representatives of the great Scottish diaspora that changed the rest of the world.

The Ulster Scots were genuine legatees of John Knox, with their fundamentalist religious zeal, their aggressive egalitarianism, and "their love of education and their anxiety to have an educated ministry," in

James McCosh's famous phrase. Two of those ministers were Francis Hutcheson's grandfather and father. John Hutcheson was pastor of Armagh when his son Francis was born in 1694. Francis received his first education at his grandfather's house. It seemed only natural and proper that he follow in their footsteps as a minister.

By then the Ulster Scots community had been through much. In the decades before Hutcheson's birth, they had endured massacre by dispossessed Irish Catholics, including the wholesale murder of men, women, and children at Portadown in 1641, and paid them back in kind. Many had signed the National Covenant, and backed the Parliamentary forces against Charles I. They had submitted to Cromwell's rule, and defied James II and the French at the gates of Londonderry in 1687. Like life in America's frontier West, life in Ulster had hardened and toughened its inhabitants into a tight-knit community. They felt surrounded by hostile forces, not only the native Irish but the Anglican officials of a "foreign" government in London. Thrown back on their own resources, Ulster Scots clung fiercely to their independent status and Scottish ways, including their Presbyterian faith.

But that faith was already changing. What was called "the new light" was spreading within the ranks of the Scottish clergy from England and Holland, and found support in Ulster. Like English Latitudinarians, some ministers had begun to question the harsh dogmas of old-style Calvinism, such as the proposition that man was innately sinful and the belief that every human being is predestined from birth for either heaven or hell. What had happened to the notion of human beings being made in the image of God, they wanted to know, and of changing one's life by accepting Jesus as Savior? We don't know whether young Francis was exposed to any of this "new light" when he attended James McAlpin's academy in County Down. But we do know John Hutcheson opposed any dilution of the old-time religion, and that later he and his son differed sharply over what direction the Presbyterian faith in Ireland should take. If Francis Hutcheson had begun to rethink his faith that early, he would get more food for thought when he arrived to study in Glasgow in 1711.

Glasgow lay across the water from the Ulster counties, and dominated western Scotland. The former medieval market town, set in the Clyde Valley, was a very different city from Edinburgh. Residents and visitors all agreed it was much more attractive. While Edinburgh was cramped, dirty, and soot-stained from thousands of foul-smelling coal fires (giving it its half-affectionate nickname of "Auld Reekie"), Glasgow was spaciously laid out in a graceful cruciform, defined by its four principal streets meeting in a central intersection. Daniel Defoe called it one of the most beautiful and cleanest cities in Great Britain. An international port city for more than a hundred years before the Act of Union, Glasgow had dispatched its ships regularly to European markets and to the Scottish settlements in the New World, in Nova Scotia (which James I sponsored), and in New Jersey. Before the Act of Union, and even before Darien, Perth Amboy was a regular stop for Glasgow merchants picking up goods and dropping off settlers in America.

In 1684 broadsides circulated in Glasgow calling for volunteers to "Province of New-east-Jersey in America," where, they said, the woods were filled with deer and elk, the sea with fish, the banks with oysters and clams. Winter ran only two months out of the year, the broadside assured readers, and natives were very few and "a help and encouragement, [rather] than anyways hurtful or troublesome." Eventually the English took over Perth Amboy and merged it into their own colonial administration, closing it to all but English merchants. Even this did not deter Glasgow merchants, who continued to do brisk business along the New Jersey coast—as smugglers.

The freewheeling, entrepreneurial character of Glasgow communicated itself to its university. The university's students numbered four hundred in 1700 (compared to around six hundred at Edinburgh), and included not only Ulstermen like Hutcheson, but a regular contingent of Englishmen from the south. The university was also much older than Edinburgh's—and suffered less interference from the local merchants or the Kirk. Whereas Edinburgh's Kirk-dominated town council appointed the majority of faculty professorships (they still controlled eighteen out of twenty-six in 1800), and voiced its approval or disapproval on the rest, at Glasgow pay and hiring remained in the hands of the university regents. This became important in the years after 1688.

The winds of change were beginning to blow through the university when Hutcheson arrived.

When William III came to the throne, the bloody persecutions and tensions of the Killing Time came to an end. Raised a Calvinist himself, William gave the Kirk the independence it had fought for, throwing out the bishops and recognizing the authority of the General Assembly. But William also insisted that the old fire-breathing, antimonarchical Covenant theology was out. Blotting out the Covenant's legacy among a clergy scattered across the country was difficult. An easier place to start was in the ministry's own training grounds, the universities. As his instrument to do this, the king chose his former chaplain and the man who would save the Act of Union, William Carstares.

Carstares did not become Principal of Edinburgh University until 1703. But his brother-in-law William Donlop had occupied that post at Glasgow since 1690. Donlop succeeded in appointing a series of regent professors who would undermine the power of the militants, while Carstares later did the same at Edinburgh. Together they recast the curriculum of Scotland's universities. Professorships sprang up in new fields such as history, botany, medicine, and law. The educational monopoly that the old-style Calvinist curriculum had once enjoyed was broken.

This also had important consequences. As the new century proceeded, young Scotsmen with brains and ambition learned to shy away from theology, as too controversial a field and too politically charged. Instead they turned their energies to other subjects: mathematics, medicine, law (Carstares set up the first chair in civil law at Edinburgh in 1710, and Glasgow followed suit in 1712), and the natural sciences— or natural philosophy, as it was called. The Carstares reforms laid the groundwork for the scientific side of the Scottish Enlightenment, and the appearance of such towering figures as Joseph Black in chemistry and William Cullen in medicine.

It also meant that for Scottish intellectuals, the study of science, medicine, mathematics, and even engineering was at least as important as literature, philosophy, history, and the arts. The enlightened man was expected to understand both. The notion of an intellectual conflict between science and the humanities, what the English writer C. P. Snow later termed the "two cultures," would have made no sense to an enlightened Scot.

Of course, all this lay in the future. Francis Hutcheson was starting at Glasgow on the traditional path, toward a master's degree in theology. But even here, new influences were making themselves felt. One of his first professors was John Simson, a new appointment as Professor of Sacred Theology and a Carstares-Donlop favorite. He was in fact Donlop's brother-in-law. It was a good thing, too, because he needed all his principal's help in his running battles with the Glasgow Kirk. Although he was detested by hard-line conservatives, Hutcheson and many others of the "Irish" contingent at Glasgow felt irresistibly drawn to him.

Simson directly challenged the harshest of the old Calvinist dogmas and offered to students a more reasonable view of man and divinity. The world around us is not the realm of the Devil; it reflects the purposes of its Creator, in its orderliness and bountiful gifts, its regularity and symmetry, and its startling beauty. Through it we can get a grasp of divinity that supplements, but does not replace, the one from the Bible. Like the teachings of Jesus in the Gospels, Simson explained, nature reveals a beneficent God who watches over the fate of His creatures and provides for their needs and desires.

This was a far cry from the terrifying fire-and-brimstone vision of the world taught by John Knox's catechisms or the sermons from the average Kirk pulpit. Hutcheson welcomed its image of a more serene and compassionate Creator and an orderly, benign creation: it became the foundation stone of his own theology. But he was also troubled by the radical direction Simson's teachings sometimes seemed to take. Simson proposed that belief in Jesus as Savior was not necessary for salvation, and that even moral and upright pagans might be saved. He cast doubt on the Trinity and on Jesus Christ as the Son of God—Christian tenets that advanced English thinkers such as John Locke and Isaac Newton had also abandoned. At one point in a lecture, Simson was even supposed to have told his students that when they read the passage from the Bible proclaiming Jesus "the highest God," they should read it "with a grain of salt."

No wonder Simson ran into such trouble with the Kirk authorities, who branded his teachings blasphemy. Simson's God of natural religion easily morphed into "nature's God" of the freethinking radical deist, who was only one remove (to an orthodox mind) from the outright atheist. Yet it was startling and amazing. Notions that had cost Thomas Aikenhead his life just fifteen years earlier were now being bandied about in theology classrooms—a measure of how much the intellectual atmosphere in Scotland had loosened up, even while Francis Hutcheson was still a student.

Hutcheson, the minister's child, could not accept his teacher's more radical teachings. Yet what troubled him about this racy, English-style natural religion was not just its detached view of God. He saw it overlapping with another troubling tendency, also stemming out of England, a kind of moral relativism. If God never did sacrifice His only son for our salvation, if He really is as distant and unconcerned about what happens to us here on earth as English deists claimed, then what happens to the moral law laid out for us in Scripture? It is, in that case, entirely contingent on personal belief. Otherwise, human beings are thrown back on their own resources, to find a way to survive in the jungle among their own brutal kind.

The figure of Thomas Hobbes loomed large and sinister in the minds of many thinkers at the beginning of the Age of Reason, and not just the young Hutcheson's. Hobbes's *Leviathan* was the description of just how such a jungle struggle for power results in the creation of the State. Human beings, realizing there is no natural moral order or constraint on their own appetites, entrust sovereign power to a single master, in order to prevent an inevitable "war of all against all," as Hobbes put it. In many ways, Hutcheson's lifework was one continuous refutation of Thomas Hobbes and all he stood for. The notion of human beings as naturally selfish and vicious, requiring the constant whip hand of the absolute State; the idea of morality as a man-made, rather than divinely inspired, set of ethical conventions—morality as a "social construct," as our modern-day Hobbesian, the postmodernist, would say—were all deeply repellent to Hutcheson.

Yet he also saw an irony: that moral relativists such as Hobbes ended up sounding like the fire-eating absolutists of traditional Calvinism. They both asserted that human beings were innately depraved creatures, incapable of a generous or self-sacrificing action without coercive iron constraints—of the Kirk's godly discipline, said the one; of the absolute State, said the other. The same conclusion, by different means.

Hutcheson believed there had to be a middle way between these two extremes, one that preserved the notion of an unquestionable moral law governing men's actions, but without the austere tyranny of a jealous God. He found some of what he was looking for in the classes of another professor, Gershom Carmichael.

If Hutcheson is the founding father of the Scottish Enlightenment, then Carmichael can claim to be its grandfather. He was one of the first teachers in Scotland to discuss Isaac Newton in his lectures. As Professor of Moral Philosophy, Carmichael intoduced his students to the great natural-law thinkers of the previous century, the Dutchman Hugo Grotius and the German Samuel Pufendorf. Hutcheson came to listen as Carmichael lectured—or, more precisely, read aloud his written notes in Latin, the common form of university teaching in those days.

The subject was the human being as he actually is, stripped of all the trappings and programming from a multitude of cultures and contexts, including religion. What was left? What philosophers called "man in the state of nature." He was at once an abstraction (after all, no one had ever really met such a creature, even in the remote, primeval forests of Africa or America) and a starting point for inquiry and understanding. He was for the student of philosophy like the model skeleton who hangs on his peg in anatomy class. He is on the one hand an artificial creation; no actual skeleton hangs together like that, and he corresponds to no person we know, either living or dead. His obvious unreality makes him, despite his macabre appearance, slightly ridiculous. Students give him absurd names and wheel him out for practical jokes and pranks.

But when class begins, we realize he reveals something important, something concealed beneath the skin, muscle, and tissue. He reveals the hidden structure, the essential anatomical parts and relationships without which none of the rest could exist. He exposes to us our own essential reality, stripped of outward appearance—he shows the bones, the marrow, the core of things.

That is what Carmichael, like his predecessors Grotius and Pufendorf, was trying to do. Pufendorf in particular struck a responsive chord in the young Hutcheson. Man in nature carries with him the spark of divine reason, Pufendorf argued, allowing him to grasp nature's governing laws. This includes the moral laws. As human beings living in society, we have certain *rights* that we bring to the table with us from our natural state, such as the right to our own life and our property. But there are also certain *obligations* we have to observe. One of the most obvious of these is obeying the laws established through common consent. But the other is the moral law governing our private conduct toward others. Without a moral law, no community is possible. Without community, there is no protection for ourselves and the things we need to survive, i.e., our property. When we realize, Pufendorf wrote, that our own self-interest dictates that we treat others as ourselves, we are ready to live among our fellow men.

Later on, Hutcheson would be more critical of this approach. "All must be Interest and some selfish View," he wrote of Pufendorf's theory. But for now it opened up a tantalizing possibility. The Presbyterian worldview and the Hobbesian one were both wrong. Man is indeed a moral creature, not by accident but by design. He carries within him the means to learn how to be virtuous and helpful to others. One big question remained: How does he learn to take that crucial step? Does he learn it the hard way, that if he is going to get along he has to go along, as Pufendorf suggested? Or is there a simpler, more uplifting way, by which we learn that virtue can be its own reward?

Even after Carmichael's classes, this remained unclear. So as Hutcheson graduated and returned to Ulster to take up his ministerial duties, he realized his education was still not complete. In fact, it was not until 1718 that it recommenced, when he set off south for Dublin.

Dublin was a city very much like Glasgow: mercantile, freewheeling, and culturally open-ended. It was the capital of the Protestant Ascendancy in Ireland. Ambitious Anglican Irishmen flocked there, hoping to find jobs working for the government or teaching at Trinity College or perhaps an undemanding sinecure with the Church of Ireland, whose intellectually alert and politically astute archbishop, William King, resided in Dublin.

Ulster Scots went, too, although the doors of Trinity College and St. Patrick's were closed to them. Competition between the two religious groups was fierce but friendly. Unlike in Scotland, or even in Ulster, Anglicans and Presbyterians had learned to mix in an atmosphere of mutual tolerance. Part of this was the need to close ranks against the Catholic Irish majority, whom the Penal Laws banned from civic life and certain professions (although somewhat later they would produce a thriving middle class in Dublin). But much of it came from a common fascination with the new cultural and intellectual trends swirling over from England: the ideas of John Locke, Samuel Clarke, Isaac Newton, and the suave aristocrat of English philosophers, Anthony Ashley Cooper, the third earl of Shaftesbury.

Hutcheson had been asked down to help set up a Presbyterian college-style academy in Dublin. He soon fell in with this eager and exuberant crowd of intellectuals, churchmen, and scholars. At their center was Viscount Molesworth, aristocratic politician and political theorist, and a friend of Shaftesbury's. Molesworth took up the soft-spoken clergyman from Armagh, and at Molesworth's dinner table, Hutcheson met or at least learned about the leading intellectual lights in London and Dublin. One of these was Jonathan Swift, who addressed the sixth of his *Drapier's Letters* to Molesworth. Another he heard about but who had died five years earlier was Molesworth's friend and patron Shaftesbury, who was a student of John Locke and the most original moral thinker of his generation. Yet another was George Berkeley, later to become a bishop, whose radical philosophical views (Berkeley believed that sense perceptions were all we could know about the world, and that we couldn't be certain there were other objects out there at all) provoked and dismayed his contemporaries. But the real bone of contention between Berkeley and the Molesworth circle, which now included Hutcheson, was political.

Berkeley had authored a pamphlet called *Passive Obedience,* which argued that rebellion, even against a tyrant, was contrary to God's will. It was a direct slap in the face to the 1688 revolution that had toppled James II. In fact, many people suspected Berkeley of pro-Stuart sympathies, which probably cost him the post of dean of St. Paul's in Dublin. Molesworth, like Shaftesbury and Locke, believed firmly in the principles of 1688, and in the idea of political liberty. They were Whigs (Shaftesbury's father had even been founder of the Whig Party), not just because they were strong Protestants but because they believed, contrary to Berkeley, that men were born with a desire to be free, in their own lives and in their political arrangements.

That notion became a ruling passion for Hutcheson. Later friends and students all described his deep commitment to the ideal of political liberty and his "just abhorrence of all slavish principles." In one of his last works, *The System of Moral Philosophy,* Hutcheson, as an admiring reviewer wrote, "boldly asserts the rights of resisting in the people, when their fundamental privileges are invaded." In fact, it is through Hutcheson that the old doctrines of right of resistance and popular sovereignty, espoused by Knox and Buchanan, merge into the mainstream of the Scottish Enlightenment, although in a more sophisticated and refined form.

Refined and *refinement:* these were important words for the Scottish Enlightenment. They went together with another term that Hutcheson picked up in Dublin, when he turned to the writings of Molesworth's patron, Lord Shaftesbury. That word was *politeness.* Shaftesbury took a term associated with the world of jewelers and stonemasons (as in "polished" stones and marble) and elevated it to the highest of human virtues. Being polished or polite was more than just good manners, as we might say. Politeness for Shaftesbury encapsulated all the strengths of a sophisticated culture: its keen sense of understanding, its flourishing art and literature, its self-confidence, its regard for truth and the importance of intellectual criticism, and, most important, an appreciation of the humane side of our character. The motto of the Shaftesburys was "love, serve." Kindness, compassion, self-restraint, and a sense of humor were, for Shaftesbury, the final fruits of a "polished" culture. Athens had achieved it in the age of Socrates; Rome, too, briefly, in the age of Horace and Virgil; and later on, Venice and Florence in the Renaissance. Now London had succeeded them as the artistic and literary capital, as well as the commercial center, of the greatest of modern "polite nations," Great Britain, the home of Newton and Locke, poets such as Pope and John Dryden, and architects such as Burlington, Vanburgh, and Christopher Wren.

Shaftesbury also explained where the highest and most sophisticated polite cultures came from. The answer was simple: liberty. "All politeness is owing to Liberty," he wrote. "We polish one another, and rub off our Corners and rough Sides by a sort of amicable Collision. To restrain this, is inevitably to bring a Rust upon Men's Understanding. 'Tis a destroying of Civility, Good Breeding, and even Charity itself. . . ." Shaftesbury joined up the notion of political and religious liberty that he had picked up from John Locke (Locke had been his father's doctor and his own tutor) with that of personal liberty, a polishing and refining of the self through friendly social interaction with others. You could not have one without the other, Shaftesbury claimed: just as human beings were meant to be free in the first, political sense, so they were meant to be free in the second, social and intellectual, sense.

The active, open, and sophisticated society of Dublin must have seemed vivid proof that Shaftesbury was right. On one side, interaction with others sharpens our minds and deepens our understanding. But it also teaches us about our obligations *toward* others—just as the encounters between Dublin's Anglicans and Ulster Presbyterians made each more tolerant of the other's point of view. Here Shaftesbury's words must have recalled for Hutcheson those of Pufendorf. What made Shaftesbury different was that he saw us serving others, not because we realized we had no choice if we wanted to get along, but because we realized we *enjoyed doing it.* Helping others, even strangers (giving directions to a lost motorist, helping a blind person cross a busy intersection) suffuses us with a sense of well-being and pleasure. For

Shaftesbury, this was the essence of morality. Being good *means* doing good for others. Virtue requires it, but, most important, our own feelings confirm it. Man was born to be with others, and born to make their lives more pleasant. "No one can be vicious or ill," Shaftesbury concluded, "except either by the deficiency or weakness of natural affection. . . . To be wicked or vicious is to be miserable and unhappy."

These words brought Hutcheson a major step closer to resolving the fundamental questions about God and man he had encountered at Glasgow. At the prompting of Molesworth and his Dublin friends, he began to put his answers on paper.

II

How do human beings become moral beings, who treat one another with kindness, regard, and cooperation, rather than brutality and savagery? Scottish Presbyterians knew how. It was inscribed in the *The Shorter Catechism,* which every child memorized: "The moral law is summarily comprehended in the Ten Commandments."

Under the influence of Carmichael and Shaftesbury and Pufendorf, Hutcheson had come to think otherwise. All human beings are born with an innate moral sense, Hutcheson believed, a fundamental understanding of the nature of right and wrong, which God gives to His creatures in His own image. "*From the very frame of our nature* we are determined to perceive pleasure in the practice of virtue, and to approve of it when practiced by ourselves or others."

In other words, we are born to make moral judgments, just as we are born with a mouth to eat and eyes to see. Moral reasoning ("what he did was good, what she did was bad") is a natural human faculty, but it differs from other kinds of reasoning, such as judging distances or adding up columns of numbers. It is expressed through our feelings and emotions. The most important is love, particularly love for others, which is the starting point of all morality. Love also proves man is not inherently selfish, as Thomas Hobbes had claimed. "There is no mortal," Hutcheson asserted, "without some love towards others, and desire in the happiness of some other persons as well as his own." A benevolent "fellow-feeling" for other creatures and a "delight in the Good of others" becomes the basis of our sense of right and wrong. We decide that what helps and pleases a person we love is good, because it also gives us pleasure. What injures him is bad, because it causes us pain to see him unhappy. We begin to realize that the happiness of others is also our happiness.

Everyone's ultimate goal in life, Hutcheson decided, is happiness. "He is in a sure state of happiness who has a sure prospect that in all parts of his existence he shall have all things he desires." Vulgar people assume, mistakenly, that this means gratification of physical desires: food, drink, sex. But for Hutcheson the highest form of happiness was making others happy. "All men of reflection, from the age of Socrates," he wrote in one of his Dublin essays, "have sufficiently proved that the truest, most constant, and lively pleasure, the happiest enjoyment of life, consists in kind affections to our fellow creatures."

It is the inner glow we feel when we make a child smile. For Hutcheson, our emotional lives reach out, instinctively, toward others, in bonds of affection and love, in ever widening circles, as our interactions with others grow and become more numerous. The basic rules of morality, including Christianity's rules, teach us how to act in the world, so that we can make as many others happy as possible.

Self-interest and altruism are no longer at odds. In our highest moral state they merge, and become "two forces compelling the same body to motion." They form "an invariable constant impulse towards one's own perfection and happiness of the highest kind" and "toward the happiness of others." Virtue is indeed its own reward. But it is the highest reward of all—a contented mind and soul.

If, three hundred years later, all this sounds ludicrously naive, we need to think again. Hutcheson was no fool. He was acutely aware of the standard objections to his view, not only from cynics like Thomas Hobbes but from his fellow Calvinists as well. He knew people could behave viciously, and hurt others. He knew human beings often ignore their consciences and the "bonds of beneficence and humanity" that bind us together in society.

But, he was asserting, that is not their true nature. As God's creatures, they carry within them the image of His infinite goodness. By using their reason and listening to their heart, they will choose right over wrong, and the good of others rather than gratification for themselves. The proof of this had come, interestingly enough, in his own life. When his grandfather Alexander died, he had left his house and estate to Francis, his favorite grandchild, bypassing in his will the eldest grandson, Hans. Francis very properly turned it down, although it would have raised his standard of living substantially. When Hans learned what his brother Francis had done for his benefit, then he, too, refused, insisting their grandfather's original wishes be carried out. The brothers spent the next several months arguing back and forth, each trying to force on the other the good fortune left to them by their grandfather—as perfect an example of altruism in action as Shaftesbury or anyone else could ask.* Human beings are not vicious by nature, was the lesson Hutcheson learned from this and a multitude of other little examples. They can do the right thing, and do right by others, and they prove it in their own lives every day.

———

Hutcheson published his first book in 1725, and dedicated it—*An Inquiry into the Original of Our Ideas of Beauty and Virtue*—to the teacher he had never met, Shaftesbury. The book made him celebrated not only in Dublin, but in England and eventually on the Continent as well. He followed with another edition in 1726, and then two years later published an *Essay on the Nature and Conduct of the Passions and Affections*. Its impact was such that when his old teacher at Glasgow, Gershom Carmichael, died, Hutcheson's name inevitably came up at the top of names to replace him.

The reaction from the Kirk establishment was overwhelmingly negative. They saw in Francis Hutcheson everything they disliked in the "new light" tradition: belief in a "natural" morality, downplaying the importance of the Ten Commandments, questioning the importance of predestination. Just that year, in 1729, they had finally forced John

———

*In the end, they agreed to split the inheritance between them.

Simson out of his chair as Professor of Theology. They were prepared to do at least the same to prevent Hutcheson from teaching.

The younger faculty members, however, saw him as a potential leader of reform. Several English students studying at Glasgow announced that if Hutcheson was not hired, they would leave the university. Even so, it is doubtful whether Hutcheson could have taken Carmichael's place if he had not had an unexpected and powerful ally waiting in the wings.

This was Archibald Campbell, Lord Islay, later the fourth Duke of Argyll. He was a remarkable man in an age of remarkable men. His grandfather was the Earl of Argyll who had been Andrew Fletcher's friend and who had lost the battle of Sedgemoor in 1685; his father was the Argyll who bested the Earl of Mar on the field at Sheriffmuir. Islay concentrated on politics rather than war, and rose to become the most powerful man in Scotland. He had strong connections both in the Lowlands and the Highlands—in the latter he was head of the great Campbell clan—as well as at Westminster and at Court. For forty years he used those connections ruthlessly to further the interests of his Whig allies and the House of Hanover.

But he was also a man with large intellectual and scientific interests. He was good friends with Robert Simson the mathematician, and a skilled amateur chemist. He provided generous patronage to Scotland's universities, particularly the University of Glasgow, where his word was virtually law. Between 1722 and his death in 1761, Islay had his hand in no less than fifty-five university appointments, not only at Glasgow but also at Edinburgh. He completed the progressive transformation of Scotland's universities that Carstares and Dunlop had begun. He created Glasgow's chair of Practical Astronomy and its first chair in chemistry. He donated plants and materials for its bonatical gardens. Some of Scotland's most distinguished scientific names, including Robert Simson, the chemist Joseph Black, and the medical theorist William Cullen, owed their careers in one way or another to Islay. Without him, in fact, Glasgow might never have played a major part in the Scottish Enlightenment.

His most important act in that regard was his support of Francis

Hutcheson. Islay recognized how useful Hutcheson could be at Glasgow, as a voice for reform and Whig ideals, and as a thorn in the side of the hidebound traditionalists. He pressured the faculty and regents at Glasgow to give way, and so Hutcheson beat his two rivals (one of them Carmichael's own son) for the post. It is a delicious irony that without the self-interested help of Islay, the most feared but also the most hated politician of his day, Hutcheson and his philosophy of moral altruism would never have enjoyed the sort of influence it did.

If the older generation of faculty resented his presence at Glasgow, Hutcheson never allowed it to become an obstacle to his teaching or writing. He carefully prepared his class lectures so that they never served as a cause for scandal. He turned out to be a brilliant teacher— so good, in fact, that his classes were always overbooked and he had to hire an assistant.

They were crowded for another reason. Hutcheson broke with ancient precedent and presented his classes on moral philosophy in English, rather than Latin. He may have been the first professor in Europe to teach in the vernacular, instead of the centuries-old language of academic learning. It not only expanded the range of students who could attend his class, but also introduced a note of informality and spontaneity into his lectures, which made their impact on hearers even greater. One of his students later described what taking a class from Hutcheson was like:

"He was a good-looking man, of engaging countenance. He delivered his lectures without notes, walking backwards and forwards in the area of his room. As his elocution was good, and his voice and manner pleasing, he raised the attention of his hearers at all times, and when the subject led him to explain and enforce the moral virtues, he displayed a fervent and persuasive eloquence which was irresistible."

Hutcheson lectured on Natural Religion, Morals, Jurisprudence, and Government five days a week, and delivered a sermon every Sunday on "the excellence of the Christian religion." Three days a week Hutcheson introduced another important innovation: discussing assigned readings directly with students, usually the ancient authors on morality such as Aristotle and Cicero. By his own example, and by exerting a gentle pressure on his colleagues, Hutcheson became a driving force behind curriculum reform at Glasgow. He pushed training in the Greek language and the ancient classics into the curriculum, as the foundation for polite learning. He helped to appoint other reform-minded colleagues to important chairs. Glasgow University soon gained a reputation for academic excellence and learning. English and Scottish observers considered its students better prepared and more intellectually engaged than those of Edinburgh—even though so many came from less than "the best families," but rather from middle-class or even poor origins.

Hutcheson's reforms at Glasgow served as the model for academic reform at the other Scottish universities later in the century. But through it all, Hutcheson never lost sight of his main goal: "to change the face of theology in Scotland," as he put it. He wanted to turn his fellow clergymen away from the hard, inflexible dogmas of John Knox and refocus their energies on the moral questions their parishioners faced every day. Hutcheson wanted the Presbyterian faith to take on a more humane, comforting face. It caused controversy. "I am already," he wrote to a friend in 1742, "called New Light here. I don't value it for myself, but I see it hurts some ministers who are most intimate with me." Nonetheless, within the Kirk he managed to create a lobbying group that later become known as the Moderate Party. It included colleagues such as William Leechman, whom Hutcheson brought in as Professor of Theology, former students such as Alexander Carlyle and Matthew Stewart (whose son Dugald would become the University of Edinburgh's most famous teacher), and ministers such as William Robertson and Hugh Blair, who chose Hutcheson as their professional role models.

All of them embraced Hutcheson's main point, that the message of Christianity was above all a moral message. The pulpit was not a place to inspire fear and terror, but to uplift and inspire. Church should be the school of men's consciences and a place to cultivate a disinterested benevolence and affection for our fellowmen. It becomes, in fact, a training ground for Shaftesbury's polite culture. Unlike their French counterparts, the great minds of the Scottish Enlightenment never saw

Christianity as their mortal enemy—not even Hume, the self-proclaimed skeptic. For the clerical disciples of Hutcheson, Church and Enlightenment were natural allies, in much the same way as science and the humanities were not pitted against each other, but were two halves of the same intellectual enterprise.

Yet Hutcheson's most lasting impact lay outside his immediate profession. It touched students such as Adam Smith, who arrived to study at Glasgow in 1737 and quickly fell under Hutcheson's spell. He sat in on the great man's lectures on moral philosophy from 7:30 to 8:30 in the morning three days a week, and then attended his main course on the philosophy of law and politics. There, Smith and other listeners would discover that the underlying principles of all human behavior were part of an "immense and connected" moral system governed by the dictates of natural law. That included "*oeconomicks,* or the laws and rights of the several members of a family," as well as "*private rights,* or the laws obtaining in natural liberty."

The crucial element in each, the part that enabled everything else to move, was always the same: liberty. Human beings are born free and equal. The desire to be free survives, even in the face of the demands for cooperation with others in society. Society acknowledges it as a natural right, which it must leave intact. That right is *universal;* in other words, it applies to all human beings everywhere, regardless of origin or status.

> As nature has implanted in every man a desire of his own happiness, and many tender affections towards others . . . and granted to each one some understanding and active powers, with a natural impulse to exercise them for the purposes of these affections; *'tis plain each one has a natural right to exert his power, according to his own judgement and inclination, for these purposes, in all such industry, labor, or amusements, as are not hurtful to others in their persons or goods.* . . .

Hutcheson took this basic principle of liberty out beyond the political realm. He not only endorsed Lockean ideas of freedom of speech and freedom of religion. He challenged other forms of oppression, which Locke and even Shaftesbury had ignored.

One was the legal subjection of women. Hutcheson defined rights as universal, and did not recognize any distinction based on gender. The other, even more important, was slavery. "Nothing," he said, "can change a rational creature into a piece of goods void of all rights." In fact, Hutcheson's lectures, published after his death under the title *A System of Moral Philosophy,* were "an attack on all forms of slavery as well as denial of any right to govern solely on superior abilities or riches." They would inspire antislavery abolitionists, not only in Scotland but from London to Philadelphia.

Francis Hutcheson had created a new political and social vision, one that went far beyond Locke or any comparable English thinker: the vision of a "free society." He is Europe's first liberal in the classic sense: a believer in maximizing personal liberty in the social, economic, and intellectual spheres, as well as the political. But the ultimate goal of this liberty was, we should remember, happiness—which Hutcheson always defined as resulting from helping others to be happy.

Freedom's ends are not selfish ones, he believed; they are in truth governed by God, through our moral reasoning. Hutcheson never worried about the dangers of letting people do or say whatever they wanted, because in his mind a free society enjoys a firm and permanent backstop, our innate moral sense, which enables us to distinguish the vicious from the virtuous, and the decent from the obscene, just as our intellectual reason enables us to sort out truth from falsehood. "The nature of virtue," Hutcheson wrote, "is thus as immutable as the divine Wisdom and Goodness."

Hutcheson's doctrine of happiness, then, had two faces. It involved, on one side, gratification of the self through a joyous and contented life. When Thomas Jefferson added "the pursuit of happiness" to his list of inalienable rights of man in the Declaration of Independence, he was emphasizing this side of Hutcheson's legacy. On the other, it was also intensely altruistic. No man stands alone, was the message his students absorbed. Hutcheson constantly enjoins us to get out and become involved in the lives of our fellow human beings. Our willingness to do so becomes the measure of who we are. His statement on this point—"action is best, which produces the greatest happiness for the greatest number"—would also ring down through the next two centuries, underpinning the utilitarian philosophy of two later Scots, James and John Stuart Mill.

That was what Francis Hutcheson taught his contemporaries: the desire to be moral and virtuous, and treat others with kindness and compassion; the desire to be free, including political freedom; and the desire to enjoy our natural rights in society, as civil rights, are *universal* desires. And why do human beings want them? Because these are the things that lead to human "happiness."

But this raised a problem for his disciples. If those desires are really so universal, why do so many societies deny people those very things? Why, given the variety of political and social systems in history, have there been so few that have delivered on Hutcheson's vision of a free society?

When Hutcheson died in 1746, he left no answer. He had been a philosopher, not a historian. He had concentrated on describing how things ought to be, rather than explaining how they actually were. It would take another Scotsman, based in Edinburgh rather than Glasgow, to do that.

CHAPTER FOUR

The Proper Study of Mankind II

The faculties of the mind have been explored, and the affections of the heart; but there is still wanting a history of the species in its progress from the savage state to its highest civilisation and improvement.

—*Lord Kames*

I

Henry Home was the son of a landed gentleman from Kames, in Berwickshire. His mother was the granddaughter of Dr. Robert Baillie, Principal of Glasgow University and an enthusiastic Covenanter in the 1640s. "I furnished to half a dozen of good fellows muskets and pikes," Baillie wrote the year the National Covenant had spread like wildfire across the south Lowlands, "and to my boy a good broad sword."

Home, who later took the title Lord Kames,* may have inherited his ancestor's fire and spirit, but the Kirk's legacy of pessimistic moral austerity left no discernible trace. Instead, he was raised an Episcopalian and learned early on the importance of a good income, as well as the pride and pleasure of being a gentleman farmer (especially when others do the heavy lifting). He attended no school or university, but was tutored at home. Since he showed a predilection for books and learning,

---

*When Scottish judges took their seats on the Court of Session, they were automatically addressed as "my Lord" and allowed to take honorary titles. Hence James Boswell's father, Alexander, became Lord Auchinleck, James Burnett became Lord Monboddo, and so on. Kames's title, which he took from his family estate, was in no way a peerage or a claim to nobility: from that point of view, Lord Kames remained a commoner for the rest of his life.

it was decided that the perfect profession for this heir to a modest country fortune was the law.

In 1712, just the year after Francis Hutcheson arrived at Glasgow, sixteen-year-old Harry Home set off for Edinburgh to start his legal education in the chambers of John Dickson, a so-called writer of the Signet, or what the English would call a solicitor. This was more than just a matter of terminology; it reflected a genuine difference between the legal systems of the two countries, and even a difference in the mentality of those who took up the study and practice of the law.

Scottish law had developed very differently from its English counterpart. They sprang up at almost the same time, in the twelfth and thirteenth centuries. But as time went on, the outlook of English lawyers and judges became increasingly insular. They looked to the custom and precedent of their own past to settle virtually every dispute—hence the term *common law*, meaning common to the kingdom of England.

The Scots, on the other hand, who had learned to cast wider for their fundamental legal principles, turned to the ancient Roman civil law. They studied the medieval legal scholars, the great "civilians," who were busy reviving that Roman legacy on the Continent. This meant that by John Knox's time Scottish law looked more like that of France or Italy than Scotland's neighbor to the immediate south. In fact, many Scottish lawyers in the seventeenth century still went to France to complete their law training rather than to England, since English legal principles made little or no sense to the Scottish mind.

To an American, the two systems might look the same. To bring a case to court, a person hires a solicitor (or in Scotland, a writer), who in turn finds a barrister (in Scotland, an advocate) to plead the case for his client before the judge. There, however, the similarity ends. The relationship between plaintiff and defendant is more than simply adversarial. The prosecution makes no opening statement; the evidence against a defendant must speak for itself. Judge and jury (and in Kame's time, there were no juries in civil trials) carry an awesome responsibility. Unlike his English and American counterpart, the Scottish magistrate does not just ask what the evidence proves. He dares to pose the crucial question: *What really happened?*

A Scottish judge's decision in a civil or criminal case looks beyond the facts to the underlying principles of fairness and equity that the case involves. His guide is not precedent but reason—hence the importance of Roman law, which later commentators even referred to as "written reason." Since the Middle Ages, in fact, Scottish legal minds had come to rely on Roman law to fill in the gaps in their own law. The judges of the Court of Session were even designated senators, as if they were the successors to the ancient Roman body.

The first professor of Scots law at the University of Edinburgh, Alexander Bayne, explained, "We consider the Roman laws which are not disconform to our own fixed Laws and Customs, to be our own Law." Later, as a distinguished judge, Lord Kames would agree. "Our law is grafted on that of Old Rome," he would write. "The Roman law is illustrious for its equitable rules, affording great scope for acute reasoning." It taught a judge above all to think independently, and not to worry too much about what other judges had said in the past. It also taught another invaluable lesson, firmly established in Scottish jurisprudence: that no person, not even a monarch, stood above the law.

The one Scottish institution left untouched by the Act of Union in 1707, besides its Kirk and its universities, was its legal system. Parliament House, once the home of self-government, now became the home of the law courts. When the teenaged Henry Home visited for the first time, he would have seen judges striding back and forth to court in their magnificent maroon silk robes (patterned after the red robes of the sovereign courts of France), the bustle of attorneys and bailiffs summoning clients to court, and he would have heard the cries of shopkeepers peddling their wares from their booths in the nearby streets and alleys. It became the center of his world. For the rest of his life, he never lived more than a few blocks from Parliament House.

Apprenticing with a writer of the Signet (so called from the royal signet ring used to authorize legal documents) was a typical way to start one's training in the law. Working with Dickson immersed Home in the complicated legal issues arising from the sale and alienation of land, and establishing hereditary title. He would have spent hours mastering the arcane rules and vocabulary of Scottish feudal landholding, a mixture of Norman French, Middle English, and Scots.

First came the various kinds of tenure, such as *ward, feu, blench, burgages,* and *mortification.* Then the obligations owed to landlords: *bonds, contracts, tacks* (a type of lease), *wadsets* (or mortgages), *venditions,* and "bills of bottomry." He would have learned how the landholding of feudal Scotland, in both Highlands and Lowlands, had been created out of military necessity. This archaic system of land ownership had survived in Scotland much as it had elsewhere in eighteenth-century Europe, although the Scots had organized and systematized it better than most. But since then, new forms of property holding—buying, selling, and leasing of land and movables—had arisen, which both overlapped and challenged the old patterns. Who was more in the right, the old landholders or the new? It was the kind of question that would occupy Home later on, and he could not have begun to address it without his earlier training in Dickson's chambers.

Home's interest in the law took a sharply different turn when he met Sir Hew Dalrymple, Lord President of the Court of Session. Dalrymple was the brother of John Dalrymple, Viscount Stair, who had died while pressing the Act of Union on a reluctant Parliament. Their father, the first Viscount Stair, was the distinguished organizer and systematizer of Scottish law, whose *Institutions* were published in 1681. The supposed "Dalrymple curse" left no mark on the elegant and convivial Sir Hew. Just the opposite. Home himself described the first time as a struggling young law clerk he met Dalrymple, and how it changed his life:

> I was kept waiting in an outer room. I heard delightful Musick upon a harpsichord in the next room, and I meditated on the hardship of there being such distinctions amongst Mankind. "Why are the people in that room enjoying such happiness, and I kept in a mean, drudging way? Were I but fortunate enough to be on the other side of that Wall."

There was only one way. This was to switch from the straightforward but less lucrative profession of writer or solicitor to the more glamorous but also more competitive world of the advocate or barrister, who represented clients in court and commanded high fees for doing so. It was also from their ranks that future judges for the Court of Session and the Court of Justiciary, Scotland's highest criminal court, were chosen.

Home quickly made up his mind. He became close friends of the Dalrymple family. The son became his roommate, and the music of the family harpsichord become a familiar sound to young Harry Home. He also threw himself into the studies necessary for admission to the Faculty of Advocates.

Scottish advocates had been practicing before the bar since the thirteenth century, and had formed their own guild, the Faculty of Advocates, in the sixteenth. The rules for admission had become increasingly strict, even scholarly. The Faculty required from its members a full course of study of philosophy and law at a university for at least two years, in lieu of formal experience for seven.

The contrast with England was striking. The English barrister received no formal academic training at all. Instead, he learned his trade at the Inns of Court in London entirely in the old medieval style of hands-on apprenticeship. Like his solicitor counterparts, the young English barrister learned to play follow-the-leader, and to obey the dictates of precedent, because there was no practical alternative.

But his Scottish counterpart was as much the product of rigorous scholarly erudition as of practical skills. Two years of overseas study, at universities in Holland or even in France, gave the Scottish bar a cosmopolitan air the English never achieved.

It also immersed the aspiring advocate even deeper in the theory of Roman and civil law. Justinian's *Codex* sat on Home's desk side by side with Stair's *Institutions* as he prepared for his final examination. Since 1664 the Faculty had required a private and public exam on the civil law administered by senior advocates, and a public speech on a civil law text chosen by the Dean of the Faculty. Home presented his on January 17, 1723, on a subject familiar from his days studying to be a writer to the Signet: the revocation and transference of legacies. He was now a full-fledged advocate and a member of the Scottish bar. He was twenty-seven years old.

Harry Home proved to be a rising star. His "tall, stooping figure," as his friend Allan Ramsay described him, and his "keen, sarcastic face" became familiar sights around Parliament House and in the neighboring taverns and oyster houses. Men and women alike found him captivating. The poet William Hamilton described him this way:

> *While crowned with radiant charms divine,*
> *Unnumbered beauties round thee shine. . . .*

As he admitted to James Boswell years later, "I got into pretty riotous and expensive society." When he found himself swamped with bills and over three hundred pounds in debt, he put the brakes on his social life and concentrated on the work.

His time in Dickson's office had given him a firm grasp of the intricacies of the law regarding land tenure, inheritance, and estates in Scotland. Combined with his immersion in civil jurisprudence, he now had the best of all possible intellectual backgrounds: a mind broadened by rigorous understanding of theory, but also steeped in the nuances of actual practice. He also turned out to be a brilliant advocate in court, summarizing cases without fanfare but with the full force of reasoned persuasion. He soon rose to become a senior examiner for the Faculty of Advocates, and then stepped in to act as curator of the Advocates' Library in 1737.

With the help of the library's keeper, Thomas Ruddiman, over the next half-decade Home turned it into a major repository for books not only on law but also on philosophy, history, geography, and foreign travel. It soon became one of the premier collections in Great Britain, and the seedbed of the Edinburgh Enlightenment. Its future keepers would include David Hume, who used the library to write his *History of England,* and Adam Ferguson, who used it for his *Essay on the History of Civil Society*. Anthropology, sociology, ethnography: almost all our modern social sciences got their start from the volumes assembled on the shelves at the Advocates' Library in Edinburgh. And it was Home who made it possible.

In this, as in so much else, his tireless energy reflected a key characteristic of the Scottish enlightened mind, its passion for organizing and systematizing knowledge. His first published book was a collection of past judicial decisions by the Court of Session, in order to help attorneys and judges to understand the future direction of Scottish law. He pored through the manuscripts of its old president Lord Fountainhall, the same judge who had met Thomas Aikenhead in Tollbooth Prison and spoken to the Privy Council on his behalf. The Advocates' Library contained his private papers, and Home was able to sift through Fountainhall's personal account of daily business in the Privy Council. It gave him invaluable insights into the interplay between politics and the law, and how issues arising from the one impinge upon and shape the judgments made in the other.

Increasingly, Home concluded that this was a normal, not an extraordinary, state of affairs. The law, he realized, was a living thing, "being founded on experience and common life," he would write later. "Our law thus comes to be enriched with new thoughts, new discoveries, new arguments, struck out by the invention of our lawyers." It is not a lifeless chain of tradition and precedent, but a flexible instrument, a means for attaining order and justice, and it must change as society changes, and human beings with it. The law is a means to an end—and what that end is depends on human desires and needs.

But somewhere, some basic principles have to stick. Somewhere there has to be a firm base on which everything else can rest; otherwise, the law becomes the plaything of power, not its master.

One such principle was reason, our rational faculty for grasping knowledge of the world and drawing conclusions from it. Another was nature: like Hutcheson, Home looked to philosophers such as Pufendorf as a guide for seeing how all human societies reflect the same underlying laws of nature dictated by God. Yet nature's laws, too, were not fixed and immutable. "The law of nature," he concluded in 1751, "which is the law of *our* nature, cannot be stationary. It must vary with the nature of man, and consequently refine gradually as human nature refines."

So what does remain stationary? What can we rely on as fundamentally true if everything else, including those qualities that define us as human beings, constantly shifts and changes? Those were the questions Home was determined to pursue.

The problem was that his research had to be squeezed into a highly successful but demanding legal career. In January 1752 he was appointed Lord Ordinary of the Court of Session, which enabled him to take the title of Lord Kames. His day regularly began sometime between 5:00 and 6:00 A.M., when he began reading and preparing for his day at court. Shortly before noon he would go to Parliament House to hear cases with his colleagues, including James Boswell's father. When the court rose at about three o'clock in the afternoon, Kames would skip dinner in order to spend time with books and manuscripts, including the Code of Justinian, Anglo-Saxon and Frankish law, and legal theorists ranging from the Hebraic and Islamic world to English commentators such as Sir Edward Coke and Sir William Blackstone.

Any actual writing usually had to wait until he could get away to the country between court sessions. Even there it had to be sandwiched in between supervising work on the farm and entertaining guests. Ramsay remembered Kames dressing for dinner, while "his clerk read over what he had written in the morning, marking his emendations and subsequent hints" for further research.

Evenings in the city were given over to social gatherings, which both he and his wife intensely enjoyed. They would invite friends to attend a concert or the theater (although in the 1740s theatrical performances were still technically illegal in Edinburgh), then return home to enjoy supper with intimates. Kames rarely got to bed until after midnight.

From the point of view of his researches, however, these convivial at-home evenings were not lost time. Kames liked to mix food and drink, including prodigious quantities of claret, with serious discussion of philosophical and legal issues. Kames's love of good company set the style and tone of Edinburgh's intellectual life for nearly a century, while his guests included a series of young men of genius who would dominate the Scottish Enlightenment.

One of these was John Millar, who served as tutor to Kames's son, then became the University of Glasgow's first Professor of Civil Law. As a teacher and scholar, Millar would virtually invent modern political history. Another was Adam Smith, who came to Edinburgh in 1746 looking for an academic job. Because none was available, Kames arranged for him to deliver a series of public lectures on rhetoric, literature, and the subject dear to Kames's heart, civil jurisprudence. Those lectures, delivered between 1748 and 1751, would become the foundation for the *Wealth of Nations*.

A third was James Boswell, the son of Kames's colleague on the Court of Session bench, Lord Auchinleck. The headstrong James quarreled frequently with his cold, reproachful father, and looked to the rough but affectionate Kames as his intermediary when things were going badly at home. After "Jamie" Boswell passed his exam to become an advocate in late July 1762, Kames brought him along on a tour of Scotland's Border country, not far from his Berwickshire estate. Boswell called Kames a man of "uncommon genius" as well as a "great character." Kames was in many ways the forerunner of the more famous father figure Boswell met when he moved to London, Samuel Johnson. In fact, Boswell even planned a biography of Kames similar to the one he did for Johnson. He never finished it—sadly, since it might have made the brilliant and sardonic judge from Berwickshire as familiar to modern readers as the learned doctor from Lichfield.

However, the favorite among Kames's young protégés was David Hume. They were distant relations—different branches of the great Border family of Home—and neighbors. The house at Kames was only ten miles from Ninewells, where David Hume had grown up. David's father died when he was a child, so Kames again stepped in as a father figure and intermediary. He reassured David's shocked mother and relations when the headstrong boy decided to give up the study of law and pursue philosophy instead.

Hume called Kames "the best friend I ever possessed" but also "the most arrogant man in the world." He described him as "an iron mind in an iron body," but noted: "He is fond of young people, of instructing them and dictating to them; but whenever they come up and have a mind of their own, he quarrels with them." In fact, Hume and Kames quarreled constantly, especially on matters of religion. David Hume had no religion. Kames was an Episcopalian (rare in Edinburgh, but not in landed upper-class Scottish circles) and detested unbelief. Kames even wrote his *Essays on the Principles of Morality and Natural Religion* as a refutation of Hume—only to become the target of the same vote of censure that hard-liners in the Kirk's General Assembly were bringing against Hume!*

As it happened, the vote against Hume failed. But it drove home the point that in the larger scheme of things, mentor and protégé were more alike than different. Both offended conventional opinion by pointing out that morality, like society itself, arose from human aspirations rather than divine ones—in Hume's words, from "mere human contrivances for the interest of society." Far more than Hutcheson, they worked to detach our understanding of human nature from its traditional theological moorings. Both saw human beings as the products of their environment, whether one was talking about the individual, as Hume did, or the collectivity, which was Kames's particular focus. They *relativized* man, in the sense that they made who we are dependent to some degree on our experience in a particular time and place, rather than solely on some inborn quality or sense.

This sense of context would become central to the Scottish view of history, anthropology, psychology, and economics. From this perspective, Hume would have to agree with Adam Smith: "We must every one of us acknowledge Kames for our master."

II

Kames's stolen hours of research, reading, and debate first bore fruit in 1732, when he published his *Essays Upon Several Subjects in Law*. He followed this with a second collection of essays on legal history in 1747, and then *Essays Upon the Principles of Morality and Natural Religion* in 1751. Together with *Historical Law Tracts* in 1758, they opened a new

---

*The *Essays,* however, did have an enormous impact on Kames's friend the Aberdeen philosopher Thomas Reid, and served as the foundation for his own philosophy of common sense. For more on Reid, see chapter 9.

chapter not only in the study of comparative law, but also in the study of human history.

The issue Kames raised was deceptively simple: Why do laws exist? What makes it possible for human beings not only to institute rules and regulations for their conduct, but also to agree to abide by them?

The answer he gave was a classic one—but now with an extra twist. Men institute laws, he concluded, in order to protect property. This was self-evident to the heir to a Berwickshire estate. But it was also rooted in every discussion of natural and civil law. A sense of property marked the starting line for all social arrangements. Any child knows that there are certain toys that belong to him, and him alone, and ones that belong to you. Roman lawyers called this a sense of *meum et tuum,* the sense that "that is yours and this is mine." We can share, and I can even pretend for a time that the tricycle I ride is really *my* tricycle. But at the end of the day, when accounts are settled, things must be returned to their proper owners—otherwise there come tears and recriminations, a sure sign that a fundamental instinct for fairness, a sense of justice, has been violated.

"That is yours and this is mine." And let's keep it that way. In other words, I'll respect yours, if you respect mine. That is why we create society, and with it government, in the first place: so that each person can enjoy what he or she has appropriated by his or her own efforts, without fear of hin-drance. "It is . . . a principle of the law of nature," wrote Kames, "and essential to the well-being of society that men be secured in their possessions honestly acquired."

Standing by itself, this was not a very original observation. John Locke, Samuel Pufendorf, even Thomas Hobbes would have said the same thing. But Kames added two points that made his readers sit up and take notice.

The first was that while Francis Hutcheson was insisting that men form governments in order to pursue the common good, Kames's emphasis on this self-interested sense of property introduced a note of realism. Kames was quite willing to believe in the notion of an innate moral sense, and man's natural sociability. His *Essays on the Principles of*

Morality and Natural Religion endorsed much of Hutcheson's point of view. It even contains Hutchesonian phrases such as, "Nature, which has designed us for society, has connected us strongly together by a partic-ipation [in] the joys and miseries of our fellow creatures." But life as an attorney had taught Kames a more realistic, if not cynical, view. Kames recognized that human beings need a more compelling reason to draw together into a binding community, and to surrender their personal freedom to others.

This is what our desire to protect our property, what we have worked for and set aside for ourselves, forces us to do. It forces us to take the plunge, to enter into this network of rights, duties, and oblig-ations with other people, because without it we will never feel secure about our property. "For without property," Kames pointed out, "labour and industry [were] in vain."

If Hutcheson was arguing that the most important instinct human beings have in common is their moral sense, Kames was saying that it is their sense of property and desire to own things. "Man is disposed by nature to appropriate"—one reason human beings are perennially adverse to common ownership of goods. It is not enough just to have goods; they must be *my* goods. Property is more than just material objects—it is a part of my sense of self. Without it, I am missing an important dimension of my personality, projected outward into the world. In fact, in eighteenth-century English, the language of Kames's works, *property* meant the same as *propriety*: those things that are *proper* to me, and to me alone. To Kames and his followers, including Hume and Adam Smith, to own *things* is in fact to own *myself*. Property makes me a whole and complete human being.

So it is not surprising, then, that human beings make the desire for property the guiding force in their lives, and devote so much time and energy to getting it, holding it, increasing it, or stealing it. "We thirst after opulence," Kames remarked in *Historical Law Tracts*. David Hume would put it even more vividly: all the other passions, including self-interest itself, have relatively minor effect on our lives, compared with the desire for property. "This avidity alone of acquiring goods and possessions for ourselves and our nearest friends is insatiable, perpetual, universal, and *directly destructive of society*."

Hume's point seems to contradict Kames's belief that property stands at the origin of society, but it actually restates it. We establish government precisely to put a check on *other people's avidity for our personal goods*. Where property is, laws and government follow, not out of keen desire for them, but out of necessity. What we want and have, others want, too, and they will do anything to get it, if we let them.

If we let them. What we might not have the time or even the inclination to do, compelling others to leave our possessions alone, the law does for us. In this way, Kames believed the law, meaning not just legal rules but their enforcement as well, served a powerful didactic purpose. It tells us our duty, toward others with regard to property and other rights, and toward ourselves. Doing injury to one person's property hurts everyone, because violating the rights of one, such as the right to property or the right to life, threatens the rights of all. In other words, the law projects a particular moral picture onto the world, which we as members of the community must share.

In its very earliest stages, as in the laws of Moses or of Hammurabi, the law simply taught men not to harm others, in their person or their possessions. Then it taught the importance of keeping promises and contracts, including the buying and selling of goods. Finally, as in the civil law code of the ancient Romans, "it extended to other matters, till it embraced every obvious duty arising in ordinary dealings between man and man."

Eventually the law's role in creating a moral order is supplemented by an internal device: the voice of conscience. "In the social state under regular discipline," Kames explained, "law ripens gradually with the human faculties, and by ripeness of discernment and delicacy of sentiment, many duties formerly neglected are found to be binding on conscience." Our innate moral sense finds a social footing, and the law is forced to catch up with the new attitudes: "Such duties can no longer be neglected by courts of law."

The happiest society, Kames concludes, is one where the law and culture, or what he and the rest of the eighteenth century called "manners," match. "The law of a country is in perfection," Kames wrote, "when it corresponds to the manners of a people, their circumstances, their government. And as these are seldom stationary, the law ought to accompany them in their changes."

And what are those changes? This was the second new twist Kames gave to his subject, one that was even more momentous and far-reaching. Kames attempted nothing less than to organize the history of the human community into four distinct stages, based on his extensive reading in comparative law, history, and geography, in order to show how each of these stages forces changes in the way people think, act, and govern their lives.

"Hunting and fishing," he explains in *Historical Law Tracts,* "were the original occupations of man." The life of the hunter and fisher, like those of the Bushmen of southern Africa and Eskimos in Kames's own day, encourages him to avoid other human beings, except members of his own family, as competitors in the daily hunt for game. Then, somewhat later, men learned to follow the animal herds and discovered how to domesticate them for their own purposes. This is the second stage, the pastoral-nomadic stage. "The shepherd life promotes larger societies" of clans and tribes, "if that may be called a society which hath scarce any other than a local connection."

Instead, the "true spirit of society, which consists of mutual benefits and in making the industry of individuals profitable to others as well as to themselves," must wait for the third stage of the human community, that of agriculture. Cultivating the fields is by necessity a communal enterprise: "this circumstance," the need for cooperation to bring in the annual harvest, "connects individuals in an intimate society of mutual support." New occupations arise—plowman, carpenter, blacksmith, stonemason—and new relationships: between craftsman and farmer, between landlord and tenant, between master and slave. New forms of cooperation, in one sense, but also new sources of conflict and the clash of competing interests.

In the first two stages of human society, Kames argued, that of hunter-gatherers and pastoral-nomads, there is no need for law or government, "except that which is exercised by the heads of families over children and domestics." It was the agricultural community that first needed additional help. Why? Because "the intimate union among a multitude of individuals, occasioned by agriculture," bred a complexity of rights and obligations no one had encountered before, and which earlier custom could not control. The law takes over, enforced by sanctions and punishment. These in turn require law enforcers, "men of weight and probity" to judge and acquit. "In short," Kames concluded, "it may be laid down as an universal maxim, that in every society the advances of government toward perfection are strictly proportioned to the advance of the society toward intimacy of union."

That "intimacy" has only gotten started at the agricultural stage, however. A further stage lies beyond, as activity shifts from the village and farm to the seaport and market town. A new society springs up, born of the buying and selling of goods and services, "commercial society." It brings even more benefits, and more cooperation, but also more complexity. It requires new laws—contract and maritime law, laws governing the sale and distribution of commodities—but also generates new attitudes and manners.

> Commerce tends to wear off those prejudices which maintain distinction and animosity between nations. It softens and polishes the manners of men. It unites them, by one of the strongest of all ties, the desire of supplying their mutual wants. It disposes them to peace, by establishing in every state an order of citizens bound by their interest to be the guardians of public tranquility. As soon as the commercial spirit gains . . . an ascendant in any society, we discover a new genius in its policy, its alliances, its wars, and its negotiations.

This was not Lord Kames speaking, or even Adam Smith. It was Smith's friend William Robertson, cleric and historian, and later Principal of the University of Edinburgh. Robertson's great contribution to the Enlightenment was to take Kames's four-stage theory and apply it to the history of Europe since the fall of Rome. By doing so, he created the modern study of history, turning Kames's evolutionary model into a way of organizing the history of Western civilization.

————————

The year was 1769, and the book was *The History of the Reign of Emperor Charles V.* Robertson demonstrated how the Dark Ages marked the return of a pastoral-nomadic society to Europe, with barbarian tribes such as the Vandals and Franks, and how the revival of agriculture, the third stage of civil society, brought with it the seeds of medieval feudalism. Then, starting in the Low Countries and Italy, merchants revived trade in its ancient home, the Mediterranean, and the fourth stage, commercial society, was born in its European guise. "In proportion as commerce made its way into the different countries of Europe," Robertson concluded, "they successively . . . adopted those manners, which occupy and distinguish polished nations." Politeness, as Lord Shaftesbury and Francis Hutcheson had understood it, now had a firm historical basis.

At each stage of civil society, Kames, Smith, and Robertson said, the way people earn their living shapes the character of their laws, their government, and their culture. Who we are depends on whether we are hunters and gatherers, or shepherds and nomads, or farmers and peasants, or merchants and manufacturers—the latter being the makers of "commercial society," or, to use a more familiar term, *capitalism*. Almost one hundred years before Karl Marx, Kames and the Scots had discovered the underlying cause of historical change: changes in the "means of production."

Kames had done two other remarkable things. First he had developed a flexible, sliding scale by which to characterize and compare different societies, in the past or the present, based on their position in the four-stage process. Modern England and France clearly fit the modern commercial stage, as did ancient Athens and Renaissance Italy. Medieval England, on the other hand, belonged to the agrarian stage, as did eighteenth-century Russia. The ancient Hebrews and the Indians of the American Plains fit the pastoral-nomadic—along with the Highland clans of Kames's own Scotland.

But none could be said to be forever fixed or static. This was the point: Human communities are in a state of constant evolution, as they slowly, sometimes inperceptibly, make their way from one stage to the next, higher stage. Kames's followers borrowed a French term for this process of social evolution. They called it "civilization," meaning a transformation of society from primitive barbarism to a civilized "polite" state.

The four-stage theory of civilization defined human history as a continuous vista of secular progress. Understanding the character of those different stages, and identifying the crucial moving parts in each, would become the task of the Scottish historical imagination for the next hundred years.

But Kames had also solved the question Francis Hutcheson had by implication posed, but never quite answered: Why, if everyone has the same desire to be free and happy, as Hutcheson had claimed, are there so many societies in which people are neither?

Now Lord Kames gives us the answer. Because, under certain primitive material conditions, when resources are scarce or in uncertain supply, the rights of the individual have to give way to the imperatives of the group. The Bushman hunter divides his kill with the rest of his little clan, whether he wishes to or not, because otherwise the group might starve. During the Dark Ages, peasants were bound to the land to produce food, because no one knew when the next attack by marauding Vikings or Saracens might disrupt the harvest and plunge the community into famine.

Under these harsh conditions, society cannot afford to trust individual choice or inclination. Men are guided instead by custom, and the personal authority of those they do trust—"the elders of the tribe" or a warrior nobility. The laws are strict, the punishments harsh.

Then, as material conditions improve, *as they inevitably will* when human beings devise new ways to increase their stock of property, the institutions governing the community also improve. In short, material progress—from the relative scarcity of the hunter-gatherer Bushmen to the relative prosperity of mercantile London and Edinburgh—brings other kinds of progress in its wake. The affluence and mutually beneficial union of commercial society "softens and polishes the manners of men," as Robertson put it. Individual conscience is prepared to do the work that laws, and fearful punishments and taboos, used to do. As a modern social scientist would say, the rules of socialization are internalized. We no longer need awe-inspiring authority figures—kings and nobles, popes and priests—to tell us what to do, or what is right and wrong. "The moral sense," Kames explained, "is openly recognized, and cheerfully submitted to." Hutcheson's community of free and active human beings becomes possible, and the old collective traditions and constraints give way to individual liberty.

Even in Scotland. On the heels of the Jacobite revolt of 1745,* Kames published his *Essay Upon Several Subjects Concerning British Antiquities.* In it Kames demonstrated that the politics of traditional Scotland was not about loyalty and devotion to the king, as Jacobites claimed, but about royal land grants, which enabled the king to reward his closest followers and secure control over the people. This was the origin of feudalism. "No Constitution," he wrote, "gives [the sovereign] such an immediate hold of the persons and property of his subjects." Scotland's traditional laws were not bulwarks of political freedom, as Andrew Fletcher and the rest had used to argue. They were in fact an invitation to despotism.

Then came the sweep of historical change. "After the arts of peace began to be cultivated" at the close of the Middle Ages, "manufacturers and trade began to revive in Europe, and riches to encrease," and the feudal system "behoved to turn extreme burdensome. It first tottered, and then fell of its own weight, as wanting a solid foundation." Feudalism loses out to trade and commerce, because it runs counter to "love of independence and property, the most steady and industrious of all human appetites." Commercial society supplies that "love of independence" in abundance. It encourages men to overturn custom and tradition, and establish a new kind of law, based on a free circulation of goods and services.

Already, in 1747, Kames recognized what Adam Smith and later

---

*For details, see chapter 6.

economists would confirm. More than any other stage of society, the commercial stage represents the greatest change from the past. This progress comes at a price: the overturning of almost everything that came before, in laws, in forms of government, even in manners and morals. Capitalism's innate capacity for creative destruction would fascinate Kames's followers, including Adam Smith, who would witness its awesome power in the Lowlands and Highlands of their own day.

III

The four-stage theory, which Kames revised and refined in his *Sketches on the History of Man* when he was nearly eighty, would live on after him. It served as the model for William Robertson and others of the "Scottish historical school," and for the great masterpiece of Enlightenment history, Edward Gibbon's *The Decline and Fall of the Roman Empire*. It defined the fields of comparative anthropology and sociology for two hundred years, and inspired a historical genre, "the story of civilization," that would last down to Arnold Toynbee's *A Study of History* and William McNeill's *The Rise of the West*. And at its core was Kames's notion that changing forms of property drove the evolution of civil society. "Without private property," he wrote in the *Sketches,* "there would be no industry, and without industry, men would remain savages forever."

Today, of course, we have grown suspicious of attempts to classify entire societies as "savage" or "civilized." The multiculturalist teaches us to see them as misleading stereotypes, which denigrate certain non-Western peoples, especially peoples of color, in order to exalt our own Western values. We try to dismiss the four-stage theory as "ethnocentric" or even racist.

It is true that the four-stage theory would help to underpin racial theory in the nineteenth century. But at the time it served a powerful and useful purpose. It enabled people to think of history as a *progressive* enterprise, with change as a normal, even desirable, feature of society, rather than an undesirable one. It also *cut across* issues of race. Enlightened Scots had no difficulty in thinking of China or Persia as "civilized" or even "commercial" societies, just as they understood primitiveness and savagery to be prominent aspects of their own white European past—or, in the case of the Highlands, in their own backyard. It immunized the Scottish historical imagination against attempts to make race determine culture. Nurture, not nature, explained human behavior and institutions. Kames himself dismissed the idea that Africans and blacks were inherently inferior to whites. Who can say, he wondered, what kind of society they might produce, if they had the occasion to exercise their powers of freedom, as European whites had?

Kames and Robertson may have been willing to make "value judgments" about other societies and peoples, but they did it without concerning themselves with skin color. The fundamental issue for them was not race but human liberty, much as it was for Francis Hutcheson. And the proof of it came in the Joseph Knight case.

Joseph Knight was an African-born slave sold in Jamaica, whose master took him to Scotland in 1769. Three years later Knight learned about the celebrated decision by the English Chief Justice Lord Mansfield* that slavery was contrary to the laws of England. Knight assumed this included the rest of Britain. Knight went to his master and demanded wages for the work he had been doing for free. His master refused. When Knight tried to run away, the master had him arrested.

When the case came before the Sheriff of Perth, however, he ruled that there was no slavery in Scotland, and that the slave laws of Jamaica had no validity in his jurisdiction. He let Knight go. Knight's master appealed, and in 1777 the case arrived at the Court of Session in Edinburgh. It was momentous enough that it was granted a full hearing in front of the full panel of judges, including Lord Kames. History was about to be made, and not just for Scot-land.

Knight's advocate told the judges, "The law of Jamaica in this case, will not be supported by the Court: because it is repugnant to the first principles of morality and justice." James Boswell had helped him to prepare his brief for Knight's freedom, with the advice of another tire-

---

*Mansfield actually happened to be a Scot, although he was educated in the law in England and served on the King's Bench in London.

less opponent of slavery, Samuel Johnson. Their argument was simple: "No man is by nature the property of another." To become the legitimate chattel of another person, he must renounce that original natural freedom. If there is no proof he has done this (and Knight's own actions clearly proved the opposite), then he must be set free.

Kames, who was now over eighty, vigorously assented. "We sit here to enforce right," he told his colleagues, "not to enforce wrong." The majority of the court agreed with Kames. They wrote, "The dominion assumed over the negro, under the law of Jamaica, being unjust, could not be supported in this country to any extent." They pronounced slavery to be against the law in Scotland, and set Knight free. James Boswell was jubilant. He pointed out to friends that although Lord Mansfield had made a similar ruling five years earlier, the Scottish decision was more significant, because it established a broader principle. It went "to the general question, whether a perpetual obligation of service to one master *in any mode* should be sanctioned by the laws of a free country." It was a vindication of the historical point Kames had been making for years, that what might have been suitable or necessary for ancient or primitive societies may not be now. Progress was possible, in law as well as in everything else.

But it was also a vindication of the Scottish approach to the law. Kames and his fellow judges had decided the case not on precedent but on "the dictate of reason," in order to assert a basic principle of equity and justice. It was a victory for the notion that man's claim to liberty is universal. What Francis Hutcheson had first asserted in his Glasgow classroom had now been confirmed by Kames and the judges of the Court of Session.

The Knight case shows Lord Kames at his best. In other respects, he is a hard man to like. If Francis Hutcheson represents the soft, humane side of the Scottish Enlightenment and the Scottish character, Kames represents its hard, cold-eyed edge. His sardonic view of the primacy of self-interest and the "thirst for opulence" anticipates what comes later in the works of David Hume, and dismays champions of Hutcheson's moral altruism.

So does Kames's enthusiastic support for capital punishment. Unlike some of his colleagues on the Court of Justiciary, he saw no conflict between a civilized legal system and hanging men for stealing sheep. "The objects of the penal laws," he argued, "are to be found among that abandoned and most abject class of men, who are the disgrace of the species." No other punishment will deter those individuals, he decided, who have "no feelings at all of honour, justice, and humanity."

This is not the sort of sentiment to endear him to the modern liberal, and it must be said that Kames handed out death sentences with a kind of relish that shocked even his fellow judges. Once in a single session he convicted and sentenced two prisoners to be hanged. That evening Kames was in particularly good spirits, boasting to his guests that "he had killed two birds that day." Another time he pronounced the death sentence on an old acquaintance, who had been an opponent at chess. "And that's checkmate, Thomas!" Kames quipped as they led the man away.

Courtesy and social niceties, key ingredients of Hutcheson's notion of politeness, meant nothing to Kames. He did not mind being vulgar. He liked to call people "brutes" or even "bitches" (in Scots it can apply to men as well as women). "Davie, how are ye, ye brute?" was a standard greeting if he met a friend on the street. Some took it in good humour, others were horrified. He ignored all questions of social rank. If he could not get an intellectual guest such as Boswell or Thomas Reid to accompany him on one of his interminable walks on his estate, he would get his estate foreman or gardener, or even one of his farm laborers, to go with him, arguing about law and social customs at the top of his lungs as they swung along across the fields, with Kames occasionally stooping to examine, or even taste, the new experimental fertilizer he had ordered laid down the week before.

In the final analysis, we find in Lord Kames and his writings the Scottish mind geared entirely toward the practical and the concrete, shorn of any sentimentality or pretense but also of any compassion. Religious feeling, too, got short shrift from Kames. Divine Providence increasingly disappeared from his analysis of man as a moral or social animal. When mortal illness finally overtook him, at age eighty-six, he greeted it stoically with his usual lack of sentimentality. His last day on the bench, he said merely good-bye to his colleagues with a jocular "Fare ye weel, ye bitches!"

James Boswell came up from London to visit him at home a month or so later, shortly before Christmas in 1782. He was shocked, and a little disappointed, to see that the approach of death had failed to lift his old mentor's thoughts beyond the mundane and trivial. There were no last words of wisdom, insight, or even regret. Nothing.

Boswell, who was a professing Christian and a believer in an afterlife, tried to corner the old man about his views on the subject. "I believe, my Lord," he said, "you have been lucky enough to have always an amiable view of the Deity, and no doubt of a future state."

Kames, sitting in his armchair, said nothing. Boswell confessed he believed the doctrine of an eternity of Hell's torment was counterproductive. "No," Kames replied, "nobody believes it."

Six days later he was dead.

CHAPTER FIVE

A Land Divided

The Highlanders are Great Thieves.
—*Cassius Dio, Roman historian, Third Century* A.D.

T wenty thousand years ago, the last great ice age buried the northern half of Europe under a massive glacier. In some places, the Eurasian ice sheet was as much as one mile thick; it acted as a primordial bulldozer, relentlessly shoving aside everything in its path. It did its most destructive work in Scandinavia and northern Britain, grinding the earth's surface down to the bare rock. When the huge ice plate finally melted and receded, it left behind a pitiless landscape of granite mountains and deep, gouged-out river valleys—the landscape of the Scottish Highlands. Only a thin, provisional crust of topsoil covered the harsh, flinty ground. It is the poorest land in Britain.

Nonetheless, over the next millennia it would become home to a succession of peoples. First, pre-Celtic Neolithic tribesmen; then the Picts, who battled the Romans along Hadrian's Wall for control of northern Britain; and then, finally, wanderers from Ireland whom the Romans termed *Scoti* (or "bandits") but who called themselves the *Gael*. Celtic by language and culture, the Gaels congregated in extended family groupings—the ancestors of the clans. By the middle of the eighteenth century there were more than 600,000 people living in this wild, inaccessible region. The agriculture produced by that poor layer of topsoil could barely support half that number.

By 1745 the Highlands were on the brink of starvation. Political events far beyond the mountains and glens were about to set off a massive upheaval, as the news spread south that the clans were on the move.

I

To an observant Scot in the 1730s and 1740s, Lord Kames's four-stage theory of social evolution was more than a theory; it was a part of everyday reality. Looking around him, he could see all four stages in action at once.

For example, Glasgow and Edinburgh were beginning to exhibit all the characteristics of "polite" commercial society. The fertile river valleys in the middle Lowlands, from Ayrshire and Lanarkshire in the Clyde Valley across the Lothians to Berwick and Roxburgh, fit the agrarian stage, as lairds and tenants labored as they always had to produce the annual harvest. In fact, the Scottish version of "fixed" agriculture was anything but fixed: a prodigious wave of agricultural improvement was about to sweep over the Lowlands. One of the most enthusiastic improvers was Lord Kames himself. He constantly experimented on his family estate with new crops, crop rotation, and different manures and fertilizers—all in order to make his land more productive. Kames even dubbed agriculture "the chief of the arts," and wrote an influential book on the subject. In it he admonished his fellow landlords and their tenants for their "stupid attachment to ancient habit and practices," and pushed them to embrace the new. After the disastrous harvest of 1740, which triggered the last widespread famine in Scottish history, many were ready to follow his lead. Change was becoming the norm in Lowland Scotland, just as it is for us living in the modern global village: change for those living on the land, as well as those in the city.

The Highlands, by contrast, seemed permanently stuck in the pastoral stage. Its inhabitants were herdsmen, living off their flocks of cattle and sheep, with farming coming in a poor second. The clan way of life fit perfectly Kames's own description of the "shepherd life, in which societies are formed by the conjunction of families for mutual defense." Once a source of strength, the clan system now increasingly isolated its members from the rest of Britain and Scotland.

In 1600, Lowlanders and Highlanders would not have been

strangers to each other. By 1700 they were. Even before the Act of Union, a series of changes had driven a wedge between the two halves of Scotland. Some were social and economic, as cities and the cash-based relations between laird and tenant uprooted the last remnants of clanship in the Lowlands. Some were religious, as the Lowlands embraced the Presbyterianism of John Knox, while the clansmen in the north tended to remain loyal to the Catholic faith or followed their chieftains into the Episcopalian Church. Others were linguistic, as Gaelic disappeared from the regions of Scotland south of the Firth of Forth but remained firmly rooted in the glens and Hebridean Islands to the north. But in every case, the next century would only deepen the split, which the events of 1745 would set in high relief.

Then, if the observer turned to the Western Isles and the remotest parts of the north of Scotland, he might catch a glimpse of the most primitive of social stages, the hunter-gatherer stage. Tiny communities of fishermen and gatherers of seaweed and whelks dotted the Hebridean coast, eking out an existence from the rocky shoreline as they had for hundreds of years. Samuel Johnson saw them when he made his tour of the Hebrides with James Boswell in 1773, and noted the crude and piti-ful huts in which they lived.

A visit to the north made any Scot immune from the romantic myth of the "noble savage." This was not a life of harmony with nature, as the disciple of Jean-Jacques Rousseau—or the modern radical environmen-talist—might think. It was a world of dreary drudgery, inhabited by a people, Johnson observed, "whose whole time is a series of distress; where every morning is labouring with expedients for the evening; and where all mental pain or pleasure arose from the dread of winter, the expectation of spring, the caprices of their chiefs, and the motions of the neighboring clans." No wonder he concluded, in one of his most famous maxims, that "the best prospect a Scotsman ever sees is the high road to London."

London, perhaps, but more likely Glasgow or Edinburgh. If hunting-gathering and pastoral-nomadic Scotland chained people to a life of destitution and ignorance, commercial Scotland opened them up to the rest of the world, and the rest of Britain. In 1740, Glasgow's great

Tobacco Lords were just coming into their own, and the wealth from their American trade was about to transform the face of the city. The teeming warehouses and counting-houses along Glasgow's business district not only looked westward over the Atlantic but also south and east, as Glasgow merchants re-exported their American tobacco cargoes to ports in France, Scandinavia, and Russia, as well as the Mediterranean.*

But it was Edinburgh that first exhibited the key advantages of life in a commercial, modern society. In 1740 it was still a small town compared with London or even Bristol. Citizens rich and poor still lived in the dank narrow alleys and wynds of the Old Town, now packed to overflowing. But the city breathed an energy and cultural vitality that every observer noted immediately. James Boswell described what it was like growing up in Edinburgh in the 1740s, with its unceasing bustle and social diversity, as he would race home after class down Horse Wynd and up Borthwick's Close, past "advocates, writers, Scotch Hunters, cloth-merchants, Presbyterian ministers, country lairds, captains both by land and sea, porters, chairmen, and cadies"—"cadies" being young men hired to do menial tasks (such as the one for which we still use the word, namely carrying golf clubs).

Secular polite culture had arrived in Edinburgh, of a sort that a Lord Shaftesbury could recognize, and despite the occasional fierce opposition of local clergy. The sound that had symbolized the good life for the young Lord Kames—a harpsichord—had become part of everyday public life, thanks to the Crosskeys Tavern off Canongate. There, owner Patrick Steel, who was also a violin maker, sponsored regular concerts by talented amateur musicians. Lord Colville on the harpsichord, Forbes of Newhall on the viola da gamba, Steel himself on the violin, and Sir Gilbert Elliott of Minto on a new instrument from Germany, the transverse flute, drew flocks of admiring ladies. A little later the Edinburgh Musical Society would soon make the city Scotland's music capital.

More daringly, dancing also penetrated the Edinburgh scene. In 1710, Edinburgh had its first public ball. By the next decade Scotland's

*See chapter 7.

leading aristocrats—Hamilton, Morton, Annandale, and Islay—could be seen dancing minuets, gavottes, and polonaises at parties or "assemblies" in private homes, much like their counterparts in London or Paris. The real breakthrough came in 1737, when ministers-in-training were allowed to learn to dance without fear of retribution, divine or otherwise. Alexander Carlyle, who was studying to be a minister at the university in the 1740s, took up dancing lessons with enthusiasm. As he confessed years later, he became quite good at it, "and had my choice of partners on all occasions."

Carlyle probably also perused *Rules of Good Deportment*, published in Edinburgh in 1720 by Adam Petrie. The *Rules* vividly demonstrated how "polite society" in Shaftesbury and Hutcheson's sense required new standards of personal behavior. Petrie's premise was that "civility is a pleasant Accomplishment" as well as "a Duty injoined by God." He explained to his fellow Scots that gentlemen walk, rather than run, in the street. They don't make faces or move their hands when they speak. They don't prod people in the stomach to emphasize a point, and "when you discourse with another, stand not so near him as to breathe in his face."

Petrie also warned against making noises when you eat, or cramming your mouth with food, which is behavior, he explained, "more suitable to a Beast than a rational creature." The polite diner does not lick his fingers at the table, or blow on his soup if it is too hot. Petrie concluded his advice on table manners by saying, "Do not smell at what you eat or drink, and it is most rude to do it to what another eats or drinks."

Edinburgh got its first daily newspaper in 1705. The Royal Bank of Scotland, the first such since the disastrous Darien failure, opened its doors in 1727, as did the Friendly Insurance Company and the Royal Infirmary. *Scots Magazine* published its first issue in 1739. It is still published today. Shops offering the physical accoutrements of polite manners—lace, gloves, linen underclothing, snuff, and gentleman's powdered wigs—became part of Edinburgh commercial life, employing local men and women. Allan Ramsay, for example, was apprenticed to a wigmaker when he arrived in Edinburgh from his home in

Lanarkshire. Once again, his education was a tribute to Scottish village schools. Although Ramsay was the son and stepson of day laborers, he learned enough Latin to read Horace "faintly in the original," as he put it. Ramsay set up his own wigmaking shop in 1707, the same year as the Act of Union, but continued his voracious intellectual interests, poring over London publications such as Addison's *Spectator* and Defoe's *Review*. In 1727 hc published his first poems, and then opened a bookstore in the Luckenbooths, beside St. Giles's church.

Ramsay understood, as other Scots soon would, that high culture could also be good business. To increase his customer base, he permitted patrons not only to buy the latest books but also to borrow them for a week or two, for a subscription fee. It was the first lending library in Britain, and soon people were following Ramsay's example up and down Scotland. At first Ramsay ran afoul of the Kirk: clerics warned that he was allowing profane and sinful works to circulate in the city, and demanded that he be shut down. The day the town council sent inspectors to examine Ramsay's bookshelves, however, they were amazed to discover them full of theological works and sermons. The city fathers decided to allow Ramsay to stay open.

He did go too far, however, when he tried to open a theater, almost within sight of the John Knox House. The Kirk attacked Ramsay's "Hellbred Playhouse Comedians who debauch all the Faculties of the Souls of our Rising Generation," and the place had to be closed. It would be several more years before plays could be performed publicly in Edinburgh; people instead went to what were called "presentations," usually in someone's private home. But a corner had been turned in the battle against the old prohibitions and taboos, and the Kirk's warning about "the Souls of our Rising Generation" shows that it knew the old Presbyterianism was losing its grip.

Commercial Scotland had another significance in the 1740s. Glasgow and Edinburgh were where loyalty to the British union ran the deepest. They were "Whig" cities par excellence, meaning committed to ties to England and parliamentary rule from Westminster, as well as the new Hanoverian kings, a succession of German-born Georges with their English prime ministers. The first generation of Scottish Whigs, men such as Principal Carstares, had had to fight for union, and saw it primarily as a way to keep a Protestant on the throne. The next generation—men such as William Robertson, David Hume, Hugh Blair, John Home, and Alexander Carlyle—could take union for granted. Those self-professed disciples of Kames and Hutcheson saw their mission as securing Scotland's rightful place as England's equal in this United Kingdom. When Robertson composed his *History of Scotland* in 1759, he could boast that "the union having incorporated the two nations, and rendered them one people, the distinctions which had subsisted for many ages gradually wear away; peculiarities disappear; the same manners prevail in both parts of the island. . . ."

One such distinction had been political. John Erskine of Grange, a jurist and leading Scottish Whig, noticed this as early as 1735. The end of independent Scotland, with its own Parliament and Privy Council, had not brought despotism and tyranny, as so many had feared. Just the opposite. "There is a wide difference," Erskine noted, "between constitutional and effectual liberty." In Scotland, he explained, "we had the first; but actual liberty was a stranger here." Even the greatest aristocrats were not really free men, "for they were lawless, and with lawlessness freedom is inconsistent." Thinking of figures such as William Wallace and Robert the Bruce, Erskine remarked, "the truth is our Scottish heroes of old savor a little of the Poles at present," Poland being the eighteenth-century equivalent of constitutional anarchy. "They fought for liberty and independency, but not [for] the country, but [for] the Crown and the grandees." Scots were beginning to realize that the passing of the old laws could be a matter of celebration rather than regret. In fact, that same year, 1735, saw the death penalty for witchcraft finally abolished.

The other distinction between England and Scotland, and just as important in the minds of Robertson and others, had been cultural and literary. Whereas seventeenth-century Scotland had little or no great literature to set beside the achievements of Shakespeare, Milton, Dryden, and Pope, today, Robertson wrote, "the same standard of taste, and purity of language, is established" in both England and Scotland.

"Purity of language"—this touched on a thorny issue in the eighteenth century, namely whether educated Scotsmen should adopt English, instead of Scots, as their primary written and spoken tongue. The social and cultural pressures for taking up English were intense. Everyone knew that England was the dominant partner in this new united kingdom. A Scotsman with drive and ambition measured his success by his success in England, and particularly in the English equivalent of the Big Apple, London. Succeeding there required learning to be and act English: Dr. Johnson's maxim about the high road to London turned out to be true in more ways than one. At the same time, one was expected to set aside the language and culture one had grown up with since childhood. But how far and how much? That was the question that the early Scottish Enlightenment confronted head-on, and with it something that has bedeviled the modern world ever since: the question of cultural identity.

In fact, Scottish Whigs such as Robertson, Adam Smith, and David Hume confronted much the same problem that Indian, Chinese, and other Third World intellectuals would encounter a century or two later: how to deal with a dominant culture that one admired but that threatened to overwhelm one's own heritage, and oneself with it. At times they tried to act as if there were really only one culture, a British culture, just as there was only kingdom, Great Britain. They even took to calling themselves "North Britons," implying that any remaining difference between the two people was merely geographic. However, no Englishman ever referred to himself as a "South Briton," and Scots knew it. No amount of political wishful thinking could close the cultural gap.

One of the first to realize this was the poet James Thomson. Born in the Scottish border country, he was not only the first nature poet and forerunner of British Romanticism; he also composed the anthem of Scottish Whiggery, which would resound down through the next two centuries as rousing choruses of "Rule Britannia":

When Britain first at Heaven's Command
Arose from out the azure main,
This was the charter of the land,
And guardian angels sung the strain:

Rule Britannia, Britannia rule the waves!
Britons never shall be slaves.

Here was the Scottish Whig ideal: we are Britons, Scots and English all, belonging to one nation and enjoying the same privileges and liberties. All the same, although it was Thomson's own home of Southdean in the Tweed river valley that inspired his poetic landscapes, and although he studied in Edinburgh and lived there for nine years, it was not until he went to London in 1726 and found a fellow Scot named Millan to publish the first part of his cycle of poems, *The Seasons,* that he found the literary success he craved.* An English, not a Scottish, reading public made Thomson one of the most celebrated writers of the eighteenth century—and English, not his native Scots, served as the vehicle for his poetic muse.

So which to use, English or Scots (not, we note, Gaelic, which hardly any urban dweller spoke)? Despite their shared origin as dialects of old Anglo-Saxon, the two languages diverged widely in vocabulary, grammar, and syntax. Enlivened by borrowings from French and Scandinavian as well as Gaelic, broad Scots could be heard up and down the streets of Edinburgh, Glasgow, and Aberdeen, as well as in the farms and valleys of the Clyde and Tweed. For centuries it had served as the language of law, government, commerce, and the Kirk. It had also spawned a rich literary heritage during the Middle Ages and the Renaissance, as even a dedicated Scottish Whig such as William Robertson readily admitted. But now, as the eighteenth century dawned, it seemed second-class. As the career of James Thomson demonstrated, any Scottish modern or "polite" culture would have to take root in the idiom from the south.

For most Scots, learning to converse and write in English was as difficult as learning a new language. Mistakes in grammar, as well as accent, would constantly give them away. David Hume conversed in broad Scots all his life, but he always regretted that he never learned to

---

*Meanwhile, Millan went on to create Britain's most prestigious publishing house, under the name he used in London: Macmillan and Company.

speak English as well as he wrote it. He confessed that he and his fellow Scots were "unhappy in our Accent and Pronunciation." It was not easy to pronounce *night* as *nite* instead of *nicht,* or say *brite* instead of *bricht.* It was hard to remember to say *old* instead of *auld; above* instead of *aboon; talk* instead of *crack;* a *gathering* instead of a *rockin';* to say "It made me very glad" instead of "It pat me fidgin' fain" or "I am angry" instead of "I'm a' in a pelter" and "I have drunk a great deal" instead of "I drang a muckle." Hume confessed to an English correspondent, "Notwithstanding all the Pains, which I have taken in the Study of the English Language, I am still jealous of my Pen. As to my Tongue, you have seen, that I regard it as totally desperate and irreclaimable."

However, the person who best and most famously represents the problems of being a Scot in Georgian Britain is James Boswell.

Boswell is one of those writers whose reputation has suffered from his own success. Generations have come to take him for granted. In his *Life of Johnson,* Boswell turned himself into a sensitive, self-effacing sounding board in order to reveal the character of someone he believed to be not only interesting and admirable, but a truly great man—much as he would have done if he had ever finished his biography of Lord Kames. His voluminous diaries suffer from the same virtues. Boswell made them an absolutely honest and candid record of his own thoughts, experiences, and emotions. They present us with "Bozzie" not as he appeared to others but as he appeared to himself: his fantasies, ambitions, missteps, anxieties, and weaknesses are all revealed in detail. They dominate our recollection of reading them—and of him. Taken together, they have created the image of James Boswell as a genial, bumbling mediocrity, who happened to compose a literary masterpiece almost by accident.

Now, finally, we are beginning to realize that Boswell was a truly gifted writer and an accomplished man, that rare combination of an intellectual with broad human sympathies as well as a deep personal honesty. He grew up in Edinburgh under the shadow of the impossibly high demands of his disapproving father, Lord Auchinleck of the Court of Session, and found an emotional and intellectual counterweight in his mentor, Lord Kames. It was Kames who encouraged Boswell's intellectual and literary interests, and who probably enabled Boswell, against his own inclinations, to complete his studies to become a lawyer.

The idea of setting off for London was Boswell's own, however. He was twenty years old when he first arrived in 1760, determined to succeed in the city that seemed the center of civilized life. He was, as he described himself, "a young fellow whose happiness had always centered in London, who had at last got there, and had begun to taste its delights." He fantasized about "getting into the Guards, being about Court, enjoying the happiness of the *beau monde* and the company of men of Genius."

One thing stood in the way of this fantasy: being Scottish. When he first met Dr. Johnson, his first stammered words were, "I do indeed come from Scotland, but I cannot help it." Johnson's reply was devastating: "That, Sir, I find, is what a very great many of your countrymen cannot help." It was a bad season for being a Scot in London. The new king, George III, had selected an extremely unpopular prime minister of Scottish origin, Lord Bute, and political feelings ran high against "North Britons." Boswell even attended a play at which the audience kept shouting over and over, "No Scots! No Scots!" The radical John Wilkes published daily diatribes against Scottish immigrants, attacking them as ignorant, grasping, and corrupt: "The principal part of the Scottish nobility are tyrants," Wilkes sneered, "and the whole of the common people are slaves."

In this hostile atmosphere, Boswell struggled with his giveaway Scottish diction, just as Hume did. When he introduced General Sir Alexander MacDonald to Dr. Johnson in March 1772, the distinguished soldier remarked, "I have been correcting several Scotch accents in my friend Boswell. I doubt, Sir, if any Scotchman ever attains to a perfect English pronunciation." Johnson replied loftily, "Why, Sir, few of 'em do. . . . But, sir, there can be no doubt that a man who conquers nineteen parts of the Scottish accent may conquer the twentieth." Later, Boswell met a Dr. Kenrick, who claimed "he taught a man from Aberdeen to speak good English in six weeks." Kenrick explained to Boswell that his great difficulty was to get the Aberdonian to stop lilting his words as he spoke, as a Scotsman did and an Englishman did not. Kenrick finally told the man, "Sir, you don't speak at all. You sing."

Today we would naturally expect this sort of prejudice and "negative stereotyping" to breed a deep cultural resentment among educated Scots, or at least a backlash. Remarkably, and characteristically, it had just the opposite effect. Boswell not only read Wilkes's anti-Scottish scandal sheet (he admired its "poignant acrimony," as he put it), but when they met he found Wilkes to be funny and charming, and they struck up a lasting friendship. Intellectuals in Edinburgh were thrilled, not offended, when in the summer of 1761 the Irish actor and "orthoepist" (or pronunciation expert) Thomas Sheridan arrived in town to offer a series of lectures on English elocution. More than three hundred gentlemen, "the most eminent in this country for their rank and abilities," attended Sheridan's lectures (one of them, we note, was Boswell). They encouraged Sheridan to enlarge on those aspects of spoken English "with regard to which Scotsmen are most ignorant, and the dialect of the country most imperfect." They even encouraged him to run a separate set of lectures for ladies. Sheridan, whose son Richard would become a celebrated playwright and author of *The School for Scandal,* sold places at his lectures for a guinea each—in today's money, almost a hundred dollars—as well as subscriptions for his forthcoming book for half a guinea. The Edinburgh town council even made him a honorary freeman of the city. All in all, it was a remarkable summer, not only for Sheridan but also for Edinburgh's elite, whose cultural anxiety evidently ran so deep that they were eager to be lectured on good English from an Irish actor.

This has led some critics to condemn the Scottish Enlightenment for knuckling under to English "cultural imperialism." But just the opposite was the case. Far from leading educated Scots to abandon or forget their Scottish identity, Anglicization seems to have encouraged them to keep it alive and intact. Kames continued to speak Scots on the bench up into the 1780s. Poets such as Allan Ramsay and Robert Burns became in effect bilingual, composing verse in good Scots or perfect Augustan English, depending on the occasion or the mood. Boswell himself spoke his native dialect during his stays in Edinburgh, and when he met Jean-Jacques Rousseau he fantasized about admonishing him in broad Scots for his eccentricities: "Hoot, Johnie Rousseau mon, what for hae ye sae mony figmangairies? You're a bonny man indeed to mauk siccan a wark; set ye up. Canna ye just live like ither fowk?"*

In effect, the Scots *became* English speakers and culture bearers, but *remained* Scots. Instead of forgetting their roots, they acquired new ones. Men such as Boswell, Hume, and Robertson freely conceded the superiority of English culture so that they could analyze it, absorb it, and ultimately master it. They refused to be intimidated, because they intended to beat the English at their own game. They would reshape the dominant English culture so that both the English and the Scots could find a home in it.

The effort paid off. Robertson and Hume taught the English how to write "philosophical history," using the four-stage theory to illuminate the past. The greatest masterpiece of Enlightenment history, Edward Gibbon's *Decline and Fall of the Roman Empire,* would be unimaginable without its Scottish school predecessors. Boswell's *Life of Johnson* would become the most famous biography in English letters—again, in *English,* not Scottish letters. And of course Adam Smith would compose the founding text of modern economics— *Inquiry Concerning the Wealth of Nations*—in a language that was, it is all too easy to forget, a foreign tongue to him.

By 1758, Horace Walpole, the son of the former prime minister, had to admit "Scotland is the most accomplished nation in Europe." Voltaire agreed: "It is to Scotland that we look for our idea of civilization." A central European observer stated that "it is now an incontestable fact that the principal authors who have adorned the British literature in these latter times, or do honour to it in the present days, have received their birth and education in Scotland." It was as neat an

---

*Which we can translate as: "Tell me, Jean-Jacques, why do you always act so strangely? You have written an excellent book; so get hold of yourself. Why can't you live like other people?" In the event, Boswell kept his thoughts to himself.

example of reverse cultural imperialism as one can find, and David Hume expressed his pleasure with it in the form of a paradox:

> Is it not strange that at a time when we have lost our Princes, our Parliament, our independent Government . . . are unhappy in our accent and . . . speak a very corrupt Dialect of the Tongue which we make use of, is it not strange, I say, that in these Circumstances, we shou'd really be the People most distinguished for Literature in Europe?

All the same, it was a rash man who could have predicted all this before 1745. At that date, Scottish Whigs knew that life even in Edinburgh was still pretty primitive compared with what was going on south of the Tweed. But they understood that change was under way, and that the changes were for the better—that the institutions and habits that still held Scotland back, such as the intolerance of the Kirk and the old feudal customs that made rural tenants so dependent on their lairds, were slowly improving. So it came as a shock when so much of Scotland lashed out violently against these changes in 1745, and the deepest, darkest aspects of Scotland's past suddenly rose up to blot out the future.

II

Many myths abound about the Highland clans. The oldest, and most persistent, is that the rising of Bonnie Prince Charlie in 1745 symbolized a cultural clash between a Celtic "Jacobite" Highlands, steeped in primeval tribal loyalties, and a modernizing, proto-industrial "Whig" Lowlands. Scottish Whigs actually encouraged this view. It implied that they and their English allies were engaged in a virtual crusade for civilization, a war against an anachronistic social order left over from Scotland's barbarous history.

The clans were an anachronism, all right, except that they were a holdover from Scotland's feudal, not tribal, past. The bonds that held the clan together were land and landholding. Their origins had as much to do with French-speaking Normans as with ancient Celts. If we want to identify the true prototypes of the Highland warriors who fought for the Earl of Mar at Sheriffmuir or Prince Charlie at Culloden, we should look not to the ancient Picts or Britons, but to the followers of William the Conqueror.

The term *clan,* of course, comes from the Gaelic *clann,* meaning "children." It implied a kinship group of four or five generations, all claiming descent from a common ancestor. And clan chieftains encouraged their followers to believe that they were indeed bound together like family. Men such as the Duke of Argyll of the Campbells or Lord Lovat of the Frasers routinely demanded a loyalty from their tenants not unlike that of children for a father. But it was entirely a fiction. The average clan—and there were more than fifty of them in 1745—was no more a family than is a Mafia "family." The only important blood ties were those between the chieftain and his various *caporegimes,* the so-called tacksmen who collected his rents and bore the same name. Below them were a large, nondescript, and constantly changing population of tenants and peasants, who worked the land and owed the chieftain service in war and peacetime. Whether they considered themselves Campbells or MacPhersons or Mackinnons was a matter of indifference, and no clan genealogist or bard, the *seanachaidh,* ever wasted breath keeping track of them. What mattered was that they were on clan land, and called it home.

"In that sense," says one prominent authority on the history of the Highlands, "one cannot really talk about a 'clan system,' only about specific clans." Those clans that appear in the first written sources were all extinct by the beginning of the sixteenth century. The ones that dominated the landscape in 1745—Fraser, Cameron, Mackenzie, Stewart of Appin, and the most famous of all, the Campbells and the MacDonalds—mostly date from the thirteenth or fourteenth century, after Norman mercenaries had come to Scotland at royal invitation and established a pattern of feudal landholding across both the Highlands and Lowlands. Norman feudalism intermingled with Celtic tribal tradition, creating a hybrid: the clan, headed by a chief with his tenants living on a wartime footing. Many of these Norman knights and their descendants, such as Fraser, Drummond, Montgomery, Grant, and Sinclair, became heads of clans. Secured in their power by royal decree and tribal superstition, they became the power brokers of medieval Scotland and a law unto themselves, just like their feudal magnate counterparts in England or France. The only difference was that while the John of Gaunts and Charles the Bolds disappeared across the rest of Europe, and eventually even from Lowland Scotland, men such as the Lords Lovat of Fraser and MacDonnells of Keppoch lived on, a source of Highland pride and legend, but also of disunity and strife.

Scottish feudal law gave the chiefs land and peasants, as well as tenants-in-chief, the tacksmen, to run things. It also gave them formal jurisdiction over persons living in the clan area, including the power of life and death. They did not hesitate to use it. Once a woman was brought before MacDonald of Clanranald, accused of stealing money from him. He ordered her tied by the hair to seaweed among the rocks, until the Atlantic tide came in and drowned her.

Another chief, Coll MacDonnell* of Barrisdale, required all fishermen on his land to pay him one-fifth of their catch. Those who failed to pay up found themselves tied to a device locals dubbed the "Barrisdale." Iron rings held a man flat on his stomach while a large stone weight was strapped to his back, and a steel spike placed under his chin. If the miscreant failed to support the stone's weight, the spike would drive up through his chin to the roof of his mouth. It is with a jolt that we remember this was in 1740, not 1140, and that there was nothing in Scottish law to protect a MacDonnell tenant from his chieftain's protection racket.

What the average clansman got in exchange for submitting to this sometimes brutal authority was land, land to work or graze in order to feed his family, and to pay his rent. Rarely did he call himself a MacDonald or a MacKinnon or an Ogilvie or whatever the clan name was; he used patronymics or nicknames instead, such as Collum mac

---

*MacDonnells were, like their cousins the MacDonalds, an independent branch of the great Clan Donald.

(meaning "son of") Fergus vic ("grandson of") Ian, or Angus *mór* (Angus the elder) or Angus *ruadh* (meaning "red"). His membership in the clan rested on the ties of custom, not kinship. He obeyed the chief, paid the chief's rent, listened to his bard's songs and stories, wore his badge, a sprig of herb or plant, in battle, and shouted his slogan because they were the *clan's* badge and slogan, just as it was the clan's land he worked. He saw the chief and his tacksmen and his bodyguards, the henchmen, not as masters, but as guardians and trustees of what ultimately belonged to everyone.

Unfortunately, this was not how the chieftains themselves saw it. Whatever sense of communal responsibility might have existed was fading fast; loyalty was becoming more and more a one-way street. Most chieftains now thought of themselves as landed aristocrats. They wore ruffled lace and drank French claret. They and their sons were educated at the universities. Families such as the Campbells and the Camerons kept fine houses in Edinburgh, although most of their followers were dirt poor. The sons of a chief continued to be raised in the traditional way, in the midst of the clan, and wet-nursed in the cottage of a humble clanswoman, whose own son became his milk-brother. He still had to prove his leadership in battle, by leading cattle raids on neighboring clans or committing acts of petty revenge. But increasingly the chieftains came to think of the clan land as their own property, and looked for ways to guarantee that their eldest sons would inherit it intact, regardless of what the clan itself might think or want. Lord Kames's iron law, "man is disposed by nature to appropriate," applied equally well to the Highland chieftain, the Berwickshire farmer, or the Glasgow merchant.

The chieftain's key ally in this push for privatizing the clan's lands was, and always had been, the Scottish Crown. This is another persistent myth: that Highlanders supported Bonnie Prince Charlie out of some ancient, mystical loyalty to the Stuarts. The truth was that the alliance between the Crown and the clan chieftains was one of mutual self-interest. The Crown recognized the chieftain's life-and-death power over his tenants, reinforced the privileged status of his family members and supporters, and protected his children's rights to his land by formal law. In exchange, the chiefs gave the king a rough version of law and order in a remote and largely inaccessible part of his kingdom. It also allowed him to play one clan against another, when it suited his own political purposes.

At various times the Stuarts banished or destroyed clans that had become nuisances or even merely inconvenient. They destroyed the Clan Donald's power in the western Highlands and islands, and handed over its lands to the Campbells. They did the same to the Clan Leod of Lewis, and the MacIains of Ardnamurchan. In 1603, James VI went even further. After a quarrel with the leaders of the MacGregors, he in effect sentenced the entire clan to death. If any man dared to use the name MacGregor again, James decreed, he was to be put to death and his property forfeit to his killer. As an additional incentive, James promised any criminal an immediate pardon if he brought a royal official the head of a MacGregor.

It was genocide, pure and simple. Within the year more than thirty-six men had been murdered or executed. James himself led the way by hanging six who happened to be in his personal custody. The clan was steadily driven from its home in Glen Strae and Glen Lyon into a life of permanent exile and banditry, regularly hunted as renegades by all the other clans in the region. One hundred fifty years later the proscription against the MacGregor name still stood. One reason the head of the illegal Clan Gregor, the son of its most famous leader, Rob Roy, joined the revolt in 1745 was the vain hope that Prince Charles might rescind the ban. In fact, it was not until 1774 that it was finally stricken off the statute books.

The real winner in the destruction of the MacGregors was Clan Campbell, which moved in and occupied their former territory. In fact, the Campbells and their most important chiefs, the Dukes of Argyll, rose to power by serving as the Crown's principal tool in controlling the other western clans. This reached its climax on the night of February 13, 1692, when the Campbells were ordered to put to death the MacDonalds of Glencoe, including women and children. The plan was botched. Most of the MacDonalds escaped, but the Campbell soldiers managed to drag thirty-six of them out into the snow and murder them, including children four and five years old. The massacre caused an uproar in Parliament and elsewhere. Lowlanders often shuddered at the barbarity and savagery of the Highland clans; but it is worth remembering that the worst examples, the massacre at Glencoe and the extermination of the MacGregors, were both done at royal order.

What was life like in a clan? Every outside observer noted that crossing the Firth of Forth into the Highlands meant entering a different world. For one thing, normal law and order did not follow him across the border. A different law, the code of the clan, applied instead. This often meant that a Highlander who came into a town such as Aberdeen or Greenock to do business or find employment, where he got into an argument with a local and killed him, could count on getting away free if he could get back home. It was the official rash enough to pursue, not the murderer, whose life was in danger. The only recourse was an appeal to the chieftain, whose concern was not guilt or innocence, but honor.

An English visitor in the 1720s stopped at one chieftain's house and remarked casually that some of the chief's clansmen had behaved with less than the sort of courtesy one expected from Highland hospitality. The chieftain, the Englishman recalled, "clapped his hand to his broadsword and said, if I required it, he would send me two or three of their heads." The visitor laughed, thinking this was a joke, "but the chief insisted he was a man of his word." Eventually the visitor talked his host out of his gruesome offer.

In his natural habitat, surrounded by his henchmen, his bard, his piper, and his servants or gillies, the Highland chieftain could be an awe-inspiring figure. What generally struck most outsiders, however, was the shabbiness and poverty of the average chief's existence. Like his followers, he was the product of a fundamental and intractable poverty.

People lived by raising cattle, sheep, and goats, and maintaining tiny plots of land for growing stands of oat and barley. In winter, "they have no diversions to amuse them," said an observer, "but sit brooding in the smoke of their fire til their legs and thighs are scorched to an extraordinary degree." Most of the year food was scarce, so clansmen supplemented their income by stealing from neighboring clans, with elaborate and daring cattle raids. A burning cross, made of two sticks tied together with a strip of linen stained in blood, summoned clansmen together, as they saw it blazing forth from mountaintop to mountaintop. As the warriors passed along the mountain trails, they watched for portents of future victory or defeat. A stag or hare or fox that crossed their path and was not immediately hunted and slain boded evil. If a barefooted woman was sighted, she had to be seized and blood drawn from her forehead with a dirk before the men could go on.

The cattle raid, the *creach,* was not only a test of leadership and honor, celebrated in bardic song. It also paid a tidy profit, when the clan could charge ransom to return the stolen cattle. The term in Scots was *blackmail—mail* being the word for "rent" or "tribute," and black the typical color of the Highlander's cattle. Blackmail determined the rhythm of life in many parts of the Highlands. Some observers estimated that at any given moment the average chief had half his warriors out stealing his neighbor's cattle, and the other half out recovering the cattle his neighbors had stolen from him.

In summer, families lived on milk and whey from their cattle, and little else. Bread was available only in the spring, which was when most work had to be done. In winter the scarcity cut deep. Deprived of other sources of protein, Highlanders often had to bleed their cattle, mixing the blood with oatmeal and frying it in the fire. Sometimes cows were bled so frequently they could barely stand. It is worth remembering that a "traditional" Highland dish such as haggis, the stuffed sheep's stomach that is the bane of visitors to Scotland and such a source of pride to its natives, would have been a great luxury to an average Highland family. "Where flocks and corn are the only wealth," Dr. Johnson observed, "he who is poor never can be rich. The son merely occupies the place of the father, and life knows nothing of progress or advancement."

Families lived in a one-room hut of mud and stone, called a bothy. The typical Highland village was a collection of bothies; to visitors at a distance, it looked like heaps of dirt in a field. It was only when they grew closer that they saw that these heaps of dirt housed human beings, with dogs, goats, and half-naked children roaming among the huts and peat fires. In poorer clans the only way to tell a chief's children from the other half-naked urchins was that they were the ones who could speak English. In fact, these were people much poorer than Plains Indians or the other pastoral-nomadic peoples civil-society theorists knew about. Poverty was the keynote to everything in the Highlands. It even determined who was loyal, and who was not, in the Forty-five. Twenty-two clans joined up with the Stuarts; ten remained loyal to the British. But the ten who stayed loyal were the most prosperous, including the Clan Campbell. By contrast, many who joined the revolt, such as the MacDonnells of Keppoch and the MacDonalds of Glencoe, were either landless or on the edges of bankruptcy. One contemporary estimated that the total yearly income of all the clans that marched for Prince Charlie did not add up to 1,500 pounds.

The Highlander's poverty was compensated by one thing: his pride as a warrior. The crucial distinction in the clans was between those who worked and those who fought. Peasants and women did the former; men, the clansmen, did the latter. Visitors found this hard to fathom. In the early nineteenth century an Englishwoman became fed up at the sight of a Highland woman laboring wearily on her family's meager plot of ground while her husband, in full Highland regalia, sat and watched. She upbraided the man's mother: How could she allow her son to sit idle like this, while her daughter-in-law did all the work? The old woman stoutly replied that if her son lifted his hand to till the soil, he would cease to be a gentleman.

As Dr. Johnson observed, in the Highlands "every man was a soldier." The clansman was trained to fight from boyhood. Armed with his double-edged broadsword,* which measured a yard long and two inches wide; his dagger or dirk; and his shield or targe, and screaming his clan's motto as he rushed headlong at his opponent, he was a formidable sight. But he was no Iron Age throwback, the "bare-arsed banditti" of English legend. He could be as familiar with handling a musket, and

---

*Sometimes mistakenly called a claymore. In fact, the claymore or *claidheamh-mór* (which simply means "big sword") was the two-handed battle sword popular in the Middle Ages, which the clans had largely abandoned for the lighter but just as deadly broadsword, with its characteristic basket hilt.

fighting in formation, as any British grenadier. For generations the principal export of the Highlands had been its surplus males, as soldiers and mercenaries for the armies of Europe. In the Middle Ages, Irish chieftains had hired them: nicknamed *galloglasses* or *redshanks* because of their exposed knees below their kilts, Scottish mercenaries had kept the Gaelic parts of Ireland safe from the English for four hundred years. They fought for the Dutch against the Spanish as the Scots Brigade, and served the princes of Germany and central Europe in their frequent internecine conflicts. Clan Mackay kept Swedish King Gustavus Adolphus supplied with a Scottish regiment during the Thirty Years' War. The men who fought at Culloden were in large part seasoned, hardened professionals, led by men with commissions in various European armies.

So, if poverty was one keynote of Highland life, war and violence was another. It is what made the Highlander admired, and feared. Daniel Defoe watched them walk the streets of Edinburgh: "They are formidable fellows. . . . They are all gentlemen, will take no affront from any man, and insolent to the last degree." But he also noted the incongruity of one of these proud men with his weapons and tartan (another myth: genuine Highlanders wore plaids in any color that pleased them, regardless of their clan) walking "as upright and haughty as if he were a lord," while driving a cow in front of him. Duels, murder, and feuding were constants in the Highlands, as was "scorning," or taking food and shelter by force from tenants of other clans when a feud was under way. Lairds routinely burned down the houses and seized the livestock of tenants who displeased them. When Lord Lochiel brought the Camerons in on Prince Charles's side in 1745, his brother Archibald passed through Cameron country warning villagers that "if they did not come off directly he would burn their houses and cut them in pieces." When some Cameron males refused, he beat them with his whip. When another hesitated, he killed four of the man's cows until he agreed to join him.

It was a way of life most Lowlanders had not known for generations, and they avoided it as much as they could. Contact could be dangerous, or even fatal. Once a member of Clan MacDonald of Glencoe passed a

Lowlander on the road near Achnacone and gave him a traditional Gaelic greeting: *"Beannachd Dia duit, a duine!"* (God's blessing on you, sir!) The Lowlander knew no Gaelic, but replied nervously it was indeed a fine day. "Foolish man," said the Highlander, "do you despise the word of God?" With that he drew his sword and killed him, and then robbed the body, taking his shoes, his musket, and a guinea piece he found in the man's coat pocket. Later he told his laird what he had done, "adding that to his mind it had been a profitable morning." Big Archie MacPhail, as he was known, was a famed cattle stealer and was never prosecuted for the murder. But he did worry at night, he told others, about being haunted by the dead man's spirit.

The English usually dismissed Highlanders as "savages" and barbarians. Enlightened Scots could be more understanding, although just as censorious. One such was Duncan Forbes of Culloden, Lord President of the Court of Session in the 1740s and friend to Lord Kames. From his estate in Inverness-shire, overlooking Drummossie Moor, he watched the clansmen around him with a critical, if sympathetic, eye. They were, he wrote, "unacquainted with industry and the fruits of it, and united in some degree by the singularity of dress and language, stick close to their antient way of life." They "depend generally on the Chiefs, as their sovereign Lords and masters; and being accustomed to the use of arms, and inured to hard living, are dangerous to the public peace." He noted that their isolation left them "the prey of their accustomed sloth and barbarity," and made enforcement of the laws impossible.

Like other enlightened Scots, what Forbes wanted for the Highlands was civilization, of which the chief beneficiary would be the Highlander himself. The key to this, according to Forbes, was to take away their weapons. "Their successors . . . must be as harmless as the commonality" in the Lowlands. When the Highlander "could not longer live by Rapine," Forbes wrote, he would be forced to "think of living by Industry." The other key was roads. "The want of Roads . . . [has] proved hitherto a bar to all free intercourse between the High and Lowlands," and prevented the spread of civilizing influences to the north.

Beginning in the 1720s, after the failed Jacobite revolt in 1715 and another in 1719, the government began building roads. General George Wade was dispatched with garrison troops to lay out an ambitious network of roads and forts. Between 1725 and 1740, General Wade boasted of having constructed 250 miles of highway, designed to link Fort William and Fort Augustus in the west to Inverness. Communication, along with military fortification, was supposed to counterbalance the Highlanders' chief military advantage: numbers.

In 1715 the Earl of Mar, a man with no military experience, had assembled a Highland force of nearly six thousand warriors in a matter of weeks. MacDonnell of Keppoch alone boasted of being able to raise five hundred fighting men. The Campbells could summon up two or three thousand. Duncan Forbes calculated that if all the Highland clans joined together in a single enterprise, they could raise more than thirty thousand troops. There was no military force in Britain capable of standing up to an army such as that. The possibility of a general rising in the Highlands frightened government officials, just as it frightened Duncan Forbes. But in 1745, Wade's network of roads was still not finished. Even worse, other events, very far away from Scotland, had drawn away the bulk of his garrisons. The roads that were completed would enable soldiers to move with speed across the heart of the Highlands, just as Forbes predicted—except that they were soldiers in the army of Prince Charlie. And Drummossie Moor, beside Forbes's house at Culloden, would become the bloody ground on which the struggle for Scotland's future would be played out.

CHAPTER SIX

Last Stand

To wanton me, to wanton me,
Ken ye what maist wad wanton me?
To see King James at Edinburgh Cross,
Wi fifty thousand foot and horse,
And the usurper forced to flee,
Oh, this is what maist wad wanton me!

—*Traditional Jacobite song*

I

Officials in the Spanish West Indies were at their wits' end. For years, English and Scottish traders had been carrying on an illegal trade along their coasts. They collected salt in the Tortugas, cut timber in Honduras, and smuggled black-market slaves to plantation owners in Trinidad and Santo Domingo. So Spanish officials began issuing warrants to local captains to act as *costa gardas* or coast-guard cutters, allowing them to stop and search any vessel they suspected of violating Spanish law. If any English smuggler found himself roughly handled as a result, he had only himself to blame.

On April 9, 1731, Captain Juan de Leon Fandino was patrolling the coast of Cuba with his ship the *San Antonio* when he spotted an English sloop, the *Rebecca,* under the command of Captain Robert Jenkins. Fandino ordered the *Rebecca* to stop and submit to a search. Jenkins, who was bound for London from Jamaica, allowed Fandino to come aboard to examine his log book and his cargo hold. According to Jenkins, the Spaniards then proceeded to tear the ship apart, including stealing his nautical instruments. When Jenkins remonstrated, Fandino had him tied to his own mast and cut his ear off as a final warning, before letting Jenkins and his crew go.

Seven years later, Jenkins had his chance to tell his story before Parliament. He brought with him his severed ear, still wrapped in a ball of cotton. He told the stunned House of Commons how Fandino had told him to give it to King George, and how the arrogant Spaniard had said that if His Britannic Majesty had been present, he would have cut *his* ear off. An MP rose to ask Jenkins what his feelings had been at this dreadful moment. "I recommended my soul to God," he replied stoutly, "and my cause to my country."

The phrase reverberated through the press and nation, and triggered a massive outcry. English public opinion demanded that Britain send a fleet to punish the Spanish. Prime Minister Robert Walpole tried to deflect the tide of war hysteria, much of it fomented by his political opponents, but in the end he could not hold it back. The official declaration of war came on October 19, 1739, with the ringing of bells and the Prince of Wales toasting the London populace outside the Rose Tavern near Temple Bar. "This is your war," Walpole told his rival the Duke of Newcastle, "and I wish you joy of it."

After a quarter-century of peace, Britain was about to enter into armed conflict with a fellow European power. It would not know peace again for a quarter-century more. The War of Jenkins's Ear, as it inevitably became known, had reverberations far beyond Spain and the West Indies. It embroiled Britain in the political crisis simmering in central Europe, and by 1742 the kingdom found itself at war with Spain's allies, including France.

Britain desperately needed soldiers for fighting on the Continent. Whitehall stripped garrisons in northern England and Scotland to the bare minimum. Realizing this, and examining its own options, France decided to take a new look at a plan it had not considered since 1719: dispatching an expeditionary force to land in Britain as a "second front" in support of James Stuart, now living in exile in Rome. What had seemed a permanently lost cause, restoring the Stuarts to the throne, now enjoyed a new lease on life—thanks to Captain Jenkins and his ear.

Jacobitism* and the effort to bring "the auld Stuarts back again" is forever linked to the history of Scotland and the Scots. But in fact Jacobitism was as much an English problem as a Scottish one. In Scotland it served largely as a vehicle for anti-English feeling, and xenophobia in general. Until 1745, however, the truly fanatical Jacobite supporters, those willing to throw their lives and fortunes away for a vanquished political ideal, tended to be English.

The Stuarts were, of course, originally a Scottish royal house. By 1688, though, when Parliament had deposed James II, the father of Queens Mary and Anne, who would succeed him, and of James, Prince of Wales, who would not, they had become very much part of the English scene—certainly far more so than their German cousins the Electors of Hanover. But Elector George, who barely spoke English, enjoyed one key virtue: he was a Protestant, whereas James Stuart (his father had died in 1701) was a Catholic. So, when Queen Anne died in 1714, Parliament gave George the crown.

Despite what English historians would later assert, it was not a popular decision. The late Anne's leading ministers had to be driven into hiding in France in order to secure the Hanover succession. With French help they set about trying to undo what was, from the perspective of many, an illegal coup d'état. Their original plan called for landing at Plymouth, not in Scotland at all, and for James to raise his army in southwest England.

It might have worked, too, except for the British ambassador in Paris. This was none other than John Dalrymple, second Earl of Stair, son of the Lord Stair who had ordered the massacre at Glencoe and had died saving the Act of Union. The younger Stair established an efficient network of spies and sources at the French court, including someone who shared his mistress with the leading Jacobite conspirator. Thanks to Stair's information, the government rounded up the ringleaders in England, and the revolt of 1715 began in Scotland instead, under the ill-fated and incompetent Earl of Mar.

Even after the collapse of the Fifteen, pro-Stuart sentiment in

---

*The term comes from the Latin *Jacobus*, or James, as in James the Pretender.

England remained strong, although harshly muzzled. Northwest England in particular was a bastion of Jacobitism, thanks to its active Catholic minority. It was not just Catholics who remained loyal to the Stuarts, however. Government spies managed to foil another serious plot in 1722, this one involving the Anglican bishop of Rochester, Francis Atterbury. Indeed, a large cross-section of the clergy of the Church of England leaned toward the Stuarts, as did many landowners and members of Parliament who described themselves as Tories, in opposition to the pro-Hanover Whigs. Historians are only now beginning to realize how important a political movement Jacobitism really was in eighteenth-century England, and how for nearly sixty years it remained a serious threat to the Whig regime.

What drew people to the Stuart cause? It certainly was not the diffident, lethargic figure of James Stuart—deemed James III of England and James VIII of Scotland by his supporters. Nor was the typical Jacobite a crude reactionary, as their Whig opponents liked to claim. Samuel Johnson, no friend to tyranny, expressed private support for the Stuart claim. So did Alexander Pope.* Lord Kames felt the pull of Jacobitism—it was probably the violence of the Forty-five that killed any lingering sympathy he had for it. Allan Ramsay wrote poems as a young man supporting the deposed Stuarts. When Prince Charlie's army marched on Edinburgh in 1745, Ramsay chose to flee the city. But he did leave his house, with its strategic view of the walls of Edinburgh Castle, open to the Highland army when it occupied the town. It later provided a useful spot for snipers shooting at the royal garrison.

So what compelled sensible, law-abiding, and enlightened individuals to admire and sometimes even support a conspiracy to overthrow the existing government? In a word, nostalgia. Jacobitism reflected a nostalgic yearning for a traditional social order in which everyone supposedly knew his or her preordained place and stayed in it. It satisfied a deep utopian longing for the perfect society—except that it looked backwards, rather than ahead, for its model of perfection.

The average Jacobite wanted to return to a community that was sta-

---

*Although scholars usually blame this on Pope's Roman Catholicism.

ble and harmonious, two qualities that eighteenth-century Britain notoriously seemed to lack. He extolled the virtues of a rural-based society and the authority of a traditional landowning class. He detested the new rising competitive capitalist society, with its getting and spending, its greedy merchants and vulgar upstarts, its contempt for the old rules, its creative destruction, as much as any Marxist. And like the Marxist, he cared deeply about "justice," which in his mind meant inferiors willingly obeying their superiors: tenants obeying their landlords, the middle class obeying the nobility, the people obeying the king and the Church.

In England, and in much of the Scottish Lowlands by 1745, this longing for the security of a stable, hierarchical social order was largely, even self-consciously, a matter of nostalgia. Just as today we still have sentimental Marxists who put bumper stickers on their cars that say "No Peace Without Justice," so eighteenth-century Englishmen were aware of sentimental Jacobites among their Tory neighbors, who secretly toasted "the king across the water."

In the Highlands, though, Jacobitism was not nostalgia but reality. The Stuarts were not symbols of "a world we have lost," but emblems of a power that existed here and now. For a century they had shored up and strengthened the authority of the clan chiefs—none of them needed reassurances from the Roman Catholic Church (very few chieftains or clans were Catholic anymore, anyway) to see the Stuarts as the only real kings they had ever known. A Stuart uprising in Scotland made sense, not just as good strategy but as an attraction of like to like. There was one person who understood that, and in the end he was the one who mattered.

II

Just before dawn on January 9, 1744, James Stuart's son and heir, Charles Edward Stuart, left his house in Rome on the pretense of going boar-hunting north of the city at Cisterna. This was to throw English spies off the scent. Instead, his younger brother Henry went to Cisterna, while Charles made his way in disguise to the Tuscan coast. There he picked up a boat bound for Genoa, and then Savona, where a

Spanish fishing smack slipped him past the watching British fleet to Antibes. Lyons was his next destination, and then on January 29 he reached Paris.

Prince Charles was twenty-three years old. In contrast to his father, he was charming, handsome, and personable. In normal circumstances he was exactly the kind of person one might want to succeed to a royal throne. That was how the French saw him: in February 1744 he had a big place in their plans.

The War of Jenkins's Ear had gone well for the British, then badly. They had scored a major success against the outmanned and outgunned Spanish fleet in the Caribbean, which had satisfied the English thirst for revenge. But then things got stuck. Spain had found a capable ally in France, which was able to launch an invasion of Germany, threatening King George's home territory in Hanover. Suddenly Britain had found itself drawn into a European land war it was neither prepared for nor wanted. As Britain's war effort began to bog down, the French saw an opportunity to smash their ancient rival once and for all. This included putting their Stuart allies back in power.

By the end of the month, the French Crown put together an expedition of seven thousand men on transports at Dunkirk under the Marshal de Saxe to take Charles across the English Channel. The British, realizing what was coming, had put together a fleet in the Straits of Dover to block them. But then a storm scattered the French fleet and sank several of the transports. Charles himself managed to escape harm, but any invasion of England was now on hold.

The Dunkirk storm, "the Protestant wind" as gleeful English commentators dubbed it, did not just sink Charles's transports. It also sank French confidence in Charles. New ministers stepped in, who believed de Saxe would be better employed fighting the British on land in Flanders rather than at sea in a risky amphibious landing on the English coast. Charles refused to give up hope, and for the rest of the year he continued to lobby for French help, but without results. In November he wrote to his father that his debts amounted to some thirty thousand crowns. "The more I dwell on these matters," he confessed, "the more it makes me melancholy." Isolated, frustrated by inaction, and furious with his French hosts, Charles had formulated a new plan: to land in Scotland with a small and trusted band of followers, and raise an army himself.

No one knows who first came up with the idea of Charles going to Scotland with no troops or resources, and with no real way out if the enterprise failed. But the notion of failure apparently never entered Charles's mind. From the very beginning, a kind of headstrong, heedless optimism seems to have possessed him, goading him on when other, more experienced heads sensed disaster. When the first hint of his plan reached Scotland in the spring of 1745, even loyal supporters called it "the mad enterprise." They hoped he could not be serious.

But he was serious. By May he had cobbled together enough money and arms from the French government to outfit two warships, the *Du Teillay* and a sixty-four-gun frigate, the *Elisabeth*. On July 12 they set sail from Belle Île for Scotland. Bad luck dogged them from the start. A British man-of-war spotted them off the Lizard, and nearly sank the *Elisabeth,* forcing her and her consignment of seven hundred men, 1,500 muskets, and twenty small field pieces to turn back. The *Du Teillay* resolutely sailed on, carrying Charles and seven companions—two English, two Irish, and three Scots—for their destination on the Scottish west coast.

On July 23 they landed on the tiny island of Eriskay off South Uist, at a point still called Coilleag a Phrionnsa, or the Prince's Shore. It was the first time Charles Edward Stuart had ever set foot in Scotland.

News of his arrival brought not joy and celebration, but shock and dismay. His first visitor was the chieftain Alexander MacDonald of Boisdale, who told him "there was nothing to be expected from the country" and that "not a soul would join him." One of Charles's companions noted that "everyone was struck with a thunderbolt, as you may believe, to hear that sentence." They began to urge Charles to leave before it was too late. He refused, convinced that the Highlanders would stand with him. When Charles finally landed on the mainland at Borrodale, he organized meetings with the other branches of the MacDonalds. Charles asked about the strange Highland dress, which he had not seen before, and about the Gaelic language. He told them he intended to raise the royal standard and claim the crown of his ancestors.

The MacDonalds, like the Camerons of Lochiel and the Murrays of Atholl, listened with mixed emotions. For nearly one hundred years they had watched the Highlands, for all its continuing poverty and problems, grow more peaceful and secure. Incidents such as the Glencoe massacre notwithstanding, serious interclan feuds were largely a thing of the past. The British Crown left them alone to enjoy themselves as Scottish aristocrats and gentlemen. Now, Charles's arrival endangered it all.

But they could not evade the thrust of his appeal, that if he returned empty-handed, he would be humiliated in front of a pack of foreigners (meaning the French), who would see that he had no friends. Out of a sense of honor, they reluctantly agreed to summon their clans to battle. But from the start they sensed their doom. Charles, and Charles alone, believed they had a chance of success. And to everyone's amazement, the government of London, out of sheer incompetence and poor planning, was about to give it to them.

On August 19, at the northern end of Loch Shiel at Glenfinnan, Charles and the clans met. Cameron of Lochiel had summoned together seven hundred men; McDonnell of Keppoch fulfilled his boast of nearly five hundred. Charles ordered casks of brandy opened to allow the Highlanders to drink King James's health. Then the assembled warriors cheered the royal standard of blue, white, and red silk and hailed their commander, *Thearlaich mac Sheumais,* or Charles, son of James. *Thearlaich* would sound to non-Gaelic ears like "Charlie." Thus, the sobriquet that Charles would carry throughout the revolt and which history remembers as a dashing diminutive, Bonnie Prince Charlie, was in fact his name to the Gaels who now rallied to obey a prince they had never met, in order to serve a king who had never sat on any throne.

Charles waited two days until the MacDonalds of Clanranald arrived. Then he sent messages to the other clans between Glencoe and Glengarry to join him, and on August 21 started off to the east.

When news reached Edinburgh that the Highland army was on the march, the inhabitants, in David Hume's words, were seized with a "universal Panic," and, he added, "that not groundless." The military situation could not have been worse. The government had stripped available troops down to fewer than three thousand, most of whom were inexperienced or "invalid" garrisons stationed in towns such as Edinburgh and Stirling, or Highland regiments such as the Black Watch, whose loyalty was suddenly very much in question. The English commander was General Jonathan Cope, who, despite warnings from Duncan Forbes in early July that something was up, had done nothing until it was virtually too late. By the time Cope decided to move his troops to block Charles's line of march, the prince had already joined up with Stewart of Appin, MacDonald of Glencoe, and Grant of Grandiston, crossed Corriearrack Pass by Wade's military road, and taken Perth. Edinburgh, the capital, was clearly next.

Cope decided his only option was to avoid Charles's army—which he believed to be twice the size it actually was—and withdraw to Inverness. This, he believed, would give clans loyal to the government a chance to rally and allow him to send reinforcements by sea to Edinburgh. There was only one problem: the Disarming Act of 1725, which had outlawed weapons and firearms in the Highlands after the last Jacobite rising, was widely ignored by disloyal clans such as the MacDonalds, but obeyed by the loyal. It in effect disarmed precisely the Highlanders Cope now needed to have armed.

Meanwhile, Edinburgh would have to fend for itself. Its reputation as a bastion of Whig and pro-Hanover sentiment began to wilt as the Lord Provost and the town council met. They showed no interest in opposing the advancing Highland army, and temporized about taking any emergency measures. Instead, organizing the defense of the city fell to two private citizens, a merchant and former provost named George Drummond and a professor of mathematics at the university, Colin Maclaurin. They immediately called for volunteers to help the undermanned royal garrison in Edinburgh Castle. Their summons brought forward a host of young volunteers, many of them students. One was William Robertson, future author of *The History of Scotland,* who was serving as pastor at Gladsmuir. Behind him came William Wilkie and John Home, both probationers awaiting their first assignments as ministers. Theology student Alexander Carlyle signed up, as did William Cleghorn, who would later beat out David Hume for the chair of moral philosophy at Edinburgh. Clerics and intellectuals, they were the future stars of the Edinburgh Enlightenment, who now put their lives on the line for the House of Hanover and the Union.

They drilled twice a day. Cannon of various sizes and from various eras were assembled on the city walls. Professor Maclaurin drew up designs to modernize Edinburgh's defenses, and vigorously supervised the building and repair work. One of his assistants was the seventeen-year-old Robert Adam. In the meantime, citizens anxiously watched the weather vanes, hoping for a change in the wind and news that Cope's army would be under sail to rescue them. On September 15 they learned instead that the Jacobite army was only eight miles from the city and closing fast.

It was the moment of truth for Edinburgh's bands of volunteers. The result was one of those episodes that epitomizes the contrast between a culture that is prepared for war, whether it wants it or not, and one that, however willing, is not. Drummond hastily drew up his four hundred volunteers at the Lawnmarket for the march down the Bow, a long, winding street through the heart of what is now the Old Town, to the West Port. Students and other citizens set off in serried ranks through the crowds, drums beating and flags flying, to meet the invaders.

To their dismay, however, the crowd sent them off not with cheers but jeers and insults, while the rest of Edinburgh quickly shut up its houses and barred its windows. The volunteers, with Drummond at their head, marched on. When they got farther down the Bow, Alexander Carlyle remembered later, "the scene was different, for all the spectators were in tears, and uttering loud lamentations."

Still they marched on. Finally, as the volunteers neared the West Port, Drummond turned around to review his troops. To his shock, they had almost all disappeared. One by one, his brave young volunteers had reconsidered their position and, with the help of neighbors, quietly melted away up a convenient wynd or into a nearby tavern. Only Carlyle, Robertson, Home, and a few others still stood sheepishly with him, muskets in hand.

Their humiliation, and Drummond's, was not yet complete. Bearing down on them was the Principal of the University, William Wishart, and a gathering of local clergy appealing to Drummond not to expose "the flower of the youth of Edinburgh" to certain death at the hands of the fearsome Highlanders. Turn back and send them home, Wishart begged him. The crowd added their entreaties, cheering and applauding. Drummond was furious, but with no troops left, his options were limited. He finally gave the order to withdraw, and the West Port gates were closed. The volunteers were to see no action that day.

Carlyle, Robertson, Home, Cleghorn, and another student volunteer, Hugh Bannatine, retired to Turnbull's Tavern to restore their pride and spirits. A couple of glasses of claret put them in a better mood, and together they swore an oath to carry on the struggle for "the security of our country's laws and liberties," as Carlyle put it, even if Edinburgh surrendered, as now seemed very likely.

In fact, the end came even more swiftly than they had imagined. The next day Prince Charles camped at Gray's Mill, two miles from Edinburgh, and sent a note asking the city to surrender. Deputies from the town council met him to discuss terms, but the two sides could not reach any conclusion. As the deputies returned to the Bow Port and ordered the gates opened, however, a detachment of Camerons that had set out earlier to reconnoiter the city walls dashed as quick as lightning through the opening and seized the guard. With a triumphant shout, the Highlanders pelted up the street to the city guardhouse, taking possession of it and then the other gates to the city. Edinburgh Castle, with its garrison of six hundred men, remained secure. But the city had fallen before most people knew it was under attack. The next morning a citizen out for a walk noticed the strange-looking soldiers standing guard on the walls. He asked a Highlander who was leaning on a cannon and smoking a pipe, surely these were not the same soldiers as yesterday? "Och, no," the man answered, "she pe relieved."

On the morning of the seventeenth, John Home and the others

watched as Charles and his troops paraded in the King's Park, just below Arthur's Seat and out of range of the Castle's guns. Alexander Carlyle remembered them as "short and dirty, and of a contemptible appearance." John Home had a more appreciative eye. The prince himself "was in the prime of youth, tall and handsome," while the Highlanders "seemed to be strong, active, and hardy men," armed with muskets, fowling pieces, swords, and even scythe blades on pitchfork handles. Their "stern countenances, and bushy uncombed hair, gave them a fierce, barbarous, and imposing aspect." Then he, Carlyle, and William Robertson slipped away to find General Cope.

They found him and his army at Dunbar, some forty miles east of Edinburgh, where he had just arrived by ship from Aberdeen. They managed to give him a detailed description of the Highland army, and Cope ordered them to act as forward scouts as his forces closed on Haddington from the west, while the rebels marched east. The two armies collided at Prestonpans, eight miles east of Edinburgh on the Firth of Forth, on September 21.

The result must have been secretly gratifying to Home and other ex-Edinburgh volunteers, however disheartening at the moment. At the first charge of the Highlanders, Cope's dragoons ran away so fast that Charles's generals thought it must be a feint. The Highlanders then lashed the royal infantry with musket volleys and, grabbing their broadswords and dirks, charged them headlong. The soldiers—professionals this time, not amateur volunteers—broke and ran. Cope and his fellow officers chased after them, calling "For Shame, Gentlemen, behave like Britons," but to no avail. It was a stunning victory, and at one stroke, to everyone's amazement, Charles found himself master of Scotland.

In Charles's mind, still unclouded by any doubts or reflections, his next move had to be southward, into England and on the road to London. Again, there seemed to be little to oppose him. The government was frantically recalling troops from Flanders because there were virtually none in England; Charles had the promise (which ultimately proved empty) of nearly five thousand armed volunteers from the northern counties of England, as well as the hope of French assistance now that the revolt had caught fire. But his generals, who understood the military realities, were less sanguine. Their troops were melting away with constant desertions, as many Highlanders, pleased with their success and their booty, simply packed up and went home. Even with additional volunteers from the Gordons, Mackinnons, and MacPherson of Cluny, Charles had no more than five thousand foot and five hundred horse. Eventually they would have to face a British force of at least six times that number.

Charles's lieutenants also doubted the likelihood of further French help (here they were mistaken; reinforcements did arrive, but too few to make any difference). In the end, they and Charles worked out a compromise. They agreed to take the army south through Cumberland, where the rough, mountainous terrain would help to disguise their maneuvers from the English. On November 3, in a dense fog, they set out from Dalkeith in two columns, one commanded by James, Duke of Perth, and the other by Charles and Lord George Murray. On the eighth, Charles's force crossed the River Esk into England. As they crossed, "the Highlanders without any orders given," according to an eyewitness, "all drew their Swords with one Consent upon entering the River, and every man as he landed on tother side wheeld about to the left and faced Scotland" to raise a salute to his homeland.

Once again the Hanoverian forces, this time commanded by old General Wade, now a field marshal, were outdone by the rebels' boldness. Charles's division of forces drew Wade east, while Charles and Perth reunited their forces and closed on Carlisle in the fog and driving rain. The royal garrison withdrew to Carlisle Castle while the city itself surrendered. The Highlanders then marched into what, in less than fifty years, would become the heart of the English industrial landscape. Kendal, Lancaster, Manchester, Macclesfield, Derby—at each town the response to Charles's coming, while not overtly hostile, was far less warm than he had been led to expect. By December 4, however, they were less than 130 miles from London.

The English natives were as amazed by the appearance of these Scottish invaders as if they had been Eskimos or Watusis. They were certainly just as ignorant of who they were and what to expect. Most could not distinguish between Highland and Lowland Scots. Since many of Charles's Lowlander volunteers chose to wear kilts and bonnets, English obervers simply described them all as "Highland savages" and let it go at that. Fears ran high that they intended to plunder their way to London, "which according to Ancient Customs will be the murdering of people of all Sexes and Ages, the Burning of Houses, and Cutting of Cattle to pieces, with Swords and dirks. . . ." When Charles and his staff stopped at one house, according to Murray of Broughton, its owner begged the soldiers not to eat her child. But as Murray said of his troops, "There is no instance in the history of any times in whatever Country where the Soldiery either regular or irregular behaved themselves with so much discretion, never any riots in the Streets, nor so much as a Drunk man to be seen."

In one sense it is idle to speculate what might have happened if Charles and his little army had decided to press on to London, but the temptation is overwhelming. Could Charles really have taken the city, proclaimed his father king at Westminster, and then crafted a political settlement that would have put the Stuarts on the throne again?

It does seem indisputable that if Charles had marched farther south, he never would have made it. Not just one, but three British armies were now converging on him, including the one commanded by King George's son, the Duke of Cumberland, recently arrived from campaigning in Flanders. Thirty thousand troops were now available for action against the Stuart army of barely five thousand. From a military point of view, those who counseled Charles to abandon his plan to march on London were right. He never had a chance.

But this raises a more interesting point: that the odds against Charles in November of 1745 were more military than political. In other words, *if* Charles had somehow evaded Cumberland (very unlikely), and *if* he had made it to London, it is hard to see how anyone could have stopped him from carrying out his plan. Despite the hopes of English Jacobites, the great majority of their countrymen were not going to rise up in support of the Stuarts; but the same majority was not ready to risk life and property to keep the Hanovers. A compromise between Parliament and the Stuarts was not only possible but probable. As early as 1739, when the War of Jenkins's Ear was starting to heat up, Robert Walpole had sent secret letters to James asking what his intentions were regarding the Church of England and the personal safety of the members of the House of Hanover, *if* the Stuarts should come back to the throne again.

If they had, the English constitution would never have been the same. The notion, enshrined since 1688, of the sovereignty of Parliament would have died on the spot. But in 1745, not only sentimental Jacobites but most Englishmen would have willingly traded it in to avoid a civil war and have a little peace and quiet.

So who had the most to lose if Charles succeeded? The answer is not the English, but the Scots.

This seems shocking, especially in view of the revolt's bloody aftermath. Yet it gets to the heart of what really mattered to key political players at the time, and to two very distinct and different groups of Scotsmen.

The first group were Charles's allies, the Highland chiefs. They had joined their fortunes to his out of a rash sense of honor and pride. To their amazement, they had succeeded. Now, as they assembled at the prince's headquarters in Derby to discuss what to do next, they realized what success might actually mean. Having a Stuart at Whitehall was not, and would never be, the same thing as having a Stuart at Holyrood. The influence of his Highland allies would inevitably shrink away in the vast labyrinth of competing and conflicting interests of Great Britain. They had every reason to help Charles secure his position in Scotland, but they had no interest in seeing him win his father's crown in England and Wales. So, military necessity apart, returning to Scotland served their larger political agenda. No wonder, then, that they stood foursquare together against going any farther.

When Lord George Murray broke the news to Charles that "it was everybody's opinion that the only party that was to be taken was to retire," the prince "was astonished at this proposition," and said, "why the Clans kept me quite another Language and assured me they were all resolved to pierce or to dye." The debate took place at Exeter House, even as clansmen lined up outside to sharpen their swords in preparation for battle. Although Charles argued and pleaded, the chieftains remained unmoved. Provoked by their intransigence, Bonnie Prince Charlie "fell into a passion and gave most of the Gentlemen that had spoke very Abusive Language," according to an eyewitness, "and said they had a mind to betray him." A second meeting that evening produced no change. Finally the prince gave up and ordered the retreat.

The retreat from Derby was a low point for the Jacobites in more ways than one. Charles fell into a pout and a funk, and refused to talk to his subordinates. His troops were equally furious. They quickly lost their earlier discipline and fell to looting the locals, leaving a trail of resentment and rage behind them. Outside Penrith they clashed with some of the Duke of Cumberland's advance dragoons, who, unlike the raw recruits at Prestonpans, stood to fight rather than run away. Rumors that the Highlanders had cried "No quarter!" and killed some of the British wounded circulated among the duke's troops, with ugly repercussions later on.

On Christmas Day the army entered Glasgow. As Charles's chief Irish adviser noted, "the Prince was resolved to punish the Town of Glasgow, who shew'd a little too much Zeal to the Government." He demanded 5,500 pounds in ransom, as well as supplies and food, including "6,000 pair of shoes, 6,000 bonnetts, and as many tartan hose." City merchants paid up with a bad grace, and it was with difficulty that some of the Highlanders were restrained from burning the city down. Nowhere else, Charles said bitterly, had he found so few friends as in Glasgow.

This was his first full encounter with that second group of Scots who had no interest in seeing him succeed: Scotland's growing middle class of merchants and professional men, as well as improving landowners. Like Robertson, Carlyle, and the other Edinburgh student volunteers, they were Whigs, but less from conviction than out of practical self-interest. Union had brought them affluence and prosperity. Just as its architects had calculated, it secured their loyalty to the new government. Union, and the Hanovers on the throne, implied a Scotland with expanding horizons and possibilities; growing commerce and trade; the

rule of law; the good things in life. Returning the Stuarts meant returning to the old Scotland. In the minds of Scottish Whigs, this was not an
option.

In the sharpest sense, the Forty-five was not a war between Scots
and Englishmen, but a civil war. The split that divided Scots transcended
class or religious divisions, or even the division between Highlander and
Lowlander. (According to one recent scholar, Murray Pittock, perhaps
as much as 40 percent of Charles's army consisted of Lowlanders.) It
was in fact a cultural split, between two competing visions of what
Scotland should be and where it could go. Charles's supporters could
not afford for Scotland to move forward, and so they were prepared to
fight and die to topple the existing Whig regime. Scottish Whigs could
not afford to go backward, and so they were willing to do anything and
make any sacrifice to keep the Stuarts off the throne.

Charles's march south had given them a chance to catch their
breath, and as he returned to Scotland to gather reinforcements, they
began to mobilize against him. What they may have lacked in martial
valor, they made up for in deep pockets and political skill. The city of
Glasgow had already raised a regiment of militia which attached itself to
the royal forces converging to retake Edinburgh. With them was a
diehard company of volunteers commanded by John Home. On January
6, 1746, they retook the capital. Charles's army, meanwhile, was
bogged down in a pointless and ineffectual siege of Stirling Castle,
which critically divided his forces and depleted him of resources such as
artillery for the rest of the campaign.

More decisive intervention came from two Scottish Whig politicians. One was Archibald Campbell, the former Lord Islay and Francis
Hutcheson's old patron, who was now Duke of Argyll. He brought the
powerful Campbell clan firmly on the side of the government, thus
securing most of the western Highlands—although, ironically, Argyll's
success in making agriculture more prosperous in the clan area made his
followers less than willing to leave their farms to risk their lives on the
battlefield.

The other, even more important at the moment, was Duncan Forbes
of Culloden. After Prestonpans he found himself, as he remembered

later, "almost alone, without troops, without arms," and "supported by nobody of common sense or courage." Nonetheless, he knew he had to act to "prevent extreme folly." Single-handedly he waged a campaign to keep the clan chieftains of the northern Highlands loyal to the house of Hanover. MacLeod, Sutherland, Munro, MacDonald of Sleat—Forbes cajoled, persuaded, and with his own money bribed them into passivity. Other clans he managed to divide, including the Grants, Gordons, Mackenzies, and Frasers. By his efforts Forbes prevented the one thing that might have saved the Stuart cause: a general rising of the clans. If any single individual can be said to have defeated the Forty-five, it is not the Duke of Cumberland but Duncan Forbes.

Of course, Scottish Whigs could use their money and political smarts to prevent Charles from winning, but they still needed a military solution to crush him altogether. Ten days after they retook Edinburgh, royal troops had another disastrous encounter with the Jacobite clans at Falkirk. Once again, British cavalry and infantry flew into a panic as the Highlanders attacked. John Home, stationed with his volunteers on a hill, watched incredulously as the redcoats broke and ran, just as they had at Prestonpans. Yet Samuel Johnson could understand the professionals' distress. "Men accustomed only to exchange bullets at a distance," he wrote, "are discouraged and amazed when they find themselves encountered hand to hand, and catch the gleam of steel flashing in their faces." It was all over in less than twenty minutes. The Jacobites took more than three hundred prisoners, including Home and his volunteers (although he led his men in a daring escape a few nights later and rejoined the royal army). "By my soul, Dick," one prisoner was heard saying to another, "if Prince Charles goes on in this way, Prince Frederick [the Prince of Wales] will never be King George!"

He was wrong. The end of Charles's hopes was at hand, in the person of the new British commander in chief, Prince Frederick's brother William, Duke of Cumberland. Despite Cumberland's later sobriquet of "Butcher" and his gross rotund appearance, he was a skillful and experienced soldier, and only four years older than Bonnie Prince Charlie. He soon set about restoring the royal army's morale. He brought them fresh artillery, something sadly lacking at Prestonpans and Falkirk, and

a new technique for their new weapon, the bayonet. By training his soldiers to lunge with their bayonets not at the charging Highlander in
front of them, but at the one to their right as he raised his arm to strike
and thus exposed himself to a lethal thrust, Cumberland now had the
tactic that could counteract the violent shock of the clansmen's charge.
His troops sensed for the first time that they could beat the Jacobites in
a pitched battle.

They had their chance to prove it on April 16, 1746. Charles's situation had now deteriorated to the point of collapse. His war chest was
empty; his men had no pay; supplies were gone; worst of all, he and his
field commander, Lord George Murray, were no longer on speaking
terms. He and his troops had been on a long line of retreat for weeks
from Cumberland's much larger army, toward Inverness. Most of his
soldiers had not eaten for two days. On the sixteenth, the sorry ragtag
force reached Culloden House, overlooking Drummossie Moor—the
home of Duncan Forbes, the man who had doomed Charles's last
chance for a Highland uprising. Charles's officers, "sullen and dejected,"
according to one eyewitness, lay down to sleep in the deserted house,
"some on beds, others on tables, Chairs, and on the floors." The
Jacobites had drained Forbes's private supply of sixty hogsheads of claret
on an earlier visit: the prince, weak from a recent bout with pneumonia, had to be content with a dram of whisky and some bread.

With Cumberland close on his heels, Charles decided the only way
to reverse his fortune was by offering battle. Murray and the other commanders were appalled by the suicidal plan, and Charles again lost his
temper. "God damn it! Are my orders still disobeyed?" he cried. Walter
Stapleton, commander of his Irish volunteers, now ventured his opinion: "The Scots are always good soldiers till things come to a crisis," he
said contemptuously. This silenced the other commanders' objections.
Now they had to fight, to prove their manhood. At the end of their
enterprise as at its start, honor compelled them to take a position they
knew to be a mistake. They and their clansmen were about to pay for
that mistake in full measure.

The next day, as the clans and other Jacobite contingents wearily
drew up their line of battle, Cumberland's army marched onto the field,

with flags, drums, and the squeal of the Campbell pipes. His army out-
numbered Charles's by two to one. Three of his fifteen regular battal-
ions were Scottish, in addition to Lord Loudun's regiment of Highland
volunteers and Campbell's clansmen. As rank after rank of redcoats
moved slowly but inexorably into position—the two armies were only
five hundred yards apart—the hearts of the Jacobite commanders sank.
"We are putting an end to a bad affair," George Murray muttered to
Lord Elcho. Even Prince Charlie's optimism faded, and for the first time
he "began to consider his situation desperate."

Numbers, discipline, and technology now took over. Cumberland
opened the battle with an artillery barrage that pounded the Jacobite
line for half an hour, killing, wounding, or scattering nearly a third of
Charles's effectives. Charles himself narrowly escaped death when a
solid shot decapitated the groom holding his horse. Meanwhile, a contingent of Campbells had seized the low stone fence that was supposed
to secure the Jacobite right, and began to pour a deadly fire into their
flank. Charles's troops still had not fired a shot, and yet the battle had
been largely decided.

However, the clansmen did not realize this. While their commanders had steadily lost their nerve, they were eager for battle. They had
scattered their enemies not once but twice, and assumed they could do
it again. At last, maddened beyond endurance by the shelling, the
Mackintoshes, who held the center of the prince's line, could no longer
be held back and charged. Without waiting for orders, Cameron of
Lochiel, sword and pistol in hand, led his "sons of the hound," as the
Camerons called themselves, after them.

Then the rest of Clan Chattan—Mackintosh, MacGillivray, and
MacBean—surged behind them, coming up "very boldly and fast all in
a cloud together, sword in hand," as one English soldier described it;
"like wildcats," said another. Most came on too fast to use the muskets
they were carrying; in their bloodlust, they threw their firearms away.
The British laid a withering fire into them as they came on, forcing the
charging Highlanders to swerve to the right, as if to evade the hailstorm
of lead and shot. "Making a dreadful huzza, and even crying 'Run, ye
dogs!'" they broke onto the British line.

But this time the British did not run. Even the Scots of Munro's regiment, which had disgraced itself at Falkirk, stood their ground. It was vicious hand-to-hand combat, with the clansmen blindly hacking and thrusting as the choking gunsmoke closed around them. "It was dreadful to see the enemies' swords circling in the air as they were raised from the strokes," said one eyewitness, "and no less to see the officers in the army, some cutting with their swords, other pushing with their spontoons, the sergeants running their halberds into the throats of the opponents, the men ramming their fixed bayonets up to the sockets."

Meanwhile, the British fire continued undiminished. The smoke became so thick that the Highlanders had to feel rather than see their way to the enemy. Clansmen were shot down in heaps three or four deep as they climbed over the bodies of cousins and brothers and "hacked at the muskets with such a maniacal fury that far down the line men could hear the iron clang of sword on barrel." Those who were not mowed down by musket fire and grapeshot died on the points of the Britishers' bayonets. "No one that attacked us, escaped alive," said one of Munro's officers afterwards, "for we gave no quarter, nor would accept of any."

The last head-on clash between a modern army and a premodern one on European soil ended when the clansmen could no longer stand up to the slaughter. First in ones and twos, then in clumps of ten or a dozen, they broke off and headed to the rear. Some, "in their fury and despair, threw stones for at least a minute or two, before their total rout began." Now the Campbells rose up, tearing down the stone wall and shouting *"Cruachan!"* as they fell on their ancient foes. Within minutes the Jacobite center and right turned and ran. The MacDonalds, holding down the left flank, soon followed.

Some chieftains refused to give up. MacDonnell of Keppoch cried out, "Oh my God, has it come to this, that the children of my tribe have forsaken me!" and charged, sword in hand, toward the enemy. He fell when a ball struck him in the arm, just as his brother Donald was shot down at the head of his company. Keppoch struggled on and took a second wound before dropping to the ground in front of the advancing line of British grenadiers. James MacDonald of Kilchonat tried to help him up, when another bullet hit the chief in the back. Kilchonat left him for dead and fled. But Keppoch was not dead, and when his natural son Angus Ban found him, he was unable to speak but still breathing. Angus and some of his soldiers (he had single-handedly rallied what was left of his father's regiment and led them off the field) managed to carry Keppoch to a small bothy filled with wounded and dying MacDonnells. There the old chieftain, who had once boasted of having five hundred warriors at his beck and call, expired, surrounded by the clansmen he had led to defeat and death.

The slaughter among the clan leadership was heavy. Grapeshot had shattered both of Lord Lochiel's ankles, and he had to be carried off the field. The only regimental commanders to escape unwounded were Lord George Murray, Lord Ardshiel, and Lord Nairne—although Nairne's brother, Robert Mercer of Aldie, was killed, as was Mercer's son Thomas. Their bodies were never found. Only three of the Mackintosh officers survived. But if the Jacobite chieftains and their tacksmen paid a heavy price for their misplaced loyalties, it was their followers who suffered most from the retributions of Cumberland and his soldiers.

We can try to make various excuses for their behavior. We can say war and its aftermath is often very nasty, and that the killing of prisoners and noncombatants is more common than most of us care to admit. There were the rumors that the Highlanders had massacred their prisoners at Penrith, which inflamed many British spirits. There was the desire on many soldiers' part to settle scores for the humiliations at Prestonpans and Falkirk. Then there was a political culture that treated rebels as traitors and the lowest of the low, undeserving of mercy or pity. And so on. But the bitter truth is that the British at Culloden behaved monstrously, in violation of all the accepted conventions of warfare at the time, and that Cumberland himself set the poorest example.

When riding across the battlefield, he came upon the twenty-year-old colonel of the Fraser regiment, Charles Fraser of Inverallochy, standing wounded and bloody in front of him. Cumberland asked him to whom he belonged. "To the Prince," Fraser replied. Furious,

Cumberland turned to an officer, Major James Wolfe, and ordered him to shoot the boy on the spot. In less than twelve years, during the French and Indian Wars, Wolfe would be the conqueror of Montreal, and would himself make the commander's ultimate sacrifice on the battlefield. Now, to his everlasting credit, Wolfe refused to obey the order, and offered to resign his commission. Instead, Cumberland gave a signal to a passing soldier, who raised his musket and shot Fraser through the head.

Cumberland did show great solicitude for his own troops, giving twelve guineas for every wounded man, and ordered up rum, brandy, biscuit, and cheese for their provision. He praised "my brave Campbells" and the Scots of Munro's regiment. But there was no mercy for the rebels, either on the battlefield or afterwards. For two days the wounded were left unattended on the field, with sentinels on guard to prevent anyone from helping them. Soldiers went from house to house in the area, rounding up rebel stragglers and executing them by the dozens. The hut in which McDonnell of Keppoch had died was set on fire, consuming his body and those of his followers, those still alive screaming horribly until they were "scorched to death in a most miserable, mangled way." A nearby hut containing eighteen clansmen was also put to the torch.

Cumberland's cavalry pursued the retreating army all along the Inverness road, riding down and killing everyone, rebel or not, whom they met. Afterwards one eyewitness came upon a horrific scene, "a woman stript and laid in a very indecent posture, and some of the other sex with their privites placed in their hands." At King's Milns, close to Inverness, he found a twelve-year-old boy, "his head cloven to his teeth." A Mrs. Robertson, widow of the late laird of Lees at Inshes, came home after the battle to find sixteen dead men in front of her door, all of them murdered by passing dragoons. She summoned her terrified servants and told them to give the clansmen a proper burial.

The atrocities redoubled when Cumberland's forces marched across the Great Glen and into the home territories of the rebel clans, in search of the fugitive prince. All summer and autumn the harrying continued, and while hundreds were killed outright, hundreds more died during the severe winter of 1746–47, or died in prison. According to John Prebble, at any given time there were more than 3,400 Jacobite prisoners being held in jails in England and Scotland, or on transports at Inverness and Tilbury. Many had been arrested for being seen "to drink the Pretender's health" or "known to wish the Rebels well." What served as a radical-chic gesture at Tory Oxford was now the equivalent of a death sentence in the post-Culloden Highlands.

Those in the transports suffered worst. A prisoner on the *Alexander and James,* its hold crammed with prisoners being taken to London for trial and execution, remembered: "They'd take a rope and tye about the poor sicks west, then they would hawll them up by their tackle and plunge them into the sea, as they said to drown the vermine; but they took speciall care to drown both together. Then they'd hawll them up on deck and ty a stone about the leggs and overboard with them." He added, "I have seen six or seven examples of this in a day."

At the same time, the rest of Scotland was returning to normal. When the city of Glasgow learned of the royal victory at Culloden, citizens rang church bells and built bonfires that blazed on through the night. The Lord Provost of Edinburgh, who had failed to defend the city against the prince's troops, was arrested and thrown into prison. George Drummond replaced him, and the young volunteers whom people had earlier laughed at and mocked were now the heroes of the hour. Colin Maclaurin, who had supervised reinforcement of the city's defense so diligently and to so little ultimate purpose, returned from his exile in York. But his health was gone, and before the summer was over he was dead. A popular and respected teacher, Maclaurin's textbooks on mathematics had made Newton's calculus standard practice across Britain. Enlightened Edinburgh mourned one of its own.

The bulk of Cumberland's army returned to Flanders. His successor, the Earl of Albemarle, divided Scotland into four military districts, and said of the Highland Scots, "Nothing but fire and sword can cure their cursed, vicious ways of thinking." But except for patrols to look for remaining rebels or the unaccounted-for Prince Charles (who was still in hiding in the Great Glen), his troops spent most of their time completing the military fortifications and roads General Wade had started two decades before, including Fort George at Ardersier Point, near Inverness. A forbidding example of the most advanced eighteenth-century fortificatory technology, it was finally finished in 1769. It has never seen a shot fired in battle.

At the recommendation of soldiers and bureaucrats, Parliament passed laws banning weapons (again), the tartan, and the kilt. This time the laws had teeth, and the threat of Cumberland's dragoons, behind them. For a generation Highlanders had to dye their plaid clothing black or brown, and learn to sew their kilts together at the crotch. Warriors hid their swords and targes in the heath, hoping that they or their children would remember where they had buried them. Year by year, the clan battle cries and the tales of ancient cattle raids began to fade from the people's memory.

Most of this, like the bloody reprisals in the Great Glen, did not touch the lives of Lowlanders. Scottish Whigs were either ignorant of, or indifferent to, what was happening. An exception was David Hume. He had acquaintances who had turned Jacobite, and he beseeched his cousin, Alexander Home of Eccles, who, as solicitor general, was prosecuting many of these cases: "Seek the Praise, my dear Sandy, of Humanity and Moderation."

Another was Duncan Forbes. He had returned to Culloden House to find the windows smashed, the furniture broken or stolen, his wine cellar drunk dry, and his tenants beaten and robbed by both sides. He also learned that twelve wounded Jacobites had sought shelter in the house after the battle, and that British soldiers had turned up and, on the pretext of taking them away to be treated for their wounds, dragged them into the forecourt and shot them. Later, when he met George II, the king asked him if the story was true. "I wish I could say no," Forbes said.

As Lord President, he presided over many trials of accused traitors that spring, and tried whenever possible to make sure that justice, rather than revenge, was served. When MacDonald of Kingsburgh was arrested because the fugitive prince had stayed at his house, Forbes offered to put up his bail himself. He warned the Earl of Albemarle, "Unnecessary severity creates pity." The ban on weapons was something

Forbes had been pressing for years, but he thought the ban on the kilt both ridiculous and too severe. He called it "a chip in porridge" and worth "not one half penny." Instead, he urged the government to put the ban on the rebel clans instead of on everyone, regardless of loyalty. The London government, which was not in the mood to distinguish between good and bad Highlanders, ignored him. Having saved the government from its worst nightmare, a general uprising of the Highlands, Forbes never received any honor or reward, not even a knighthood.

Forbes did, however, have the satisfaction of seeing through a piece of legislation that he considered key to breaking the power of the chieftains. This abolished the ancient, hereditary jurisdictions of chieftains over their clansmen, including the so-called regalian rights, which made them virtual kings in their territories. At the same date, Lord Kames was writing his *Essay Concerning British Antiquities,* pointing out that the old Scottish law had been set up to keep tenants under the thumb of their feudal overlords. Now Forbes oversaw the creation of a new legal framework for the Highlands, shattering the age-old dependence of clansman and peasant on the will of his chief. It established a new principle, that the Highlander was a free individual, who could contract to work his own land and keep the proceeds for himself.

Forbes even introduced a new system of written leases, which freed the tenant from compulsory services in kind to his landlord, including service with the sword. No Highland chieftain could ever again summon up a private army to fight his neighbors—or the British Crown. But the change was also supposed to benefit the tenant as well, by letting him work to pay his laird rather than fight for him. The fact that it did not quite work out that way was not entirely Forbes's fault; the Highland Clearances were still a long way off, and something no one could have foreseen in 1748.

Instead, like other Scottish Whigs, Forbes watched with relief the disarming of the Highlands and the disruption of clan life. They had just had a brush with disaster; no one wanted to see it repeated. Looking back, Alexander Carlyle said, "God forbid that Britain should ever again be in danger of being overrun by such a despicable enemy." According to John Clerk of Penicuik, news of Culloden "gave universal joy" not only to Whigs "but there were even Jacobites who were at least content at what had happened." Thanks to the rebellion, "all trade and business in this country were quite at a standstill." Now, Clerk noted with pleasure, "peace and quietness began to break in."

Scotland was ready for the next stage of its future.

III

There are many aftermaths to Culloden and the Forty-five.

Prince Charles spent five months hiding from Cumberland's troops. With a price of thirty thousand pounds on his head, he wandered hungry and sick from one sanctuary to another, endangering everyone who gave him shelter. At one point he traveled disguised as an Irish maidservant with Flora MacDonald, daughter of MacDonald of Milton, to her future father-in-law's house at Kingsburgh, on the Isle of Skye. Escorted on foot to Elgol, he was able to catch a boat to the mainland, and on September 19, 1746, he made his rendezvous with the French privateer *L'Heureux.* He returned to France until 1748, when the terms of the peace treaty between France and Britain deported him to Italy. He lived the rest of his life in Rome a corpulent alcoholic, blaming the failure of the revolt on everyone except himself. When his father died in 1766, Charles became the Stuart claimant—but by then it was a meaningless claim. On January 31, 1788, the man who more than any other was responsible for bringing death and destruction to the Highlands expired, still admired by too many of the people whose lives he had ruined.

The notion that Culloden destroyed the Highland clans is a myth; the traditional ways had been dying for years. Long before, without realizing it, the chieftains and the Crown had conspired to obliterate the old system of loyalties and mutual dependence in order to consolidate their own power. The battle was the clans' last stand, just as the myth states. The glory was gone. But the sordid reality of that way of life lingered on for decades: the poverty, the bruising punishment of the weak and helpless, the sullen hopelessness.

More than a quarter-century after Culloden, Samuel Johnson and James Boswell made their famous visit to Scotland. From the western Highlands they traveled to the Isle of Skye, and from Skye to Raasay. Raasay, a narrow, barren island fifteen miles long and only three miles wide, was MacLeod land and the scene of some of the ugliest reprisals of the Forty-five (committed, we note in passing, not by the English but by fellow Scots, including MacLeod clansmen from the loyalist side). By 1773, however, the bitterness of those years had faded. The captain of Boswell and Johnson's boat to Raasay was Malcolm MacLeod, who had escorted the prince to Elgol. Now sixty-two, MacLeod struck Boswell as a perfect "representative of a Highland gentleman"—although he wore breeches and a plaid jacket instead of a kilt. Boswell found him "frank and polite, in the true sense of the word."

Boswell and Johnson even stopped in on Flora MacDonald, now a middle-aged married lady, and drank gin with her and her husband. Johnson slept on the same bed Prince Charles had used when he stayed there disguised as Betty Burke. Flora had even saved the sheets the prince had slept in (she would eventually be buried in one of them). Boswell stayed up to visit with his hosts, and was distressed to learn that they were "under a load of debt and intended to go to America." In 1774 they did as they promised and emigrated to the colonies, just in time to be caught up in another revolt against the British Crown.

During his stay, Johnson observed that "the clans retain little now of their original character." The people had lost their taste for war: "their contempt of government is subdued, and their reverence for the chiefs abated." In general, he noted with satisfaction, progress in Scotland has been "rapid and uniform." It was finally becoming a civilized country. "What remains to be done," he concluded, "they will quickly do, and then wonder, like me, why that which was so necessary and so easy was so long delayed."

Still, the fate of the Highlands and Highlanders bothered him. Before the Forty-five, "every man was a soldier, who partook of national confidence, and interested himself in national honor. To lose this spirit, is to lose what no small advantage will compensate." This led Johnson to wonder whether in fact any nation ought to become "totally commercial," or whether "it be necessary to preserve in some part of the empire the military spirit."

It was an acute and profound point. But in fact Scottish Whigs had been there a decade or two ahead of him. As they watched the new Scotland take shape around them—a nation that men such as John Home and William Robertson had risked their lives to see emerge from the shadows of the past—they would see much to celebrate and extol. But always a small doubt remained: a sense of loss, of something missing from the modern cultural universe they and their generation, more than any other, could take credit for creating. And for them as well as for Scots ever after, the symbol of that something would be the Highlanders who fought and died at Culloden.

CHAPTER SEVEN

Profitable Ventures

August, around, what Public Works I see!
Lo! Stately Street, lo! Squares that court the breeze!
See long Canals and deepened Rivers join
Each part with each, with the circling Main
The whole enlivened Isle.

—*James Thomson*, Liberty, *1736*

I

Scottish Whigs had helped to defeat Jacobitism in order to give birth to a new enlightened Scotland. They got their wish—with a vengeance. The years after 1745 witnessed an explosion of cultural and economic activity all across Scotland, as if the collapse of the Jacobite and Highland threat had released a tremendous pent-up store of national energy. It was economic "takeoff" in the full modern sense.

Scots were not the first, or certainly the last, people to experience it. But they were the first to recognize it for what it was, and to realize how economic growth could suddenly transform an entire society for (on the whole) the better. As the century proceeded, merchants, scholars, clerics, and professional men—a Scottish middle class—pushed themselves front and center. Progress was no longer just a question of creating a polite or even commercial society. Scots were engaged in creating the new capitalist future of the world, with its self-renewing productive growth and "economies of scale," and Adam Smith would be its prophet.

The epicenter of this transformation was Glasgow. It became the emporium of Scotland, a thriving international port city on the

Atlantic, commanding the sea routes south and east. In 1707, Glasgow had fought hard against union, since it cost the city its independent political clout. Within a generation, however, Glaswegians carved out a place for themselves in Britain's trade with the American colonies, particularly the trade in tobacco. The men who confronted Prince Charles with their sullen resistance, and raised a regiment of militia to oppose him, enjoyed a perspective on the world that extended to America, Scandinavia, and Russia. After 1745 they became cutthroat competitors for the market in tobacco with their English rivals.

A decade after the Act of Union, the first Glasgow-owned ship had made the seven-week voyage to the tobacco landings on the Chesapeake Bay. By 1727 there were fifty vessels making the trip every year. In 1741 Glasgow shippers dropped off 7 million pounds of tobacco on their wharves at Port Glasgow; in 1752, they were unloading 21 million, three times the volume of just eleven years earlier. From that point on, the rate of growth, as well as the total volume of trade, continued to accelerate, while the British Empire expanded. In 1758, the year after Robert Clive conquered India and the year before James Wolfe captured Quebec and Canada, Scottish tobacco imports from America were larger than those of London and all English ports combined.

Yet the biggest growth in the market was still to come. The true "golden age" of Glasgow and her wealthy tobacco importers, the so-called Tobacco Lords, came in the decade and a half before the American Revolution. In 1771 the trade rose to an incredible 41 million pounds; it totaled more than a third of all Scottish imports, and almost two-thirds of all the nation's exports. Scottish merchants were a regular part of life in such ports as New York, Philadelphia, Baltimore, and Alexandria, Virginia. Almost half of all American trade in tobacco was in Scottish hands. William Lee wrote his fellow planter Landon Carter in 1771, "I think it self-evident, that Glasgow has almost monopolized Virginia and its inhabitants." As the most recent historian of the Glasgow trade puts it, "By the 1780s, the city was a player on the world stage."

The men who made Glasgow a world player came from different

backgrounds and circumstances. A few were sons of local artisans and clerics. One, Hugh Wylie, was a sea captain who saved enough money to buy a share in one of the big importing houses. Most, though, were well-to-do Lowlanders, including sons of landowning families. Others belonged to long-established Glaswegian families such as the Bogles, the Dunlops, and the Murdochs, who had been in the American trade since the seventeenth century. Almost all served time in Virginia or Maryland as tobacco warehouse managers (or factors) before returning to Glasgow.

The appellation Tobacco Lords was a tribute to their wealth and power, but also expressed a paradox. Business, rather than birth, had conferred on them an almost aristocratic status. As they walked along the Gallowgate with their scarlet cloaks, satin suits, and gold-tipped canes, awed citizens stepped off the pavement to let them pass. Their town houses and gardens were noted on Glasgow street maps with the same respect as the estates of great peers in county surveys. They were a ruling class made entirely by money—money hard earned and, it must be said, money freely spent.

The Big Three were William Cunninghame, Alexander Spiers, and John Glassford. In the half-decade before the American Revolution, their three firms controlled over half the Glasgow tobacco trade. The rest of the market was divided among their lesser rivals: Bogles, Murdochs, Dunlops, Oswalds, Buchanans, and Ritchies.

William Cunninghame was born in 1715, and started his career working in a tobacco warehouse in Virginia. In 1775 he was rich enough to loan his brother-in-law Robert Dunlaw 150,000 pounds, perhaps $60 million in today's money (albeit over ten years). His company owned fourteen warehouses just in Virginia, and his famous company ships such as the *Patuxent* and the *Cunninghame* regularly set records on the seven-thousand-mile, three-month round trip to the mouth of the Chesapeake Bay. The *Cunninghame* alone made the run fifteen times in seven years. Cunninghame built himself a magnificent town house in Glasgow that cost over 10,000 pounds, while Alexander Spiers's mansion nearby ran to nearly 5,300 pounds. Spiers, Bowman, and Company had had a total capitalization of just over 16,000 pounds in 1744; in 1773 it was worth 152,280 pounds. Spiers's personal fortune made him one of the richest men in Britain.

How did they do it? Some pointed to Glasgow's geography. Like the rest of western Scotland, its westerly projection into the Atlantic made it uniquely situated to benefit from American trade. A journey from Port Glasgow, the heart of Glaswegian shipping, to Charleston, South Carolina, or Annapolis, Maryland, could shave two to three weeks off the same trip from London or Bristol. Faster time meant lower costs, of course, and quicker return on investors' money. Many of those investors were also immediate family members. This was another feature of the big Glasgow firms: their reliance on a loyal circle of uncles and aunts, nephews and sons-in-law, to pool capital and lay off risk.

This "clannishness" of Scottish business firms, past and present, used to be supposed to be crucial to their success. This is a myth. Similarly, the economic advantage Glasgow enjoyed on the Atlantic end of the tobacco run was more than offset by the long trip to re-export it into the Mediterranean and the Baltic—which is where one could make real money. Instead, the secret of the Tobacco Lords' success lay in their balance sheets: their ability to summon up capital from a wide variety of sources, while ruthlessly cutting costs. Investment money for ships, warehouses, and inventories (since Scottish firms, unlike their English rivals, bought the tobacco from planters outright instead of selling it abroad on commission) came from a wide variety of sources, including banks set up to finance the trade. Between 1740 and 1770 no less than six banks were chartered in Glasgow for this purpose, including the Glasgow Ship Bank and the Thistle Bank.

In addition, partners were paid only 5 percent interest on their shares. The rest of their profits, an overwhelming sum of money in good times, had to be plowed back into the business. The result of all this was that the Glasgow tobacco trade was one of the most heavily capitalized industries in Britain, giving merchants the flexibility to expand when things went well, or sit out the storm when they did not.

The eighteenth-century Glasgow tobacco trade was run by entrepreneurs in the classic sense: men who took risks in order to make money, and who paid the price when their enterprises failed. One of the oldest participants, the Bogle family firm, had to go into receivership in 1772 when it could no longer pay its debts. Established figures such as Hugh Wylie, George McCall, James Dunlop, and William French all went through the ordeal of bankruptcy. But, for every firm that went under, new syndicates of investors took its place. This was a constantly self-renewing industry, drawing on fresh outside blood and investors even as competition compelled everyone to keep costs down and services at their deliverable best. Glasgow's tobacco trade offered up an image of capitalism in its purest and most dynamic form.

It was by watching the city's tobacco trade that Adam Smith, professor at the University of Glasgow from 1751 to 1764, made his first real acquaintance with large-scale business enterprise, and with the businessmen who ran it. Smith struck up a close acquaintance with John Glassford, who kept him informed of events in America and also took a keen interest in Smith's progress with his *Wealth of Nations.* Glasgow Provost Andrew Cochrane organized a Political Economy Club, whose members included Smith, Glassford, and another wealthy tobacco merchant, Richard Oswald. Cochrane even presided over a special session of the Glasgow Town Council on May 3, 1762, when Professor Smith was made an honorary burgess of the city.

This sort of thing happened because the Glasgow merchant community, like other middle-class Scots, ranked education almost, though not quite, as high as good business sense. Most merchants could read Greek and Latin as well as a ledger and balance sheet. The heirs of firms such as Glassford, Ingram regularly went for one or two years at the university. Several almost certainly sat in on Adam Smith's lectures on philosophy and jurisprudence, just as their fathers had attended Francis Hutcheson's classes. Their numbers at the University of Glasgow grew as the century wore on. In fact, by one count fully one-half of the students enrolled by 1790 were sons of "industry and commerce." This compares with less than 8 percent at Cambridge University in the same period—indicating how much the Scots, and Glaswegians in particular, not only talked about the alliance between commerce and "politeness" or cultural excellence, but lived it as well.

"The connection between Commerce and the liberal arts is so well known," wrote Glaswegian John Mennons, "that such as cultivate the latter naturally seek the patronage of those who are the greatest friends to the latter." Education and the arts did find generous patrons among the Tobacco Lords. Affluence and long months between the departure and return of shipping fleets meant that Glasgow's elite had plenty of time on their hands. Alexander Bogle alleged that "all the merchants in Glasgow . . . are quite idle for one half or two-thirds of the year" when their ships were at sea and so had to find other ways to keep themselves occupied. They joined the Literary Society of Glasgow, and the Sacred Music Institution, and founded the Hodge Podge Club, which invited luminaries such as Adam Smith and Thomas Reid to speak. They gathered in the coffee room of the Tontine Hotel for polite conversation or a glass of rum punch, the drink of choice among the Tobacco Lords and Glasgow's West Indian merchants.

It was tobacco merchant George Bogle who cast the deciding vote on the university board of regents enabling Francis Hutcheson's friend William Leechman to become professor of theology, over the objections of Presbyterian hard-liners. And it was John Glassford and his partner Archibald Ingram who put up the initial funding for the most farsighted cultural project in the city's history, the brainchild of the Glasgow Enlightenment's most unusual and eccentric figure.

Francis Hutcheson first noticed him sitting in on his lectures in the 1730s. Although Robert Foulis was not a regular student, Hutcheson was so impressed with this "singular worthy soul," as he called him, that he offered to hire Foulis as his classroom tutor. Foulis was working class, the son of a maltman and apprenticed to become a barber. However, his thirst for learning had driven him into Hutcheson's classroom as well as that of professor of mathematics Robert Simson. Foulis became devoted to Hutcheson's vision of education as a means of teaching human beings to be free and good. But because he had no university degree (although he read Greek and Latin fluently, as did his younger brother Andrew), a career in teaching was closed to him. The next best thing, he decided, was to open a bookshop, as a kind of import-export business in enlightened ideas and culture.

Like Allan Ramsay before him, Foulis used his bookshop as a vehicle for branching out into other cultural projects. He soon turned from just selling books to printing them. In 1741 he and his brother became the official "university printers," and since they both knew Latin and Greek, their editions of ancient classical texts were far more accurate than those of any other Scottish or even English publisher. The Foulis brothers' meticulous attention to detail even extended down to designing new and clearer typefaces for Roman and Greek letters, with the help of the university's type founder, Alexander Wilson. Their edition of Homer's *Iliad* in 1756 defined the state of the art, and won a medal from the Edinburgh Society for Encouraging Arts, Sciences, Manufactures, and Agriculture—a rare tribute to a Glaswegian from a rival sister city.

The award, like the edition itself, went to the heart of what Foulis saw as his personal mission: to make the "practical" arts such as printing, engraving, and stencilmaking as important and significant to polite society as the "fine" arts, such as painting, sculpture, and music. It was to pursue this that in 1753 Foulis established his School for the Art of Design, with the help of Glassford and Ingram. The University of Glasgow gave its imprimatur to the school, making it an official appendage of the university, like Foulis's press and bookshop. Adam Smith helped him find rooms for classes and faculty, and Britain's first academic school for design was launched.

Foulis hoped that his classes in sculpture, drawing, and printmaking would become as essential to the curriculum as philosophy, mathematics, or theology. "It is to be wished," he said, "that all Universities were also academies, in order that artists should never be without learning, nor learned men without a taste for those arts, that in all enlightened ages, have been deemed liberal and polite." He deliberately set up his printmaking classes to appeal to local linen and cotton manufacturers, as a place to devise new patterns and designs for their cloths.

In Foulis's mind, the practical was inseparable from the theoretical. There was no sense of the artist or the intellectual pursuing a "higher" or more spiritual goal than the craftsman or businessman. Everyone, the artist and the artisan, the philosopher and the mechanic, the scholar and the manufacturer, was engaged in the same project: creating a polite, humane, enlightened culture. This intermingling of the practical and the intellectual was in fact a keynote of the Glasgow Enlightenment. It explains why engineer James Watt, who helped build Scotland's first dry dock at Port Glasgow in 1762, was just as highly regarded by university professors such as Adam Smith and Joseph Black as he was by Glasgow's merchants, and why type maker Alexander Wilson could also be named Professor of Practical Astronomy in 1760.

After its promising start, Foulis's academy faltered. "The fine arts do not ripen quickly," he wrote to anatomy professor William Hunter, "especially in a cold climate." The academy was forced to close its doors in 1775, and Foulis had to sell the pictures he had accumulated in the academy's art gallery to cover his debts. His brother Andrew died at the same time. Depressed and financially ruined, Robert Foulis caught pneumonia and passed away in November 1776.

His great dream had failed. But Foulis had put into play a basic principle of his teacher Francis Hutcheson's view of art in relation to life. This was that God had made human virtue beautiful as well as useful, and that physical beauty, or "uniformity amidst variety," was, like the arts, essential to human happiness. It is the spirit of Scottish neoclassicism, and would carry over in the works of two other Scots—Edinburgh men this time, not Glaswegians—Robert and James Adam.

In any case, Glasgow's breakthrough was complete. The Foulis Press had spawned a host of imitators and offshoots. The number of books printed in Glasgow increased by 500 percent. By the 1770s the city could boast of fourteen booksellers, as well as three engravers, four architects, two marble cutters, an imported-carpet warehouse, two coach builders, fourteen saddlers, three fine jewelers, and twenty-three different cabinetmakers—not to mention twenty-six hairdressers and thirteen barbers. Service industries and consumer goods, or what the more old-fashioned still called luxuries, were now a fixed part of the Glasgow scene, as newly acquired wealth poured into desirable new channels like a river into a multitude of streams and tributaries. "Whenever capital predominates," Adam Smith noted, "industry prevails, which increases the real wealth and revenue of all its inhabitants." This "trickle down" economics turned overseas tobacco money into local jobs, just as the smart tobacco dynasties diversified their investments into the wine and sugar trade, marine insurance, linen and cotton textiles, and iron foundries. Mercantile Glasgow laid the foundations for industrial Glasgow in the nineteenth century. Even after the tobacco trade declined, the city's capitalist base turned out to be self-perpetuating. Once started, economic growth was hard to shut down.

Economic growth proved to be the engine of change in other ways, as well. When the Glasgow Town Council decided to demolish the city's old West Port in 1749, it opened up croft land west of Glasgow to development and purchase. Many leading tobacco lords bought parcels for their mansions, with gardens opening onto the new streets laid out north to south: Virginia Street, Havannah Street, Jamaica Street, Queen Street, Dunlop Street (named after the merchant family), Buchanan Street (ditto). The Buchanans themselves had built their residence, Virginia House, slightly east of these later residential developments, with an arrow-straight drive leading to the front door. The tide of urbanization soon swept on past them, however, dotting the vicinity with houses and shops, and their long drive became Virginia Street instead.

In 1740, 17,000 people lived in Glasgow. In 1780 the population had swelled to over 42,000. Developers had laid out thirteen new streets and squares in the new western district of Glasgow, in hopes of attracting merchants and other homebuilders to an affluent urban lifestyle very different from that of the crowded old inner city. Streets were wide (twenty-three meters across in the case of Jamaica Street), with flagstone sidewalks on either side, and urban planners banned unpleasant or noisome businesses, such as skinning or tanning factories, and tallow and soap works. Surveyor James Barrie laid out an entire residential suburb on the Ramshorn and Meadowflat Crofts, by extending Miller, Queen, and Buchanan Streets northward. Back Cow Loan, the rural dirt track Prince Charlie had used to enter Glasgow in December of 1745, became Ingram Street, in honor of tobacco merchant and financier Alexander Ingram.

As with Foulis's academy of the arts, not everything went according to plan. Construction took time, lots sat empty for long periods, and conditions in the crowded old city remained a nuisance. But a new middle-class urban community was taking physical, as well as economic, shape. Its institutional emblem was Glasgow's Chamber of Commerce, the first in Britain, formed on New Year's Day, 1783, with a hefty round of rum toasts. Its more obvious and visible emblem was Barrie's George Square, laid out in his Meadowflats development between Queen and Frederick Streets. Unfortunately, by the time building actually began at Meadowflats in 1787, Glasgow had been upstaged by another, even more successful design for the new urban lifestyle: Edinburgh's New Town.

II

"Look at those fields," George Drummond said to a young friend who was standing beside him at a window looking north of Edinburgh Castle. It was 1763. Drummond, the belated hero of the city's failed resistance against the Jacobites, was approaching the end of his fourth consecutive, and last, term as Lord Provost. He was seventy-five and the most revered figure in Edinburgh. Certainly no one laughed at the commander of the Lawnmarket volunteers now.

Drummond was staring out across the North Loch, at the empty area beyond that residents knew by the charming name of Barefoot's Park. He pointed and turned to his guest.

"You, Mr. Somerville," he said, "are a young man and may probably live, though I will not, to see all these fields covered with houses, forming a splendid and magnificent city." Drummond explained how this could be done, by draining the North Loch and building a causeway linking it to the old town. "I have never lost sight of this object since the year 1725," he confessed, "when I was first elected provost." Now Drummond's dream was about to come true.

Everyone recognized that as modern cities went, Edinburgh left much to be desired. It was "that most picturesque (at a distance) and nastiest (when near) of all capital cities," according to the poet Thomas Gray. Clustered at the foot of Edinburgh Castle, the city earned its nickname "Auld Reekie" from the forest of chimneys belching smoke from fires that burned coal at the rate of five hundred tons a day, choking residents and visitors alike. Its central avenue, the so-called Royal Mile, was a dark, narrow canyon of rickety buildings, some stacked ten or even twelve stories high, thronging with people, vehicles, animals, and refuse.

To visualize what Edinburgh was like in 1763, one has to imagine a network of shadowy, twisting streets, each branching out into a bewildering labyrinth of wynds (or through alleys) and dead-end courts and closes, all lined with blackened, narrow-faced houses and tenements. The typical tenement saw several families jammed together on each floor, all sharing a common stairway—the servants and lower classes occupying the lowest and highest stories, and the upper and middle class—including nobles and supreme court justices like Kames and Auchinleck—ensconced in the middle. Daniel Defoe said, "I believe that in no city in the world so many people have so little room." Sanitation was nonexistent. Pigs, sheep, and the occasional cow wandered the pavement. A familiar figure in the neighborhood was the "Wha' wants me?" man, who carried a portable toilet (with small, discreet black curtain) for the use of passersby. For residents, a cry of "Gardy loo!" (from the French: *"Prenez garde à l'eau!"*) from an overhead window was the only warning before a chamber pot was emptied on the heads of anyone in the street or courtyard.

When Defoe visited, Edinburgh still had a population of less than thirty thousand. By 1755 it had grown to almost sixty thousand, all crowded into the same tight, medieval urban space. To relieve the congestion, citizens had constructed some new buildings and carried out renovations of others. After a disastrous fire, Parliament House had been extensively rebuilt. The Royal Infirmary had gone up in 1727, and the Edinburgh Exchange in 1753 (both involved architects from the Adam family). There was even an attempt to create a couple of model residential developments, one at James's Court in the late 1720s and the other at George Court. One of the first homeowners there was Sir Walter Scott's father. But the truth was that there was simply no room for any extensive building in the confines of the old city, which was also, thanks to overcrowding, a natural breeding ground for disease and epidemics.

––––––––

Now, in the flush of confidence following the defeat of the Forty-five, the Edinburgh Town Council, under Drummond's prodding, decided to do something about the congestion. It proposed buying up enough land north of the city to permit the construction of what would eventually be an entirely new city, to be called the New Town. Its goal was "to enlarge and improve this city, to adorn it with public buildings," to celebrate Edinburgh's growth of "husbandry, manufacturers, general commerce, and the increase of useful people." The proposal concluded with this stirring exhortation to loyal Scotsmen:

> What greater object can be presented to their view, that of enlarging, beautifying, and improving the capital of their native country? What can redound more to their honour? What prove more beneficial to SCOTLAND and by consequence to UNITED BRITAIN?

With this in view, in March 1766 the city fathers sponsored a competition for developing the one hundred or so acres of land above the North Loch as a single residential area. Architects and builders could submit whatever kinds of plans they wished. The only requirements were that there had to be room for two churches, and that each house had to be a maximum height of three stories totaling forty-eight feet from basement to wall-head, to give the New Town an even skyline.

Three months later the award went to a twenty-one-year-old mason named James Craig. The choice seems odd. He was certainly no rising star as an architect; his only other claim to fame, then or later, was that he was the nephew of poet James Thomson. Yet personal connections—the standard "it's not what you do, but whom you know"—seem to have played no part in the decision.

Craig's plan was simple, almost mechanically so. It consisted of a gridiron of three principal longitudinal avenues intersected by a series of north-south streets, with two large open squares at either end. Its real virtue, however, was that Craig had grasped at once the political agenda behind the New Town proposal. It showed in his choice of street names—George Street, Hanover Street, Princes Street (after the Prince of Wales and his brother the Duke of York) and Queen Street—and the names he gave to the two open squares: St. Georges Square, after the patron saint of England, and St. Andrews Square, after the patron saint of his native Scotland. Two east-west streets were named after the national flower of each kingdom, Rose Street and Thistle Street. Craig capped it all by laying out the streets and avenues in the shape of a Union Jack (the town council finally decided that was going too far and modified the design into its present shape).

Nevertheless, the point was made. The New Town would commemorate the new Whig Scotland, a modern commercial society that was to be the equal partner of its neighbor to the south, with Edinburgh its modern capital.

When Craig learned he had won the competition, he printed up a copy of the plan for the public to see, and put at the top a passage from his uncle's poem "Liberty":

> *August, around, what Public Works I see!*
> *Lo! Stately Street, lo! Squares that court the breeze!*
> *See long Canals and deepened Rivers join*
> *Each part with each, with the circling Main*
> *The whole enlivened Isle.*

When Thomson had composed the poem in 1736, the only place in "the whole enlivened Isle" of Britain to find "stately Streets" and elegant squares had been in England. Now, Craig and the Edinburgh Town Council were saying, it was Scotland's turn.

Development got under way almost at once. The first building, the Theatre Royal, went up in 1768—a monument to refined taste and polite culture, and a rebuke to the old Presbyterian culture that had condemned and banned "the lies of the theatre." In 1772 the North Bridge connecting the New Town with the Old Town was finished, launching another spurt of development that did not let up until the American Revolution. Once peace returned in 1783, the rest of the development filled in fast, until only the far western quadrant remained.

Who moved in? Most of the buyers of building lots, or *feus* as they were called, were members of Edinburgh's commercial class. Only one great aristocrat, Sir Laurence Dundas, built himself a mansion in the New Town facing St. Andrews Square (today it houses the Royal Bank of Scotland). Otherwise, unlike similar residential developments in London or in France, the New Town left no room for large, aristocratic residences or private parks. Its residents were by and large representatives of the new Scotland: merchants (including many members of the Town Council itself), bankers, well-to-do master craftsmen, professional men, clerics, and professors from the university.

Purchasing the grounds and building a house of the acceptable height and in the New Town's standard yellow-gray sandstone was expensive—around two thousand pounds—but not prohibitively so in the affluent Edinburgh of the 1770s and 1780s. Coach builder John Home (no relation to the writer) bought his lot on the south side of Princes Street; wright John Young, who was also a member of the Town Council, initially bought on George Street, although the city had to buy the lot back from him in order to build St. Andrews Church. The church's architect, William Pirnie, liked the neighborhood so much that he, too, bought and built in the New Town. Upholsterer John Brough was another resident; so was the philosopher David Hume.

Hume decided to move out of his home in James Court because it had become too small. He bought a lot on the northwest corner of St. Andrews Square, one block north of Princes Street. He liked the spot because of the view: like Queen Street to the north, Princes Street had houses on only one side of the street, so that residents looked onto gardens and the picturesque (at least at a distance) view of Edinburgh proper, now dubbed the Old Town. Hume planned for himself a house, coach-shed, and stables, and set to work finding a builder. "I am engaged in building a house," he wrote to a friend, "which is the second great operation of human life." The first, he explained, was marriage (Hume was a bachelor). What finally arose was a tidy and confortable urban town house—"a small house," he used to say, although "a large house for an author." Hume let his old place to James Boswell, and happily settled into life in his fashionable new neighborhood. "Our New Town," he wrote enthusiastically to a correspondent, "exceeds anything you have in any part of the world."

Edinburgh's New Town was, and still is, a model of successful urban planning (although, interestingly, it took almost twenty years before it began to break even). It is the model, one might almost say the ideal, of all middle-class residential suburbs and "planned communities," from Milton Keynes and Hampstead in England to Scarsdale (New York) and Reston (Virginia). It combined elegant urban living with beautiful natural views, charming, flower-lined parks, and discreetly convenient shops, taverns, and oyster houses clustered around Shakespeare Square. It formed a coherent, visually harmonious community, yet was open to all.

Two groups, and two only, were left out. The first were aristocrats, since there was no space allotted for their usual mansions and parks. Although some did eventually buy and build, particularly in later stages of the development, the New Town's rule required that their houses could look no different from, or any larger than, those of their middle-class "tradesmen" neighbors.

The second group was the laboring masses and working poor. Increasingly, the Old Town became their preserve, as more and more wealthy people left its narrow, teeming streets to find a place in the wide-open spaces north of the city. Class division in Edinburgh was no longer vertical (servants and laborers in the attic, well-to-do in the middle, artisans and shopkeepers at street level) but horizontal. A distance, physical as well as cultural, had opened up between those who were affluent enough to escape the dirty and unpleasant "inner city" and escape to the suburbs, and those who were not. To us, it is a familiar story, even depressingly so. Without knowing it, Edinburgh's New Town had opened a new chapter in modern urban history, the social and cultural costs of which we are still struggling to overcome.

In the 1780s, however, this class segregation was one of the things that made moving to the New Town so appealing. Demand for lots was running high when the city fathers prepared to develop the last and westernmost section of Craig's original plan, Charlotte Square. That development would make the New Town even more famous, by linking it to the single most important architect in Britain: Robert Adam.

III

Robert Adam transformed the art of building in the modern world, and it is worth taking time to understand how and why.

His father, William Adam, born and bred in Kirkcaldy in Fife, "had established himself the universal architect of his county." He was Master Mason of North Britain for the Board of Ordnance, and had executed famous commissions across the country, including the Royal Infirmary in Edinburgh and the Glasgow University Library. But William Adam's interests extended beyond just architecture. He invested his money in the Pinkie coalfields, the manufacturing of Dutch pantiles, and a brewery, as well as a large landed estate, which he named Blair Adam, near Fife. He belonged to that first generation of Scottish "improving" landlords who were remaking the face of the rural Lowlands. From their father, Robert Adam and his brothers learned a very important lesson. It was not enough for an architect to make beautiful or visionary buildings; he must also make a lot of money.

William Adam's own reputation rested on his connection to the new, sophisticated architectural style coming up from London, the style called Palladian after the Renaissance Italian architect Andrea Palladio. Although its best-known exponents were aristocratic English amateurs such as Lord Burlington, many of the finest examples of the style came from the brains and drawing tables of Scotsmen working in England, such as James Gibbs (a former student of Christopher Wren, and builder of London's St. Martin-in-the-Field) and Colen Campbell.*

---

*One of Campbell's earliest efforts was the Tobacco Lord mansion Shawfield House, which he built in Glasgow in 1712. It impressed and inspired Lord Burlington, the father of English Palladianism; so one could with justice argue that Shawfield House was actually the first neo-Palladian edifice in Britain.

Campbell had even put together a popular and influential book of plates highlighting the trend, called *Vitruvius Britannicus*. It showed how British builders of large houses and public buildings were moving away from French and Italian models to create a new classical architecture that was also distinctly "British"—hence the book's title. The book's success was yet another example of how Scottish intellectual discipline and energy could take an English idea or insight and turn it into a powerful instrument for remaking the intellectual, social, political, or in this case visual, landscape.

The hallmarks of this British Palladian style were clean lines (lots of smooth stone walls and friezes shorn of excess frills or decoration) and monumentality: massive porticos with large classical pillars or pilasters, topped by gleaming white round domes in the manner of Rome's Pantheon, and flanked by row upon row of marble steps. Everything was designed to impress the onlooker with the grandeur of the building as well as the importance of its wealthy owner. Scotsmen Campbell and Gibbs used it to great effect in England, but it was William Adam who made it the fashionable style in Scotland as well, beginning with his renovations in the late 1720s of Hopetoun House, the country residence of the well-connected Hope family.

William remained loyal to the Palladian canon all his life. Porticos and domes, deeply cut lines and decorative motifs, heavy window surrounds with double flanked giant pilasters on either side—whether public building or private residence, it did not matter. Everything had to impress, and everything had to conform to the classical order as defined by Palladio in his books on architecture. Yet it was precisely this fashionable and successful style that his sons would rebel against, beginning with Robert.

Robert Adam was born on July 3, 1728. He was, according to an early biographer, "from his infancy of a feeble constitution, which frequently seems the attendant of genius and refined taste." He went to the Edinburgh High School at age six to learn his Latin, and then to the University of Edinburgh. There he studied mathematics with Colin Maclaurin and soon fell in with that same crowd of young, intellectually alert Whig students: John Home, Alexander Carlyle, William Wilkie, and William Robertson, who also happened to be Robert Adam's first cousin. It is even possible that he may have joined their ill-fated company of volunteers, although he would have been barely seventeen. He certainly helped Maclaurin with his rebuilding of Edinburgh's walls and defenses.

His real education began, however, when he left the university to apprentice for his father. Since William Adam was Master Mason for the Board of Ordnance, part of that work included construction of Fort George for the British Army. Adam turned out to be quite adept at military architecture, perhaps in part from his exposure to the late Colin Maclaurin's visionary plans (or perhaps in spite of them). In any case, his work designing and supervising the building of parapets, glacis, and reinforced trenches made him financially independent—indeed, he is said to have made over ten thousand pounds. His father's death in 1748 also left him with a small estate, Dowhill, whose most prominent visual feature was a semiruined medieval tower—something that would inspire some of his later experiments with the neo-Gothic.

But Robert Adam had bigger plans than just building forts. His father's business had gone to his older brother John. If he was going to achieve fame and money as an architect, he would have to do it on his own. In 1749 Robert made his first visit to London to see the English Palladian style for himself. That experience "first began to curb the exuberance of his fancy and polish his taste," as a friend later wrote. He then decided he needed to go to Italy, not just for a brief visit but for an extended stay, in order to build up a visual data bank of classical designs and motifs—cornices, friezes, figures, bas-reliefs, vases, altars, columns, windows, and doorways—which he could use for his own designs. He joined forces with his younger sibling James, and together they decided Robert should go to Italy for four years to do nothing but see and draw. They scraped together five thousand pounds to pay his expenses, and in the spring of 1754 he set off. It was in both their minds an investment in their joint future, which would, if they did it right, pay them back many times over.

The visit to Rome, Naples, Venice, Vicenza, and other famous sites revealed to Robert Adam just how far from the original classical perfection and proportion of the ancients later modern imitators, including Andrea Palladio himself, had fallen. Brother James agreed: when he did his own Italian tour in 1760–63, he found the villas Palladio had designed for wealthy Venetian patrons "ill-adjusted both in their plans and elevations." In Robert's judgment, thanks to the Italians, "all Europe has been misled, and has been servilely groaning under their load for three centuries past."

They had been misled above all by the heavy, ponderous scale of Roman buildings such as the Pantheon and the Colosseum. It was true that on the outside, ancient temples and palaces showed "the strength, magnitude, and height of the building." But, as Robert noted, "on the inside of their edifices the Ancients were extremely careful to proportion both the size and depth of their components and panels." If their public buildings paid attention to proportion and the human scale, their domestic ones did so even more. "And with regard to the decoration of their private and bathing apartments, they were all delicacy, gaiety, grace, and beauty."

This point was effectively demonstrated by Robert's trip to Spalato (modern-day Split) to see the remains of the retirement residence of the Roman emperor Diocletian. Robert spent five weeks there, surveying and drawing. The palaces's light, elegant colonnades and surrounding gardens with views of the mountains and the sea confirmed everything Robert believed about the true classical style: the builders' goal had been not to overawe or weigh down the viewer, but to please and delight. The result was "not only picturesque but magnificent."

The term *picturesque* captured the new architectural style that was taking shape in Robert's mind, and that would eventually set off a revolution in modern building and design. The architect, Adam decided, had to learn to compose the elements of his building in much the way an artist composes the elements of a painting: the setting, foreground and background objects, points of perspective, even the lighting, all had to be taken into consideration before construction could even start. Just as a picture should provide the spectator with a new view of his world, so should a building.

The other key word was *movement*. Robert Adam had become fed up with the rigidly inflexible uniform façades of doctrinaire Palladianism and neoclassicism. Movement in architecture meant "the rise and fall, the advance and recess, with other diversity of form, in the different parts of the building," as it stood before the viewer. To achieve it, Adam was ready to break another neoclassical taboo by using decoration. He saw that the discreet use of decorative elements—statues, vases, trophies, rams' heads, twisting acanthus, grotesque faces and masks—could "add greatly to the picturesque of the composition." Adam was even willing to accept the occasional use of trefoil and quatrefoil leaf designs from the medieval Gothic, something that would make the average British Palladian faint dead away.

His brother James was even more emphatic on this. James was in many ways the real theorist of the pair, and in his diary from his Italian travels he jotted down the key ideas that he and Robert would publish, almost word for word, ten years later in their *Works in Architecture.* James Adam advocated the use of decorations because they "give such amazing magnificence and render an edifice so wonderfully interesting to every spectator. . . . This, then, is the great secret of beauty in architecture and what every artist who would please must study with the greatest attention."

James also advanced another notion, which has continued to influence architects down to our own day: form must follow function. " I am more persuaded than ever that architecture is capable of receiving any sort of character one pleases to give it, so that nobody would be at a loss to say to what purpose such a building was put."

This meant various things, but two stand out. First, obviously, was that a church or a temple should look like a church or a temple, a house like a house, and not vice versa. But the Adam brothers would also assert that an architectural style must be flexible enough to compose and decorate any type of building. Therefore any building could be made to be beautiful, not only a town house or a commercial building, but even a warehouse—or a factory.

If European architecture had been "servilely groaning" under the burden of a misleading neo-Palladian dogma "for three centuries past," then the time had come to set it free again. The place to do that was

London. Robert Adam returned to Edinburgh in 1757, but stayed only long enough to gather up and organize his drawings and materials. He then set off for London to establish himself and begin scouting up the necessary connections that would enable him to launch his own architecture business.

Fortune, and friendship, worked to his advantage. He managed to arrange meetings with two of the most influential Scots living in London. One was Chief Justice Lord Mansfield, who promised to help Robert with "all his interest." Eventually, Robert would work on his country estate at Kenwood. The other Scot, even more important, was John Stuart, Lord Bute.

Bute was the nephew of the Duke of Argyll, a Scottish peer in his own right, and virtual monarch of the Isle of Bute. But he owed his real political prestige to the fact that he had been tutor to the new king, George III. The king made him his chief political adviser, and then, in 1761, First Lord of the Treasury. Bute was probably the worst prime minister of the century—given his competition, no mean accomplishment. But he had sense enough to try to surround himself in a hostile England with talented and ambitious Scots, and his private secretary happened to be Adam's old friend John Home. Home introduced the two.

The first meeting was not a success. Bute's natural temper, according to one observer, was "dry, unconciliatory, and sullen." Afterwards, Robert stepped outside and "fell acursing and swearing. What! Had he been presented to all the princes of Italy and France and most graciously received, to come and be treated with such distance and pride by the youngest earl but one in all Scotland!" The second and subsequent meetings went better, though, and with Bute's help, Robert Adam began to secure his first significant commissions. Whatever else history may say about Bute, he does deserve thanks for recognizing the talent and genius of Robert Adam, so much so that in November 1761 Bute secured for him the title of Architect of the King's Works—a title Robert shared with William Chambers, who also happened to be a Scot.

Even with Bute's help, it took nearly three years before Adam's architectural business began to bring him substantial financial reward. Many of the buildings he built or decorated in the next ten years are familiar names to students of architecture and art history: Harewood, Compton Verney, Croome, Luton Hoo, Kedleston, Lansdowne House, and Syon House. Robert learned to supervise everything connected with his projects, not just the architecture and the construction inside and out, but what we today would call the interior decorating, including the furniture, rugs, doors, chimney pieces, and display porcelain. Everything had to reflect the neoclassical vernacular he and James (who joined his brother in London after his Italian tour in 1763) were bent on creating, a language of design that would create a new visual lifestyle down to the last detail, even the window latches and candle snuffers.

Where did this Adam style come from? Part of it was inspired by the archaeological discoveries in southern Italy at Pompeii and Herculaneum, which showed Europeans for the first time what ancient domestic interiors really looked like. Part of it, too, came from a source of ancient building ideas that, it is astonishing to realize, had been almost unknown to previous architects: Athens in Greece. Neither Adam brother had been there but another Scottish artist, James Stuart, had. He and Nicholas Revett had lived in Athens from 1751 to 1755, and had brought back an inventory of drawings and etchings that they published in their multivolume *Antiquities of Athens.* It became as influential as Campbell's *Vitruvius Britannicus* in changing the visual taste of a generation. But its most immediate effect was to reinforce the insights of Robert Adam that the key to all ancient design was the projection not of weight and power, but of elegance and sophistication. Refinement, one might even say. So here were the elements for constructing a setting for the social morality of Shaftesbury and Hutcheson, not to mention the new urban Scotland.

This fit nicely with the other great, but more unexpected, source of inspiration for the Adam style: the writings of Lord Kames. Kames's theory of art, summarized in his *Elements of Criticism,* was that beauty truly is (as the cliché has it) in the eye of the beholder. Human beings have an innate sense of beauty, which objects—paintings, houses, landscapes, a bar of music or a couplet of poetry—trigger in our consciousness. The job of the artist, Kames suggested, was to create and arrange those elements that would generate that response.*

This notion of beauty as a universal human response to certain objects had a huge impact on both brothers, and particularly James. But unlike Kames, they did not believe that there was a single objective formula for achieving it. Instead, the artist had to be willing to be flexible and adaptable, even to the point of breaking all the rules, in order to bring out what was, after all, a subjective response from his audience or patron. Robert Adam confessed in a letter to Kames that this approach "may do harm in the hands of rash innovators or mere retailers in the art, who have neither eyes nor judgement." But by knowing his material thoroughly, by supervising every nuance and detail, as Robert Adam did, and, of course, by drawing on his own sense of the "picturesque," the skilled artist or architect could bring it off.

Yet the ideas of Kames and the Scottish Enlightenment entered into the Adam brothers' program in a more subtle way. The point of turning to the ancient Romans, Greeks, Etruscans, and even Egyptians was not merely to copy their designs, but to translate their sense of refinement and beauty in a new, modern idiom. The new design style would provide a visual environment to remind moderns of the virtues of their ancient predecessors, but would also be suited to contemporary living. Progress was possible, in the arts just as in society. By drawing on the best of the past, by combining and recombining it with elements already at hand, the Adam brothers believed they could turn domestic architecture into a civilizing instrument. It could offer material comfort together with moral uplift: it would pass on to modern Britons the spiritual power of ancient Greece and Rome, while still providing the viewer with "great variety and amusement."

To our eyes, jaded by nearly a hundred years of modernist pseudo-Bauhaus starkness and streamlining, the result may seem frilly and fussy.

---

*It was not very far from what Francis Hutcheson had said on the subject in *An Inquiry into the Original of Our Ideas of Beauty and Virtue*. In fact, both Adam brothers must have heard a great deal about the late Glasgow professor from their cousin William Robertson, and from other friends who intensely admired Hutcheson.

Robert Adam's Drawing Room from Lansdowne House (now housed at the Philadelphia Museum of Art) and his "Etruscan Room" at Osterley Park, with their gilded stucco, blue and gold trophy panels, and liberal uses of pastel reds and greens, remind us painfully of another eighteenth-century domestic style, French rococo—a style the Adam brothers actively detested. We miss what contemporaries, who had grown tired of the cold, empty, and impersonal interiors the Adam style replaced, all recognized in the brothers' work: the promise of becoming "modern ancients," as it were, combining Stoic moral seriousness with a sense of individual freedom and comfort. The Adam brothers themselves were convinced they had revived an ancient standard of artistic perfection for a modern audience. "We flatter ourselves we have been able to seize, with some degree of success, the beautiful spirit of antiquity, and to transfuse it, with novelty and variety, through all our numerous works." Whether they had carried this off or not, "we shall leave to the impartial public."

Insofar as that impartial public consisted of wealthy patrons in both England and Scotland, the answer was resoundingly positive. In 1764 their bank account at Drummonds stood at 6,620 pounds. Seven years later, in 1771, it had grown to over 40,000 pounds. Robert Adam had become a man of substance. He owned a splendid house off St. James's Park, where he entertained friends such as the famous actor David Garrick and visitors such as David Hume and James Boswell, and played golf in the park. He also sat as member of parliament for Kinross-shire. He employed the best craftsmen and artists he could find for his projects: Thomas Chippendale for furniture, Joseph Rose for plasterwork, Josiah Wedgewood for porcelain, Matthew Boulton for ironwork, and painters such as Angelica Kaufmann and her husband, Antonio Zucchi, for frescoes and painted friezes. According to a letter Hume wrote to Adam Smith, the Adam brothers employed more than three thousand craftsmen in their English workshops alone, while still maintaining an equally active business in Edinburgh.

Yet they almost destroyed it all with their one great failure, Adelphi Terrace. It was to be their crowning glory (the name Adelphi came from the Greek for "brothers") and the Adam version of the New Town: a magnificent residential apartment complex or "terrace" rising up from the mudflats along the Thames, at Durham Yard, north of Westminster. The plan combined elegant apartments above, with startling river views, and warehouses and commercial wharves underneath: as complete a fusion of politeness and commerce as one could expect.

Constructing it brought an epic battle with the London City Council that ultimately required an Act of Parliament to resolve. The Adam brothers managed to tie up most of their personal fortune in Adelphi Terrace. Finally, with great fanfare, it opened in 1771. Robert Adam himself took apartment number 4; David Garrick and his wife settled into number 6. Josiah Wedgewood agreed to open a pottery showroom in the galleries below. The British government also contracted to use the lower floors and wharf space, which was supposed to defray costs. But in the end the government reneged. Robert and James Adam lost almost everything; only the massive scale of their architecture business, with important commissions pouring in by the week, saved them from bankruptcy. David Hume, who had advised them against it, confessed "my wonder is how they could have gone on so long." It was in fact a pure ego play, akin to the real-estate-development mogul's ego, with which we are today so familiar. As with Robert Foulis, the dream failed—but the terrace remained (until it was demolished in the 1930s), and the subterranean complex of galleries became the foundations, literally, for another great urban project: the London Embankment.

What Robert Adam had attempted at Adelphi Terrace—applying the Adam style to middle-class urban living—he had a second chance to do with Charlotte Square in Edinburgh's New Town. It marked his triumphant return to his native Scotland, after having conquered the wealthy and powerful in England. It was the last remaining piece of James Craig's original plan—the city did not even own the land when Craig was drawing his final sketches—and the city fathers had decided that the natural candidate for completing it was Robert Adam. Work began in 1792, just as his health was failing, but Adam labored to give the project the pictorial harmony he believed all domestic architecture deserved.

The result still looks very much as it did when it was finally completed in 1820, almost thirty years after Robert Adam's death. The three-story terraced houses, with their elegant Corinthian pilasters in the center topped by full-bodied sphinxes at each end, surround an open square on four sides, while streets enter at each corner. The façade of the north side reproduces exactly that of the south side, giving the square the sort of architectural unity the city fathers wanted for this west end of the New Town. Built in the pale yellow-gray sandstone that characterizes so much of the New Town, Charlotte Square still projects a serene, almost glowing effect.

Like so many of Robert Adam's later designs, exteriors at Charlotte Square stayed simple while the interiors became more ornate. At number 1, which has the best original interior, and number 7, the so-called Georgian House, we can still get a sense of how he adopted his unique stylistic idiom to the environment of the Edinburgh upper middle class (Charlotte Square attracted lots of lawyers and doctors). But the real revolution he introduced was in the floor plans, adding a new feature he had experimented with in town houses he had built in London's Portman Square. This involved installing separate back staircases for servants and domestics, away from the main hall. This not only added to the family's privacy, along with separate "tradesmen's entrances," but also marked a major social change. In the new design for middle-class living, servants, like children, were to be seen and not heard. The logistics of domestic life were made as unobtrusive as possible, much as they are now. The focus of the middle-class home, like that of the noble's country house, becomes "presentation of self": polite, refined, and highly individual in character.

Robert Adam died in 1792. At the time of his death, he was working on eight public buildings and twenty-five private ones, most of them in Scotland. William Robertson, by then Principal of the University of Edinburgh, said of his cousin, "I have lived long and much with many of the most distinguished men in my own times, but for genius, for worth, and for agreeable manners, I know none whom I should rank above the friend we have lost." Coming from a man who had been the intimate friend of David Hume and Adam Smith, it was the highest possible compliment.

At his funeral, the pallbearers included the Duke of Buccleuch, the Earl of Coventry, the Earl of Lauderdale, Lord Frederick Campbell, and William Pulteney, whose house at Bathwick was one of Robert's last completed commissions. The titled and powerful bore his coffin to Westminster Abbey, where he was interred—ironically enough, next to his fellow Scotsman and old rival, Sir William Chambers.

Together they had revolutionized the artistic scene in Britain. Chambers had persuaded George III to create the Royal Academy, and acted as its first treasurer. Thanks to Chambers, Robert Foulis's dream of a public institution devoted exclusively to the training of artists, painters, and sculptors had come to life in the very heart of the British capital. Chambers also trained the man who would become the most important neoclassical architect of the nineteenth century and a great admirer of the Adam style, the Englishman Sir John Soane.

Robert Adam, meanwhile, had carried out the sort of cultural conquest every Scottish Whig dreamed of: he had gone south and made the taste of Englishmen bend to the will and imagination of a Scot. In fact, his impact reached out beyond Britain and across the Atlantic. The Adam brothers' manifesto of their new design idiom, *Works in Architecture,* became a fixture in the library of every American interested in art and taste. As early as 1775, George Washington was borrowing elements for the building of Mount Vernon. Charles Bulfinch studied with Adam in London, and brought the full "Adam style" with him back to America, where it became the foundation for both the Federal style and Greek Revival. Bulfinch's designs for the United States Capitol and his Massachusetts House of Delegates make Robert Adam the spiritual father of American public building. Thomas Jefferson even bought lengths of prefabricated ornamentation in the Adam style from London, for chimney pieces and panels at his private mansion at Monticello.

Another Scottish Adam disciple, Charles Cameron, made an even more amazing cultural journey. An exhibit of his architectural drawings attracted the admiration of Catherine the Great, who invited him to come to Russia to work on her various private palaces. Cameron left for St. Petersburg in 1774 and proceeded to shake up the jaded and worn-out Russian architectural establishment. He extensively rebuilt Catherine's Great Palace at Tsarskoe Selo, and designed the façade and various rooms for her son's palace in Pavlovsk. Cameron's Green Dining Room at Tsarskoe Selo (now Pushkino) and Grecian Hall at Pavlovsk are brilliant adaptations of the Adam style, and they made neoclassicism the architectural idiom of imperial Russia.

Through Cameron, Robert Adam's artistic vision reached out toward the Urals; through Bulfinch and Jefferson, to the foothills of the Appalachians. Adam's neoclassicism was the first truly international style in the modern West, much in the same way that Scottish-style commercial society was about to become the paradigm for modern capitalism.

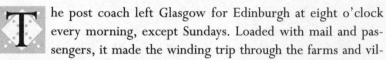

CHAPTER EIGHT

A Select Society:
Adam Smith and His Friends

I

The post coach left Glasgow for Edinburgh at eight o'clock every morning, except Sundays. Loaded with mail and passengers, it made the winding trip through the farms and villages of Lanarkshire and West Lothian, with an overnight stop halfway. It was one of only two coach lines in Scotland, and in 1760 the trip took a day and a half. But it allowed a traveler such as Adam Smith to reach Edinburgh by noon, spend the afternoon and evening there with friends and colleagues, and then return to Glasgow by dinner the next day. Nor was Smith the only commuter. The chemist Joseph Black, political scholar John Millar, and other Glasgow intellectuals regularly made the same trip. In fact, for more than forty years the post coach was the linchpin, one could almost say the lifeline, connecting the twin halves of the Scottish Enlightenment, Glasgow and Edinburgh.

Scotland offered a third center of civilizing and modernizing activity, namely Aberdeen. It would play its crucial role in the making of the modern world, too, as we will see. But in the years after the Forty-five, Glasgow and Edinburgh were truly the "twin cities" of enlightenment and change. In a crucial way, they complemented each other. Glasgow was more innovative and practical; it knew how things were made and how to get things done. Older attitudes, including a deep-rooted Calvinism, were stronger there, but thanks to its commercial success, it was also more freewheeling. James Watt, engineer and self-taught philosopher, was a natural in Glasgow. He would have seemed a fish out of water in Edinburgh.

Edinburgh was more artistic and literary, more intellectual in the abstract sense. It still is. In the eighteenth century it was home to writers, poets, and painters, rather than engineers and experimental scientists. But we should not overdraw the contrasts. What really made Edinburgh different, and what attracted outsiders as diverse as Adam Smith, Benjamin Franklin, and the young Robert Burns was its close-knit community of scholars and thinkers, who were willing to take up new ideas while putting old ones to the test of discussion and criticism. Edinburgh was, as contemporaries said, "a hotbed of genius." It sharpened minds, inspired originality, and intensified that sense of purposeful activity that every thinker, writer, or artist needs to be truly productive and creative.

Only London and Paris could compete with Edinburgh as an intellectual center. But unlike those two world capitals, Edinburgh's cultural life was not dominated by state institutions or aristocratic salons and patrons. It depended instead on a circle of tough-minded, self-directed intellectuals and men of letters, or "literati," as they called themselves. By the standards of 1760, it was remarkably democratic. It was a place where all ideas were created equal, where brains rather than social rank took pride of place, and where serious issues could be debated with, in the words of Lord Shaftesbury, "that sort of freedom which is taken amongst Gentlemen and Friends, who know each other well."

This was in part because everybody was the neighbor of everyone else. Passing down from the High Street, each turn of any given close offered the house or lodging of another writer or intellectual. Allan Ramsay, Lord Kames, David Hume, William Robertson, William Fergusson, John Home—all lived virtually within shouting distance of one another. Edinburgh was like a giant think tank or artists' colony, except that unlike most modern think tanks, this one was not cut off from everyday life. It was in the thick of it.

Edinburgh's intellectuals fully entered into the Old Town's traditions of boisterous and informal society. Given the close and intimate quarters, social barriers went by the board. An English visitor was amazed to discover that the "shrine of festivities" for Edinburgh's best families was a local oyster house, with huge tables piled high with oysters, over which men and women stood swigging flagons of porter, and then leaping onto the dance floor for a series of high-stepping reels and flings. Edinburgh people, he noted, are "exceedingly fond of jovial company," and it was true of the city's literati, as well.

Some, like David Hume, grew up associating good food and drink with intellectual discussion at Lord Kames's dinner table. Others simply liked good food and drink, especially drink. The closes and wynds of Edinburgh flowed with alcohol. Drinking, according to one contemporary, "engrossed the leisure hours of all professional men, scarcely excepting even the most stern and dignified." Half the bench of the Court of Session, he reckoned, were well-oiled before they met in the morning: which may have had something to do with the shrewd, raucous, and often hilarious comments by judges such as Kames and Lord Braxfield.

"When St. Giles bells played out half-past eleven in the morning," writes one historian, "each citizen went to get a gill of ale, which was known as his 'meridian,' although before breakfast he had paid a similar visit." People did business deals, signed legal documents and wills, organized their university lectures, or planned a father's funeral with the help of a glass or a dram. Many of the city's most important intellectual movements began with a gathering in a tavern. Discussion of a pressing political or theological issue without bottles on the table and loud gusts of laughter was inconceivable. *In vino veritas,* "in wine, the truth," as the ancient Romans said—and the people of Edinburgh, who were great admirers of the Romans, did their best to live up to the maxim.

The drink of choice was not whisky (still considered crude and provincial) or beer, but claret. Plentiful supplies of Bordeaux wine were the legacy of Scotland's medieval ties to France, "the auld alliance," and every Scottish gentlemen was a connoisseur, with his own preferred vintages and his private cellar. After 1707, as the English taste for port or sherry began to seep northwards, continuing to drink claret became almost a patriotic act. John Home even composed a short verse about it:

> *Clear-eyed and proud the noble Caledonian stood,*
> *His claret old and his mutton good.*

"Let him drink port,"the Saxon cried,
He drank the poison, and the spirit died.

A gentleman or writer would be routinely identified as a "two-" or "three-bottle man," depending on how much claret he consumed at a meal or single sitting.

But, unlike the modern writer, he did not consume his alcohol as part of a solitary purgatory. He did his drinking surrounded by charming and lively company, and usually under the auspices of one of Edinburgh's numerous social clubs. There was the Tuesday Club, the Poker Club (named after not the card game but the fire poker, for stirring things up), the Oyster Club (of which Adam Smith was a regular member), the Mirror Club, and many others. Most mixed serious intellectual business with imbibing and socializing. The Mirror Club, which met at a tavern in Parliament Square, promoted papers and discussion on the cultural improvement of Scotland's landowning class. The Rankenian Club tackled philosophical topics in its tavern, and kept up a regular correspondence with the philosopher George Berkeley (Berkeley admitted that its members were among the few critics who really understood his theories).

The most important of these clubs was the Select Society. It was founded in 1754 with the help of Allan Ramsay the painter, son of the old bookseller and poet. As its name implied, it saw itself as a gathering place for Edinburgh's elite—except this was an intellectual, not a social or political, elite. The original thirty-two members included William Robertson, John Home, David Hume, Adam Smith, Kames's erudite colleague Lord Monboddo, Alexander Carlyle, and Hugh Blair. Later members included Adam Ferguson, who joined in the spring of 1756, and Lord Kames himself. As with Monboddo and Kames, most of its titled members took their peerages with their service on the judicial bench. The rest owed their prominence to their pens, or to their status in one of the middle-class professions.

For ten years it was the central forum of Edinburgh's republic of letters. A paper or talk presented there received a fairer and more rigorous hearing than it could from any academic or university audience. As one participant put it, the informal proceedings made "the *Literati* of Edinburgh Less Captious and Pedantick then they were elsewhere." The astonishing diversity of the views and experience of its members made it particularly valuable. By 1760, writes historian Richard Sher, the Select Society included "virtually every . . . prominent man of letters and taste in the Edinburgh vicinity, as well as a host of physicians, architects, military officers, merchants, magistrates, and above all lawyers."

Lawyers, yes, but also Presbyterian ministers. Membership in the Select Society overlapped with all the other important intellectual associations in Edinburgh, including the Poker Club, founded in 1762, and the Edinburgh Society for Encouraging Arts, Sciences, Manufactures, and Agriculture in Scotland, which became the Select Society's successor when the original club dissolved in 1763. It also provided the editorial board for the very first *Edinburgh Review,* which included the distinguished professor of moral philosophy from Glasgow, Adam Smith. And at the core of each we find the same list of names, all of them prominent clergymen: William Robertson, John Home, Hugh Blair, Alexander Carlyle, John Jardine, and, slightly later, Adam Ferguson. We met most of them before, as Edinburgh volunteers in the Forty-five, and exponents of the Whig cause. Now, twenty years later, they dominated the discussion of ideas and issues. They were in fact the great movers and shakers of the city's cultural life.

This, too, made the Scottish Enlightenment unique. At its core was a group of erudite and believing clergymen (unlike the various *abbés* of the French Enlightenment, who were by and large skeptics, and clerics only as a matter of convenience and income). They resolutely believed that a free and open sophisticated culture was compatible with, even predicated on, a solid moral and religious foundation.

Robertson and the rest saw the doctrines of Christianity as the very heart of what it meant to be modern. Robertson said, "Christianity not only sanctifies our souls, but refines our manners." As Hugh Blair put it, religion "civilizes mankind." Refinement and civility now meant much more than just polite manners and fine taste in clothes and music. They referred to a historical process in which the entire cultural frame of society—the political and the moral, as well as the literary and artistic—comes to reflect the same stimulating and liberating power of social interaction. Through the complex connections of commercial society "the mind acquires new vigour [and] enlarges its powers and faculties" and "*industry, knowledge,* and *humanity* are linked together by an indissoluble chain." It makes men free, and enlarges their power to do good. Virtue and enlightenment move together step by step.

To the enlightened Edinburgh clerics, Christianity both epitomized this cultural process and described its final goal. The moral teachings of Christianity were in effect a shortcut to refinement, but only if the Church itself reflected that refinement. Beginning in 1751, Robertson, Blair, Home, and their friends took on the task of bringing the Kirk into the modern world, even in the teeth of bitter opposition from Presbyterian hard-liners.

The battle raged back and forth in the General Assembly and in a series of public controversies. The old conservatives, the so-called Evangelicals, had the advantage of numbers and the backing of rural congregations, which were by and large satisfied with the old fire-and-brimstone style. The Robertson group had the advantage of organization and unity of purpose, plus the support of educated laymen in places such as the Select Society, the landed nobility, and the press—the voice of "enlightened public opinion." They called themselves the Moderate Party, to set them apart from both the religious extremism of a Kirk that still officially approved the execution of Thomas Aikenhead, and the religious skepticism of men such as the English deists—or their friend David Hume. Their hero was Francis Hutcheson, and they offered a compassionate, enlightened Presbyterianism that they believed would be in step with modern commercial society.

The Moderates boasted champions such as Robertson, by then the most famous historian in Britain, and John Home, author of the enormously successful historical drama *Douglas.* The best the Evangelicals could offer was a minister from East Lothian named John Witherspoon, who published a devastating anti-Moderate satire called *Ecclesiastical*

Characteristics, * which was so well written and funny that even the Moderates admired it and bought copies. In one passage, Witherspoon offered this mock advice to the aspiring enlightened clergyman on how to write his Sunday sermon:

1. All his subjects must be confined to social duties— as opposed to religious doctrines.
2. There must be no reference to an afterlife.
3. His authorities must be drawn from pagan writers, and none, or as few as possible, from Holy Scripture.
4. He must be very unacceptable to the common people.

Very telling, especially the last point, which reminded people how Robertson and his friends from groups such as the Select Society represented a new kind of cultural elitism. Yet the very fact that the Moderates' most formidable opponent had to resort to a secular literary genre, the satire, to score his points showed who was really winning, and who was losing, the overall battle.

In 1756 the Moderates managed to prevent an official censure of David Hume by the General Assembly. In December of that year the pillar of the old orthodoxy, Reverend George Anderson, died. Hugh Blair was already minister at St. Giles, Edinburgh's biggest church. Five years later William Robertson was named Principal of the University of Edinburgh, and Blair became its Professor of Rhetoric. Reading the handwriting on the wall, Witherspoon accepted an offer from the American colonies he had declined before: to become president of the College of New Jersey in Princeton. In that guise he will reappear in the next chapter, playing a very different role from that of Moderate-basher and defender of the old-time religion. But in 1768, his departure for America marked the final triumph of the Moderates and their vision of an enlightened Church of Scotland.

---

*The title was a swipe at the Earl of Shaftesbury and his famous essays, which influenced all the leading Moderates, including Hutcheson himself. See chapter 3.

We have mentioned that one of the Moderates' heroes was Francis Hutcheson. Another, at least by 1759, was Hutcheson's former pupil Adam Smith. His early lectures given in Edinburgh at the behest of Lord Kames heavily influenced their notion of poetry and literature, or *belles lettres,* as a cultural bellwether, and of clear, elegant English as the best vehicle for modern literary communication (the model Smith himself had proposed was Jonathan Swift). They were also impressed by his *Theory of Moral Sentiments,* which reworked Hutcheson's theory of an innate moral sense. William Robertson used Smith's lectures on natural law and the four-stage theory of civil society for his own history of Europe—so much so that Smith privately accused him of plagiarism!

All this shows that long before he published his *Inquiry into the Nature and Causes of the Wealth of Nations,* Adam Smith was a prominent and influential figure in Edinburgh circles. He attended the meetings of the Select Society and the Poker Club, and went to the dinner parties of even nonintellectual citizens. As a guest he could be trying. He rarely spoke, but when he did, it was usually at great length. Alexander Carlyle remembered Adam Smith as "the most absent man in Company that I ever saw, Moving his Lips and talking to himself, and Smiling, in the midst of large Company's." Once, when he had started on a long harangue criticizing a leading Scottish politician, someone discreetly pointed out that the man's closest relative was also sitting at the table. "Deil care, deil care," Smith muttered, "it's all true."

II

Adam Smith was born in Kirkcaldy, just across the Firth of Forth from Edinburgh, in 1723. His father, Adam Smith, Sr., was trained in the law, and served as a customs inspector in Kirkcaldy. It was not a cushy job. One of the unforeseen results of the Treaty of Union had been a huge increase in smuggling along Scotland's coasts. His father's frustrations in trying to intercept the operations of local smugglers, most of whom were otherwise law-abiding citizens and merchants, were an early lesson for the younger Adam Smith in how human ingenuity will find a way to defy government rules and regulations, such as customs tariffs, when they fly in the face of self-interest. Here is how Smith would put it in his *Wealth of Nations,* almost fifty years later: "The natural effort of every individual to better his own condition . . . is so powerful a principle, that it is alone, and without any assistance, not only capable of carrying on the society to wealth and prosperity, but of surmounting a hundred impertinent obstructions with which the folly of human laws too often incumbers its operations."

Words that have made every socialist, and every liberal of an altruistic Hutcheson mold, gnash his teeth! But the truth is that it was Adam Smith who snatched Hutcheson from the burning embers to which the skeptic David Hume had consigned him, and who tried to find a way to keep the idea that human beings have an inborn moral sense, and natural regard for others, alive as a basic principle of human nature. We usually think of Adam Smith as an economist, and the founder of the study of political economy, or "the dismal science"—and there certainly are pages of *Wealth of Nations* that are dismal. But Adam Smith thought of himself primarily as a moral philosopher, and almost all his studies came down to answering the basic questions Hutcheson had raised. Why are human beings on average good rather than bad? Why do they choose (on the whole) to lead constructive lives, getting up in the morning to go to work and raise a family and build relationships with other human beings, instead of (on the whole) murdering and plundering them?

The answers Smith came with up were different from Hutcheson's, because by now he had to confront the challenge of Lord Kames's cynical realism and that of his disciple, David Hume. In many ways Smith is the fusion of the two sides of the Enlightenment, the "soft" side represented by Hutcheson—with its belief in man's innate goodness, its faith in the power of education to enlighten and liberate, and its appeal to nature—and the "hard" side represented by Kames and Hume, with its cool, skeptical distrust of human intentions and motives. A fusion, but also a tension runs all through Smith's work, a tension that is never fully resolved. It is the tension that runs through all of modern life and culture, in fact—a tension between what human beings ought to be, and occasionally are, and what they really are, and generally remain. Smith's great achievement was to have the courage to confront that tension head-on, to describe it and analyze it, and then leave it to others in the future to understand it in their own way. It is this, not his role as the supposed high priest of capitalism, that has made him one of the great modern thinkers, and makes him still important to us today.

Adam Smith was a man of thought and contemplation rather than action. He almost became a minister, although he was never ordained. He should have been a lawyer, like his father, but when he went to the University of Glasgow in 1737, he fell instead under the spell of Francis Hutcheson. At Glasgow, Smith absorbed the twin traditions of Scottish learning, the study of natural and civil law, and afterwards wrote brilliant and influential lectures on both. In every respect his education was Scottish; all the leading influences on his thought were entirely Scottish-based. Although he did go to England to study at Oxford for seven years, he found nothing of value there. He summed up his experience there in his description of the average university as a "sanctuary in which exploded systems and obsolete prejudices find shelter and protection, after they have been hunted out of every other corner of the world."

Yet Smith did not hesitate to use Scottish universities as a base for his work and activities. His public lectures in Edinburgh in 1750 and 1751 earned him enough of a reputation to bring him back to Glasgow as professor of logic, and then as Hutcheson's successor to the Chair of Moral Philosophy. At first Smith tried to emulate the informal, animated lecture style of his great teacher, but he soon gave up and resigned himself to reading his notes aloud from his desk. What drew students was not Smith's style, but the substance of his lectures, which were nothing less than an attempt to fulfill the great project Hutcheson had envisioned decades before, of creating a science of human behavior as coherent and irrefutable as the physical science of Isaac Newton. It would begin with a "natural history of man as a political agent" and end with "the general principles of municipal law, political oeconomy, and the law of nations." This would have been a daunting task in any case, but by 1755 it was even more so, because now Smith, like everyone else, had to work under the shadow of David Hume.

If Adam Smith is the first great modern economist, then David

Hume is modernity's first great philosopher. His literally unorthodox views made him a legend in his own time. One day, after he had bought his house in Edinburgh's New Town, he was going home by taking a shortcut across the deep bog left by the draining of the North Loch. As he walked along the treacherous and narrow path, he slipped and fell into the bog. Unable to extricate himself, he began calling for help as darkness started to fall. An old woman, an Edinburgh fishwife, stopped, but when she looked down and recognized him as "David Hume the Atheist," she refused to help him out. Hume pleaded with her and asked her if her religion did not teach her to do good, even to her enemies. "That may well be," she replied, "but ye shall na get out o' that, till ye become a Christian yoursell: and repeat the Lord's Prayer and the Belief [i.e., the Apostolic Creed]." To her amazement, Hume proceeded to do just that, whereupon, true to her word, the old lady reached down and pulled him out.

The story reveals a great deal about Hume the man: his self-deprecating sense of humor (the story comes out of one of Hume's letters); his keen awareness of the clash of cultures in the meeting between the philosopher and the fishwife; but above all his awareness, even relish, of his status as an outsider, even within his own country and city. It was not just Hume's religious views that made him the outsider and renegade, however. For more than two thousand years Western philosophers had praised the primacy of reason as the guide to all human action and virtue. Plato, Aristotle, Augustine, Aquinas, Descartes, Locke, Hobbes, and even Hutcheson could all agree with that great time-honored consensus, that the job of reason was to master our emotions and appetites. With one earth-shaking book, his first, Hume reversed this. "Reason is," he wrote, "and ought to be, the slave of the passions."

That "ought to be" stood two thousand years of philosophy on its head. Hume quietly pointed out that human beings are not, and never have been, governed by their rational capacities. Reason's role is purely instrumental: it teaches us how to get what we want. What we want is determined by our emotions, our passions—anger, lust, fear, grief, envy, but also joy, love of fame, love of contentedness, and, paradoxically, our desire to live according to rational principles—or in the last case, to recognize the dictates of necessity and act accordingly. It is not reason, however, that teaches us this, but habit, a frame of mind that associates certain effects with certain causes or actions. We are, in the end, creatures of habit, and of the physical and social environment within which our emotions and passions must operate. We learn to avoid the passions that destroy, and pursue the ones that succeed—in order to get what we consider our just desserts, and gratify our self-interest.

A Treatise of Human Nature appeared in 1734, when Hume was only twenty-six. Yet it contained the seeds of almost everything he would write for the next forty years, and the seeds of a new philosophic outlook for the West. Other thinkers, of course, had recognized the importance of self-interest in human affairs. Lord Kames, as founder of the civil society school, had stressed its paramount role in the creation and formation of all social ties. But Hume carried this to a new level.

For Hume, self-interest is *all* there is. The overriding guiding force in all our actions is not our reason, or our sense of obligation toward others, or any innate moral sense—all these are simply formed out of habit and experience—but the most basic human passion of all, the desire for self-gratification. It is the one thing human beings have in common. It is also the necessary starting point of any system of morality, and of any system of government.

If Hume had made a dog's breakfast of Hutcheson's moral theories (Hutcheson was horrified when he first read the *Treatise,* and did what he could to prevent Hume from getting a university appointment), he gave a similar disturbing twist to the question Lord Kames had started out with: Why does society exist? He agreed with his mentor that it was there to protect property. But Hume also pointed out that we are surrounded by a seething, crawling cesspool of passions, our own as well as those of others. Left to ourselves, with no external constraints, the result would be a murderous chaos—Hume certainly saw Hobbes's view of man's natural depraved state as more realistic than Hutcheson's more exalted vision. Yet no society, even the best organized, can possibly police each and every outbreak of self-gratification at the expense of others. There aren't enough minutes in the day. Any appeal to reason is hopeless, since "reason is, and ought to be, the slave of the passions": and the passions are the root of the problem.

So, in order to survive, Hume concluded, society has to devise strategies to channel our passions in constructive directions. Through social rules and conventions and customs, internalized by its members and made into regular habits, it turns what might be socially destructive impulses into socially useful ones. The passion of lust becomes licit within the confines of marriage—which not only prevents social discord, but actually helps to propagate the society's members. Anger and bloodlust are rightly condemned as socially disruptive—that is, unless they are unleashed on the battlefield against society's enemies.

The passion of avidity could, if left without limits, destroy all social bonds, as each member of society robs and plunders his neighbors, and is plundered in turn. However, canalizing that desire and pushing it in a constructive direction makes it work to the benefit of society. Instead of robbing a bank, why not open one? One can make more money with less work and stress, and help his neighbors at the same time. In short, the passion of avidity becomes socialized—"refined" as William Robertson might say—and generates a sense of property. We can have what we want, when we want it, society tells us, just as long as we do not take it at the expense of the rights of others.

"There is no passion, therefore," Hume concluded, "capable of controlling the interested affection but the very affection itself, by an alteration of its direction." And he went further: "Men are not able radically to cure either in themselves or others that narrowness of soul which makes them prefer the present to the remote," or, in other words, the short-term to the long-term. Men cannot change their nature. All they can do is create social and political arrangements that "render the observation of justice the immediate interest of some particular person, and its violation their more remote." Hence the origin of government, and hence the best possible social framework within which human beings can operate, based on a secular Golden Rule: I won't disturb your self-interest, if you don't disturb mine.

This is the best we can hope for, in a world in which men are governed by self-interest, and "even when they extend their concern beyond themselves, it is not to any great distance"; in which morality is largely a matter of convention and ingrained habit; in which the laws of nature offer nothing to help, and appeals to reason fall on deaf ears; and with an empty sky above, devoid of divine guidance or even a supernatural presence. This world offers a form of liberty—the freedom to pursue one's own self-interest—and a form of authority: the power of the magistrate "to punish transgressors, to correct fraud and violence, and to oblige men, however reluctant, to consult their own real and permanent [long-term] interests." But, Hume had to conclude, there is nothing particularly exalted, or inspiring, about the nature of civil society.

What did his contemporaries make of all this? A large part of the response to Hume was, very understandably, negative. It comes as no great surprise that Hutcheson was horrified, or that the Kirk's General Assembly tried to have him censured, or that he failed to get a university appointment not once but twice. But much of the response was respectful, and at times slightly celebratory, even among those, such as Edinburgh's literati, who were deeply disturbed by the implications of Hume's philosophy. This was not explained merely by his affable personality, which made him a popular guest at dinner parties and club meetings, or his elegant command of written English (although he always spoke it with a heavy Scottish burr). It arose from his own confidence in the future of civil society, which seems strange given its less-than-noble origins, and from his optimism about modern commercial society in particular.

The work that made him a major figure in British letters was his collection of *Political Discourses,* which Andrew Millar published in London in 1752, followed by other collections and reissues of earlier essays over the next half-decade. In them, Hume pointed out what seemed to him obvious: society's effort to canalize human being's passions into constructive channels *does* work; we do learn from past failures and manage over time to improve how government works and how it administers justice and protects civil rights. The whole growth of the British constitution from feudal despotism to modern liberty was proof of this. History revealed to Hume a growth of human industry and cooperation over time, as well as a growth of personal liberty of the sort Hutcheson and others celebrated. And central to it was the role of commerce, as the great engine of change:

> It rouses men from their indolence; and presenting the gayer and more opulent part of the nation with objects of luxury, which they never have dreamed of, raises in them a desire of a more splendid way of life than what their ancestors enjoyed. . . . Imitation soon diffuses all these arts; while domestic manufactures emulate the foreign in their improvements. . . . Their own steel and iron, in such laborious hands, become the equal to the gold and rubies of the INDIES.

Commerce and liberty; liberty and refinement; refinement and the progress of the human spirit were all interrelated. And every Scottish Whig could applaud Hume's statement that "it is impossible for the arts and sciences to arise, at first, among any people unless that people enjoy the blessing of a free government."

But Hume also threw out a warning. Liberty was a fine thing, but it required a counterbalancing principle—something to remind us that human beings are creatures of their passions and that, left entirely to themselves, they become their passions' slaves. Jacobites and Tories had had a point: no society can survive without some stable center of authority. The power of government is needed to redirect those potentially destructive passions, to "punish transgressors," and ultimately to preserve the conditions under which liberty can be enjoyed. "In all governments," Hume wrote, "there is a perpetual intestine struggle, open or secret, between Authority and Liberty, and *neither of them can ever absolutely prevail in the contest.*"

Politics in modern society, then, must involve a tension between two conflicting, but complementary principles: liberty, which preserves individuals, and authority, which preserves society. Authority that is absolute and uncontrolled ends by destroying society itself; Hume foresaw what the history of totalitarianism would teach the rest of us. But he also realized that even in the freest society, "a great sacrifice of liberty" has to be made to authority, which, he wrote, "must be acknowledged essential to its very existence."

How much of a sacrifice is, of course, the key question, for eighteenth-century Britons as well as for us. Hume never quite answered it, although he did, in his essays and his *History of England,* explore the conditions under which the question can be posed. However, it may be that Hume thought there was no real answer. He may have simply decided that the struggle is perpetual, and that we only realize we have gone too far when it is already too late.

As a philosopher and as a friend, Hume made a huge impact on Adam Smith. Smith read and understood him more thoroughly, perhaps, than any other contemporary. His own writings would be inconceivable without Hume's peculiar take on the "progress" of civil society, and on what an imperfect, trial-and-error process it really is.

Hume swept away all that was pretentious and sanctimonious from the Scottish intellectual scene. Even his most telling opponent, Aberdeen's Thomas Reid, acknowledged him to be one of the great philosophers of the age. Smith himself probably would have endorsed the German philosopher Immanuel Kant's remark on first reading Hume, that it awakened his mind from its "dogmatic slumbers." Hume had certainly cleared the air of illusions and made it free from cant. But there was still the question of what to build afterwards, and this is what Smith now undertook.

III

His starting point brought him back to where Hutcheson and Hume had first diverged. What makes us good? Is morality inborn, as Hutcheson insisted, a gift from God and nature? Or is it something that has to be imposed from outside, as Hume suggested, a system of punishments and rewards that mold us into creatures fit for society?

As he shuttled back and forth between Edinburgh and Glasgow in the 1750s, lecturing to students at one end and listening to papers at the Select Society at the other, Smith was thinking of ways to resuscitate

Hutcheson's original notion of an innate moral sense. But if Hutcheson had been right in one sense, that morality is something we carry inside us from birth, he had forgotten about the need for what Smith would call the "awful virtues": discipline, self-restraint, moral rectitude, and righteous anger at wrongdoers. The virtues of the ancient Stoics and of the Calvinist Kirk were just as necessary to life in society as were civility and compassion, because they policed the sometimes volatile frontiers of our dealings with others. How ironic it must have seemed, that the clergyman Hutcheson should overlook their importance, and that the skeptical agnostic Hume should understand how they contained and channeled our most explosive impulses!

In fact, Smith was trying to build a notion of an inborn moral sense that was more basic and instinctual, and less abstract, than his former teacher's notion. He eventually found it in what he called "fellow feeling," a natural sense of identification with other human beings. When we see someone suffer, we suffer. When we see others happy and celebrating their good fortune, it raises our own spirits. To be a social creature, part of the world of men, is to experience the joy and sorrow, and the pleasure and pain, of others.

This "fellow feeling" and identification with others leads to our first moral judgments. We use it first to judge others' actions toward us (what makes me feel happy is good, and what makes me sad is bad), and then our own actions toward others, as we watch their reactions. Then, finally, we use it to judge the motivating passions behind those actions (here Smith accepted Hume's basic point, that human beings were largely governed by their passions, not reason). Society acts as a mirror to our inner self, by reflecting back to us the reactions of others, and becomes our guide to what is good and evil in the world. "Were it possible," Smith wrote, "that a human creature could grow up to manhood in a solitary place, without any communication with his own species, he could no more think of his own character . . . than of the beauty or deformity of his own face."

Bring him into society, however, Smith stated, "and he is immediately provided with the mirror which he wanted before." He will see that some of his passions—anger, for example, or lust—trigger other people's disgust and disapproval, while others—bravery in the face of adversity or love or fame—get the opposite response. We learn to adjust our passions accordingly, we "internalize" that approval and disapproval, and concentrate ourselves on those that make us loved by others—and by ourselves.

H. L. Mencken once defined conscience as a little voice that says "someone might be watching." For Smith's *Theory of Moral Sentiments,* that someone is myself, my social self. "When I endeavor to examine my own conduct," he wrote, "I divide myself, as it were, into two persons. . . . The first is the spectator, whose sentiments with regard to my own conduct I endeavor to enter into, by placing myself in his situation, and by considering how it would appear to me, when seen from that particular point of view. The second is the agent, the person whom I properly call myself. . . . The first is the judge; the second the person judged of." The moral human being is by nature a divided self, united by the voice of conscience, which is the voice of others who watch and listen and judge. Postmodern morality tells us constantly, "Don't be judgmental"—yet Adam Smith was saying that being judgmental is the essence of what makes us moral beings.

It is also about being accountable to ourselves as well as to others. "Nature, when she formed man for society," Smith explained, "endowed him with an original desire to please, and an original aversion to offend his brethren. She taught him to feel pleasure in their favourable, and pain in their unfavourable regard." But again, the approval of others is not enough by itself. We are not by nature entirely "other-directed" beings. We also need to meet the approval of our own inner judging self, which understands when we really are what we approve in other people: honest, trustworthy, generous, compassionate. It is this capacity for self-judgment that, Smith argued, makes us "really fit" for society.

So being moral requires an interplay of imagination. It demands that we put ourselves in another person's place, and put another person (someone making judgments) in our place. It leads us to promote the well-being of others, by making them as happy as ourselves—here

Hutcheson's altruistic instincts come back into play. At the same time we want others to leave our own happiness undisturbed—and here Smith gave a more sympathetic account of Hume's Golden Rule: I'll leave you alone, if you leave me alone, so that we can both be happy.

This, then, becomes the mission of good government. "The wisdom of every state or commonwealth endeavors, as well as it can, to employ the force of the society to restrain those who are subject to its authority, from hurting or disturbing the happiness of one another. The rules which it establishes for this purpose, constitute the civil and criminal law of each state . . . [and] a sacred and religious regard not to hurt or disturb in any respect the happiness of our neighbor . . . constitutes the character of the perfectly innocent and just man." Hutcheson and Hume, at last, find common ground.

For Adam Smith, our moral life, as well as our cultural life, is a matter of imagination. The richer the inventory of objects for its diversion, and the deeper our own fellow feeling, the happier we become, but also the more we can perceive happiness in others.

> Our imagination, which in pain and sorrow seems to be confined and cooped up within our own persons, in times of ease and prosperity expands itself to every thing around us. We are charmed then with the beauty of that accommodation which reigns in the palaces and oeconomy of the great; and admire how every thing is adapted to promote their ease, to prevent their wants [and] to gratify their wishes. . . . We naturally confound [this ease and beauty] in our imagination with the order, the regular and harmonious movement of the system, the machine or oeconomy by means of which it is produced.

So already, in the fourth book of the *Theory of Moral Sentiments,* we meet that crucial term *economy,* at first in its narrow meaning, referring to the households of the rich and mighty, and how "the pleasures of wealth and greatness . . . strike the imagination as something grand and beautiful and noble, of which the attainment is well worth the toil and anxiety which we are so apt to bestow upon it." But Smith also employs it in the more modern sense, as the "machine or oeconomy" by which that wealth is produced—in other words, commercial society.

And here imagination turns out to be the driving wheel of that system as well. Our imagination, the inner picture of ourselves being as rich and comfortable as a Duke of Argyll or a Bill Gates, spurs on our efforts, focusing and directing our energies toward a single purpose. "It is this *deception*," Smith adds (with my emphasis),

> which rouses and keeps in continual motion the industry of mankind. It is this which first prompted them to cultivate the ground, to build houses, to found cities and commonwealths, and to invent and improve all the sciences and arts, which ennoble and embellish human life; which have entirely changed the whole face of the globe, have turned the rude forests of nature into agreeable and fertile plains, and made the trackless and barren ocean a new fund of subsistence, and the great high road of communication to the different nations of the earth.

The rich man is the man with the most fertile imagination, in other words; his eyes really are bigger than his stomach. By devoting all his efforts and those of his employees and tenants to his land or his warehouse or factory, he ends up producing far more than he can consume himself:

> The rich consume little more than the poor [after all, you can drive only one Rolls-Royce at a time] and in spite of their natural selfishness and rapacity, though they mean only their own conveniency [and] their own vain and insatiable desires, they divide with the poor the produce of all their improvements. They are led *by an invisible hand* [my emphasis] to make the same distribution of the necessarities of life, which would have been made, had the earth been divided into equal portions among all its inhabitants. . . . Thus, without intending it, without knowing

it, [the rich] advance the interest of the society, and afford means
to the multiplication of the species.

The *Theory of Moral Sentiments* made Smith famous. To his dying day,
he thought of it as a better book than The *Wealth of Nations*—and in fact,
as we can see, it contains all the seeds of that later work. It won the
warm approval of Hume (although he did not change his mind about his
own theories). The book also won great praise for its "solidity" and
"truth" from Edmund Burke, then a rising member of parliament and
author of *The Theory of the Sublime,* who wrote to Smith that "a theory
like yours founded on the Nature of man, which is always the same, will
last." German intellectuals read it with fascination, particularly
Immanuel Kant, who asked plaintively, "Where in Germany is the man
who can write so well about the moral character?" Voltaire summed up
the feelings of many French *philosophes* when he exclaimed, "We have
nothing to compare with him, and I am embarrassed for my dear com-
patriots."

Admiration for the book did not necessarily extend to approval of
every idea in it. Some reviewers wanted to know if Smith was saying
that we have no higher standard of morality than the one society
imposes on us. What if society demands of us actions that are actually
evil? Are we condemned to be social conformists forever? Smith replied
no, "we soon learn . . . to set up in our minds a judge between ourselves
and those we live with," who weighs our actions according to an impartial standard, so that "real magnamity and conscious virtue can support
itself under the disapprobation of all mankind." But the conformity
problem would not go away, and it would haunt every Enlightenment
figure who treated morality as essentially a matter of social utility.
Instead, it would take a renegade French musician, Jean-Jacques
Rousseau, and a former Army chaplain from the Highlands, Adam
Ferguson, to break that issue wide open and explore the new ethical
horizons that it opened up. The result would be the birth of the
Romantic movement, which proposed a different relationship between
the inner self and society—one born of conflict rather than coopera-

tion, in which our happiness seems possible only at the expense of others, and vice versa.

All this seemed a long way off, though, particularly to Smith. His most important work still lay ahead. It was the indirect result of his friendship with the eighteen-year-old Duke of Buccleuch, one of Scotland's wealthiest aristocrats. The English politician and future Chancellor of the Exchequer Charles Townshend had suggested that Buccleuch take Smith as his tutor for his Grand Tour of Europe (Smith and Hume had given Townshend a copy of the *Theory of Moral Sentiments*). The Grand Tour was the rite of passage of wealthy adolescent Britons in the eighteenth century. It involved visiting western European cities such as Paris, Amsterdam, Venice, and Rome to taste the artistic, social, and often sexual fruits of the culture of the Continent. It often could last a year or more. Smith, worn out by his teaching and administrative chores at Glasgow (he had become Dean of the Faculty in 1760), happily accepted the invitation, and set out with his young pupil for the Continent in February 1766.

The reader who expects the trip to have been a fiasco, with the young Buccleuch turning out to be a holy terror, a kind of aristocratic Tom Jones, is going to be disappointed. In fact, Buccleuch seems to have been a sweet, rather shy boy, not overburdened with intellect but serious enough for Smith to give him Hume's *History of England* to read on the way. A strong bond of affection and trust developed between them, strong enough that when they returned, Buccleuch offered Smith enough money to quit teaching and to write his next big book—a sort of eighteenth-century "genius grant." The book Smith completed in 1775 was, of course, his *Inquiry into the Nature and Causes of the Wealth of Nations,* which appeared in print that following spring.

It was the logical follow-up to Smith's earlier lectures on civil and natural law, but also to the themes of his moral theory: How and why do human beings learn to cooperate, and what makes for a constructive, useful life as opposed to a destructive one? Its strictly "economic" chapters, especially in Books One and Two, touched on subjects that certain French thinkers, the so-called Physiocrats, had taken up in their writings. Smith knew their work, and met several of them during his stay in

Paris with Buccleuch. However, he does not seem to have taken much of what they said to heart, and he came back from his Paris visit very unimpressed (judging from their letters about Smith, the feeling was mutual). The real inspiration for his subject was his fellow Scots and the work they had done over the past three decades on the history of civil society, of how "commerce and manufactures gradually introduced order and good government, and with them, the liberty and security of individuals." Lurking in the background of the *Wealth of Nations* are Kames, Hume, Robertson, and even Hutcheson. It is not only Adam Smith's masterpiece. It is also the *Summa* of the Scottish Enlightenment, a summation of its exploration of the nature of human progress—and its salute to the triumph of the modern.

Starting with chapter 1, Smith explains how the business of civilization gets done, by isolating the basic principle that explains all social improvement: the division of labor. This is Smith's term. The idea itself probably originated with David Hume, who called it "the partition of employments." We use another, perhaps better, word for it: *specialization*.

The notion itself is simple. When we concentrate our energy on one task rather than several, we increase our productivity. Instead of herding and fishing and farming for our living, as primitive man or the Highland clansman did, we just farm. The result is we grow more than enough to feed ourselves, enough in fact to sell to others. Later, instead of dividing our time between growing and then bartering or selling our produce, we decide to leave the farming to someone else and concentrate on just buying and selling. We become merchants, and soon discover we can earn far more than the farmers and peasants who sell us the fruit of their labors.

And so on, at each stage of civil society's progress. The division of labor, Smith believed, was the inevitable rule everywhere; it occurred at every stage and in every human activity. But its role becomes particularly pronounced in commercial society. As we continue to specialize and become increasingly more productive, the fruits of our labor are no longer things we consume ourselves. They become "commodities," literally the things that make our lives comfortable, which we buy and sell in exchange for other goods. We start to think about our labor in a new way. We look for ways to improve what we make and save time in making it, in order to sell it at market to get the things we really want. Capitalism is born, the system of economic production behind commercial society, a system whose productivity and inventiveness put all the rest in the shade.

The reason is that capitalism brings an intellectual as well as an economic change. It alters the way we think about ourselves and about others: we become buyers and sellers, customers and suppliers, who strive to improve the quality and quantity of our output, in order to gratify our needs. Eventually, Smith states, the division of labor produces people who do nothing but think about improvements: engineers such as his friends James Watt and Alexander Wilson, scientists such as Joseph Black, and those "whose trade it is not to do anything, but to observe everything"—philosophers, teachers, and professional managers of every sort.

The division of labor, in short, applies not just to physical labor, such as growing carrots or selling tobacco or making nails, but to intellectual labor as well. "Each individual becomes more expert in his own particular branch," Smith explains, "more work is done upon the whole, and the quantity of science is considerably increased by it." It lays the necessary foundation for technological innovation, as well as the gift of cultural refinement. Society finds space for its white-collar professionals, people who have time to do nothing but write, paint, teach, compose music, count numbers, or plead cases in court, all for the gratification of the rest of our fellow citizens.

Smith had finally defined the link between commerce and cultural progress, which the rest of the Scottish Enlightenment had written about and celebrated, but not really proved. But he also opened up a broader point, and gestured toward another, often overlooked advantage to living in a modern commercial society. As the fourth stage of human progress, it produces more, in greater quantities, than any of its predecessors. It is so productive, in fact, that it can supply the wants and needs not only of those who work, but of those who don't. In the early drafts of *Wealth of Nations,* Smith strongly emphasized this (unfortunately, most of it did not make it to the final published version). He conceded that capitalism generates a great inequality of wealth, with a very few commanding the great bulk of commodities and a great part of the rest sharing what is left. But even so, Smith wanted to know, "in what manner shall we account for the superior affluence and abundance commonly possessed by even the lowest and most despised member of Civilized Society, compared with what the most respected and active savage can attain to."

The answer is again division of labor, in which "so great a quantity of everything is produced, that there is enough both to gratify the slothful and oppressive profusion of the great, and at the same time abundantly to supply the wants of the artisan and the peasant." Better to be a poor man in a rich country than a rich man in a poor one. It was a lesson in comparative advantage that Smith and his generation saw played out in the Scottish Highlands. Later on, the modern West learned it again as it watched floods of Third World emigrants gladly give up their homes in Bangladesh or Guatemala for the most menial jobs they could find in London or New York.

On this point, as on so many in the *Wealth of Nations,* Smith shared his friend Hume's delight in irony. Commentators sometimes suggest that irony is the most characteristic attitude of the modern mind. Certainly the enlightened Scots had it in abundance. It sprang from their pursuit of intellectual detachment in observing human affairs, in noticing how our intentions and expectations so often differ from our actual performance. In Smith's case, that detachment allowed him to see that the charity cases of commercial society's "universal opulence" included not only the indigent and homeless at the bottom of the social scale, but the rich and famous at the top. It also led him to perceive the real significance of self-interest as a human motivation.

Division of labor is one universal condition for the making of civil society. The other, even more essential and universal, is self-interest. Smith describes it in Hume's terms: as a passion or emotional impulse rather than a cold rational calculation, or what other philosophers liked to call "self-interest rightly understood." Self-interest acts like an emotional spur. It is an inner compulsion to better ourselves and our cir-

cumstances, which forces us to take action even when we do not particularly want to. It is in fact the drive behind the division of labor.

Contrary to popular misunderstanding, Adam Smith never supposed that everyone is driven solely by self-interest in a material sense.
He knew that many of us, perhaps most, are not. Certainly very few
people are so driven that they make great sacrifices and efforts in order
to gratify its demands. But enough do to make a difference. They force
the pace of progress forward, prodded along by their imaginings of
wealth and fortune, just as *The Theory of Moral Sentiments* foresaw. The
surplus they produce, in a world governed by scarcity, spills over to the
rest of us. "It is not from the benevolence of the butcher, the brewer, or
the baker, that we expect our dinner," Smith wrote in one of the most
famous passages of the *Wealth of Nations,* "but from their regard to their
own interest."

Of course, Smith was not the first to propose this paradox, that self-
interest, even greed, is actually beneficial to society and to the human
species. The Dutch moralist Bernard Mandeville had said the same thing
almost a century earlier, arguing that what most moralists condemned
as vices were actually virtues, in their beneficial effect on the economy:

> *Luxury employ'd a million of the poor,*
> *and odious pride a million more;*
> *Envy itself and vanity*
> *were ministers of industry;*
> *Their darling folly, fickleness*
> *In diet, furniture, and dress,*
> *That strange ridic'lous vice, was made*
> *The very wheel that turn'd the trade.*

Smith carried Mandeville one step further, however, revealing an
even deeper paradox and a greater irony: the pursuit of our own self-
interest actually causes us to reach out to others. This is true of all societies, as Hume and Kames had realized; the Bushman soon realizes that
the hunt goes easier when he has help, instead of having to do it all himself. But Smith's bold insight was to realize that it was the genius of cap-

italism to carry both of these characteristics, the pursuit of self-interest *and* the need for cooperation, to their highest pitch. On the one hand, it multiplies the opportunities, and lessens the amount of direct physical labor, necessary to pursue that interest. On the other, the relentless search for customers to buy, and for suppliers to sell, results in a vast network of interdependence, binding people together in far more complex ways than is possible in more primitive conditions. "In civilized society [a person] stands at all times in need of the cooperation and assistance of great multitudes," Smith wrote, "while his whole life is scarce sufficient to gain the friendship of a few persons."

Then still another paradox, and a further irony: the interdependence of the market begets independence of the mind, meaning the freedom to see one's own self-interest and the opportunity to pursue it. We recall that for Hutcheson, human happiness had been about personal liberty, the capacity to live one's life as one saw fit without harming others. For Kames, it had been about owning property, which gave us our sense of "propriety" and identity as human beings. Now Smith put the two together. By entering and competing in the great interactive dynamic network of modern society, at once impersonal but also indispensable to happiness, we become fully free and human. Independence in this sense becomes the hallmark of modern society, just as dependence on others or "servility" becomes the hallmark of primitive societies and institutions. "Nobody but a beggar," Smith admonished, "chuses to depend chiefly upon the benevolence of his fellow-citizens." Yet this has been the essential fate of the vast majority of humankind through most of history, as slaves toiling for their masters, as peasants handing over the harvest to their feudal lords, or as members of the tribe or clan dependent on their chieftains' command for life or death—hapless creatures whose quality of life rests entirely on whether their chief is "gentle Lochiel" or a brute like Coll MacDonnell. Capitalism breaks that cycle, and offers the conditions under which we forge our own happiness: independence, material affluence, and cooperation with others.

Today, more than two hundred years later, three great myths still surround Adam Smith and his *Wealth of Nations*.

The first is that Smith believed that the wealth of capitalism was generated by some great, guiding "invisible hand." In fact, the term, which appears in *Wealth of Nations* and *The Theory of Moral Sentiments,* is meant to be taken, once again, as irony. Smith did believe that capitalism produces its own kind of natural rational order, based on the market and its complex, interlocking system of self-interested exchange. To a superficial observer it might appear as if everyone were moving according to a single directing mind or "invisible hand." But his real point was not that a market-based order was perfect or even perfectible. Rather, it was more beneficial, and ultimately more rational, than ones put together by politicians or rulers, who are themselves creatures of their own passions and whims.

Here Smith's chief target was what he termed, and what has been known ever since, as "the mercantile system." He found it exemplified in theory in a book by another Scot, Sir James Steuart, titled *Inquiry into the Principles of Political Oeconomy,* and in practice in the British government's handling of its overseas empire.* Steuart's *Inquiry* appeared in 1767, and although Smith pronounced the book an "ingenious performance," everything about it infuriated him. Steuart was a strong believer in state intervention to develop trade and expand economic growth. He even argued that without the government's constant attention, its foreign trade might actually grind to a halt, leaving the nation vulnerable and destitute.

This was the sort of justification for punitive tariffs, export subsidies, and government-granted trade monopolies that Smith saw at work in Britain's overseas empire, and which he was determined to fight. He wrote of Steuart's work, "I flatter myself, that every false principle in it, will meet with a clear and distinct confutation in mine." In fact, Books Three and Four of the *Wealth of Nations* are a devastating analysis of the attempts by successive governments to manipulate the powerful productive forces of overseas trade, foolishly believing they could

---

*Steuart had been, interestingly enough, Charles Stuart's private secretary during the Forty-five and had been pardoned afterwards, living quietly in Edinburgh until his death in 1780.

increase wealth by government dictate, when in fact they usually did the opposite.

The centerpiece is Smith's scathing critique of London's policy toward the American colonies—which, by the time he was writing in 1775, had reached a critical point. Smith followed the American crisis, not only from recent news reports and Parliamentary debates, but also from his tobacco merchant friends such as Glassford and Ingram, who had lived in Virginia and Maryland and knew the situation firsthand. They understood, as Smith did, that Scotland was perfectly poised to benefit from a policy of free trade with America, and that London's shortsighted efforts to bend the Americans to its will would not only cripple their own business there (which it did), but would cost Britain her empire as well. "There are no colonies of which the progress has been more rapid than that of the English in North America," Smith wrote, and yet thanks to its monopolistic policies, "Great Britain derives nothing but loss from the dominion which she assumes over her colonies."

Smith's critique reached out beyond colonial monopolies to all kinds of unwanted government meddling in economic affairs. This is the second myth about *Wealth of Nations,* that in it Smith invented the notion of laissez-faire capitalism, in which the government has little or no role to play. In fact, the phrase *laissez-faire* comes from French economists, not Smith, who does not use the term at all. And contrary to the myth, Smith did see an important role for a strong national government. He saw it as necessary for providing a system of national defense, to protect the society and its commerce with its neighbors. It also must provide a system of justice and protection of individual rights, particularly the right to property: "[I]t is only under the shelter of the civil magistrate that the owner of that valuable property, which is acquired by the labor of many years, or perhaps of many successive generations, can sleep a single night in security." And it is needed to help defray the expenses of essential public works, such as roads, bridges, canals, and harbors.

Beyond that, however, Smith saw any other form of government interference as having all kinds of unintended consequences. History offered innumerable examples of governments and rulers, often with the best intentions, trying to change or adjust their nation's economic life, with disastrous results. Roman emperors had attempted to regulate the sagging economy of the Late Empire, and had destroyed it instead. Spain had tried to maintain a monopoly on the flow of bullion from the New World, only to bankrupt itself. Smith worried that Britain and its policy in America was headed down the same road.

To Adam Smith, belief in a free market was not an intellectual dogma, but a basic lesson of history. It was time for rulers to learn from their mistakes, and let commercial society follow its own course:

> All systems either of preference or of restraint, therefore, being thus completely taken away, the obvious and simple system of natural liberty establishes itself of its own accord. Every man, as long as he does not violate the laws of justice, is left perfectly free to pursue his own interest his own way. . . . The sovereign is completely discharged from a duty, in the attempting to perform which he must always be exposed to innumerable delusions, and for the proper performance of which no human wisdom or knowledge could ever be sufficient; the duty of superintending the industry of private people, and of directing it towards the employments most suitable to the interest of society.

This is the Adam Smith with whom we are all familiar: the great prophet of free-market capitalism as a system of "natural liberty," and the great enemy of any and all attempts to tinker with that system, whether for the sake of political power or social justice.

But there is another, less obvious Adam Smith who is also appears in the pages of *Wealth of Nations*. He, too, was a player in a contemporary debate raging in Edinburgh, about the new "commercial spirit" sweeping across Scotland and what it might mean for the future. This Adam Smith also flies in the face of the third myth about him and his greatest work, that it is basically an apologia for big business and the merchant class.

In fact, while *Wealth of Nations* speaks highly of free markets, it treats businessmen themselves in a very different light. To begin with, Smith saw the important beneficiaries of the free market not as businessmen but as consumers. "Consumption is the sole end and purpose of all production; and the interest of the producer ought to be attended to, only so far as it may be necessary for promoting that of the consumer." This was precisely what the existing British system failed to do. It put the interest of the producers and merchants ahead of that of consumers, who only want low prices and a ready supply of goods. Merchants often prefer the opposite. In fact, Smith understood that much of the British government's disastrous trade policies came at the instigation of the London merchants themselves, who wanted to protect their livelihood. "It is the interest of every man to live as much at his ease as he can," Smith notes in Book Five, and that rule applies as much to the businessman as it does to the landed aristocrat or university professor.

His overall picture of the typical businessman is certainly unflattering, and reading it must have made some of his Tobacco Lord friends slightly uncomfortable. He notes that while they often complained about high prices, "they say nothing concerning the bad effects of high profits." He speaks of their "mean rapacity" and "monopolizing spirit" and suggests that "the government of an exclusive company of merchants is, perhaps, the worst of all governments for any country whatsoever." Most of this was aimed at the business community in London, which had instigated and benefited from the corrupt old imperial system, rather than Glasgow. Smith's point was that the free market was as much a check upon the greed and power of the merchant as it was on an interfering king or government bureaucrat.

But Smith saw another, more systematic corruption flowing from commercial society, one that was more pernicious and worried him deeply. Even as capitalism increases specialization, and more sophistication in the overall output of goods and services, the individuals caught up in the process become narrower in their interests and less concerned with what happens outside their shop, office, or showroom. They come to weigh everything in terms of their job, of profit and loss, and lose sight of the larger picture. This worry appeared years before in one of Smith's lectures, and is worth quoting in full:

Another bad effect of commerce is that it sinks the courage of mankind, and tends to extinguish martial spirit. In all commercial countries the division of labor is infinite, and every one's thoughts are employed about one particular thing. . . . The minds of men are contracted, and rendered incapable of elevation. Education is despised, or at least neglected, and heroic spirit is utterly extinguished.

Preventing this kind of "mental mutilation," Smith says in the *Wealth of Nations,* deserves "the most serious attention of government." It is in fact the one place where Smith actually commends a genuinely active role for civic institutions: creating a system of education that will counteract this "deformity" of the human character by the division of labor.

Through capitalism we gain, but we also lose. The loss, Smith felt, was felt most among the lowest classes—his particular example was employees in a pin factory—whose cramped place in the chain of production leaves no room for the enlargement of the mind and spirit, which the freedom of commercial society should open up. Smith in fact defined the problem of the "assembly line" mentality of factory workers almost two decades before the Industrial Revolution got fully under way—the problem that Karl Marx and his followers would call alienation. It was especially worrisome to Smith, because "in free countries, where the safety of government depends very much upon the favourable judgement which the people may form of its conduct," a mass of ignorant, culturally degraded citizens easily becomes an immense drag on the system. They become easy prey to demagogues and applaud every attempt to undermine the foundations of that "natural liberty" which they have enjoyed in the first place.

So, while Smith had given one set of issues its final, definitive shape—the link between commercial society, refinement, and liberty—he had opened up a whole new territory for discussion and debate, the cultural costs of capitalism. In fact, he and his Edinburgh friends had been arguing about this for almost a decade, even before Dr. Johnson had wondered during his Scottish tour whether any society benefitted from becoming entirely "commercial" in its mentality and attitudes. The Scots, including Adam Smith himself, had firmly answered No.

The person who put the matter in the strongest terms was another member of the Select Society, and founder of the Poker Club, Adam Ferguson. Born in Perthshire, along the border between the Highlands and Lowlands, he had gone to Edinburgh to study for the ministry. There he became friends with the other future Moderate literati. But he missed the traumatic events of 1745–46 when he accepted a post as chaplain to the Black Watch regiment in Flanders.

It was an experience that profoundly altered his perspective from that of his contemporaries. They, as we saw, considered Prince Charles's Highland followers uncouth barbarians, and looked forward with undisguised relish to the demise of their society and culture. As chaplain, Ferguson had come to know the Highlanders firsthand and understood that for all their crude habits and harsh aggressiveness, they were men of honor, with an undeniable sense of courage, loyalty, and generosity toward friend and foe alike. In fact, they reminded Ferguson of no one so much as the warriors of the Homeric poems, and the ancient Spartans and Roman legions. The very qualities that his Moderate friends admired in their beloved Greeks and Romans, Ferguson found alive and well in the Scottish Highlands. The destruction of that way of life meant the destruction of something precious, Ferguson decided, and Scotland and the Scots would be the poorer for it.

Ferguson expanded his argument far beyond Scotland and into the very nature and history of civil society itself. In fact, that became the title of his book *Essay on the History of Civil Society,* published in 1768. In it, Ferguson helped himself to generous portions of Kames and Hume, as well as Adam Smith and Jean-Jacques Rousseau—and another, largely forgotten figure, Andrew Fletcher. The result was a volatile mixture of typical, cold-eyed Scottish political and social analysis, and flights of almost romantic poetry in praise of primitive peoples everywhere, but particularly in the ancient world and among Native Americans. Ferguson found in them what he had found in his Highland regiment: honor, integrity, and courage, which commercial society, with its over-specialization and mental mutilation, destroyed.

This was one of Ferguson's most striking points. Far from being "civilized" and advanced in their attitudes, the ancient Greeks and Romans were in fact, by modern standards, true primitives. A world of differences separated them from us, a world created and defined by the rise of capitalism. As Ferguson showed, modern civilization had erected an enormous barrier, cutting off "polite" nations not only from their "barbarous" neighbors, but from their own past as well. He quotes with approval a Native American chief telling a British official in Canada, "I am a warrior, not a merchant." It is a sentiment that would have been shared by an Achilles or a Hector, or even a Cato or a Pericles—not to mention a Highland chieftain such as Lochiel. "Their ardent attachment to their country," Ferguson wrote of the ancients, "their contempt of suffering, and of death, in its cause; their manly apprehensions of personal independence, which rendered every individual, even under tottering establishments, and imperfect laws, the guardian of freedom to his fellow citizens . . . have gained them the first rank among nations."

All these qualities were being steadily eaten away in the new, self-centered, modern society taking shape around them. Today "the individual considers his community only so far as it can be rendered subservient to his personal advancement and profit." Human beings become weak and soft, and lose their sense of honor and courage. They must have their creature comforts, no matter what. Freedom itself becomes a commodity, to be sold to the highest bidder—or seized by the strongest power.

Ferguson saw history moving along the same lines as his fellow Edinburgh literati, but the ultimate destination would be very different from what the prophets of progress had forecast.

> The boasted refinements, then, of the polished age, are not divested of danger. They open a door, perhaps, to disaster, as wide and accessible as any they have shut. If they build walls and ramparts, they enervate the minds of those who are placed to defend them; if they form disciplined armies, they reduce the military spirit of entire nations; and by placing the sword where

they have given a distaste to civil establishments, they prepare for mankind the government of force.

The last stage of modern history would be not liberty but tyranny, unless something was done to prevent it. Left to itself, commercial society would become humanity's tomb.

Ferguson's book had an enormous impact when it came out. It contained one of the first uses of the word *civilization* in English, and coined the term *civil society* as synonymous with modernity itself. It made Ferguson almost as famous as Adam Smith, and on the Continent almost as influential. The German Enlightenment particularly admired it, including the father of modern nationalism, Johann Gottfried Herder, and the founder of German Romanticism, the poet Friedrich Schiller. But Ferguson's closest reader would be Wilhelm Friedrich Hegel, who incorporated many of Ferguson's ideas and even phrases into his own philosophy of history, which Karl Marx would take up and develop. In fact, Marxism owes its greatest debt to Ferguson, not Rousseau, as the most trenchant critic of capitalism—and as the great alternative to Adam Smith as the prophet of modernity.

Admiration among his fellow Scots was more measured. Hume disliked the *Essay;* he saw it as a surrender to a kind of romantic primitivism, which the controversy over the Ossian poems had recently set off.* Adam Smith was miffed by the fact that Ferguson had stolen many of his insights from Smith's own lectures, including the part about the decline of the martial spirit in capitalist society. The real disagreement was not over content, however, but the tone. Smith and Hume clearly saw the shortcomings of a society organized completely around the gratification of self-interest and the calculation of profit and loss. They saw the virtues of premodern "rude" societies disappearing, along with their vices, and understood that we pay a heavy price for the division of labor and specialization in a modern complex economy.

But they believed firmly that the benefits were worth the price. A

---

*For details, see chapter 11.

society that could finally feed everyone, not just a chosen few; that could relieve the poverty and misery of even the weakest and least productive of its members; that recognized the sovereignty of the individual and his rights, and agreed to leave him alone to pursue his own ends; that put a premium on treating others with kindness and deference rather than disdain and exploitation; and, finally, that a society that recognized that it was better to do business with other nations than to try to conquer them, was not one on the verge of tyranny, but just the opposite. These were the conditions of modern liberty. If the ancients had constructed a version of freedom that lacked these essential ingredients, then they, not we, were the poorer for it.

And if commercial society offered new problems, it also offered solutions. Steps could be taken to correct course, and counteract the "bad effects of commerce" Smith and Ferguson had defined, even the cultural ones. One such solution was education, and Smith, in the late sections of *Wealth of Nations,* strongly urged public support for a system of schools that would make sure the benefits of a civilized culture reached as large a public as possible. Not surprisingly, his model was Scotland's own system of parish schools, which "has taught almost the whole common people to read, and a very great proportion of them to write and account." Smith knew that a modern capitalist society without a decent system of education was committing suicide, politically as well as culturally.

Another solution was one that many of Smith's Edinburgh friends had embraced, including Adam Ferguson: the creation of a citizen militia. This was a sore subject for Scotsmen. Ever since the Forty-five, they had been denied the use and ownership of weapons, and Parliament's passage of Militia Acts in 1757, and then during the American war, deliberately left the Scots out. Ferguson had become a virtual firebrand on the issue. He organized the Poker Club specifically to "stir up" public support for creating a Scottish militia. He also wrote pamphlets on the subject, as did John Home and other Moderates, arguing that a citizen militia was a way to keep alive the traditions of physical courage and martial spirit in a commercial society.

Why did the Scottish Enlightenment embrace the militia cause so strongly? Lurking in the background, perhaps, were uncomfortable memories of the volunteer companies of 1745 and that ill-fated march through Edinburgh. When liberty is threatened, can anyone expect young men raised in a cushy commercial environment to risk their lives on the battlefield against tough and hardened warriors? Obviously not, unless they have help. Not material help in this case, but cultural help, something that taught them self-sacrifice, discipline, and loyalty, and gave them confidence in their own physical powers and those of their weapons. This, Ferguson and the rest believed, militia training could do. And Adam Smith came to agree with them. Although he warned in *Wealth of Nations* that a citizen militia could never equal the discipline of a professional army in peacetime, he did believe a few campaigns in the field could harden them into an effective fighting force. The record of citizen soldiers in modern times, from Saratoga and Gettysburg to El-Alamein and Omaha Beach, tends to bear him out.

The agitation for a Scottish militia failed to move legislators in London. But it did set a new standard for later debates about the future of free societies, and the place of military virtues and military arms in them. The idea that a free people needed to keep and bear arms in order to defend their liberty was an ancient one, reaching back to the Greeks and forward to Andrew Fletcher. But now Ferguson and his friends had added something new, a social-psychological dimension. By owning weapons and learning to use them, a commercial people can keep alive a collective sense of honor, valor, and physical courage, traditions that no society, no matter how sophisticated and advanced, can afford to do without.

Here again, we see how the force of the debate had shifted. The issue was no longer how to make Scotland "civilized" and modern. That had been done. The question now was, having crossed that irrevocable line, what could be preserved of what came before? A watershed had been passed, and everyone knew it.

The *Wealth of Nations* was published on March 6, 1776. In February of that year, another masterpiece had appeared, the first volume of Edward Gibbon's *Decline and Fall of the Roman Empire*. Although English, Gibbon modeled his work closely on the Scottish and Edinburgh historical school: for all intents and purposes, he was intellectually a Scot. One of his closest friends was Adam Ferguson, but his other heroes were Hume and Smith, whose new book Gibbon called "the most profound and systematic treatise on the great objects of trade and revenue which had ever been published in any age or century." When Hume wrote to Gibbon praising his new history, Gibbon said the letter "repaid the labour of ten years."

On August 25, 1776, David Hume died after a long illness. His funeral drew a huge crowd, as his body was carried in a pouring rain from his house in the New Town to the Old Calton Burying Ground. Although Hume dismissed the idea of an afterlife to the very end, his last hours were calm and serene. Joseph Black described them in a letter to Adam Smith: "When he spoke to the people about him [he] always did it with affection and tenderness."

Earlier, on July 4, a different world-shattering event took place across the Atlantic. The American Revolution lurks in the background of every chapter of *Wealth of Nations,* just as it occupied the attention of so many of Smith's colleagues and friends.* Yet in certain ways, the reverse was also true. Scottish ideas, and Scots, were having a large impact on the events unfolding in the American colonies.

---

*In fact, Smith pointed to the Continental Army as his chief example of how a trained citizen army could compete with such professionals as the British redcoats.

PART TWO

Diaspora

In the evening the company danced as usual. We performed, with much activity, a dance which, I suppose, the emigration from Skye has occasioned. They call it *America*. Each of the couples, after the convolutions and evolutions, successively whirls round in a circle, till all are in motion; and the dance seems intended to show how emigration catches, till a whole neighbourhood is set afloat.

—*James Boswell,* Journal of a Tour to the Hebrides, *1773*

CHAPTER NINE

"That Great Design": Scots in America

Call this war by whatever name you may, only call it not an American rebellion; it is nothing more or less than a Scotch Irish Presbyterian rebellion.

—Anonymous Hessian officer, 1778

atching events unfolding in America in the autumn of 1775, Adam Smith wrote in *Wealth of Nations:*

> They are very weak who flatter themselves that, in the state to which things have come, our colonies will be easily conquered by force alone. The persons who now govern the resolutions of what they call the Continental Congress, feel in themselves at this moment a degree of importance which, perhaps, the greatest subjects in Europe scarce feel. From shopkeepers, tradesmen, and attornies, they are become statesmen and legislators, and are employed in contriving a new form of government for an extensive empire, which, they flatter themselves, will become, and which, indeed, seems very likely to become, one of the greatest and most formidable that ever was in the world.

In this, as in so much else, Smith proved prescient. Even he, however, could not have guessed how far that process of creating a "new form of government" or growing that "extensive empire" might go. Nor could he realize to what extent his own fellow Scots, including his friend David Hume, could take at least some of the credit for it.

As we have seen, Smith's view of what was happening in Britain's American colonies was informed by his friends in the Glasgow tobacco trade, several of whom had lived there. His interest in America was primarily economic. He saw it, and its prosperity, as the unintended result of a mercantile system gone haywire, which ended up enriching colonists who were supposed to be exploited, and emptying the pockets of Britons who were supposed to be benefiting from imperial dominion. As he put it, "The rulers of Great Britain have, for more than a century past, amused the people with the imagination that they possessed a great empire on the west side of the Atlantic." But the people were beginning to discover that "the effects of the monopoly of the colonial trade . . . [are] more loss than profit." Now they were saddled with a rebellion, and a war; and while Smith realized his own sensible advice for compromise would be ignored by the government in London, he also saw that the loss of the colonies would force a change in the direction of Great Britain, including Scotland—a change almost as dramatic as the change in the thirteen colonies themselves.

I

Scottish ties to North America dated back as far back as the reign of James I, when he conceived his ill-fated plans for a Scots colony, "Nova Scotia," in Canada. It was a long way from the icy, rocky shores of Nova Scotia to the sun-drenched beach of Darien, but the same dream inspired both: the get-rich-quick scheme of settlers effortlessly tapping the fabled resources of the New World, with the government skimming the thick cream from the top. Nova Scotia failed, less disastrously than Darien, since Scots did continue to settle and live there, but both experiences taught Scottish merchants and entrepreneurs a basic truth: that only patience and hard work brought wealth from the American possessions. Even before the Act of Union, Glasgow and Greenock merchants were busy laying down their lines across the Atlantic. By 1707, Glasgow families such as the Bogles had been doing business in the middle colonies for nearly three decades, much of it through illegal smuggling.

Scottish merchants penetrated the Chesapeake Bay and the James, Potomac, and Delaware Rivers, and operated as far north as Boston. Scottish settlers started arriving as early as the 1680s, and as Britain's role in North America expanded, the Scottish presence grew with it. One expert summarized the Lowland Scot presence in colonial America this way: "They permeated the official establishment, especially in the southern colonies, and provided several colonial governors. They supplied clergy for the Episcopalian and Presbyterian churches. They served as tutors . . . and many went on to establish schools." Most of eighteenth-century America's physicians were either Scots or Scot-trained. In short, Scots became indispensable to the running of colonial government and to cultural life, especially in the Southern and Middle Atlantic states. By the middle of the eighteenth century, Norfolk, Virginia, was virtually a Scottish town.

But this was only the first wave. America became the final destination for all three branches of the Scottish ethnic and cultural family: Lowlanders, Highlanders, and Ulster Scots. The first Ulster Scots turned up in 1713. In Worcester, Massachusetts, they were much in demand as Indian fighters and as a tough barrier between the English settlers and the "savage wilderness" beyond. When they tried to build a Presbyterian church, though, their neighbors tore it down. Between 1717 and 1776, perhaps a quarter of a million Ulstermen came to America, 100,000 of them as indentured servants. They did not remain servants for very long, as colonists soon discovered that Ulster Scots were not born to be obedient.

The Highlanders were last. Many were refugees from the Forty-five who settled along the Cape Fear River of North Carolina. MacLeods, MacDonalds, MacRaes, MacDougalls, and Campbells found themselves in a land where their native Gaelic isolated them even from their Scots neighbors, and in a climate and landscape totally unlike the one they had left behind. Flat, low-lying, humid marshes, red clay soil with scrub-pine forests; but the land was cheap and available, and the Highlanders carved out farms for themselves and their families. This is where Flora

MacDonald and her husband would settle when they came to America; thousands of others would make the same trip over the next fifty years. The volume and the points of destination grew as the Highlands emptied itself of people well into the next century. Today there are probably more descendants of the Highland clans living in America than in Scotland.

A transfer of people also involves a transfer of culture. At the same time that a new, refined Scotland was taking hold in its urban capitals and then spreading its influence to the rest of Europe, the older, more traditional Scotland was finding a new home in America, and thriving. A strange time warp was under way. The very same "backward" cultural forces that the Edinburgh and Glasgow Enlightenments were overmastering in order to create a modern society, including the old-time Presbyterianism, were about to generate their own version of progress. By the time enlightened Scotland reached American shores, the two would meet in a kind of cultural cross-current: the United States, as a republic and a nation, would be the result.

The people who best represented that traditional Presbyterian Scot culture were the Ulster Scots, or, as the Americans called them, the "Scotch Irish." They were Irish by geography only. In their settlements in the northern counties of Ireland, they had struggled to preserve the twin characteristics of their Scottish forebears. The first was a fierce Calvinist faith. The other was a similarly fierce individualism, which saw every man as the basic equal of every other, and defied authority of every kind. The man who claimed to be better than anyone else had to be ready to prove it, with his words, his actions, or his fists.

These volatile ingredients had been forged in fire in the religious conflicts of Northern Ireland, and in battles against both Catholic neighbors and English masters. A sense of personal independence, stubborn pride, and fierce family honor took root in the Scotch-Irish character. It kept the Ulster community intact through a century of triumph and disaster, and when its members began to leave Antrim, Armagh, Down, and Derry for a better future, they carried it with them to America.

The first great wave of Scotch-Irish emigration began with the failed harvest of 1717, which forced people to choose between moving and starving. A merchant from Philadelphia, Jonathan Dickinson, noted that summer "we have had 12 or 13 sayle of ships from the North of Ireland with a swarm of people." He also noted their appearance: tall and lean, with weatherbeaten faces and wooden shoes "shod like a horse's feet with iron." The women wore short, tight-waisted skirts and dresses, showing their bare legs underneath, which shocked Quaker Philadelphia. Another wave of Ulster Scots followed in the 1720s; so many, in fact, that the British Parliament demanded an inquiry, wondering whether they would completely depopulate the Protestant element in Ireland before they were done.

Some never made it. The trip on overcrowded ships could be hazardous, even murderous. One ship from Belfast to Philadelphia ran out of food midway. Forty-six passengers died of starvation, and the rest had to turn to cannibalism, with some eating members of their own families. The numbers kept coming, however, until by 1770 at least 200,000 had settled in America. In the first two weeks of August 1773 alone, 3,500 emigrants turned up in Philadelphia, looking to start a new life.

Where did they go? A few stayed and found work at their ports of entry, such as Philadelphia or Chester. But most fanned out west, traveling deep into three great river valleys and mountain ridges: up the Delaware Valley into southeastern Pennsylvania; south across the Potomac into the Shenandoah Valley, and then even farther south, beyond the Piedmont ridge into the Carolinas.

From the point of view of the colonial government and locals, they had come at the right time. English emigration to America had fallen off; and non-English settlers such as Germans and Huguenot French had not yet appeared in large numbers. The Scotch-Irish settlements began pushing the frontier farther and deeper into the Appalachians. Unlike many of their earlier English predecessors, they did not expect an easy time of it. Prepared for the worst, they carved a new life for themselves out of the wilderness, taking land from neighbors or natives when it suited them. The habits of colonizing Ireland and seizing arable land from Catholic enemies carried over to the New World. Their insatiable desire for land, and the willingness to fight and die to keep it, laid the foundation of the frontier mentality of the American West.

They settled in small farm communities, usually on the lee side of a ridge or in a creek hollow, clustering together according to family or region, like their remote Highland ancestors. A typical farm consisted of a "cowpen" or livestock corral of a sort familiar to a Lowland or Border farmer, and a cabin built of logs. The archetypal dwelling of the American frontier, the log cabin, was in fact a Scots development, if not invention. The word itself, *cabine,* meant any sort of rude enclosure or hut, made of stone and dirt in Scotland, or sod and mud in Ireland.

Across southwest Virginia, North Carolina, and eventually Tennessee, their extended families spread out—Alexanders, Ashes, Caldwells, Campbells, Calhouns, Montgomerys, Donelsons, Gilchrists, Knoxes, and Shelbys—establishing a network of clanlike alliances and new settlements. They named their communities—such as Orange County (in North Carolina), Orangeburg (in South Carolina), Galloway, Derry, Durham, Cumberland (after the Border county in England), Carlisle, and Aberdeen—after the places and loyalties they had left behind. In North Carolina they founded towns called Enterprise, Improvement, and Progress; and in Georgia and western Virginia, towns called Liberty.

Placenames and language reflected their northern Irish or southern Lowlands origins. They said "whar" for "where," "thar" for "there," "critter" for "creature," "nekkid" for "naked," "widder" for "widow," and "young-uns" for "young ones." They were always "fixin'" to do something, or go "sparkin'" instead of "courting," and the young 'uns "growed up" instead of "grew up." As David Hackett Fisher has suggested, these were the first utterings of the American dialect of Appalachian mountaineers, cowboys, truck drivers, and backcountry politicians. The language was also shamelessly intimate and earthy: passersby were addressed as "honey" and children as "little shits." They dubbed local landmarks Gallows Branch or Cutthroat Gap or Shitbritches Creek (in North Carolina). In Lunenberg County, Virginia, they even named two local streams Tickle Cunt Branch and Fucking Creek.

Neighbors, including the Indians, soon learned to treat them with respect, not to say fear. One Englishman described an Ulster Scot neighbor: "His looks spoke out that he would not fear the devil, should he meet him face to face." They did not bear much resemblance to their compatriot, Francis Hutcheson. Instead, Ulster Scots were quick-tempered, inclined to hard work followed by bouts of boisterous leisure and heavy drinking (they were the first distillers of whisky in the New World, employing native corn and rye instead of Scottish barley), and easy to provoke into fighting. The term used to describe them was *rednecks*, a Scots border term meaning Presbyterians. Another was *cracker*, from the Scots word *craik* for "talk," meaning a loud talker or braggart. Both words became permanent parts of the American language, and a permanent part of the identity of the Deep South the Ulster Scots created.

One reason their cultural impact was so widespread was that they were constantly moving. It was said that no Scotch-Irish family felt comfortable until it had moved twice. Even before the Susquehanna and Cumberland valleys were fully settled, they were pushing into Virginia and the Carolinas. The governors of those colonies, Scots themselves, welcomed the new settlers; Ulster Scots began arriving in large numbers in the 1720s and 1730s, and under Governor Gabriel Johnson, a native of Dumfriesshire, expansion came to include Highland immigrants after the Forty-five. By 1760, North Carolina was practically a Little Scotland: a "Mac-ocracy," in the words of one of the Ulstermen's enemies. By the end of the century, some were moving on to Georgia, and as far south as the Savannah River.

The Scotch-Irish South was a breeding ground for a type of strong, independent man and woman, a school for natural leaders. Andrew Jackson was son of an Ulster Scot immigrant, Hugh Jackson, a wealthy weaver and merchant from Carrickfergus. In 1765 he led a group of emigrants to America into South Carolina. His son was a typical product of the tight-knit, tough, and quarrelsome culture of Ulster Scot Carolina, and chose his wife from a similar Scotch-Irish clan. Another immigrant, Captain Robert Polk, had joined the parade of emigrants from County Donegal for the New World slightly earlier. His son settled in Virginia, and his five children, Robert's grandchildren, ended up in Mecklenburg County, North Carolina. James Knox Polk was born there in 1795, eventually representing his state as senator and still later serving as twelfth President of the United States.

Patrick Calhoun and his wife, Catherine Montgomery, left Ireland for America in 1733, with their four sons. Patrick junior married a Caldwell, descendants of a Borders family also settled in South Carolina, and his son John C. Calhoun would become South Carolina's most powerful politician.

John Henry emigrated from Scotland around 1730; he numbered among his relations on his mother's side that stalwart of the Moderate literati William Robertson. He settled in Hanover County, Virginia, which was quickly becoming home to Scots and Ulster Scot families, and married another relative, Sarah Syme. Their son Patrick Henry was born in 1736. His most famous maxim, "Give me liberty or give me death," abruptly but perfectly encapsulates the mentality of these back-country Scottish communities, in which living as you pleased—a crude homegrown version of Hutcheson's notion of man's moral liberty—was a matter of birthright. In 1768 Mecklenburg County even told the North Carolina colonial assembly, "We shall ever be more ready to support the government under which we find the most liberty."

Defending that liberty against all challengers required force of will and a keen sense of valor. Here, in America, a warrior ethos took root, which was as fierce and violent as that of any Highland clan. President Andrew Jackson would remember his mother telling him, "Never tell a lie, nor take what is not your own, nor sue anybody for slander, assault, or battery. Always settle them cases yourself." One day she scolded him: "Stop that, Andrew. Do not let me see you cry again. Girls were made to cry, not boys." "What are boys made for, mother?" he asked. She answered, "To fight."

Jackson spent his life fighting, both as a soldier and as a gentleman of honor in duels that took the lives of two opponents. Dueling, and the code of honor that went with it, became embedded in Southern culture. Men defended themselves with their fists, knives, and muskets. Training with a gun and target practice were standard parts of a boy's, and sometimes a girl's, training for dealing with the real world. Running battles or feuds between backcountry families were as common, and as vicious, as any between Scottish Borders dynasties or Highland clans—the epic

Highland clashes of Campbells and MacDonalds would later be matched in backcountry America by those of Hatfields and McCoys.

To see justice done, men were prepared to take the law into their own hands. In the Carolinas, bands of vigilantes or Regulators criss-crossed the territory in the late 1760s, stamping out local hooligans and waging war on interlopers. This vigilante attitude was epitomized by a Scots Borders descendant from Pittsylvania County, Virginia, named Captain William Lynch. He ruled as virtual dictator of his county, punishing wrongdoers and warning lawless elements that "we will inflict such corporal punishment on him or them, as to us shall seem adequate to the crime committed or the damage sustained." "Lynch's Law," and the punishments and hangings it inflicted, also became part of American culture—an ugly part, but a legacy of a harsh world and a harsh, unforgiving people.

The Presbyterian Ulster Scots also brought over their burning hatred of Episcopalians (especially since, as British subjects, they had to pay taxes for the established Anglican Church in America). When one Anglican missionary tried to preach in the Carolina mountains, the locals "disrupted his services, rioted while he preached, started a pack of dogs fighting outside the church, loosed his horse, stole his church key, refused him food and shelter, and gave two barrels of whiskey to his congregation." The missionary, an Englishman, learned to hate his would-be Scotch-Irish converts with a passion. "They delight in their present low, lazy, sluttish, heathenish, hellish life," he wrote, "and seem not desirous of changing it."

Religious feeling was not all negative. The years in Ireland had kept the original evangelical fervor of John Knox's Kirk intact. For all their wild and "heathenish" ways, Ulster Scots dipped deep into the emotional resources of Scottish Calvinism. They worshiped in "prayer societies" and large "field meetings"—the ancestor of the American revival meeting. They turned to their ministers for inspiration and support, and took comfort in a hellfire-and-damnation style of Christianity. The skeptic Robert Burns mocked the dramatic flair of Scottish evangelical preachers in "The Holy Fair":

Hear how he clears the points o' Faith,
Wi' rattlin' an' thumpin'
Now meekly calm, now wild in wrath
He's stampan an he's jumpan!

But the Scots and Scotch Irish laity loved it, and it became the hallmark of Southern—and American—religion from then until the present. It also forged a link between the Presbyterian "People of the New Light," as the immigrants call themselves, and the intense Protestant revivalism taking place in the 1730s and 1740s, which historians call the Great Awakening.

The Great Awakening transformed the culture of colonial America, touching its inhabitants with the spark of promised redemption, and daring them to challenge orthodox assumptions and institutions. It set the stage for the American Revolution. The man most often associated with it is the New England minister Jonathan Edwards, and his church in Northampton, Massachusetts. But in fact Scottish Presbyterians were front and center in the movement from the start.

The Great Awakening's basic notion was that the past had passed, and the future was alive with possibilities for celebrating the glory of God. Jonathan Edwards preached that the coming of Christ's kingdom, the millennium, would begin in America. Anyone—not just Presbyterians but all Protestant sects, even the hated Episcopalians—could be touched by God's grace; all the righteous would eventually join together, regardless of denomination or place of origin, to form a single great "Christian commonwealth." Righteousness, not birth or status, determined one's place in the coming kingdom of God. It was a revivalist message that echoed the themes of Scottish Calvinism since Knox's day. Not surprising, then, that Presbyterians became its most enthusiastic partisans, or that the arrival of the Ulster Scots in the middle colonies of Pennsylvania, New Jersey, Virginia, and Maryland provided the initial spark.

At the center of the explosion were minister William Tennant and his sons. A recent scholar has concluded, "The Tennants were probably the single most important clerical force in the progress of the Great

Awakening." William Tennant, Sr., was born in Northern Ireland, educated in Edinburgh, and in 1704 ordained as a minister in the Anglican Church. However, the moment he set foot in America, in 1718, he felt drawn to the faith of his ancestors and his wife's family. By 1720 he was a Presbyterian minister in Bucks County, Pennsylvania, at the edge of the frontier, and in the midst of a thronging Scotch-Irish immigrant community in Neshaminy.

He soon realized that he had far more Ulster Scots parishioners than he could deal with, and far fewer trained clergy than he had counted on. So he decided to open his own school of theology in a log cabin (naturally) next to his church, which became known as "Log College." It was the first Presbyterian academy in the middle colonies. One of its first graduates was his son Gilbert. Hard and fearless, Gilbert Tennant would have made a worthy companion to Andrew Jackson, or perhaps William Wallace. "Taller than common size," he was "a man of great Fortitude, a lover of God, ardently jealous for His glory, and anxious for the salvation of sinners." He went on to Yale College and returned to Pennsylvania to cheer the revivalist tour of George Whitefield in 1740, which ignited the Great Awakening in Protestant congregations all along the eastern seaboard.

It was a crucial moment. The Pennsylvania synod had decided to shut down William Tennant's Log College because of his aggressive assertion that the clergy should inspire, not just rule over, its congregation. He defied them and set off a split within the Presbyterian Church in the colony, between the orthodox Old Side, and the New Side, who recruited their laity into their cause. By 1744, Gilbert Tennant was the New Side minister for the church in Philadelphia and the Tennant version of Presbyterian "New Light" was reaching out to New Jersey and New England.

To inspire students and future ministers for the New Side, the Tennants and their allies decided to create a new Presbyterian college in New Jersey. It opened its doors in 1747, and eventually moved to the town of Prince Town, or Princeton. It was supposed to be a revivalist antidote to the "corruption" of institutions such as Harvard and Yale. The college even chose Jonathan Edwards as its honorary president, although he died less than three months after moving to Princeton to assume his duties. A new president—Aaron Burr, Sr., father of the future vice president of the United States—was named, and by then the schism between Old Side and New Side Presbyterians was beginning to heal. Princeton became a haven for revivalist religion everywhere, regardless of denomination: even the Baptist leader Isaac Backus encouraged sons of his flock to go there.

One alumnus was a young Philadelphian named Benjamin Rush. Although Rush was English, not Scottish, by origin, he was the first of a succession of Americans for whom a Scottish education was the transforming event of their lives. He spent his childhood surrounded by key figures in the Presbyterian Great Awakening.* When he went to Princeton the college president was Samuel Davies, who had spent years of his life preaching the gospel in the Scotch-Irish backcountry of Virginia. He stressed to Rush's Class of 1760 "the vast importance and absolute Necessity of entering upon Public Life with A NEW HEART and A NEW SPIRIT." After graduation, Rush apprenticed with Philadelphia's leading physician, John Redman, who was also a Log College graduate. Other doctors he met encouraged Rush to travel to Scotland to study medicine, and in 1767 he left for Edinburgh. It was a trip that would change his life—and incidentally change the course of education in America.

He arrived in Liverpool on October 21. Thanks to Benjamin Franklin, who was then living in London, Rush had letters of introduction to various Edinburgh luminaries (during Franklin's visit in 1759, he had been given the keys to the city). He even met David Hume at a dinner party—"his person was rather ungenteel and clumsy," Rush wrote in his diary, "he spoke but little, but what he said was always pertinent and sensible." However, Hume's evident religious skepticism, and the relaxed attitude about religion generally among Hume's Moderate friends, disturbed the young Benjamin Rush, suffused as he was with the ardent afterglow of the Great Awakening.

---

*When Gilbert Tennant died in 1764, Rush wrote a glowing eulogy in his memory—it was his first published work.

From that point of view, he felt more comfortable with the Kirk's tradition-minded Popular Party, especially the party's champion, John Witherspoon. Witherspoon was forty-three years old when Rush met him at his fast-growing parish in Paisley, near Glasgow. Witherspoon was a strong, energetic, squat-faced man with thick, bushy eyebrows; he was a skilled theologian and a brilliant preacher. He was no rock-ribbed, fire-eating reactionary, however. He had been the classmate of William Robertson, Hugh Blair, and the other Moderates, and had received the same humanistic education in the classics, philosophy, and science. Witherspoon grasped the strengths and foibles of his Moderate opponents better than most, and he had used his knowledge with devastating effect in his *Ecclesiastical Characteristics,* the anti-Moderate satire that had made him famous and admired, even in Moderate circles.

It was Witherspoon who had pointed out that the new "enlightened" Presbyterian Church of Robertson and the rest was really a kind of elitism, reinforced by their dependence on powerful political patrons such as Lord Islay. He took the title "Popular Party" with pride: he and his fellow Evangelicals were truly preachers to the people, the farmers and shopkeepers and apprentices and tenant laborers who made up the backbone of the Scottish Kirk. The people deserved a say in who their ministers were, he believed, and in how the Gospel would be preached.

It was the sort of forthright democratic attitude Benjamin Rush, son of the New Light, could identify with, and he was not alone. For, as he explained to Witherspoon, his visit to Paisley was not a pleasure trip. Rush was there on business. He was there to persuade Witherspoon to accept the post he had been offered a year ago November, to become the new president of Princeton College in America.

II

Princeton, or Nassau Hall as it was sometimes called after its principal building, had had a run of bad luck. It had gone through five presidents in twenty years—one of whom, Jonathan Edwards, had died less than three months after accepting the post. The college needed a president who could give it continuity and stability, and its trustees believed

Witherspoon had the right qualifications and the proper orthodox Presbyterian spirit to do that. They also believed that Witherspoon could help the Church heal its New Side–Old Side schism, since Witherspoon had the respect of both groups (the head of the Old Siders, William Alison, was a fellow Scot). On November 19, 1766, they wrote to Witherspoon, offering him a salary of 146 pounds sterling, as well as use of a house and garden, and land for "winter fuel and pasturage." They closed with, "we ardently pray, that Providence may make your way plain before you for the acceptance of [our] choice."

At first glance, it seems odd that Witherspoon would even consider such an offer. His reputation in Scotland was made; Paisley was a rapidly growing city, and he felt duty-bound to stay and oversee the church he had been building there. He had already turned down offers from Dublin, Dundee, and the Scottish church in Rotterdam. Besides, as he explained to the trustees and to Benjamin Rush when he came to visit, his wife was very wary of the long and dangerous voyage to America. It was a prospect to daunt anyone, especially someone with a settled and comfortable life.

Yet the fact remained that Witherspoon, like many other Scottish Evangelicals, felt drawn to America. Since the 1750s they had been fighting a losing battle for control over their Kirk. At the same time they had seen the Presbyterian churches in the colonies newly awakened to the spirit of the Lord. A suspicion took hold in their minds, that the place God had destined for the new covenant with His chosen people might not be Scotland after all, but America. A Scottish colleague who had heard about the Princeton offer wrote to Witherspoon, urging him to accept it: "I have long thought it the intention of Providence . . . to fix the great seat of truth and righteousness in America; and that New Jersey seemed to promise fair for being the nursery of the most approved instruments for carrying on that great design, in that wide continent."

Similar thoughts must have occurred to Witherspoon, as well. The opportunity to shape "that great design" and make the College of New Jersey its educational epicenter seemed too good to miss. We will never know whether Rush's own appeal affected his final decision. But on

February 4, 1768, Witherspoon informed him his doubts were resolved and he would take up the presidency of Princeton. "Pray that it may be for the Glory of God and the publick interest," he wrote Rush, "for it is a very hard piece of work—and more against my worldly interest than you yet know but I will not draw back."

On May 10 he informed his saddened parishioners that he was leaving them and Scotland forever. On the eighteenth he and his wife boarded a ship at Greenock bound for America. They reached the mouth of the Delaware River on Saturday, August 6, after a harrowing trip of nearly eleven weeks. That Sunday, John Witherspoon landed at Philadelphia, greeted by a throng of church officials and well-wishers. Five days later they set out by carriage for Princeton. As Witherspoon and his wife came up the drive that night, they found Nassau Hall, the building that housed the college and its students, ablaze with light. The students had asked permission to illuminate the college in honor of their famous new president, and had hung Nassau Hall with dozens of candles, lamps, and lanterns, an iridescent beacon in the surrounding darkness.

Once in office, Witherspoon proved to be the opposite of the stereotypical narrow-minded Evangelical hard-liner. He intended to make Princeton not only the best college in the colonies, but in the entire British world. The model he chose was his own Scottish alma mater, the University of Edinburgh, and its curriculum would be the rigorous humanistic one that Hutcheson and others had introduced at Glasgow. Witherspoon saw education not as a form of indoctrination, or of reinforcing a religious orthodoxy, but as a broadening and deepening of the mind and spirit—and the idea of freedom was fundamental to that process. "Govern, govern always," he told his faculty and tutors, "but beware of governing too much. Convince your pupils . . . that you wish to see them happy, and desire to impose no restraints but such as their real advantage, and the order and welfare of the college, render indispensable." Under his guidance, Princeton became a vital meeting ground of America's evangelical fervor and Scotland's modernizing humanism—and a principal conduit for the flow of Scottish ideas into the culture of the colonies.

Some of this was in place even before Witherspoon arrived. Samuel Blair, one of Princeton's Ulster Scot founders, had said the school's curriculum should "cherish a spirit of liberty and free enquiry," so that every religious denomination, not just Presbyterians, enjoyed full freedom of conscience. Students were also introduced to a wide range of advanced secular, as well as theological, study. After one and a half years of Latin and Greek, they pressed on not only to traditional subjects such as logic and rhetoric, but also to history, geography, and science. Princeton's founders believed, as Witherspoon did, that science was the ally, not the opponent, of religion. It was the sort of view of education anyone trained in a Scottish university would understand: that of a basic unity of all human knowledge, which every student can be exposed to and can ultimately master.

What Witherspoon brought to this was his own dedicated energy. He swept into Princeton like a human dynamo. In addition to serving as president, and as principal orator of the college, Witherspoon was also chairman of the Philosophy Department, of the History Department, and of what today we would call the English Department, and gave sermons in the college chapel every Sunday. In addition, he tutored students in French and Hebrew.

He then reorganized the college-sponsored grammar school attached to Princeton and took over as headmaster. As one would expect a Scot to do, he doubled the amount of formal training in English in the grammar school's curriculum, and added English literature and composition to the college entrance requirements. He focused the curriculum on subjects central to the reforms Francis Hutcheson and his allies had earlier carried out in Scotland, particularly the classics, moral philosophy, and rhetoric and criticism—or what his old Moderate antagonists would have called *belles lettres*. He included massive doses of reading in all these subjects, not just the great ancient philosophers, but also modern ones. These included his fellow Scots and his Moderate opponents, such as Hutcheson, Kames, Ferguson, Adam Smith, and even David Hume. Witherspoon's attitude was that even if you disagreed with a philosopher or thinker, you still needed to read him in order to appreciate his arguments and refute them. So Witherspoon's students found themselves inundated with a host of thinkers Witherspoon disapproved of, but whom, in "the spirit of free inquiry," they were expected to understand and digest. As a result, Witherspoon's influence ranged far beyond his own views and positions, and pointed in directions he himself could not have foreseen.

Witherspoon did chart his students' intellectual progress in other ways. He encouraged them to reorganize Princeton's two student clubs along Scottish lines, as places for intellectual discussion as well as conviviality. Two of his best students, James Madison, who was just eighteen, and Aaron Burr, stepped in to help. Witherspoon also organized debates and speeches almost every evening in Nassau Hall, so that Princeton students, as he put it, "may learn, by early habit, presence of mind and proper pronunciation and gesture in public speaking." On those evenings Witherspoon threw the doors open to the public, encouraging Madison, Burr, and the rest to sharpen their wits and loosen their tongues before a large audience on a wide variety of subjects, including political topics—topics so volatile and controversial (this was at the time of the Boston Massacre) that locals began to get alarmed.

All this was part of Witherspoon's vision of Princeton as a place not just for teaching students and would-be ministers, but also for training future public leaders. It was one reason he wanted Princeton to be as "inclusive" as possible. Princeton drew students from all the colonies, not just New Jersey. He encouraged non-Presbyterians to attend, such as the Episcopalian Virginian James Madison. Even more amazingly, he recruited Native American students and blacks, such as the future teacher and minister John Chavis. Witherspoon wanted his students to think of themselves as Americans, and to think of themselves as obligated to lead America to a new future.

That future was very much on his mind, and on his students' minds, as 1770 ushered in what promised to be a decade of conflict between the colonies and Britain. These were the years of the Boston Massacre, protests against the so-called Intolerable Acts, and the first meetings of the Committees of Correspondence. In the midst of this tense and confusing crisis, Witherspoon had no doubts where he stood. Whatever his feelings as a Briton and a Scot, his loyalties were now with his adopted home. He had chosen the Popular Party in Scotland, he said, because he was opposed to "lordly domination." Now the same issue was at stake. America must be free to fulfill its place in God's "great design," and if the mother country refused to permit that freedom, then Americans had to be ready to take matters into their own hands.

Witherspoon published his first words of support for the American cause in 1771. Three years later, as events brought delegates from all the colonies together for the first Continental Congress, he composed his *Thoughts on American Liberty*. He urged the Congress to start thinking of America as a nation, with a distinct national interest. Although they should still avow their loyalty to Britain and its laws, they had to take a firm stand against Parliament's efforts to tax and regulate their affairs. It was time, America's most distinguished educator urged, to begin drawing up plans for union. He made much the same point in a pastoral letter to all the Presbyterian churches in the colonies, saying that he preferred "war with all its horrors, and even extermination, to slavery, riveted on us and our posterity."

In the predawn hours of April 19, 1775, British troops marched into Lexington, Massachusetts, to find one hundred or so local volunteers drawn up on the village green to oppose them. Shots were fired; eight militiamen died, ten others were wounded, and the rest scattered. All that day British regulars and Massachusetts Minutemen exchanged gunfire, as the American Revolution drew its first blood. When news of the fighting reached the other colonies, supporters of armed struggle sprang into action. Ulster Scots in the Shenandoah Valley took up the cause with alacrity; in Rockbridge County, Virginia, they even named their new county seat Lexington, in honor of the fallen. In North Carolina, Scotch-Irish volunteers gathered in Charlotte and, at midnight on May 20, declared Mecklenburg County to be free and independent from the British Crown.

The most pressing priority was turning the uprising in the separate colonies into a single national movement. This was partly a military problem: without a unity of command, the rebels had no chance of holding their own against their vastly superior British foes. It led to the creation on June 14, 1775, of the Continental Army, under the command of General George Washington. But it was also a political issue: how to convince colonists to think of themselves as part of a large whole, dedicated to a single purpose and requiring equal sacrifice from everyone? Fortunately, the Great Awakening had already pointed the way, and no one was more keenly aware of the deep resources waiting to be tapped there than John Witherspoon. American unity required more than just rational planning; it needed a strong moral base, and Witherspoon pointed out where to find it.

In March 1776 the British evacuated Boston; the scene of conflict was shifting from New England to New York. On May 15 the Continental Congress took the first tentative steps toward separating itself formally from Britain. Two days later Witherspoon stepped to the pulpit in Princeton and delivered a sermon he later published as *The Dominion of Providence over the Passions of Men*. It began with a survey of the role of God's Providence in world history—of how, as the Psalms had put it, "not a sparrow falls but God knows it." This was because, as Witherspoon explained, God ultimately knows and wills everything that happens in His creation, especially the fate of His chosen people. His benevolence had protected the Jews, and then the early Christians; it had guided the Reformation, and then extended it to the shores of America. Now God was guiding the turbulent events in the colonies, even as the powers arrayed against them seemed destined to triumph.

Witherspoon's next sentence rang out from the pulpit like a bell reverberating over the landscape:

> I am satisfied that the confederacy of the colonies has not been the effect of pride, resentment, or sedition, but of a deep and general conviction that our civil and religious liberties, and consequently in a great measure the temporal and eternal happiness of us and our posterity, depended on the issue.

What was at stake was not just taxes or the rights of freeborn Englishmen, but the principle of a Christian commonwealth dedicated to God. In fact, the political and religious issues were inseparable.

"There is not a single instance in history in which civil liberty was lost and religious liberty [kept] entire." The final proof, in Witherspoon's mind, that this rebellion was part of God's divine plan was that so many different religious denominations—Presbyterians, Congregationalists, Baptists, yes, and even Episcopalians—had come together to support it. "He is the best friend to American liberty," Witherspoon asserted, who combined commitment to political freedom with a commitment to God. If Americans could do this, "there will be the greatest reason to hope, by the blessing of God, for prosperity and success."

A Christian commonwealth dedicated to liberty and God: no political vision could possibly be further removed from the principles of a David Hume or an Adam Smith. But in America in 1776 it struck precisely the right note. When historians emphasize the role that secular political ideas played in inspiring the American Revolution, and point to Thomas Jefferson, John Adams, and James Madison—who actually did turn to David Hume for guidance, as we shall soon see—they sometimes overlook the powerful religious dimension of the revolt. Witherspoon's invocation helped to tip the balance in the minds of thousands of colonists who might have been hostile, or at least cool, to the idea of political rebellion against their sovereign king. It was the authentic voice of Protestant America. Witherspoon mobilized a revivalist fervor that the revolution needed to succeed, and that the new nation would inherit.

Certainly contemporaries recognized it. *The Dominion of Providence* went through nine editions, with publishers in Philadelphia, London, and Glasgow. The Edinburgh editors of the *Scots Magazine* strongly condemned it, and concluded that "the unhappy commotions in our American colonies" were due almost entirely to "clerical influence," and that "none . . . had a greater share . . . than Doctor Witherspoon." Horace Walpole, son of the former prime minister, rose in Parliament to speak. "There is no use crying about it," he said. "Cousin America has run off with a Presbyterian parson, and that is the end of it." Everyone knew whom he meant.

On June 28, 1776, Witherspoon was in Philadelphia as part of the

New Jersey delegation to the Continental Congress. They were there to draw up a declaration of American independence.

III

Revolution thrust on all Scottish immigrants, and on Americans of recent Scots or Ulster Scots extraction, a set of difficult choices. Should the colonists rebel or not rebel, in order to secure their rights? If they did rebel, should one join with them or remain loyal to the British Crown?

Recent immigrants, particularly those from the Highlands, tended to choose the Crown. Remarkably, even some of those who had fled in the wake of the Forty-five remained loyal to the government that had done so much to drive them from their homes. When Flora and Allan MacDonald heard the news about Lexington, Allan immediately offered his services to the loyalist side. He became second-in-command of the loyalist militia raised from the Highlanders in the Cape Fear region, under one Brigadier Donald MacDonald, a British officer dispatched to North Carolina—who also happened to be a cousin. Their Highland militiamen, complete with bagpipes and broadswords, ran afoul of the rebels at Moore's Creek at the end of February 1776. Leading the charge was another Cape Fear Highlander, Donald MacLeod, who died with nine musket balls in him; thirty or so others also fell until the loyalists fled in confusion. The field belonged to the rebels—most of whom were almost certainly Ulster Scots.

In the Mohawk Valley in New York, Highland immigrants rallied to the British colors under two veterans of Culloden—one who had served on the Jacobite, the other on the Hanoverian side. The old Hanoverian, Alexander MacDonald, declared that "nothing can cure the madness that prevails all over America but the sternest of measures." He led an ugly and savage guerrilla-style war in the valley, pitting Indians against rebel settlers, and Highlanders against Continental regulars. Incidents such as this, and the fighting at Moore's Creek, made Scottish immigrants synonymous with loyalist or "Tory." They became easy targets for abuse. John Witherspoon even penned an *Appeal to the Natives of Scotland*, urging them to reconsider on grounds of self-interest. Independence, he insisted, would make their new American home "powerful and opulent to a degree not conceived." Eventually Britain and America would be bound together by ties of another kind, of free trade (he even quoted David Hume on this point!). They were not giving up their old roots, but were gaining new ones.

But by and large the Scots stood firmly against revolution. When it ended, most would end up paying for their decision by having to leave, as the newly independent Americans made it clear that they were no longer welcome:

Tories, with their brats and wives,
Should fly to save their wretched lives.

Allan and Flora MacDonald returned to their original home, on the Isle of Skye—coming full circle after a life of constant adventure and turmoil. One hundred fifty thousand other Loyalist exiles, at least a fifth of them Scots, left for the remaining British dominions in the Americas. At least one-half went to Canada, and nearly 35,000 of those to Nova Scotia, Scotland's original foundation in North America. After the opulence of life in the thirteen colonies, immigrants found conditions there austere. Some nicknamed their new home "Nova Scarcity." But the American Revolution did have this unexpected consequence: it infused the British dominions in Canada with a bracing dose of Scotsmen who would play an important part in the making of the country in the next century.

Ulster Scots, on the other hand, had no such qualms. A long-standing hatred of the English drove them into the arms of the Sons of Liberty and the rebel cause. They were, said one appalled New Englander, "the most God-provoking democrats on this side of Hell." Another in Philadelphia said, "a Presbyterian loyalist was a thing unheard of." Some, such as William Stark, commander at Bunker Hill, found a leading role in the fight, but most played a humbler part, like Andrew Jackson's family. Two of Jackson's brothers enlisted in the

South Carolina militia, and one was only sixteen when he was killed in action. Andrew himself joined the militia at the incredible age of twelve, was wounded in battle and captured, and, when he refused to clean a British officer's boots, received a saber cut across the skull that left a permanent scar. In prison he contracted smallpox and malaria. His mother nursed the wounded, and died of exhaustion before the war ended.

The Scotch-Irish from places such as Mecklenburg and Orange counties in North Carolina, Augusta and Rockbridge counties in Virginia, and Bucks and Chester counties in Pennsylvania supplied the cause of independence with more than just patriotic fervor. Debate now rages among historians about how skilled the average American colonist really was with firearms and whether most even owned or had fired a musket. One thing seems certain, however: the typical frontier Scotch-Irish settler had grown up with firearms, including the use of the rifled musket, which, the British general Howe had to admit, they had "perfected with little knowledge of ballistics." They would supply the backbone of George Washington's Continental Army. One estimate (probably exaggerated) had it that half the army at Valley Forge were Ulster Scots. Certainly they brought military experience, leadership, and a fighting spirit to a revolution that badly needed all three.

Daniel Morgan of North Carolina raised a regiment of volunteer rifles, beat British regulars at the Battle of Cowpens, and then was instrumental in frustrating the British general Cornwallis's campaign in the Carolinas. Virginia-born and frontier-hardened George Rogers Clark turned the tables on the British in the Ohio Valley when he and his band of rangers made an epic journey to capture Fort Vincennes.

Henry Knox's father had arrived in Boston from Ulster in 1729. Henry was twenty-five when the rebellion broke out; although he had no soldiering experience, in less than a year he was head of General Washington's artillery. He personally led Washington's raid on the Hessians in Trenton on Christmas Eve, 1776, and earned accolades for service in subsequent campaigns. He became major general in 1781, at age thirty-one. A key member of Washington's inner coterie, Knox later served under him as the new nation's first secretary of war. He pushed hard for the creation of a national militia in 1790, although Congress turned him down. Knox did, however, manage to take the first steps toward the creation of a national military academy at West Point, New York.

James McHenry grew up in County Antrim in Ulster, and was educated in Dublin, probably at a Presbyterian academy. He emigrated to Philadelphia in 1771, and while the rest of his family founded a prosperous import business in Baltimore, McHenry chose to study medicine at the College of Philadelphia with Benjamin Rush. The war drew them both into the Continental Army as physicians, although McHenry turned from army medicine (he was senior surgeon of the army's mobile field hospital at Valley Forge) to staffwork, becoming secretary to General Washington and then to Lafayette. McHenry also went on to sit as secretary of war, both for Washington and for John Adams. When the threat of war with France flared, he ordered a series of forts built along the East Coast. The one in Baltimore would later bear his name, and the British siege of Fort McHenry in 1812 would inspire another American of Scottish extraction, Francis Scott Key, to pen the "Star-Spangled Banner," the American national anthem.

Important contributions to the American war effort did not just come from Ulster Scots, however.

John Paul's father was a gardener on a wealthy estate in Kirkcudbrightshire in extreme southern Scotland. However, his son had no interest in remaining on land. He was drawn irresistibly to the sea, and made his first voyage to Fredericksburg, Virginia, on a Scottish merchant ship at age thirteen. A brilliant seaman, he soon became master of his own ship; unfortunately, command brought out that part of his character which would plague him all his life: his vanity, his quickness to quarrel, and his ferocious temper. When he was charged with murdering one of his crewmen in 1773, he decided to skip Britain for Virginia, where he changed his name by adding to it a surname, Jones. The colonies were on the brink of rebellion: it was the perfect opportunity for a daring adventurer and skilled seaman. John Paul Jones won commission as lieutenant on the *Alfred,* the very first ship in the Continental Navy. On November 1, 1777, he took command of the *Ranger,* and with it and later his French-outfitted *Bon Homme Richard* he became America's first naval war hero. His vanity and restless ambition prevented him from playing a more important role in the navy after the war; but his epic sea battles, and his famous maxim, "I have not yet begun to fight," embodied the kind of do-or-die spirit that would eventually enable the struggling revolution to prevail.

A similar spirit overtook the delegates at the Continental Congress that steamy summer of 1776. Witherspoon, as part of the New Jersey delegation, knew the risks that this sort of undertaking involved. Within a year, British troops would invade Princeton. They would ransack Nassau Hall and burn the splendid library that Witherspoon had worked so hard to assemble. But at this point his attention was entirely fixed on the nation's future. "It has been often said," he wrote, "that the present is likely to be an important era to America. I think we may safely say, it is likely to be an important era in the history of mankind." He believed that the Congress had more than just a duty to declare independence; its job was to lay the foundation for the creation of a new nation. "We have the opportunity of forming plans of government upon the most rational, just, and equal principles. I confess," Witherspoon added, "I have always looked upon this with a kind of enthusiastic satisfaction." It was, he believed, something that had never happened before in history. If they failed, it might never happen again.

The Continental Congress included a host of other delegates of Scottish or Ulster Scot extraction: at least nineteen, in fact, out of fifty-six signers of the final Declaration, or fully one-third.* In addition to Witherspoon, there was William Hooper of North Carolina, whose father was a Scottish Congregationalist from Boston. There was Thomas McKean of Delaware, son of a farmer and tavernkeeper from the Scotch-Irish settlement in Chester County, Pennsylvania. The Pennsylvania delegation was full of Scottish descendants, including James Smith; George Taylor, who had come over from northern Ireland as an indentured

---

*Scholar Duncan Bruce insists the number should be twenty-one: he adds Abraham Clark of New Jersey and Lewis Morris of New York to the list originally compiled by genealogist William Scott.

servant; and the native-born Scot James Wilson, who came from Carskerdy and was educated at St. Andrews and (probably) Glasgow—and whom we will meet again shortly.

The influence of Scottish education was also much in evidence, with Witherspoon, Wilson, and Benjamin Rush, who sat as a Pennsylvania delegate, and Thomas Jefferson. While Jefferson never attended any Scottish university, his alma mater at William and Mary College had been recently overhauled on the Scottish model. His closest teacher, William Small, had been a native-born Scot educated at the University of Aberdeen. The most arresting phrases in his draft of the declaration, "we hold these truths to be self-evident" and "the pursuit of happiness," owed their lineage to the Scottish school. In addition, the final copy of the Declaration itself was written by an Ulster Scot (Charles Thomson, secretary to the Continental Congress); it was publicly read aloud to the citizens of Philadelphia by an Ulster Scot, and first printed by yet another Ulster Scot.

In Scotland itself, meanwhile, politicians, ministers, philosophers, merchants, and ordinary people lined up on either side of the conflict. In Parliament, Scots were now a prominent part of the governing establishment, and two sat in Lord North's cabinet as he guided Britain into war. Alexander Wedderburn was serving as Solicitor General, and Robert, Lord Dundas, as Lord Advocate for Scotland, while Lord Mansfield acted as chief spokesman for His Majesty's Government in the House of Lords. On the other side, the flamboyant Lord George Gordon, rabble-rousing orator and anti-Catholic bigot, proudly proclaimed the cause of American independence.

The merchant elites in both Glasgow and Edinburgh stoutly backed the government, and offered to raise volunteer regiments to help put down "those damned rebels." At stake was more than just the loyalty of North Britons. Their material self-interest was also on the line. Merchants worried that American independence would cripple their lucrative transatlantic tobacco business. In fact, the war had brought an embargo on American goods, which rocked the foundations of most of Glasgow's great merchant houses: by 1776 a few were ready to topple. William Cunninghame was an exception. As the American crisis had begun to heat up, Cunninghame had quietly bought up inventories of Virginia and Maryland tobacco from his rivals. When the war came, and the price skyrocketed, he graciously consented to sell the tobacco back to them—at an astronomical profit. It was the proceeds from the deal that enabled him to construct his splendid house on Virginia Street, and to emerge as the most successful—and the most cunning—of all the Tobacco Lords.

The American Revolution also made Scottish Highland regiments the backbone of the British Army. In the course of the fighting, the number of active Highland regiments doubled. Clansmen, prevented since 1745 from possessing weapons of their own, rediscovered their martial livelihood and their traditional costume of kilt and bonnet, serving in units raised by their landlords. Regiments such as Fraser's Highlanders, MacDonald's Highlanders, and the Argyll Highlanders fought in Virginia, New York, and the Carolinas, while others, such as the Atholl Highlanders and Lord Seaforth's, took the places of other British garrisons in Ireland, Gibraltar, and India. MacDonald's 76th Highland Regiment surrendered with other British forces at Yorktown, and according to one of its officers, their captors, who included several Scottish emigrants, urged them to desert. However, the officer noted proudly, "not a single Highlander allowed himself to be seduced by these offers, from the duty which he had engaged to discharge to his King and country."

The revolution splintered the political loyalties of the Scottish Enlightenment. Although William Robertson was convinced that one day "America must in some future period be the seat of the empire," he chose to support the government in London. David Hume, the archetypal North Briton, worried that hanging on to these far-flung imperial possessions would ruin the British government, both financially and morally. His sympathies lay entirely with the colonists. "I am an American in my principles," he told Benjamin Franklin in 1775, "and wish we would let [them] alone to govern or misgovern themselves as they think proper."

Like Hume, Adam Smith saw more at stake in the struggle than just American liberty versus the sovereignty of Parliament. He sensed the stirrings of forces that would eventually tear Britain apart if it failed to deal with them by changing its imperial policies more in the direction of free trade. His own solution was to give the colonies representation in Parliament—something that, given the current balance of forces at Westminster, was impossible. The only other sensible course, then, had to be—let them go. "It is surely time," he wrote in the closing sentence of the *Wealth of Nations,* "that Great Britain should free herself from the expense of defending those provinces in time of war, and of supporting any part of their civil or military establishments in time of peace. . . ." By abandoning a lost cause abroad, Smith argued, Britain would have to confront the realities at home, "the real mediocrity of her circumstances," as he put it, and the stagnant state into which her affairs had fallen.

The allies of Witherspoon in the Evangelical Party were more passionate in their support of the American cause. John Erskine, Witherspoon's friend and colleague, wrote a pamphlet in 1769 titled *Shall I Go to War with My American Brethren?* to which the answer was a resounding *No!* When war broke out, others followed suit, protesting the war and condemning London's hard-line attitude. Their position sprang from more than just solidarity with their Presbyterian counterparts in the colonies. They also worried that the government might turn to England's Roman Catholics for support of its policy by giving them a Catholic Relief Bill, offering an olive branch to Catholics and, by extension, to the papacy in Rome, in exchange for help in suppressing the revolt in America. This rather farfetched fear touched not only Scots, but Englishmen as well. In 1780 it triggered the most violent riots London had ever seen. Egged on by the unbalanced but charismatic Lord Gordon, the mob burned Catholic churches and then ransacked the house of Chief Justice Mansfield, attacked the Bank of England, and opened up the Fleet and King's Bench prisons. The riots took ten thousand soldiers to suppress. Two hundred and eighty-five persons died and another twenty-five were hanged.

It was a particularly low point for Britain, and for North Britons in particular. Had Hume lived to see it, it would have confirmed his sense that the country had entered a period of dangerous decadence, and that certain drastic steps were needed if the United Kingdom was to save itself and avoid dissolving into bankruptcy, chaos, and even revolution. Meanwhile, Britain was embroiled in an unpopular war not only with the thirteen colonies, but also with France, Spain, and Holland. Had Hume lived even longer, he might have appreciated the irony of seeing Britain's ancient French foe going through the very revolution he most feared—because of the debts they had run up helping the Americans.

IV

Scottish Americans, of course, did not win the American Revolution. It was the alliance with France that did that, and which finally guaranteed British consent to American independence at the Treaty of Paris in 1783. But just as Scots and their Scotch-Irish cousins supplied some of the crucial muscle and inspiration for the American cause, so they played an equally important role in creating the new nation afterwards. Indeed, two additional Scots decisively shaped its character, even though neither ever set foot on American soil.

John Witherspoon had started things moving when the Continental Congress was drafting the first attempt to create a national union, in the Articles of Confederation. There he spoke to the issue that was becoming increasingly important to him, America's place in the future of the world. "I do expect," he said to the assembled delegates, "a progress, as in every other human art, so in the order and perfection of human society." Why, he asked, should the Congress fail in propelling it forward? "It is not impossible," he said, "that in future times all the states in one quarter of the globe may see it proper by some plan of union to perpetuate security and peace." Let America, Witherspoon urged the delegates, be the model for such a European union and "hand down the blessings of peace and public order to many generations."

But the Articles of Confederation proved an abysmal disappointment. Too weak at the center, too fragmented in its granting of powers to the individual states, the American republic seemed doomed to fail. Pessimists such as John Adams even wondered whether the American experiment in self-government would fail with it.

To prevent this, delegates assembled in Philadelphia once again in the late spring of 1787, to draw up a new plan of union. Although Witherspoon did not attend, the Constitutional Convention did offer an indirect tribute to his efforts as America's foremost educator. Of twenty-five college graduates at the convention, nine were Princeton graduates, while only four were Harvard graduates, and even fewer were from Yale. The two plans put before the delegates for a new constitution were both authored by Princeton men. William Paterson, the son of an Ulster Scot tinsmith, attended Princeton shortly be-fore Witherspoon arrived, but had been instrumental in getting him there. He produced the so-called New Jersey Plan, which strongly supported the rights of the small states against the large, such as New York, Virginia, and Massachusetts.

The alternative plan, the one that was, with some modification, eventually adopted as the blueprint for the American Constitution, was authored by one of Witherspoon's closest disciples, James Madison. He came from one of central Virginia's wealthiest families, and was part of the state's Episcopalian squirearchy, which was disdainful of religious enthusiasts of the Great Awakening, and proud of its links to England. Yet he had gone to Princeton, where he became deeply attached to President Witherspoon, and even delayed graduation in order to continue special work with him. This included tutoring in Hebrew, and exposure to the most advanced of the Scottish thinkers, from Hutcheson and Kames to Adam Smith and David Hume.

It was above all to Hume, Witherspoon's avowed nemesis, that Madison found himself drawn. Detached, ironic, charming but devastating when engaged in intellectual debate, always interesting and frequently outrageous: Hume represented a new kind of intellectual persona that Madison admired and cultivated, both as a thinker and as a public figure. He also embraced the basic premises of all Scottish social science: that human beings act the same when they find themselves in similar circumstances, and that uniform human causes produce uniform effects. It enabled him to zero in on the question that had stumped not only speculators on the makeup of a future American republic, but also the grand classical tradition of political analysis running from Aristotle to the universally admired—even Kames and Smith quoted him—French philosopher Montesquieu.

How can a self-governing republic rule over a vast expanse of territory, which a future United States of America must inevitably do, without becoming an empire, and therefore acquisitive and corrupt? There seemed to be no clear answer. Montesquieu had summed up an entire body of thought in his *Spirit of the Laws*, published in 1748, which postulated that only a small community, composed of persons who all knew one another or nearly so, could perpetuate true liberty. A large continental republic was doomed. Geographic distance and conflicting interests, arising from differences in social development, bred civil conflict; the only solution would be tyranny, the rule of the strong in order to maintain order. Rome had succumbed to this ironclad rule, the experts said. If the former American colonies, stretching from Maine to Florida and pressing beyond the Appalachians to the Mississippi, tried to create a strong national government, they would succumb, too.

Madison thought otherwise. His rejection of accepted wisdom rested on his reading of a little-known text by David Hume published as part of his *Essays, Moral, Political, and Literary*, titled, "The Idea of a Perfect Commonwealth." In it, Hume broke with Montesquieu and proposed that a large or "extended" republic, for all its its geographic and socioeconomic diversity, might turn out to be the most stable of all. "In a large government which is modeled with masterly skill," Hume declared, "there is compass and room enough to refine the democracy." The masses find a place for themselves in the first level of elections and selection of magistrates. "Although the people as a body are unfit for government," he wrote, "yet when dispersed in small bodies"—such as individual colonies or states—"they are more susceptible both to reason and order; the force of popular currents and tides is, in great measure, broken." Meanwhile, the elite spend their time coordinating the movements of the various parts of the whole, rather than plotting its overthrow. "At the same time," Hume observed, "the parts are so distant and remote, that it is very difficult, either by intrigue, prejudice, or passion, to hurry them into any measures against the public interest."

As Douglass Adair has suggested, Hume's words must have struck

Madison like a hammer blow. He incorporated them into his plan for the new American constitution in his "Notes on the Confederacy," published in April 1787, just eight months before he wrote his essay defending the Constitution as part of the *Federalist Papers*. In it (the tenth *Federalist*) Madison laid bare the heart of the new American system. The theme was not unity, but countervailing interests; in contemporary terms, gridlock. Federal versus state power, executive versus legislative, and judicial versus them both: add the disparate economic interests of bankers versus farmers, slaveholding southerners versus commercial-minded northerners, and thirteen semisovereign political units, plus indirect elections at the senatorial and presidential level to frustrate the raw, crude will of the people—and what you have is not chaos, as the critics might expect, but stability, and above all liberty.

Gridlock at the public level guarantees liberty at the private level: this was the dirty little secret Madison dared to unveil in the *Federalist Papers*. If scholars sometimes joke that David Hume is the "real" author of the Tenth *Federalist,* it is not just because it lays out Hume's vision of an extended republic managing to govern itself into perpetuity. It is also because it co-opts Hume's skeptical, cynical understanding of human motives into an American context. Madison states, "if men were angels, there would be no need of government"—a thoroughly Hume-like aphorism—and in the eternal struggle between liberty and authority in a modern society, the only way to preserve the one is to perpetually hobble the other.

The two other key figures in the making of the new constitution were both of Scottish extraction, and, like Madison, steeped in the ideas of the Scottish Enlightenment. Alexander Hamilton was the son of a West Indies Scottish merchant, and prominent in New York political circles. He enthusiastically endorsed Madison's federal plan, and helped author the *Federalist Papers*. Hamilton even signed the Constitution in defiance of the wishes of his own state of New York. But his vision of a strong nationalist government probably owed less to Hume than to Adam Smith's mercantilist nemesis, James Steuart (although he knew the *Wealth of Nations* almost chapter and verse).

The other was a native-born Scot, the lawyer James Wilson. Born in

Carskerdy, he attended St. Andrews and sat in on classes at the University of Glasgow before emigrating to Philadelphia. He found work as a tutor at the College of Philadelphia (later the University of Pennsylvania), which was, like Princeton, Scottish-dominated, before training for the bar and becoming a wealthy attorney in Carlisle, Pennsylvania, arranging land deals for his Ulster Scots clientele. His neat, tight-lipped, bespectacled figure became a familiar sight on the floor of the Constitutional Convention, where he spoke at virtually every session—more than anyone else, in fact, including Madison. It was Wilson who reconciled Madison's plan for a strong national government with his opponent's desire to preserve popular sovereignty, and it was Wilson who thrust into the midst of the debate the ideas of the man most associated with that third great center of Scottish Enlightenment, Aberdeen: the philosopher Thomas Reid.

Aberdeen sits on the Highlands' east coast, comfortably nestled along a bay opening onto the North Sea. It was an active trading port; surrounded by fertile farmland, it became a thriving city with two distinguished educational institutions, King's College, founded in 1495, and Marischal College. Thomas Reid was born only twenty miles from Aberdeen in 1710. The son of a minister, he entered Marischal at the age of twelve—not too precocious by Scottish standards—and took his degree in theology. Reid was what contemporaries identified as a Moderate, and owed his first post with the church in New-Machar to aristocratic patronage rather than election by the congregation— indeed, when he showed up, there was a riot and troops had to be called in. Eventually, however, his congregation came to like his sincere piety and straightforward manner, as well as his hardheaded, flinty intelligence. It was while serving as minister at New-Machar that Reid read the book that would change his life: David Hume's *A Treatise of Human Nature.*

At first he was puzzled, then shocked—and then finally outraged by what he found. It was not just Hume's religious skepticism, or his provocative assertion that morality was largely a matter of convention rather than conviction. What infuriated Reid most was the suggestion that seemed to permeate the entire book, that our world is not really as it seems: that our perception of the world, and the conclusions we draw from it, including our notions of right and wrong, are uncertain at best. That is why human beings come to rely on habit and accepted convention, Hume concluded, as well as the occasional insights of philosophers. They need these things to guide humanity through a reality that is itself ultimately unknowable. It is the sort of cautious, skeptical view summarized a century later by Benjamin Disraeli: "Few ideas are correct ones, and which they are none can tell, but with words we govern men."

Reid considered this pretentious nonsense. The world was not a mysterious maze, Reid protested. It was an open and well-lit vista, rich with material for making clear judgments about up and down, black and white, and right and wrong. "Settled truth," he wrote, "can be attained by observation." Reality is not one step removed from us by our own limitations, but knowable and graspable by our own experience. All it took was ears to listen and eyes to see. "The evidence of sense, the evidence of memory, and the evidence of the necessary relations of things, are all distinct. . . . To reason against any of these kinds of evidence is absurd. . . . They are first principles, and as such fall not within the province of reason, but of common sense."

That last term stuck. When Reid left New-Machar to become a "regent" or teacher at King's College in Aberdeen in 1751, he became the central figure in a school of philosophy with which Aberdeen would be forever associated, the philosophy of common sense. Reid, James Beattie (his colleague at Marischal College), and Edinburgh's William Hamilton (who edited Reid's works after his death) all argued that all human beings came equipped with an innate rational capacity called common sense, which allowed them to make clear and certain judgments about the world, and their dealings with it. Common sense tells us that the world consists of real objects that exist in time and space. Common sense tells us that we can understand and navigate our way through that reality, and common sense tells us that the more we know about that outside world, the better we can act on it, both as individuals and as members of a community.

Knowledge is power—all Scottish philosophers recognized this—and the route to knowledge is through experience. But Reid insisted that that power belonged to every man, regardless of any other attributes. Human progress rests on expanding that capacity to its utmost and to as many people as possible, so that we can all become truly, morally free. It may not be going too far to call Reid's philosophy a science of human freedom, and it is not difficult to see why it had such appeal to Americans, both of the revolutionary generation and later. It democratized the intellect, by insisting that the ordinary man could be as certain of his judgments as the philosopher was. Of course, ordinary men can make mistakes—and so do philosophers. And sometimes they cannot prove what they believe to be true—but then philosophers often have the same problem. But on some fundamental things, such as the existence of the real world and certain basic moral truths, they know that they do not have to offer any proof. These things are, as Reid put it, "self-evident," meaning that they are "no sooner understood than they are believed," because they "carry the light of truth in itself."

Reid's full-bodied attack on skeptics and moral relativists won him plaudits in Scotland—in 1764 he took over the chair of Moral Philosophy at the University of Glasgow which had once belonged to Francis Hutcheson and then Adam Smith—and in Europe. In America, however, his impact was huge. Thomas Jefferson knew his writings, and put Reid's best-known work on his recommended book list. It was very probably from Reid that he borrowed the idea of "self-evident truths" for the Declaration of Independence. He also put Reid at the center of his planned curriculum for the University of Virginia (Hume was very carefully left out).

John Witherspoon was certainly familiar with Reid's commonsense philosophy. So was Benjamin Rush: he told his friend Tom Paine to use Reid's key catchphrase as the title of his treatise on the necessity of American independence. It would go on to become the single most popular pamphlet of the American Revolution, with Reid's motto emblazoned across the top: *Common Sense*. Reid's ideas shaped American theories of education for the next hundred years. It helped to produce a cultural type that some consider typically American, but which is just as much Scottish: an independent intellect combined with an assertive self-respect, and grounded by a strong sense of moral purpose.

But it took the brittle, mercurial James Wilson to make Reid part of the grammar of American governance. Both at the Constitutional Convention and afterward, Wilson revealed how a philosophy of common sense could smoothe over the problems arising from Madison's federalist blueprint, and how it also offered the best way to view the Constitution's most startling and also most puzzling innovation: the creation of a United States Supreme Court.

On the one hand, the Supreme Court embodied a basic principle everyone could agree on, that self-government could only function under the rule of law, with an independent judiciary interpreting its key provisions. On the other, the possibility that such a court could, under the banner of "judicial review," overturn duly approved legislative acts raised the hackles of those who saw Congress as enactors of "the will of the people," an equally important principle. Wilson showed his colleagues, however, that they were wrong to worry about such a conflict. The purpose of a Supreme Court was not to "disparage the legislative authority" or to "confer upon the judicial department a power superior, in its general nature." Instead, it added a power to the federal government that it would desperately need, the power of reflection, in order to decide whether a particular law fit within the frame of the Constitution. Judicial review would act not in defiance of the will of the people, but in addition to it, since judges would sit not as a body of legal experts but as a body of citizens. In Wilson's mind, the Supreme Court would be one of the United States' most democratic institutions; it would be, in Wilson's words, "the jury of the country."

The comparison was telling. Wilson saw being a "judge" as more than just a professional or legal designation. He used it in Reid's sense: a judge is someone who makes judgments about the world, in matters of fact, of right and wrong, and of truth and falsehood. Wilson's idea also reflected the role of the judge in Scottish law, whose job in court was not just to be a legal referee, but to find out what happened. From Wilson's point of view, there was no essential difference between judge and jury (in Scotland, panels of judges did act in the place of juries). Both did the same thing in a trial or hearing: ask questions, weigh the facts presented, and then render a verdict, a judgment. The first relies rather more on his knowledge of the law, in order to make judgments. The second, in turn, has to rely on its most important resource: common sense. A Supreme Court for the nation would combine both. Its primary obligation would not be to the law, however, but to the community as a whole. As Wilson put it, "a judge is the blessing, or he is the curse of society." It depended on whether he chose to use his common sense in deciding cases, or whether he chose his own professional vanity and ambition.

Wilson had hoped to be the Supreme Court's first chief justice. That post went to John Jay instead. But Wilson did become an associate justice, and although his years on the bench were mired in controversy, he tried to use his approach to the law to create a distinctly American brand of jurisprudence. He lived by Reid's maxim, "I despise philosophy and renounce its guidance; let my soul dwell in common sense." He always insisted that decisions be written in clear and straightforward language, avoiding any legal or technical jargon, so that any citizen could read and understand them (Wilson's insistence on this point impressed another Supreme Court judge who applied the same principle when he became chief justice, namely John Marshall). In Wilson's mind, this was part of a judge's responsibility to the principle of self-government, and part of the public's education in the rule of law: because, as Wilson observed, the entire basis of the rule of law in a democratic society was "the consent of those whose obedience the law requires." The better ordinary people understood the law, the better for the law, and the better for democracy.

This Wilson had also learned from Reid: that ordinary men could understand the law, because they were by nature equipped to do so. He endorsed Reid's view that the common man was "a man of integrity" who "sees his duty without reasoning, as he sees the highway." It led Wilson to trust people to do the right thing, particularly the American people (although he was no populist, and was very conservative on matters such as extending the franchise). The jury system was his model, not just for how the law works in a free society, but for how democracy works, as well. Its fundamental building block was man as knower, and as judger; a person who trusts his own senses, his grasp of the facts, and his grasp of right and wrong. A person who can recognize when he has the solution to a problem, or someone else does, and who goes along with what the majority finally decides.

Such a person—Common Sense Man, we can call him—was a necessary adjunct to the federal system Hume had inspired and Madison had created. Reid had been Hume's great foe. Yet here, in America, Reid now rode in to his rescue. The only way such a complicated architecture of counterbalancing powers and "countervailing interests" could avoid permanent gridlock, and getting stuck in the same rut, would be if the people who made it up were able to agree on certain fundamental truths, "self-evident truths," as Reid would say. In that way, they could trust their own judgment and that of others to arrive at a compromise solution to the crises that would inevitably arise.

Reid once defined common sense as "that degree of judgment which is common to men with whom we can converse and transact business." Where no one was clearly in charge, common sense would have to reign. It was the moral of modern democracy, as the exponents of the Scottish school had conceived it, and as Scots in America, at least, had brought it into being.

CHAPTER TEN

Light from the North:
Scots, Liberals, and Reform

I

T he cantakerous grandfather of the Scottish school, Lord Kames, died in 1782, at age eighty-six. His protégé, David Hume, had preceded him in death by six years. Adam Smith followed in 1790. Two years later Robert Adam died, and William Robertson a year after that. Boswell passed on in 1795, and Thomas Reid in 1796.

The front rank of the Scottish Enlightenment was gone. But over the next three decades their impact became decisive, as their works, students, and disciples spread their message far beyond Scotland. Edinburgh, now decked out in gleaming neoclassical splendor, came to stand for a type of modern intellectual culture that the rest of Europe understood to be quintessentially Scottish.

Inquisitive, penetrating, unsentimental; impatient with pious dogmas or cant; relentlessly thorough, sometimes to the point of pedantry; rational, but buoyed by a tough-minded sense of humor and a grasp of the practical. We see these qualities reflected in the portraits by Sir Henry Raeburn of the leading Scottish minds of the age: dressed in black coats with elegant white cravats, their strong, clean-shaven faces and clear features projecting an air of imperturbable self-confidence that their predecessors, for all their accomplishments, never knew. And no wonder. Having helped to create one new nation—America—Scots now set about saving another—their own.

Since 1780, Britain had entered a period of crisis. It had lost the war to prevent American independence, and had taken a beating at the hands of the French and Spanish. Its politics were stuck in permanent factionalism and gridlock. A sense of malaise had settled over its ruling class, while popular unrest, encouraged by the French Revolution, spread across the provinces. In 1797 mutiny broke out in the British navy; Ireland was on the brink of revolt; the Bank of England, symbol of the nation's stability, had to suspend cash payments.

For nearly a hundred years the main cultural current in Britain had flowed from south to north. Now it reversed itself. Out of Scotland came thinkers, politicians, inventors, and writers who would restore Britain's self-confidence, and equip it with the tools to confront modernity on its own terms. They remade its politics. They galvanized its intellectual and educational institutions; they gave it a new self-image and a new sense of its place in history. They also redid its infrastructure and refitted its empire. The "Scottish invasion" of the first three decades of the nineteenth century prepared the way for the great triumphs of the Victorian age.

The keynote of the new Britain was self-confidence: confidence in its own powers, confidence in its future, confidence in its relationship with the past. Edinburgh epitomized this energy and optimism. It had grown up from a provincial town of just 50,000 persons as late as 1760 to an internationally recognized capital of nearly 100,000 by the turn of the century. It had burst its old boundaries. New buildings swarmed over the new South Bridge to the south, and residential terraces and graceful curved streets or "crescents" appeared to the north and west of Robert Adam's Charlotte Square.

The Adam style had given birth to a permanent Greek Revival, with an army of offshoots and imitators. One, Robert Reid, completed Charlotte Square with his West Register House and gave Parliament House a new, harmonious neoclassical façade. Another, William Playfair, turned Calton Hill overlooking the New Town into an Acropolis of elegant porticoed buildings and monuments. More than any other architect, Playfair gave Edinburgh the look to match its sobriquet of the "Athens of the North."

The University of Edinburgh had also outgrown its bounds and desperately needed a new home. On November 2, 1789, Principal William Robertson opened a public subscription to construct new buildings suitable "to the flourishing state of that seminary of learning," which now educated "not only a great part of the Youth of Scotland, but many students from different places in the British Dominions, as well as Foreign Countries." Robert Adam supplied the overall plan; it included a double pavilion of buildings, and a central tier with a dome and a massive, columned portico. Adam died before much of it had been built. Then events abroad, with the coming of the French Revolution and war with France, stopped construction completely. Almost thirty years would pass before William Playfair finished what Adam had started. But the new university, like its original design, expressed a sense of civic pride in Edinburgh's rise as a center of learning, both for Britain and Europe.

It offered an honor roll of distinguished teachers. William Cullen, professor of medicine, friend to Adam Smith, and mentor to the American Benjamin Rush, had died in 1790. But there was still Joseph Black, discoverer of carbon dioxide and professor of chemistry, and John Playfair, the architect's father and a brilliant mathematician. Above all, there was Dugald Stewart, who had replaced Adam Ferguson in the chair of moral philosophy in 1785. For the next quarter-century he would influence the mind of Europe and the English-speaking world to a degree no Scotsman ever equaled, before or since.

He was born and bred to the academic life. His father succeeded Colin Maclaurin in the University of Edinburgh's chair in mathematics. Young Dugald attended both Edinburgh and Glasgow, and was versatile enough to substitute for his father as math professor, as well as for Adam Ferguson in moral philosophy. When Ferguson retired and Stewart took his place at age thirty-two, he brought with him a depth and breadth of learning probably unmatched by anyone else teaching at a British university. As one student recalled him: "He was of middle size, his forehead was large and bald, his eyebrows bushy, his eyes grey and intelligent, and capable of conveying any emotion, from serene sense to hearty humor. . . ." Mathematics, natural science, jurisprudence, history, political economy, ethics, the philosophy of mind—these were the fields over which Stewart ranged at will and which he opened up to successive generations of devoted students. He was the *Encyclopaedia*

Britannica in the flesh (almost literally, since he wrote the preface for the famous third edition, published after his death, in 1822).

Dugald Stewart served as the intellectual bridge between the Scottish Enlightenment and the Victorian age. The jurist Henry Cockburn remembered, "To me, Stewart's lectures were like the opening of the heavens. I felt I had a soul." His pupils included no less than two future prime ministers, Lord Palmerston and Lord John Russell. (The latter's English father told him "there was nothing to be learned at English universities," and sent him to Edinburgh instead.) They also numbered a future First Lord of the Admiralty (Lord Minto), a future Lord Chancellor (Henry Brougham), members of Parliament by the handful, and a cluster of leading philosophers. Through Dugald Stewart, "the Scottish philosophy" touched nearly every aspect of public life in Britain, for Stewart was not just a revered teacher; he was also a great synthesizer and organizer, who put the disparate works of the Scottish school together as a system, the foundation for what we call classical liberalism.

For example, it was Stewart who put Adam Smith on the intellectual map. Prior to Stewart's lectures on him in 1798, most Edinburgh people knew little about Smith except, as Cockburn (who attended that first class) noted, "that he had recently been a Commissioner of Customs, and had written a sensible book." Stewart's lectures turned *Wealth of Nations* into the fountainhead of all economic theory, and made the book virtually Holy Scripture to generations of Edinburgh-educated thinkers, economists, and politicians—who in turn spread its influence to Oxford, Cambridge, London, and the rest of the English-speaking world.

Stewart merged Smith's moral realism with the commonsense philosophy of Thomas Reid, who had been his own teacher at Glasgow. Stewart became Reid's great champion at Edinburgh, almost his alter ego. He gave Reid an air of sophistication, smoothing out his more robust edges and making him attractive to the liberal English temper, just as he did with Smith. In fact, Stewart proved to have more success with English readers than any Scot before him, offering up a smooth synthesis of the Scottish school in a prose "as pleasing and as regular as their own rich fields bounded by hedgerows."

For example, Stewart downplayed the "common" aspect of the commonsense philosophy, and implied it should really be read as "good sense"—in other words, that our commonsense judgments reflect "that prudence and discretion which are the foundation of successful conduct." While the foundations of truth were still equally available to all human beings, it was also clear that, in that respect, some are more equal than others. A trained political economist such as Adam Smith, Stewart would argue, will have more insight into the laws of human behavior, and be better able to predict how a certain fiscal policy will compel people to act, than the people themselves. Likewise, an experimental scientist such as Joseph Black will be able to offer a more comprehensive and more precise account of our daily reality than our own untrained and unscientific understanding.

Indeed, for Stewart, *science* became a powerful, even loaded, word. It represented the operations of the human mind at its highest pitch and turned our common experience of the world into a window on truth itself. The advance of science marked an aspect of human progress as important as civilization itself, Stewart believed; in fact, for him, it virtually defined progress. And although the other aspects of life—art, literature, ethics, politics, and political economy—remained important, Dugald Stewart wanted every student of human nature to strive for the same level of exactitude and precision as the chemist, the physicist, or the biologist.

Of course, other Scottish thinkers had talked about politics as an exact science—David Hume had even written an essay on it. But they had looked for a scientific model as a way to *understand* politics and human conduct. Stewart was looking for a scientific way to *organize* it, and perhaps even create something new and better. He taught his students, including future prime ministers, to see the legislator in almost the same position as the experimental scientist or the inventor: applying mind and method to matter, in order to facilitate human happiness. Stewart was no utopian; this was not a blueprint for building a new society from scratch. Rather, he saw "the science of legislation" in Adam Smith's terms, removing the obstacles that hinder the natural progress of commercial society and its social order. But he did introduce a new notion to the Scottish school. Political progress could take place in the same way it took place in mathematics or chemistry: by exhaustive investigation and research, by developing a clear theory that explained the facts, and then applying it.

Stewart conceded that a true "political science" might not have been possible in the past. But now, in modern Britain, it was. This was Stewart's other major point. Commercial society was not just more civilized or more productive or more rational than its predecessors; it was qualitatively different from every society that had preceded it. It broke the mold, in a profound sense, of the four-stage theory of civilization. A new dividing line now appeared in history: between the "modern" and the "premodern," meaning all those efforts at organizing the human community over thousands of years, which had all had their moments of glory and then had come to grief. Something new, great, and permanent was here—the modern world—and the possibilities were limitless.

This buoyant sense of optimism is partly what drew Dugald Stewart to the French Revolution. Stewart was in Paris that fateful summer of 1789, and it was with great excitement that he watched the dramatic events unfolding: the formation of the National Assembly, the storming of the Bastille, the Declaration of the Rights of Man and Citizen. A new constitutional order was being born, he believed, based on justice, law, and natural right. He was repelled when the great spokesman of the old Whig Party, Edmund Burke, wrote his *Reflections on the Revolution in France,* forecasting doom, death, and dictatorship. Stewart's student, James Mackintosh, wrote an impassioned reply vindicating the French revolutionary cause. Even the occasional outbreaks of mob violence did not deter Stewart. He wrote to a friend in late November 1791, "The little disorders which may now and then occur in a country, where things in general are in so good a train, are of very inconsiderable importance."

Then, over the next year, it turned out Burke had been right all along. Edmund Burke, Irishman and Episcopalian, was a strange figure in relation to the Scottish school. He knew many of its members; they heavily influenced his own view of history. But he had rejected their most characteristic conclusion, that the great driving force in the progress of civilization was economic change. Burke insisted it was the other way around: it was the elaborate network of civilized "manners," meaning morality, law, and tradition grown up over generations, that made a system of commercial exchange based on trust possible, and hence human progress possible. He wrote, "Even commerce, and trade, and manufacture, the gods of our oeconomical politicians, are themselves perhaps but creatures" of a higher moral order embedded in the fabric of society. Strip that away, he warned, and the entire edifice would come crashing down.

A far cry from Dugald Stewart's liberal optimism. In the event, Burke's dire predictions were borne out in almost every detail—including, after his death in 1797, his strong conviction that the revolution must inevitably give way to a military dictator such as Napoleon. It gave Edmund Burke a posthumous reputation for prescience and sagacity that no other British political thinker could challenge. Certainly Stewart looked rather foolish; he was virtually ostracized by Edinburgh society. James Mackintosh publicly apologized for having challenged Burke, and turned into a stalwart critic of the French regime, and of revolutions in general.

But in Stewart's mind the issue of political progress persisted. He spent the next ten years making the lecture hall ring with his original conviction. A modern society deserved a modern political system, based on liberty, property, and the rule of law. If the French experiment had failed because it had gone too far, that did not mean that something less sweeping and more measured was not possible for Britain—and particularly for Scotland.

Although everyone could now acknowledge that the union with England had been a blessing, it was also clear that the new society that had taken shape in Scotland had outgrown the tight constrictions first imposed in 1707, and then reconfirmed after 1745. Thanks to a rigidly high property qualification, barely one man in twenty had the vote. Economic growth had created an affluent middle class in Glasgow and

Edinburgh and Aberdeen that had no voice in how their affairs were governed. "There was no class of the community," wrote Henry Cockburn years later, "so little thought of at this time as the mercantile. . . . They had no direct political power; no votes; and were far too subservient to be feared." Instead, political power resided with the lairds and landowners, and with the government's longtime representative on Scottish affairs, Henry Dundas, or Lord Melville. Cockburn described him, with understandable exaggeration, as "the absolute dictator of Scotland," who "had the means of rewarding submission and of suppressing opposition beyond what were ever exercised in modern times by one person in any portion of the empire."

Dundas, or "King Harry the Ninth" as he was known, did control a vast network of patronage and appointments, and nearly half of Scotland's seats in Parliament. In good times his political machine had kept Scotland on an even keel. In bad times it provoked hostility and frustration. And the 1790s were bad times, not just in Scotland but across England as well. Glasgow weavers had struck in 1787 against rising food prices; harvests failed in 1792 and then again in 1795 and 1796, as the specter of starvation spread across the land (it was, in fact, the backdrop for the first serious wave of Highland clearances). In July 1792, at Fortune's Tavern in Edinburgh, a group of citizens calling themselves the Scottish Association of the Friends of the People launched a National Convention for a Britain-wide program of reform.

In England, the coming of war with France in 1793 led to a massive crackdown on every suspected "subversive" or "Jacobin" individual or group the government could get its hands on. For twenty years radicals had demanded extension of the franchise, and a voice for ordinary men in Westminster. Now, with the French crisis and the Scottish National Convention as an excuse, they faced savage retribution. Several went on trial for their lives; those in England were acquitted, but Prime Minister William Pitt suspended habeas corpus.

The bad harvests compounded the crisis. Magistrates in Berkshire organized a system of "outdoor relief" or welfare payments for the destitute based on the price of bread, and in October 1795 London broke into violent demonstrations against the opening of Parliament and against the King, Pitt, and the war against France. Two years later things had become so bad, with more suspensions of habeas corpus, a mutiny at the naval base at Spithead, and legislation banning gatherings of more than fifty persons, that opposition Whigs walked out of Parliament in protest.

It was during this crisis that Dugald Stewart introduced his first course on political economy. He was determined to chart a new direction for Britain, just as a coterie of his former students—Francis Horner, Francis Jeffrey, Henry Cockburn, Henry Brougham, and a transplanted Englishman, Sydney Smith—were determined to turn the Whig Party from political pariahs and has-beens into standard-bearers for change.

The group was a volatile mix of youthful spirits, powerful intellects, and burgeoning egos. What drew them together was their commitment to Stewart's vision of political progress. Smith was a minister, a gifted writer, and a genuine wit. Horner, "grave, studious, honourable, kind," was studying to be a lawyer, since Edinburgh was a lawyer's town, although he had tremendous gifts as a mathematician (at twenty he translated Euler's standard work on algebra into English and composed a short biography of the German mathematician, both of which were published) and scientist. Horner regularly rose two hours before breakfast to do his chemical experiments, and spent his time away from the law books at lectures on anatomy and physiology.

Francis Jeffrey was also a lawyer, and, although not yet thirty, one of Scotland's best. The house he bought at Craigcrook, three miles from Edinburgh, was the hub of its robust intellectual society. It still stands, a crenellated Renaissance castle remodeled by Jeffrey's friend William Playfair, where at three o'clock every afternoon writers, artists, painters, lawyers, and university faculty would gather for dinner. At Jeffrey's table, "the talk [was] always good, but never ambitious, and those listening never in disrepute." In fact, Edinburgh's social pace was as relentless as ever, a habit left over from the days when everyone lived next door to one another in the Old Town. Long afterwards, Henry Cockburn calculated that in the first thirty years of his marriage, he and his wife never spent more than one night a month at home alone. Friends, men and women, met night after night at dinner and supper parties, with sumptuous supplies of food, drink, and intellectual discussion.

"It was," Cockburn admitted, "a discussing age." None of the great intellectual breakthroughs of those years would have been possible without the incessant give-and-take of after-dinner table talk, with flashing wits, sharp ripostes, bursting laughter, glittering candles, and glowing, ruby-red glasses of sherry and port. As in old Edinburgh, drink opened the doors for free intellectual exchange. The demands of patriotism and a war against France replaced claret with sherry and port (making John Home's earlier dire prediction come true*), and among the lesser orders, whisky was making a steady progress. This was the final unexpected consequence of Union; the massive increase of taxes on all alcoholic beverages meant that illegal distilling was the only alternative. In 1708, only 50,000 gallons of whisky were produced in all of Scotland; by 1783 the Highlands alone were putting out nearly 700,000, and the Lowlands more than a million. Robert Burns worked briefly in that loneliest of all jobs, whisky excise agent. He gained his keen appreciation of the Scottish countryside while scanning the hills and crags for that telltale smudge of smoke on the horizon, marking an illegal still.

The *Scots Magazine* in those years noted that Scotland is "the most drunken nation on the face of the earth"—worse even, it confessed shamefacedly, than the Irish. The dinner parties of the smart and respectable flowed with alcohol. Courtesy demanded that after dinner the host offer a toast to each guest in turn, with a respectful nod and flourish of the hand, intoning "your health" or some suitable sentiment with each glass. Then each guest did the same thing, first to the host then each of the other guests. This meant, as Henry Cockburn noted, that "when there were ten people, there were ninety healths drunk." Henry Brougham remembered being one of a group drunkenly roaming the streets afterwards, wrenching brass knockers off doors and stealing street signs before the Edinburgh night watch could catch them.

---

*See chapter 8.

At one party at Craigcrook, a visiting Englishman (the English were not exactly famous for their sobriety) watched with astonishment as, after innumerable healths and toasts, one of Jeffrey's guests, an eminent fellow lawyer, "put his wineglass in his pocket and saying, 'We have sat long enough' threw up the window and leapt through it to the grass plot and, being followed by the rest, they drank champagne and played at leap-frog."

Yet on intellectual matters, and especially politics, these hardy carousers were deadly serious. It was at one of these soirées that Sydney Smith casually suggested to Jeffrey reviving the old *Edinburgh Review,* which had gone defunct in 1757. The idea caught fire: here was a chance to turn a rather routine literary chore, reviewing books, into a powerful vehicle for enlightened liberal opinion, not just on politics but on a whole range of topics, including literature, philosophy, and science. Smith, Jeffrey, and Horner took on the job of writing the essays and reviews for the first issue, to appear that following June of 1802; but the first issue of the new *Edinburgh Review* did not actually appear until October. The reason was that another person had pushed his way onto the project, someone they did not entirely trust, but whom they realized they could not do without: Henry Brougham.

Brougham was the youngest of the group, only twenty-four, but he was in some ways already the most intellectually accomplished. He was an Edinburgh man by birth; his mother was a niece of William Robertson.* He represented Dugald Stewart's intellectual ideal more than any other of Stewart's students. Horner called him "an uncommon genius, of a composite order," determined to master every branch of human knowledge; with a mind that could bring mathematical precision to each, and a gift for brilliant prose as well. Like the rest, he was trained as a lawyer. But he also read papers on mathematics to the Royal Society in London (the youngest man ever to do so), founded the Edinburgh Society of Physics in 1796, and then, together with Horner, the Edinburgh Chemical Society. When he joined the Edinburgh

---

*This related him to two earlier interesting figures: Robert Adam and Patrick Henry.

Review, he was finishing a two-volume masterwork on colonial policy, which James Mackintosh pronounced the most enlightened work on how to run the British Empire since the *Wealth of Nations*. Like the rest of the group, he knew all the classical authors and major figures in English literature, almost by heart. He was also a devoted Whig.

Jeffrey and Smith realized Brougham would give enormous assets to the new review, and he was certainly eager to join. The problem was his personality. Overbearing, vain, sarcastic, temperamental, at times almost emotionally unstable: with his dark, piercing eyes, long, pointed nose, and rapid-fire delivery in a slight but unmistakable Scottish burr, Brougham was a dangerous man to cross, at a dinner party, in a courtroom, or in the pages of a literary journal. He was, in short, insufferable; but he could not be denied. He wrote nearly one hundred pages of prose for the *Review*'s opening issue, with six different articles: three on "Travel," one on the sugar colonies, one on optics, and one on geology. Thereafter, although Jeffrey served as principal editor, it was Brougham more than anyone else who gave the *Edinburgh Review* its characteristic tone—and its controversial success.

The impact of that first issue was, as Henry Cockburn described it, "electrical. And instead of expiring as many had wished, in their first effort, the force of the shock was increased in each subsequent discharge." Everyone in Scotland and England recognized that the *Edinburgh Review* represented "an entire and instant change of everything that the public had been accustomed to in that sort of composition." It was the first literary journal to appeal to a broad but educated and serious reading public, not just scholars and literati, but informed citizens, lawyers, doctors, government officials, and, of course, politicians. Its goal was not simply to entertain, or even to educate; it sought to keep readers up to date on the latest state of progress in every important field of human endeavor, and addressed its readers as partners in a single great undertaking, the progress of modern society.

The editors also realized an important secret in publishing, that information is made more memorable when it is tinged with bias. The *Edinburgh Review*'s motto was, "The judge is condemned when the guilty is acquitted." The magazine became famous for its likes and dislikes, although "hatreds" might be a better word—in politics, of course, as the unashamed voice of reform Whigs, but also in literature. It lambasted the Lake Poets and savaged the rising star of the Romantic movement and fellow Scot, Lord Byron, who replied with his satiric poem *English Bards and Scotch Reviewers.* The editors swung verbal punches at the radical leader William Cobbett (who dismissed them as "shameless Scotch hirelings") and the Tory poet Robert Southey. Years later, John Stuart Mill's wife, Harriet Martineau, upbraided Sydney Smith for the savagery of their book reviews. "We *were* savage," came the reply, "I remember how Brougham and I sat trying one night how we could exasperate our cruelty to the utmost."

Yet the cruelty was part of what drew the large audience. Although it riled some of those who were political allies, such as the radical Whig reformer Samuel Romilly, who complained, "the Editors seem to value themselves principally upon their severity," it made even their enemies read the *Review.* At the end of 1803, after a year of publication, Smith wrote to Jeffrey from London, "it is the universal opinion of all the cleverest men I have met with here, that our Review is uncommonly well done, and it is perhaps the first in Europe."

For more than a century, and even after it changed editors in 1827, the *Edinburgh Review* was the most politically influential, the most intellectually exciting, and the wittiest reading matter in the English-speaking world. As Walter Scott said, "No genteel family can pretend to be without it." It inspired a host of imitators, including *Blackwood's Journal* and the *Quarterly Review* (both also published in Edinburgh), *The Westminster Review, The North American Review,* and *The Atlantic Monthly.* From college rooms in Aberdeen and Oxford to legal chambers in London and Bombay, and government offices in Ottawa and Melbourne, the arrival four times a year of the new issue of the *Edinburgh Review,* with its blue and yellow cover, was a major event.

What was the key to its success and impact? Part of it was due to its publisher, Andrew Constable, who insisted that the editors pay their reviewers generously. This meant that Jeffrey, and later McVeigh

Napier, could hire the best writers in Britain. Their stable of authors included Sir Walter Scott, William Makepeace Thackeray, William Hazlitt, John Stuart Mill, Thomas Macaulay, G. H. Lewes, Nassau Senior, and Sir James Stephen. Also, despite their clear political bias, the editors always made it clear that literary quality, and intellectual integrity, came first. They made readers feel that the *Edinburgh Review* was, despite its name, a *British* publication, with a British sense of national culture. And publishing a piece in the *Edinburgh Review* made an aspiring author part of an elite; to be known as "an Edinburgh Reviewer" made people stop and stare at dinner parties or literary gatherings—although sometimes it made other people stand up and walk out.

Above all, the *Edinburgh Review,* for all its political wrangling and literary raillery, communicated a sense of high national purpose. The editors had one mission: to create what Dugald Stewart had said was indispensable to a modern nation, an "enlightened public opinion." They wanted to take the mantle of reform away from working-class radicals such as Cobbett and ideological extremists such as the utilitarian philosopher Jeremy Bentham and place it on the shoulders of Britain's middle class. Jeffrey saw the middle class as the heart of the nation, and the cutting edge of progress. "The example of the middle classes descends by degrees to the ranks immediately below them," he wrote in 1803, "and the general prevalence of just and liberal sentiments . . . are thus spread by contagion through every order of society. . . ."

The contagion of progress: the *Edinburgh Review* aspired to be its carrier. Yet when Jeffrey wrote that sentence, its staff was already breaking up. Smith had returned to England. James Mackintosh was in India. Francis Horner, having passed the bar, decided to move his practice to London. After his bibulous farewell dinner in 1803, the group of friends staggered from Fortune's Hotel to Manderson's chemist shop, where they twisted off its enormous bronze serpent sign, which Brougham carried home as a souvenir. A few months later Brougham himself was heading to London, as well. The scene of battle was shifting, from Edinburgh to the corridors of power in Westminster.

II

On January 21, 1806, Brougham and Horner sat together in the gallery of the House of Commons, watching Prime Minister William Pitt fend off the latest Whig challenge to his long-standing primacy. Two days later Pitt was dead. Although he had been the leader of their enemies, the Tories, the *Edinburgh Review* editors owed him a grudging respect. Pitt had fought hard to bring Britain back after the depths of decline, following the nadir of the 1780s and the American Revolution—fighting often against his own party. He had turned to Adam Smith to revivify British commerce under the banner of Free Trade. He had even praised the *Wealth of Nations* as "the best solution of every question connected with the history of commerce and with the system of political economy," six years before Stewart made the book liberal Holy Writ.

But in other areas, Pitt had failed. His attempt to reform the electoral system had gone down to defeat; so had abolition of the slave trade. Despite the Act of Union with Ireland in 1801, legal emancipation for Roman Catholics seemed a long way off. The coming of war with France had forced Pitt to throw off his reformist clothes, and his crackdown on radical elements with the suspension of habeas corpus and the so-called Gagging Acts had an air of hysteria, even desperation, about them. Although Nelson's victory over the French fleet at Trafalgar in 1805 meant Britain was safe from invasion, the nation, and its political class, were at deadlock.

The temper of the times, and of the ruling Tories, was epitomized by the legacy of Edmund Burke. His impassioned defense of the English tradition of constitutional liberty, and his suggestion that 1688 was the only revolution England ever needed, had been turned into a justification for inertia. Any further changes, it was argued, would precipitate disaster, as they had in France, and a collapse of law and order. Parliament's role was to keep the lid on the simmering pot of popular discontent, and if it occasionally boiled over, then the lid had to be pushed down harder.

Jeffrey, Horner, and Brougham were working to change the direction and terms of the national political conversation. They had started it in the pages of the *Edinburgh Review;* now they looked to Parliament itself. Horner was already contemplating taking a seat in Parliament when Henry Brougham arrived in London. He joined the Whigs' exclusive social club, Brook's, and then attended his first dinner party at Holland House, in the heart of fashionable London.

It was a glittering palace of London intellectual and artistic life, the center of Whig politics, and the hub of London's "Scottish connection." Lord Byron was poking fun, but also telling the truth, when he wrote:

Blest be the banquets spread at Holland House,
Where Scotchmen feed, and critics carouse.

The leading intellectual lights at Holland House were all Scotsmen. James Mackintosh was one. Another was John Millar, the brilliant and popular University of Glasgow professor, whose *Historical View of the English Government* had been dedicated to the former leader of the Whigs, Charles James Fox.

Millar first introduced the notion of class conflict into the understanding of modern history. He was also one of the first scholars to discuss the history of women and the history of sex as part of the larger story of civilization, or "the rise of opulence and refinement." Millar argued that the advent of commercial society brought sweeping changes in the lives of those who were otherwise excluded from a significant social role in prior stages of civilization. Women, children, servants, peasants, and the laboring class, even slaves (Millar cited Kames's 1774 decision freeing the Jamaican Joseph Knight), all benefited from commercial society's expansion of opportunity and the breakdown of the age-old patterns of rigid patriarchal authority.

As a society becomes economically more active and affluent, Millar explained, "the lower people, in general, become thereby more independent in their circumstances." They "begin to exert those sentiments of liberty which are natural to the mind of man." But here Millar warned of a looming collision, as the people rise up to demand their liberty and the rulers try desperately to hang on to their old position and power. The result must inevitably be revolution. It had happened in Britain once before, Millar argued, during the English Civil War. It had happened again in France, in 1789.

The people will not, indeed cannot, give up their struggle. Responsibility for avoiding revolution, then, belongs to the rulers and ruling class. And it was in order to avoid Millar's dire prediction from coming true that Brougham wanted to turn the Whig Party into the self-conscious champions of reform.

Even for someone of Brougham's ego and abilities, it was a daunting undertaking. Since their earliest beginnings the Whigs had been dominated by great landed English families, and their efforts to raise the fortunes of merchants, shopkeepers, and "the lower classes" always had an offhand air of *noblesse oblige*. Brougham set out to broaden their base and elevate their sense of purpose, first by reaching out to leading radical elements, then by orchestrating a steady public-relations campaign, to make his own progressive views appear as the official Whig view, and vice versa.

The battle began with Brougham making speeches, publishing articles in the *Edinburgh Review* (he wrote more than fifty-eight in the magazine's first five years), and using his private legal practice to generate publicity for the cause. His very first speech in Parliament, even before becoming an MP, was as spokesman for Manchester and Liverpool merchants protesting new trade restrictions. The Whigs, not the Tories, now emerged as the champions of free trade. In court, he successfully defended against libel charges the author of a piece condemning flogging in the British army, pointing out that distinguished British officers had condemned the practice in print, in far stronger language. As a result, the Whigs "owned" the issue of army reform.

When Brougham finally entered Parliament in 1810, the year his teacher Dugald Stewart retired, he proved unstoppable, despite his testy temper and overbearing manner. He rose to the front rank of Whig orators, and forced the party into the lists as the champions of "the people" and the enemies of "privilege." He acted as defense counsel to Queen Caroline in the trial for her divorce from the king, skillfully turning her into a symbolic victim of heartless tyranny and a heroine to ordinary people around the country. He made speeches and wrote a string of articles on slavery, preparing the nation not only for ending the slave trade (which the Whigs finally forced through in 1807), but for its final complete abolition.

But the real battle still loomed on the horizon: parliamentary reform.

Although the English political system had been expanded and elaborated after two revolutions and a century of empire, it had not modified its basic principles since the days of Henry VIII. It was still dominated by the personal patronage of powerful aristocrats, who not only sat in the House of Lords, but could virtually name their friends and relatives to the House of Commons, through their control of county seats and local constitutencies, or "boroughs." There was no rhyme or reason for deciding who could vote, or where: although the numbers of voters had grown substantially over the eighteenth century, they still represented a tiny minority of adult male Englishmen and Welshmen, barely one in eight—and an even tinier minority of Scotsmen, scarcely one in twenty.

Even more seriously, it remained fixed in a feudal, premercantile mindset. The big agricultural counties, and their landlords, dominated Parliament. Britain's urban population found itself virtually frozen out, especially the new industrial cities. One of Brougham's followers, Thomas Macaulay, pointed out that northern London, "a city superior in size and in population to the capitals of many kingdoms," was totally unrepresented. "It is needless to speak of Manchester, Birmingham, Leeds, Sheffield, with no representation," he added, "or of Edinburgh or Glasgow, with a mock representation." This was not government by property, as its defenders claimed, but government "by certain detached portions and fragments of property . . . on no rational principle whatever." The issue was, Macaulay concluded, "not whether the constitution was better formerly, but whether we can make it better now."

Thomas Babington Macaulay was an example of just how far a young man could go in those years, if he had talent, ambition, and wrote for the *Edinburgh Review.* He was the son of a Scottish abolitionist from Inverary who moved to London, where he became the prime mover in the evangelical reform- and abolition-minded circle known as the "Clapham sect." Although Zachary Macaulay's precocious son went to Cambridge instead of Edinburgh or Glasgow, and trained for the English rather than the Scottish bar, he knew the Scottish historians almost by heart, and automatically fit in with the *Edinburgh Review* set now living in London. It was Brougham who recommended him to Francis Jeffrey as a potential reviewer, and it was his essay on John Milton in the August 1825 issue that made Macaulay famous almost overnight. By defending Milton's revolutionary politics in the English civil war, and his role in the execution of Charles I, Macaulay turned England's most famous epic poet, the author of *Paradise Lost,* into a champion of the radical Whigs. He became the latest sensation at Holland House dinner parties, leaving guests agog at his eloquence and erudition. Four years later, Lord Lansdowne, another of Dugald Stewart's English pupils and leading Whig, offered him one of the seats in Parliament under his control. In the election of February 1830, Thomas Macaulay entered the House of Commons.

By now the demands for reform had reached critical mass. The year before, the Tories, under the Duke of Wellington, had consented to another major topic in the Whig reform program, Catholic emancipation, but now they dug in their heels on making any further changes. The country was in a deep economic depression. In the Midlands of England, workers and businessmen joined together in the Birmingham Political Union; in the south, laborers rioted and burned farm machinery. After twenty-three years as the party in opposition, the Whigs sensed that their moment had come. On November 2, Wellington made his speech in the House of Lords denying any need for a reform bill. On the fifteenth the Tories lost their last vote and Wellington, the Iron Duke, went to Buckingham Palace to resign.

Five hundred miles away, in far-off Lothian, a team of day laborers were breaking stones in a seaside quarry when the news came that the Tories were out of power. One of them, Alexander Somerville, who later wrote *Autobiography of a Working Man,* remembered: "We took off our hats and caps, and loud above the north wind, and the roaring sea, shouted 'Henry Brougham forever!'"

The Whigs were in. In the new cabinet were no less than four former Stewart pupils: Lansdowne, Palmerston, Sir John Russell—and, of course, Henry Brougham. In his explosive, mercurial way, Brougham was the driving force behind the Whig program for reform. It was not as radical as some wished (no vote for working-class Britons and no secret ballot), but it was far more advanced and comprehensive than anything that had ever been proposed by a sitting government.

Brougham would, however, play no role in promoting it in his former arena, the House of Commons. The only position available for him in the Whig cabinet was lord chancellor. The new prime minister, Lord Grey, distrusted Brougham, as many of his own party did; even the prospect of having him as chancellor, a politically minor post, made them uneasy. When the cabinet learned that Brougham had accepted, one of them murmured, "Then we shall never have another comfortable moment in this room."

But taking his seat in the upper house as Lord Brougham, he made huge efforts to push the bill through. And sitting as England's most important judicial figure, he also began reforming its legal system and the Court of Chancery. He abolished the abuses and bottlenecks that had tied up lawsuits for generations (and which are described in comic yet horrifying detail in Charles Dickens's *Bleak House*) and pushed England's common-law system forward to meet the modern age.

Instead of Brougham, the party's leading orator in the Commons was the Scottish abolitionist's son, and in the end Macaulay's contribution was more far-reaching and profound. His speeches gave the Reform Bill a historical grounding, and therefore a legitimacy, that even its most fervent supporters had never imagined was there. Thirty-three years old, upright and motionless, "a little man of small voice, and affected utterance, clipping his words and hissing like a serpent," Macaulay hammered away day after day and in speech after speech. Each time he came back to the same point. This was a decisive moment in

English history, and the history of Britain, and that humanity's political progress now required another turn of the wheel.

It was all, or virtually all, the Scottish school, evoked as justification for a new way to see political change: as reform, an action that preserves at the same time as it alters and improves. Macaulay was quite capable of playing the demagogue, as other Whigs did, warning listeners of the tumult and even bloodshed that could erupt if the bill failed to pass. "The danger is terrible," he would say. "The time is short. If this bill should be rejected, I pray to God that none of those who concur in rejecting it may ever remember their votes with unavailing remorse, amidst the wreck of laws, the confusion of ranks, the spoliation of property, and the dissolution of social order." He stressed, "The great cause of revolutions is this, that while nations move onwards, constitutions stand still."

But most of his oratory evoked a larger historical canvas, as depicted by the leading figures of the Scottish school from Kames and Hume to Ferguson and Millar. It told of man's progress from barbarism to civilization, of which an essential part was the growth of political liberty, and participation in self-government. He packed into his speeches a wealth of historical detail and imagery, which he later reused in his classic *History of England*: "In listening to him," said one spectator, "you seemed to be like a traveler passing through a rich and picturesque country by railroad." He mentioned the great figures of the English past, and familiar moments in the securing of constitutional liberty: Magna Carta, the Petition of Right of 1628, the Glorious Revolution of 1688—moments sacred to Tories as well as Whigs. This was another, he said: parliamentary reform was another step "in one great progress" toward Englishmen securing their rights and the nation securing its freedom. In this sense, he suggested that the Reform Bill was a matter of historical inevitablity. "Good or bad, the thing must be done," he said at one point, "a law as strong as the laws of attraction and motion [in physics] has decreed it."

Macaulay had found a way to fuse the conservatism of Edmund Burke, whom he greatly admired, with the radicalism of Brougham. The

English constitution, with its unique brand of self-government, had saved itself through reform in the past, he asserted, and it was about to do so again. His speeches created a historical framework for Brougham's political liberalism, and moved the assumptions of the Scottish school directly into the heart of Britain's political consciousness. And in so doing he may have saved the Reform Bill.

At last, on the night of March 22, 1831, the bill came up for its crucial second reading. Macaulay described to a friend the drama as the house "divided" (that is, as members passed through opposite doors to register their vote) and the Whigs realized they had 302 votes in favor, but still had no idea how many the opposing Tories could muster:

> The doors were thrown open and in they came. . . . First we heard that they were three hundred and three—then the number rose to three hundred and ten, then went down to three hundred and seven. Alexander Baring [later Lord Ashburton, and another Dugald Stewart pupil] told me that he had counted and that they were three hundred and four. We were all breathless with anxiety, when Charles Wood who stood near the door jumped on a bench and cried out—"They are only three hundred and one." We set up a shout that you might have heard to Charing Cross—waving our hats—stamping against the floor and clapping our hands—The tellers scarcely got through the crowd—for the House was thronged up to the table. . . . You might have heard a pin drop as [Chief Whip] Duncannon read the numbers. Then again the shouts broke out—and many of us shed tears. . . .

As Macaulay left (it was now past four o'clock in the morning), he hailed a cab. The first thing the driver asked was, "Is the bill carried?" Macaulay answered, "Yes, by one." "Thank God for it, sir," the man replied.

The last chance the Tories had was the House of Lords. On October 8 the Reform Bill came before the upper house, and Brougham made a final speech in support of it, the longest ever given in the House of

Lords. He finished dramatically, kneeling before the hushed house, his arms stretched out over his head, as he pleaded, "I solemnly adjure you—I warn you—I implore you—yea, on my bended knees, I supplicate you—Reject not this Bill."

Yet reject it they did, by a wide margin. The question was what to do next; the country demanded reform or revolution, yet the Lords were adamant. It was Brougham who came up with the solution. There could be no compromise on the bill itself, he told the rest of the cabinet. It would be a mistake "to sacrifice a tittle of our principle or a grain of the Confidence we had gained in the House of Commons and Country by any thing like negotiation." Instead, he urged, the government should threaten to create enough new peers to allow the bill to pass. It was pure political brinksmanship. If the House of Lords did not budge, they would see their influence diluted and their hallowed institution destroyed—and the Reform Bill would still pass.

It worked. The new King, William IV, agreed in advance to create sixty new peers if the upper house refused to pass the bill as it was, without amendments. The House of Lords gave way, and on June 7, 1832, the Reform Bill became law.

Exactly 125 years earlier, the Scottish old regime had abolished itself, under an onslaught of English-inspired ideas and hardball politicking by the Crown. All at once, Scotland found itself thrust into the glare of the modern world. Now the roles had been reversed. Scottish ideas and political brinksmanship had toppled the English old regime, and nailed together a constitutional formula suitable for a modern nation, both north and south.

The actual changes in English politics were less than met the eye. The number of male voters rose from perhaps one in eight to one in five—hardly popular democracy, let alone mob rule. The landed interest lost many of their old nomination boroughs, but otherwise remained firmly in power. The industrial cities won representation for their middle class, but not their workers. In Scotland and Ireland, change was more sweeping because there was so much further to go. Henry Cockburn, as Solicitor-General for Scotland, oversaw the Whigs' Scottish Reform Bill that same year, which raised the number of voters from 4,500 to more than 65,000. Eight new burgh constituencies were created, with Dundee, Perth, and Aberdeen winning a seat apiece. But the old landed aristocracy was as important as ever, and the urban middle class was kept firmly in check. And, as in England, there was still no secret ballot.

But the direction of the future was clear, as was how to get there, thanks to Brougham and Macaulay. The British constitution had a new, self-conscious principle: change as reform, rather than revolution. Even the Tories learned the lesson Macaulay had set forth: "the great cause of revolutions is this, that while nations move onwards, constitutions stand still." In fact, the next major expansion of the electorate, the Second Reform Bill of 1867, which gave the vote for the first time to members of the working class, was a Tory measure passed by a Tory government. By then the Whigs were calling themselves Liberals. Their chief was Dugald Stewart's former pupil Lord Russell; their leader in the House of Commons was William Gladstone, son of a Glasgow businessman, who would be prime minister the following year. Yet another Liberal MP and son of a Scot, John Stuart Mill, even tried to amend the bill to include votes for women—without success.

In British politics, reverence for the past was giving ground to the demand for change. The forward-looking, results-driven manner of Scottish liberalism had won out. However, that backward-looking Burkean impulse discovered a new outlet in the realm of culture, and revealed unexpected reserves of strength—thanks to another Edinburgh man, Scotland's greatest writer.

The Last Minstrel: Sir Walter Scott and the Highland Revival

But I hae dreamed a dreary dream,
Beyond the Isle of Skye;
I saw a dead man win a fight,
And I think that man was I.

n 1805, Walter Scott gave a correspondent this portrait of himself:

You would expect to see a person who had dedicated himself much to literary pursuits, and you would find me a rattle-skulled half-lawyer, half-sportsman, in whose head a regiment of horse has been exercising since he was five years old; half-educated—half crazy, as his friends sometimes tell him; half-everything.

He did not mention that he had been crippled with polio as a boy, which left him with a permanent limp and a vicarious taste for action and adventure (hence the cavalry-regiment fantasies). Or that he was raised an Episcopalian in a country that, despite the tidal waves of change in the eighteenth century, was still overwhelmingly loyal to its Presbyterian heritage. He also did not add what the correspondent probably knew anyway: that he was Britain's most celebrated living poet. Within a decade he would be the best-known novelist in the world.

Sir Walter Scott (he became a baronet in 1820) single-handedly changed the course of literature. He gave it, for better or worse, the place it still occupies as part of modern life. By the same token, he gave Scotland a new identity, one to tide it over into the industrial age. His reward for these services has been to be consistently underrated and downplayed, both as a writer and as an intellectual. Virginia Woolf once said, not entirely disrespectfully, "he was the last minstrel and the first salesman for the Edinburgh municipal gas company." Edwin Muir called his novels "a mere repetition of the moral clichés of the time."

Both judgments do him a disservice. Sir Walter Scott knew better than his critics what he was really doing. He also saw more clearly than most of his contemporaries that the Scotland of even recent memory was passing into oblivion, and that the loss was not just a matter of regret. It was a cultural tragedy, both for the Scots and for the modern world. Scott salvaged what he could from the incoming tide of progress, without vainly trying to hold the waters back. He offered modernity its self-conscious antidote: a world of heroic imagination, to balance the world of sober, and sometimes dismal, fact.

I

The Scotts came from a Border family that had emigrated to Edinburgh in the early eighteenth century. Walter Scott, Sr., was a hardworking, if not particularly distinguished, writer to the Signet. It was assumed that his son, despite his early bout with polio, would do the same. The younger Scott did nothing to suggest he had other plans. He was in fact a rather unpromising student in Luke Fraser's class at Edinburgh's High School, certainly compared to the brilliant lights who came just before and after him, Francis Jeffrey and Henry Brougham. He tried writing some poetry, but the result did not prompt him or anyone else to suggest he give up studying law when he got to the university in 1784.

There Scott took classes with Dugald Stewart on moral philosophy and with David Hume, the philosopher's nephew, on Scottish law. He absorbed the assumptions and methods of the Scottish school; he became friends with Adam Ferguson's son, and was suitably awed by the august presence of Principal William Robertson. He even became friends with the future editors of the *Edinburgh Review*. But Scott also found himself drawn to what was happening outside the university.

After class he haunted Edinburgh's famed lending library, which Allan Ramsay had founded sixty years before. There he saw, and later met, the current darling of Edinburgh literary circles, Robert Burns. He had read English novelists such as Fielding and Samuel Richardson, and their Scottish counterparts Tobias Smollett and Henry Mackenzie. But the authors who impressed him most were Ramsay, John Home, and Robert Fergusson, who were trying to save what they could of Scotland's history and folkways, including its Gaelic and Scots heritage, before it washed away in the flood of cultural change.

Two celebrated figures illustrated the rewards and pitfalls this involved. Raised as a farmhand, virtually self-taught, Robert Burns arrived in Edinburgh in 1787 with a reputation as a boy genius. His literary mentors had encouraged him to write verse in the standard highbrow classical vein, which Burns could do perfectly well. But he sensed that his true talent lay in turning the everyday speech, songs, and stories of the people he had grown up with into poetry, and communicating to readers the latent power, eloquence, and nobility of the ordinary man and woman. It made Burns Scotland's most beloved poet, even today. But it disappointed his mentors, sank his career, and eventually drove him out of Edinburgh. His failure also drove him to drink, cutting short his life at thirty-seven.

The tragic case of Robert Burns served as one kind of warning; James Macpherson and Ossian were another.

In 1759, John Home, the celebrated dramatist and Moderate cleric, was vacationing at Moffat in southern Scotland when he received a visitor. This was James Macpherson, a would-be clergyman from Ruthven, who knew Home had a deep interest in ancient Scottish history and culture. Both men were also admirers of James Thomson, the founder of the British school of nature poetry, who had also translated old Scottish songs and ballads into English verse. Now Macpherson excitedly told Home that during one of his rambles across the Highlands, he had discovered a manuscript with several examples of ancient Gaelic poetry.

Home wanted to see them. Macpherson asked if he could read Gaelic. Home said no, but suggested that Macpherson do a translation of one of the poems and bring it by for examination.

A day or two later Macpherson returned with an excerpt of a poem by the legendary ancient bard Ossian, called "The Death of Oscar." Home was astounded. Like most of his Edinburgh literati friends, Home had found most Gaelic literary remains to be pretty crude and pitiful, for all their historical interest. But this was eloquent, sweeping, breathtaking. It was a tale of epic heroes and romantic maidens, of battlefield valor and lost love, of spirits on the wind and haunting mountain scenery. It contained passages of genuine literary power: "Dermid and Oscar were gone. They reaped the battle together. Their friendship was as strong as their steel; and death walked between them and the field."

Clearly, Macpherson had discovered not just another Gaelic songster, but the Scottish equivalent of Homer. Back in Edinburgh, Home showed the poem to Hugh Blair, the dean of Scottish letters and doyen of good taste. Blair was equally impressed, and insisted that Macpherson show him the rest. Within the year, with Blair's help, Macpherson had published a collection of translations of Ossian, titled *Fragments of Ancient Poetry.* Blair praised the works fulsomely as "poetry of the heart." Although they were written in a barbarous age, and for a savage people, Blair exclaimed, they showed "a heart penetrated with noble sentiment, and with sublime and tender passions, a heart that glows, and kindles the fancy, a heart that is full, and pours itself out." Of one passage where Ossian's hero, Fingal, is wounded, and, as the poem says, "he rolled into himself, and rose upon the wind," Blair exclaimed, "I know no passage more sublime in the writings of any uninspired author"—meaning outside the Bible.

The book was an overnight sensation. In one fell swoop, Ossian had shattered Enlightenment literary orthodoxy, which assumed a primitive people could not produce great art. On the contrary, as Hugh Blair said, it was evident that "as their feelings are strong, so their language, of itself, assumes a poetical turn." Here was revealed, through the poetic art, "the history of human imagination and passion." Macpherson had opened up a whole new field for research, that of Gaelic prosody, and became a national celebrity. He also hinted to his mentors that there was more to come.

Things might have turned out better if Macpherson had stopped with that first volume. But he insisted on finding and "translating" more and longer selections, finishing up with *Temora: An Ancient Epic Poem* in eight books, which he published in 1763. By then critics were wondering aloud if he was not in fact making the whole thing up as he went along. The battle over Ossian's authenticity grew to an incessant clamor; thirty years later the young Walter Scott was still writing an essay for Dugald Stewart on it. On one side stood Macpherson, Blair, and those who insisted that the poems were genuine and the Gaelic equivalent of the *Iliad* or *Odyssey,* true masterpieces of primitive genius. But the very fact that the poems were so carefully crafted made critics such as Horace Walpole, David Hume, and Dr. Johnson suspicious. Others, such as Thomas Gray and Edward Gibbon, wavered back and forth.

Walpole found the poems dull—"it tires me to death to read how many ways a warrior is like the moon, or the sun, or a rock, or a lion"— and pronounced them a "fraud." Hume's objections were sociological: "it is indeed strange," he wrote to Gibbon, "that any men of sense could have imagined it possible that above twenty thousand verses, along with numberless historical facts, could have been preserved by oral tradition, during fifty generations, by the rudest perhaps of all the European nations, the most necessitous, the most turbulent, and the most unsettled"—namely, the Highland Scots.

Dr. Johnson, sensibly enough, wanted to know where the originals were, and why Macpherson always promised to produce them, but never did. When he and Boswell did their tour of the Hebrides in 1773, they brought along their copies of Ossian to compare with what the local natives could remember of the Gaelic tales. Sometimes the verses checked out; often they did not. Johnson pronounced them clever forgeries, and Macpherson furiously responded, even threatening to beat the older man up.

There matters stood until 1805, when the Highland Society of Edinburgh undertook a full investigation of Macpherson's papers after his death. Their research showed that the critics had been correct.

Macpherson had used some genuine Gaelic fragments in his text, but the bulk, including the poem's elaborate subplots, were his own invention. From that point on, "Ossian" became synonymous with literary hoax.

But, having lost the battle, Macpherson also won the war. In the end, as Hume observed, people believe what they want to believe—and they wanted to believe in Ossian. The image of an aging, bearded bard crouched on a mountaintop composing tales of vanished heroes, gods, and maidens stirred the eighteenth-century imagination. The Ossian poems were translated into every major European language, including Russian and Hungarian. They launched European romanticism in its earliest phase. They seemed to confirm Jean-Jacques Rousseau's idea that people in primitive cultures are nobler, purer, and more creative than their counterparts in more "advanced" cultures—an idea that survives in the multiculturalist passions of our own day.

The best of Macpherson's efforts, *Fingal,* would inspire poets as diverse as Lord Byron, Robert Burns (who said Ossian was "one of the glorious models after which I endeavor to form my conduct"), William Blake, Samuel Taylor Coleridge, Tennyson, and Goethe. The German philosopher J. G. Herder and the French poet Chateaubriand took the Ossian poems as models of what a great national literature should look like. *Fingal* was Napoleon's favorite reading; he even commissioned the painter Jean-Auguste Ingres to decorate his palace at Malmaison with scenes from the poems. Macpherson himself was buried in Westminster Abbey in 1796, not far from the tomb of his most famous opponent, Samuel Johnson.

Macpherson had also triggered a vogue for all things old and medieval, both on the Continent and in Britain. People became fascinated by long-forgotten chivalric poetry and epics, which correct taste had once denounced as barbaric and "Gothick," and by Celtic folk culture. The hunt was on for other ancient poems, songs, and ballads, and one of the hunters was Walter Scott. He knew Macpherson's work was largely a "tissue of forgeries," but he also knew that a rich oral tradition really did survive in rural Scotland, much of it very old. He had encountered some of it firsthand at his father's house, when elderly Highland clients visited, some of whom had fought at Culloden, and could recite stories about the battle and other great deeds of warriors and chiefs.

In 1792, as he was waiting to enter the Bar, Scott made a walking tour of the Border country: Rosebank, Upper Tyneside, and the Cheviot and Eildon Hills, with Ettrick Forest behind them. This was his ancestral home, a vista of rolling hills, forests, and ruined abbeys, a beautiful but violent land that had known centuries of battles and "rieving wars" between Lowlanders and English, and among Lowland clans such as the Douglasses, the Maxwells, and the Homes. With the help of a friend, Scott heard and wrote down a number of the ancient "riding ballads," which celebrated the exploits of the daring raiders and brigands who had haunted the hills a century or more ago, and which were still known to their descendants. The next year he toured Perthshire and the eastern Highlands, returning several times over the next decade to the Border country to collect more ballads. In 1799 he was made deputy sheriff* of Selkirkshire, which allowed him to expand his search. Finally he decided to approach an Edinburgh publisher, John Ballantyne, with an idea: "I have been for years collecting old Border Ballads, and I think I could, with little trouble, put together such a collection from them as might make a neat little volume, to sell for four or five shillings."

The "neat little volume" appeared in February of 1802. Scott was immediately swamped with praise. He had managed to do honestly what Macpherson had done dishonestly: collect surviving specimens of an oral tradition—in Border dialect, not Gaelic—sift through the variants, and set it all down on paper. What it revealed was a literary heritage even more impressive than Ossian's, since it was genuine—a lusty celebration of long-lost battles and fighting men:

> *Now Liddesdale has ridden a raid,*
> *But I wat they had better hae staid at home;*
> *For Michael o' Winfield he is dead,*
> *And Jock o' the Side is prisoner ta'en.*

---

*The official term is sheriff-depute. It is not as romantic a job as it sounds, more like an assistant district attorney.

The ballads offered a sense of dramatic pathos:

> *For Mangerton House Lady Downie has gane,*
> *Her coats she has kilted up to her knee;*
> *And down the water w' speed she rins,*
> *While tears in spaits fa fast frae her ee.*

There was sardonic and stoic humor, as in Johnny Armstrong's farewell before his execution for murder, or "Armstrong's Good Night":

> *This night is my departing night;*
> *For here nae longer must I stay;*
> *There's neither friend nor foe o' mine,*
> *But wishes me away.*

> *What I have done thro' lack of wit,*
> *I never, never can recall,*
> *I hope ye're a my friends as yet,*
> *Goodnight and joy be with you all!*

And passages of haunting beauty:

> *Adieu, the lily and the rose,*
> *The primrose fair to see;*
> *Adieu, my lady, and only joy!*
> *For I may not stay with thee.*

Scott had opened up a new world, in which ordinary men and women spoke with an eloquence preserved over generations. It was a voice that even men of letters had to acknowledge was genuine poetry: a Scots voice he recorded accent for accent, word for word, both in his poems and later in his novels. *Scottish Border Minstrelsy* sold out in England as well as Scotland, with translations into German (the brothers Grimm, fellow collectors of oral tradition, held it in high regard), Swedish, and

Danish. An American edition made him famous across the Atlantic, and inspired collectors of American folk culture such as Washington Irving.

Scott published a second volume in 1803, and then a third—but this time of his own work, in acknowledged imitation of the archaic style of Scottish tradition. *The Lay of the Last Minstrel* did Ossian one better: it created a modern, poetic, anticlassical idiom based on medieval forms, as Macpherson had tried to do, but with a stronger sense of historical context:

> *Moor, moor the barge, ye gallant crew!*
> *And gentle ladye, deign to stay!*
> *Rest thee in Castle Ravensheuch,*
> *Nor tempt the stormy firth today.*
>
> *The blackened wave is edged with white;*
> *To inch and rock the sea-mews fly;*
> *The fishers have heard the Water-Sprite,*
> *Whose screams forebode that wreck is nigh.*

Although they were fiction, everything about the poems rang true: the language; the setting, thanks to Scott's painstaking research in old history and law books; and the love stories, which, although set in medieval garb, appealed to modern men and women.

The Lay of the Last Minstrel launched Scott's writing career and filled a temporary void in literary taste. Burns was dead. The Lake Poets were still largely unknown; Byron's first published work was a year away. So Scott became Britain's reigning poet and a Scottish national hero. He avoided alienating the official literary establishment as Burns had done; he was also honest about what he was trying to do, which Macpherson had not been. By combining Ossian and the Romantic school's taste for drama, strong emotions, and breathtaking scenery, and the Scottish school's hardheaded sense of historical truth, Scott had struck on a formula for literary success.

He created for his readers a magical realm of the imagination. Here was a vanished time and place, of romantic heroes in chain mail, of blushing heroines, ruthless villains, and mysterious sages, along with genuine historical events and battles, all described accurately to the last detail—and all set in a real Scottish landscape, from the Lowlands and Borders (in *Marmion*) to the Highlands (in *Lady of the Lake* and *Lord of the Isles*). Through the success of his works, Scott single-handedly created a new industry, that of Highland tourism. Each summer, post coaches, inns, and ferry points were filled with men and women on their way to visit Loch Katrine, the setting for *Lady of the Lake,* or tramp the Trossachs, or find some new glen or vista that reminded them of their favorite passage from *Rokeby* or *The Bridal of Triermain.*

Lady of the Lake sold twenty thousand copies, plus two thousand copies of the deluxe edition. When his epic poem, *Marmion,* was finished, publisher Archibald Constable offered him one thousand guineas for it, sight unseen. Constable was also publisher of the *Edinburgh Review,* to which Scott submitted articles. Scott and editor Francis Jeffrey had been friends since High School, despite their political differences. For while Jeffrey was a dedicated Whig, even a radical one, Britain's best-selling author was a Tory and a fierce enemy of reform and revolution.

What drew educated Scotsmen such as Scott to the conservative Tory camp rather than to the liberal Whigs? Not all were benighted reactionaries or Dundas place-seekers, despite what Whigs claimed. Under William Pitt, the Tories had supported a cause dear to the hearts of many Scottish Presbyterians, antislavery—that was the issue, for instance, that drew Thomas Macaulay's father to their ranks. Tories were also the party of patriots. The Whigs in Parliament had opposed war against France, and had even gone on strike to undermine it. But the Tories had been forthright "hawks" from the start, promising no peace with a regime built on terror, regicide, and conquest. Their Great Britain was now the last bulwark of Europe's freedom.

The wars against the French Revolution and then Napoleon struck a strong nerve in Scotland. The old, middle-class Scottish commitment to the British Union had discovered a new outlet. Its visible expression was Edinburgh's National Monument dedicated to Scotland's war dead, which William Playfair got under way on Calton Hill after a public subscription raised 24,000 pounds for it. In the end it proved too ambitious, even for Playfair. But its twelve unadorned Doric columns standing stark against the Edinburgh sky make it seem a more fitting monument today than if it had been finished—and fitting also as the culmination of Edinburgh's neoclassical age.

Gripped by patriotic fever, everyone joined the militia. Parliament had finally relented and permitted volunteer militia regiments to be raised in Scotland. Adam Ferguson's dream of forty years earlier was finally realized, and Edinburgh's middle-class intellectuals signed up with enthusiasm. "We were all soldiers," Henry Cockburn remembered of the uncertain days in 1803, when Napoleon threatened Britain with invasion, and Whigs and Tories joined forces to defend the island. Cockburn himself ended up commanding a company of infantry. Henry Brougham joined the artillery and served the same cannon as William Playfair. Francis Horner enlisted in the so-called Gentleman Regiment as a private, and could be seen prowling the Edinburgh streets with his musket. Walter Scott, with his boyhood fantasies about "a regiment of horse," gravitated to the cavalry.

Despite his physical handicap, he proved a keen and skillful officer, and became quartermaster of his regiment. Cockburn recalled, "It was with him an absolute passion. . . . He drilled, and drank, and made songs, with a hearty conscientious earnestness which inspired or shamed everybody within the attraction." Scott took his mounted saber practice with deadly seriousness, galloping at the target and swinging his sword with a shout of, "Cut them down, the villains, cut them down!" as if he were really doing battle with a French cuirassier.

Patriotism fired his view of Scottish politics, as well. As with many middle-class Scots, the outbreaks of popular unrest in the 1790s, in both Scotland and England, terrified him. He saw their blue-collar instigators as traitors, and grimly supported the government's harsh repression as the Black Watch patrolled Ayrshire and the approaches to Kilmarnock. Scott hated revolution as much as he loved his country, and for the same reason. For all his genuine sympathy with ordinary people, violence and attacks on the principle of property left Walter Scott cold. And so he, like the rest of urban Scotland, did nothing to stop the ugly episode that would scar the nation for the next fifty years: the Highland Clearances.

II

The Clearances are the saddest chapter in Scottish history. So many misconceptions surround the terrible "clearing," or eviction of tens of thousands of Highland residents from their ancestral lands by their landlords, that it is worth taking time to get the story straight.

The most outrageous misconception is the charge that somehow the English were really to blame. In fact, the principal instigators of these mass evictions were the Highland chieftains themselves, and their Scottish farm managers or "factors." In fact, some of the aristocrats who were most sentimentally attached to the traditions of Highland culture, such as the Chisholms of Strathglass and Alistair MacDonnell of Glengarry, were the most remorseless evictors. In their minds, they had little choice. Faced by an increasingly competitive agricultural market, and the need to liquidate enormous debts (Glengarry's alone amounted to more than eighty thousand pounds, with yearly rents of less than six thousand pounds), chieftains looked for ways to make the land pay. This meant rewarding farmers who could afford higher rents, for example, or specialists in cost-effective agriculture, such as sheep and cattle farming.

Adam Smith's division of labor had finally arrived in the Highlands. When it did, it swept aside everything in its path. It spelled the end of the traditional Highland village community, the *baile,* with its complex and unspoken web of rights, powers, and obligations sheltering in the glen. When the chief began to think in terms of profit and "improvement," rather than rewarding generations of loyalty and service, the old way of life, fragile even in the best of times, was doomed.

Nor were the Clearances the result of the defeat at Culloden. Almost fifty years lapsed before the first forced clearings of villages and farms got under way, to open the land up for grazing. Landlords were responding to economic rather than political pressures. However, what the Forty-five did do was sever the formal bond of service between landlord and tenant. Duncan Forbes had hoped this would free the tenant's hands to acquire and work the land for himself. It did just the opposite, in that it freed the hands of the chieftain to treat his people as temporary tenants, who could remain on his land if they could afford it—but would have to go if they could not.

The same thing had happened in the Lowlands in the early eighteenth century. There, however, the land was more fertile, the opportunities for alternate employment more numerous, and the culture not as self-limiting. This was the other key: the Highland chiefs abandoned the old ways, because it profited them to belong to the modern world. Their followers did not, because they could not. So they ended up paying the price of progress.

The price, in human terms, was terrible. On the Isle of Skye, more than forty thousand people received writs of removal; in some places, one family was left where there had been a hundred. On the lands of the Countess of Sutherland and her husband, Lord Stafford, old men in the 1880s could still remember the names of forty-eight cleared villages in the parish of Assynt alone. When people refused to leave, the more ruthless factors burned them out. "Our family was very reluctant to leave," Betsy McKay, who had lived in Skail in the valley of Strathnaver, remembered years later, "and stayed for some time, but the burning party came round and set fire to our house at both ends, reducing to ashes whatever remained within the walls." Another eyewitness, Donald McLean, remembered pulling one old lady out of her house at Strathnaver after it had been fired. The woman was paralyzed with fear, "uttering piercing moans of distress and agony, in articulations from which could be only understood, '*Oh, Dhia, Dhia, teine, teine*—Oh, God, God, fire, fire.'" Between 1807 and 1821, between six thousand and ten thousand people were forcibly herded off the Sutherland lands, to make way for sheep farms. "For some days after the people were turned out one could scarcely hear a word with the lowing of the cattle and the screams of the children marching off in all directions."

The Sutherlands, like most landlords, did not actually want to drive their tenants away. They intended to settle them along the coast in crofting villages, hoping that tenants displaced by sheep could make a living fishing or gathering kelp—and continue to pay their rents. At one point, more than 25,000 people worked in the Hebrides cutting, gathering, and drying seaweed to sell to fertilizer manufacturers. But the crofts were too small (on Skye they averaged less than one-half acre) to allow most families to feed themselves. No one wanted to confront the real problem, which was that there were more human beings in the Western Highlands than the land could support, clearances or no clearances. Communities became dangerously dependent on the potato to support them, since an acre of potatoes could feed four times as many mouths as an acre of wheat or oats. The hills of Wester Ross and Sutherland were soon thick with row upon row of potato plants. It was a disaster waiting to happen—and in 1846, it did. If the Clearances had not already forced thousands to emigrate to America, the Scottish potato blight might have been as catastrophic as the Great Famine in Ireland.

The Clearances also affected different parts of the Highlands in different ways. In the south and east, in Argyll, Perthshire, and east of Inverness, it probably raised the standard of living for those who remained, as a mixed economy based on sheep, cattle, wheat, barley (with a portion for whisky distilling), fishing, and linen weaving took root. In the West, and on islands such as Skye and Mull, where the land was poor to begin with, the alternatives were bleak. Many had to choose between emigration and starvation. In the first three years of the nineteenth century, more than ten thousand people left for Nova Scotia and Canada; by the 1820s it was twenty thousand a year, most from the Western Highlands, Ross-shire, and Sutherland. In 1831 the population of Kildonan parish was one-fifth of what it had been in 1801.

Nor is it true, as some charge, that the Scottish upper classes uniformly approved of what was happening. Some pretended it was all part of the continuing advance of "civilization" over uncomprehending ignorant savages. But others spoke out. While most Scottish journals and periodicals, including the *Edinburgh Review,* ignored the Clearances, Robert Bisset Scott's *Military Register* became an unexpected voice against "improving" landlords and chieftains. Edited for and by former British army officers, the *Register* knew that many Highland soldiers, after risking their lives for the empire in Spain and India, had come back to find their homes gone and their families dispersed. The *Military Register* published full accounts of the atrocities in Sutherland and even helped to get an indictment against the man responsible (he was later acquitted).

Another soldier, David Stewart of Garth, was also landlord and chieftain of more than eight miles of territory between the rivers Lyon and Trummel. His father, although an ardent supporter of Union, had been a chieftain in the old style:

> *Hospitality's prince,*
> *To guests and relatives kind,*
> *Good chieftain of tenants,*
> *Who frowns not when rent is behind.*

The son and heir made a career for himself in the 82nd Highlanders, serving in nearly every campaign of the Napoleonic Wars. When his commanding officer asked him to put together a chronicle of the origin of the Army's Highland regiments, David Stewart used it as a vehicle to write a detailed history of the people and communities he had grown up with and loved. His *Sketches of the Character, Manners, and Present State of the Highlanders in Scotland* appeared in March 1822. It was the first sympathetic nonfictional account of that part of Scotland that most people, including many Scots, had ever read. It surveyed the customs and traditions of the Highland clans, and gave a map of their territories. It also bitterly attacked the impact of the Clearances: "It can never be for the well-being of any state to deteriorate the character of or to extirpate a brave, loyal, and moral people, its best supporters in war, and the most orderly, contented and economical in peace."

David Stewart, like most opponents of clearance, may have not have realized that no one could stop it. It was rooted in an economic reality, and social forces, beyond anyone's control. But he did grasp the costs involved, both in human and cultural terms. The end result, he warned, would be "to root out the language of the country, together with a great proportion of the people who speak it." This, ironically, at the very time when the rest of the country was celebrating and honoring that heritage, thanks to his friend Sir Walter Scott.

Walter Scott did not ignore the Clearances, nor did he support them. He saw the necessity of them, but also wrote, "In too many instances the Highlands have been drained, not of their superfluity of population, but the whole mass of the inhabitants, dispossessed by an unrelenting avarice. . . ." But he also felt that there was nothing that he, even as Scotland's leading spokesman, could do to prevent the day coming when "the pibroch may sound through the deserted region, but the summons will remain unanswered."

Scott also had other priorities he had to balance. And although his name was and is synonymous with the Highlands, Scott himself was interested in preserving *all* aspects of Scotland's history and culture, including that of his own beloved Borders. What was happening in Sutherland and the Western Isles was, in his mind, only one instance of how the onslaught of the new Scotland was sweeping aside the legacy of its past. He was determined to fight the battles he could win, and with the weapons he had at hand.

A break with his friends at the *Edinburgh Review* gave him unexpected room to maneuver. In 1808 he published *Marmion,* his third epic set in medieval Scotland. More than 2,000 copies sold in less than two months. Four years later, sales had surpassed 28,000—unheard of for a narrative poem. But Francis Jeffrey's forbearance had run out. He panned *Marmion* in the *Review*: "To write a modern romance of chivalry, seems as much a phantasy as to build a modern abbey or an English pagoda." Although they remained friends, Scott stopped writing for Jeffrey. Then, when Henry Brougham published an incendiary political piece that seemed to support the idea of violent revolution, Scott broke off relations altogther. He dropped Constable as his publisher and joined forces with other Scottish Tories in creating a conservative alternative to the *Edinburgh Review,* the *Quarterly Review.*

Scott now found himself at the head of an ideological coterie, a group of conservative writers and poets who turned the *Quarterly Review* and then *Blackwood's Edinburgh Magazine,* founded in 1817, into witty, intelligent counterweights to Jeffrey, Horner, and Brougham. They wanted to "dust the jackets of the Whigs," as the *Quarterly*'s first editor, William Gifford, put it, and so they did. Gifford, Scott, John Croker, and John Lockhart, who later edited the *Quarterly* and was Scott's son-in-law and biographer, became major alternative voices in the British literary scene. They were joined by a leader in the English Romantic movement, Robert Southey, and *Blackwood*'s John Wilson and James Hogg, a former shepherd and self-taught poet whom Scott had met while collecting ballads in Ettrick. Unlike their *Edinburgh Review* rivals, most were not interested in politics in the conventional sense. They wanted to offer to their audience a new way of seeing the world, which was actually an old way: through the lens of custom and a reverence for the past, including the vanishing folkways of rural Scotland.

They mocked the buoyant liberalism of Brougham and Dugald Stewart and its "scientific" pretensions, just as they mocked its belief in political progress. Instead, as part of their new way of seeing, they looked back with a renewed respect at the ancient Highland loyalty to the house of Stuart and Prince Charles. More than half a century had passed since the bloodshed and sordid horrors of Culloden. The story began to take on a warm, attractive glow as a Highland romantic epic of heroism and villainy, of intrigue and bravery, complete with comely maidens such as Flora MacDonald and handsome heroes such as Bonnie Prince Charlie himself.

The result was a burgeoning neo-Jacobitism, the original romantic Lost Cause. The ongoing interest in folk culture and oral tradition helped to feed and sustain it, especially after the publication of James Hogg's *Collection of Jacobite Songs*. It swept up Robert Burns, who declared himself a Jacobite, although he came from traditionally pro-Hanoverian Ayrshire. He even wrote "Charlie He's My Darling" and "The White Cockade" as battle songs for the long-dead cause. Another poet, Carolina Oliphant, Lady Nairne, did the same with "Will Ye No' Come back Again," which became so popularly identified with the Forty-five that people conveniently forgot it was composed more than half a century later.

These reactionary neo-Jacobites were hankering after a vanished world of strong men and women (Flora MacDonald became a posthumous Scottish national heroine), of emotional loyalties rather than economic calculation, of heroic self-sacrifice rather than rational self-interest. The events of 1745 were turned into a parable, as they still are to some people, of the doomed struggle of traditional values against a soulless modernity. Scott himself was not immune to this nostalgic appeal. "I am a bit of a Cavalier," he wrote in 1800, "not to say a Jacobite." But he was too much the student of history, and of Dugald Stewart, to accept the rosy myth of Bonnie Prince Charlie without reservations. The Jacobites mattered more to him as an important chapter in Scotland's history than as a weapon for scoring political hits in the present.

Modernity's smug contempt for the past infuriated him. It was what he most disliked about Presbyterianism, after John Knox and his followers had blithely destroyed ancient churches and monasteries, and blotted out ageless popular customs and reverence for the monarchy. The *Edinburgh Review* crowd did not seem to him all that different. Scott had launched himself on a one-man campaign to reverse that legacy of hostility, or at least indifference, toward Scotland's past. His narrative poems had been one aspect of this. He also built a house at Abbotsford in his beloved Border country, as a kind of museum of Scottish history, preserving and displaying relics such as the Earl of Montrose's sword, Rob Roy's long-barreled gun, and suits of armor and antique crossbows—each object conjuring up for his visitors a vanished time and place, and the people who had inhabited it. He even chose the spot because it stood near the site of a medieval clan battle.

Then, one day in the autumn of 1813, while rummaging through the drawers in an old cupboard, Scott came across a relic of his own past. It was the half-finished manuscript of a novel he had started years before, based on the Forty-five and the stories he had heard about it as a boy. As he thumbed through it, it occurred to him that this might be another way to inspire a broad audience to appreciate Scottish history: through prose fiction. He had already decided it was time to move on from poetry: Lord Byron had published *Childe Harold's Pilgrimage* the previous year, and proved that he could execute narrative historical poems even better than Scott could. So Scott brought the pages downstairs to his study. He sent a portion to his publisher, John Ballantyne, and by the time he was back in Edinburgh in January 1814, he had finished the whole first section, with a provisional title: *Waverley: 'Tis Fifty Years Since.*

Those who have never read it may be surprised to learn that the novel's main character, Waverley, is not a Scot at all but an Englishman, an officer in the British army who is garrisoned in Scotland on the eve of Prince Charles's landing. Waverley meets a Highland chief, Fergus MacIvor, and his sister Flora, and, inspired by their courage and passion for the prince's cause, becomes a Jacobite himself. It is a story of divided loyalties and clashing cultures, of a man torn between his love for a noble but doomed cause, symbolized by the beautiful Flora, and his own sense of duty. Readers, including his publisher, were blown away by it. When it appeared in July 1814, it outsold all of Scott's previous works—and created a whole new literary genre, the historical novel.

Even the *Edinburgh Review* was captivated. It wrote of the "surprise that is excited by discovering, that in our country, and almost in our own age, manners and characteristics existed, and were conspicuous, which we had been accustomed to consider as belonging to remote antiquity or extravagant romance." Of course, the people who were, even that summer, being expelled from their homes in Sutherland and Ross might have told the reviewer that. But no one in 1814 was listening to them. Scott, almost by accident, had become their voice, however indirectly and imperfectly. Through the Highland shepherds, crofters, and fishermen he put into his novels (which, all critics agree, are Scott's best literary characters), the voice of rural Scotland reached a wider audience than anyone could have imagined.

Scott followed *Waverley* with *Guy Mannering,* then *Old Mortality* and *Rob Roy.* The books poured off his desk at an astonishing rate. They were the capstone of those years that Lord Byron, not without some jealousy, called "the reign of Scott." The novels made him the best-paid author in Britain; by now he was earning close to ten thousand pounds a year in royalties and advances. They also created a mass market for novels and novelists on which every one of his English successors could capitalize: Jane Austen (whom Scott admired and championed), Charles Dickens, William Thackeray, George Eliot, Anthony Trollope, and all the other great names of nineteenth-century literature on the Continent as well: Balzac, Hugo, Flaubert, and Tolstoy. The historical novel became a distinct art form, a way of making the past come alive through an intriguing blend of imaginative fantasy and meticulous fidelity to historical truth—a form that has proved more successful with modern readers than history itself. Tolstoy could never have conceived a work such as *War and Peace* without Scott's example, or Hugo a work such as *Les Miserables*; other historical fiction writers, from Balzac and Alexandre Dumas to Bulwer-Lytton (*The Last Days of Pompeii*), Lew Wallace (*Ben-Hur*), and Jules Verne, owed Scott a similar debt—not to mention the best of all his Scottish successors, Robert Louis Stevenson.

Scott had not only invented the modern historical novel, but one of its enduring themes: the idea of cultural conflict. He revealed to his readers that the development of "civilization" or modernity does not leave clean or neat breaks; one stage does not effortlessly pass on to the next. They overlap and clash, and individuals get caught in the gap. Waverley and the heroes in *Ivanhoe* and *Redgauntlet* find themselves culturally at odds with their world, and even with their own identities. His novels, whether they are set in the Highlands, in medieval England, or in Palestine, reveal history as a series of "culture wars": Frank versus Saracen (in *The Talisman*), Jew versus Christian (in *Ivanhoe*), Norman versus Saxon, Scotsman versus Englishman, Lowlander versus Highlander, Presbyterian versus Episcopalian.

And which side is superior, and which deserves to lose, is never fully resolved. Scott detested the old-style Scottish Calvinism—but in a novel such as *Old Mortality,* he treated it sympathetically and left no trace of his own feelings. Virginia Woolf remarked of Scott's novels, "part of their astonishing freshness, their perennial vitality, is that you may read them over and over again, and never know for certain what Scott himself was or what Scott himself thought." Scott the novelist introduced a key ingredient of the modern consciousness, a sense of historical detachment—something that Macaulay (who was a great admirer of Scott) and other historians of the early Victorian age still lacked.

Part of that detachment arose from an insight Scott shared with

David Hume and the rest of the Scottish Enlightenment: that the modern world generates opposing tensions, which cannot be resolved without destroying the whole. Scott was aware of such divisions in himself—between the romantic poet and the historical scholar, between the lover of nature and the student of science, between the sentimental Jacobite and the hardheaded lawyer, between the staunch Tory and the admirer of progress (he was the first person in Edinburgh to install gas lighting in his house). And he was aware of the same split in Scottish culture. "The Scottish mind was made up of poetry and strong common sense," he wrote to a friend, "and the very strength of the latter gave perpetuity and luxuriance to the former." The credit for defining the artist as a person who can hold two inconsistent ideas at once goes to F. Scott Fitzgerald. The credit for realizing that that is precisely what all modern men can do—indeed, *must* be able to do—belongs to Sir Walter Scott.

III

The Waverley novels thrust Scott onto the public stage (although they were published pseudonymously, everyone knew who wrote them). He became friends with the mighty and great in London and at Whitehall. Following Napoleon's defeat at Waterloo, he traveled to Paris to meet his hero, the Duke of Wellington, as well as the Russian Tsar. He also became friends with the Prince of Wales, soon to be George IV. The prince had already offered him the post of Poet Laureate, which Scott declined—the idea of having to compose a poem every year to celebrate the king's birthday, or for other state occasions, was too much even for this staunch Tory. But in 1815 they finally met in London.

The Prince of Wales was fat, lazy, lecherous, vain, and inconsiderate. He was a drunkard who practically lived on cherry brandy. He had abandoned his wife and betrayed his old political allies, the Whigs. But he was also a cultured and intelligent man, who had read Ossian and knew *Waverley* almost by heart. The prince's admiration for his work, and his undeniable charm, won Scott over. In turn, Scott began to impress on the man who would soon be king the idea that his mission should be to restore to Britain its rich historical legacy, including the legacy of Scotland. He could be the new Bonnie Prince Charlie, Scott explained, a romantic monarch for a modern empire.

One place to start was to recover the lost regalia of the Scottish monarchy: the Sword, Sceptre, and Crown. They had been stored away in Edinburgh Castle after 1707 and then forgotten. The Prince gave Scott permission to enter the castle to conduct the search. After a long and dramatic hunt through the dark cellars, corridors, and storerooms of the old fortress, which drew enormous public interest and crowds, they were finally found in a dilapidated chest. To Scott, they were the sacred symbols of Scottish nationhood. When one of his assistants jocularly offered to place the crown on the head of a nearby young lady, Scott shouted, "By God, no!" and snatched it away. The recovery of the Scottish regalia earned Scott his baronetcy, and prepared the way for the next step in restoring Scotland's vanished glory.

It is not true, as is sometimes claimed, that the King's visit to Edinburgh in 1822 was Scott's idea. The Prince of Wales, now George IV, had been planning a tour of his British dominions for years, and following his state visit to Ireland, Scotland was the next stop. When he announced his plans to Edinburgh's Lord Provost, the Provost turned to Scott, now Sir Walter Scott, for help. Scott, in turn, called on David Stewart of Garth, the sharp-tongued soldier and critic of the Sutherland clearances, for ideas on how to stage the ceremonies to accompany the royal visit. In the end, it was Stewart as much as Scott who devised the pageantry for "the king's jaunt" that August, pageantry that changed irrevocably the relationship between England and Scotland, and capped the Highland cultural revival—even as that culture was vanishing forever.

The King made his view of the visit clear when he said, "I dislike seeing anything in Scotland that is not purely national and characteristic." For an enthusiastic reader of *Waverley* and *Rob Roy*, that meant Highland attire and display, with kilts, bonnets, tartans, bagpipes, and Gaelic battle songs, so those were what Walter Scott and David Stewart decided to provide. Of course, the King had never seen actual Highland dress, except on soldiers in the Black Watch or other Scottish regiments. They wore the shorter version of the kilt, the philabeg or *féileadh-beag,* which strapped around the waist with a yard or so of plaid attached at the shoulder, instead of the *breacan an féileadh,* the full twelve yards of plaid baggily belted in the middle, which had been the traditional dress of Highland males for centuries. On the other hand, the philabeg used less material, was easier to wear, and was less redolent of rural poverty and sleeping out of doors on an empty stomach. So the King's visit made it the new "authentic" Highland kilt. It has remained so down to today—just as the visit turned Scottish history into *Highland* history, with Lowlanders and Borderers largely forgotten.

If the King had no idea what real Highlanders looked like, neither did most Edinburghers. The ceremonies Stewart and Scott devised were to be as much a lesson in Scottish history for Scots as for George IV, and as much a salute to their country as to the King. It was the first state visit by a reigning monarch since 1650, and the first since the Union. This was Scotland's chance to shine in the eyes of its King and the rest of the world, a chance to establish its place in the British Empire. For that reason, its organizers decided, too much would probably not be enough.

That July, Scott's house at Castle Street was a workshop of activity. Every day from seven in the morning until past midnight, a steady stream of messengers, visitors, porters, and officials came and went, while Scott drew up designs, protocols, invitations, lists of guests, and orders of predecent during ritual ceremonies. Everything was to be as it had been before 1707, with a parade of state and regal splendor down High Street such as Edinburgh might have seen in the days of James IV.

Some things had to be changed, however. There was no longer a Scottish Parliament, so no "riding of the Parliament" was possible. Other ways of celebrating Scotland's political traditions had to be worked out. Scott and Garth turned the Royal Company of Archers, for example, into a sort of King's bodyguard of Scottish peers and aristocrats. Likewise, the Highland dress everyone would wear for the ceremonies had to be suitably martial, including targes, broadswords, and dirks, with a *sgian dhu,* or short dagger, inserted at the top of the stocking. This would remind onlookers of Scottish courage and valor, whether on Dunrossie Moor at Culloden or, more recently, on the battlefields of Spain, India, and Waterloo.

Yet, ironically, despite all the insistence on things Highlandish, very few Highlanders were actually going to be there. Walter Scott had sent a formal invitation to MacLeod of MacLeod and other great chieftains, summoning them and their followers to a modern-day version of the gathering of the clans to greet their "chief of chiefs." But only five showed up. Campbell of Breadalbane brought fifty men wearing tartans—not their own tartans, but one the Earl had designed in Edinburgh and sent to them. The MacGregors of Griogaraich were there, as bodyguards to the Regalia. Their chief, Sir Ewan MacGregor, was looking forward to finally erasing the family's long history of royal disgrace. The flamboyant Alistair MacDonnell of Glengarry also showed up. He had been the inspiration for *Waverley*'s Fergus McIvor and looked the part, with his pipers, henchmen, and foresters in attendance—and proceeded to make an obnoxious nuisance of himself through the whole visit, to the disgust of both Scott and Stewart.

The Drummonds of Strathearn sent a contingent, as did, more surprisingly, the Duchess of Sutherland. She had been stung by the criticisms of her clearance policy in David Stewart's recent book, and was determined to show the proper Highland spirit. Everyone agreed they were the scruffiest of the lot: "[S]o inferior, indeed, was their appearance," according to Donald MacLeod, "that those who had the management refused to allow them to walk in the procession. . . . They were huddled in an old, empty house, sleeping on straw and fed with the coarsest fare while the other clans were living in comparative luxury."

So the vast majority of participants in this "plaided panorama" (as Scott's son-in-law called it) ended up being members of Edinburgh's Celtic Society and the Strathfillan Society: gentry and middle-class citizens, most with Highland names or roots, but almost all with no experience of clan life. In that sense, they were like most people who wear kilts today. Indeed, the authorities preferred it that way. When Walter Scott tried to send for some men from the Earl of Atholl, Henry Dundas, a man who was still mindful of the recent violence around Glasgow and earlier troubles in the Highlands, said no. "I think we have fully as many of the Gael, real or imagined, as is prudent or necessary."

On the eve of the King's visit, the *Edinburgh Observer* ran this editorial:

We are all Jacobites now, thorough-bred Jacobites, in acknowledging George IV. . . . Our king is the heir of the Chevalier, in whose service the Scotch suffered so much, shone so much, and we will find many a Flora MacDonald amongst the "Sisters of the Silver Cross," and many a faithful Highlander attending his Throne. . . .

The city was in a frenzy. It had filled up with visitors from across Scotland, who watched General Stewart and the Celtic Society's tartaned contingents drilling on the meadow between Queen Street and Heriot Row. Lords, lairds, archers, soldiers, and militiamen gathered in the streets, with pipes blaring and flags and banners waving in the summer sun—and at night, in the soft glow of Edinburgh's new gas street-lighting.

On Wednesday, August 14, the royal yacht was spotted in the Firth of Forth. The cannon on Castle Hill signaled the news, as the crowd gathered to join the march down from Edinburgh to Leith to greet the King. Scott rowed out to meet his monarch on board. "Sir Walter Scott!" the King exclaimed, "The man in Scotland I most want to see! Let him come up!" With a grin, George IV toasted his loyal servant with a tumbler of genuine Highland whisky. Scott put the glass in his pocket as a souvenir (later, in his excitement, he sat on it and crushed it).

The next day the visit proper began. By one estimate, 300,000 people, or more than one-seventh of Scotland's population, greeted the King as he came ashore with cheers and more cannon salutes, and as the cavalcade made its way up Leith Walk to Edinburgh's High Street. Walter Scott led the way in an open carriage to rapturous applause; then came the trumpeters, yeoman cavalry, grenadiers, dragoons, soldiers from various Highland regiments and the Scots Greys, heralds, grooms, archers: then the Knight Marischal, the Barons of Exchequer, and the Lords of Justiciary and Sessions in their scarlet robes, the White Rod, Lord Lyon Depute, the Lord High Constable—and then the King.

Fat, scarlet-faced, breathing heavily and barely able to walk, this latter-day Bonnie Prince Charlie slowly made his way up High Street to the Toll Gate, where the Lord Provost presented him with the keys to the city, and then took him across to St. Andrews Square and crowd-lined Princes Street. Turning around, the King was astonished to see more thousands of people standing in rows on Castle Hill, a living mountain of humanity watching and waving. When he waved back, the city resounded with a tremendous cheer.

On Saturday came the King's reception under the gleaming chande-liers at Holyrood House. David Stewart of Garth came to the King's chamber to examine the "authentic" Highland costume he would wear for the evening. It was the full treatment: pleated tartan kilt with the pattern of the house of Stuart, trews or plaid tights, sporran bag in front, and feathered bonnet. Stewart looked at George IV's bloated red face, his enormous belly hanging over his kilt, and tights stretched skin-tight around his bulging, flabby thighs. Discretion dictated his next words. "Ye make a varry pretty figure," he told his monarch, and sent him out to greet his rapturous guests.

It was a strange moment. This peculiar form of Scottish clothing, which had only recently been dismissed as barbaric frummery, and had even been outlawed, was now proper dress for royalty. The overweight heir of the house of Hanover, the great-nephew of the Duke of Cumberland who had fought and slaughtered kilted clansmen for con-trol of the destiny of Scotland and Great Britain, was now wearing the same tartan pattern as the mortal enemies of his ancestral house. Later that week, at the banquet sponsored by the Edinburgh Town Council which lasted six and a half hours, tartan kilts again turned up in profu-sion, on people who only twenty years earlier would not have been caught dead in them.

This shift of cultural mood was all due to Sir Walter Scott. He was not the first to rescue Highland culture from the rubbish-heap of his-tory. But he was the first to make it high-minded and respectable, with an appealing romantic panache, which has made it an indelible part of the historical imagination ever since. It was part of his larger plan for the royal visit: a reconciliation of ancient enemies, Hanover with Stuart, England with Scotland, and the past with the present.

Most historians and writers poke fun at the royal visit, and for good reason. It is tempting to yield to outrage at its falsification of Scottish history, and its hypocrisy in claiming to exalt Highland culture even while that culture and its people were being eradicated, thanks to the Clearances. Even people at the time recognized the royal visit's exaggerated ridiculousness. Scott's son-in-law John Lockhart dubbed it "a collective hallucination." It was also a largely Tory celebration. The Whigs at the *Edinburgh Review* had their attention firmly fixed on parliamentary reform. Henry Cockburn does not even mention it in his autobiography.

The visit's air of phoniness was compounded by its aftermath, when wool manufacturers such as Wilson's of Bannockburn began taking orders for the newly popularized kilt. People wondered which of the innumerable patterns or "setts" of tartan to buy. It was Wilson who began the practice of naming particular setts after specific Highland clans. There may have been some validity to this: families living in a clan area did tend to weave tartans that looked alike, and that distinguished them from their neighbors. But the real mark of clan identification was the badge worn on the hat or on the arm, such as a sprig of juniper (the badge of the MacLeods) or white heather (the MacIntyres). Clansmen generally wore whatever plaid patterns they liked, and the louder the better.

The army started the practice of using the tartan as identification, as part of the uniform of Highland regiments. The Black Watch was first in 1739, with its somber blue, green, and black plaid. Others followed suit. Clan members then began using their clan's regimental tartan, although with no sense of exclusiveness. In fact, when the Highland Society of London began in 1815 to collect patches of existing tartans and approached various chieftains to find out which belonged to which clan, it was amazed to learn that most had no idea.

All this "confusion" came to an end twenty years after the Royal Visit, when two Bohemian brothers, claiming to be the illegitimate grandsons of Prince Charlie himself, appeared on the scene with their own tartan pattern book, portentously titled *Vestiarum Scoticum*. James and Charles Sobieski Stuart, as they called themselves, had selected seventy-five different setts, each linked to a specific clan, from a sixteenth-century manuscript they claimed had once belonged to Mary

Queen of Scots's father confessor—although they could never quite produce the manuscript when others asked to see it. It was MacPherson and Ossian all over again, with a very similar result. Tartans became all the rage in England as well as Scotland. Queen Victoria insisted on them for her Highland retreat at Balmoral Castle. Clan chieftains, and even Lowland aristocrats, suddenly decided they had better line up a "true" clan pattern or get lost in the rush.

So one could say the great Highland revival began with one fraud and ended with another. But this would be unfair to its genuine adherents, including Scott. After all, his moment of glory after the royal visit was brief. His publisher and partner, John Ballantyne, went bankrupt in 1825. Rather than go bankrupt with him, Scott promised to pay his creditors everything he owed them. In exchange for keeping his position as sheriff and clerk of court in Edinburgh, and living at Abbotsford rent-free, he agreed to spend every penny of his royalties from all future books to pay off the debt, which amounted to more than 100,000 pounds.

"I will be their vassal for life," he wrote in his journal, "and dig in the mine of my imagination to find diamonds." All thought of retiring as the distinguished laird of Abbotsford was now impossible. The work broke his health; he suffered a stroke in 1830, but continued writing. "He that sleeps too long in the morning," he said, "let him borrow the pillow of a debtor." He had paid off more than half before he died in 1832, the same year Parliament passed the measure he hated and feared, the Reform Bill.

When he heard the news of Scott's death, his Whig neighbor Henry Cockburn wrote in his journal, "Scotland never owed so much to one man." And in fact, Sir Walter Scott had done something remarkable. He had managed to generate another Scotland parallel to the one about to be thrust into the new century. A Scotland of the imagination, a place where honor, courage, and integrity could still survive, and even thrive, within the individual. Scott had created a new national identity, based on the myth of the strong and noble Highlander. It was available not only for Scots but for the rest of Britain, which could take comfort and pride in the notion that north of the Tweed the old, premodern virtues were still being kept alive. Later, of course, people of Scottish descent outside Britain would help themselves to it, as well—as anyone knows who has attended a St. Andrew's Society dinner in New York or Melbourne and watched the profusion of kilts and *sgian dhus.*

This new Scottish identity complemented, but did not compete with, the one that modernity was forging. For one thing, Scott had made it essentially democratic, since it was open to anyone with a spark of imagination, and imagination, Adam Smith had shown, was the basis of modern society itself. For another, unlike Ossian's mythic past, which "breathed old age and decay," it was essentially hopeful about the future, even if the old ways were fading away. The lesson Scott taught the modern world was that the past does not have to die or vanish: it can live on, in a nation's memory, and help to nourish its posterity.

CHAPTER TWELVE

Practical Matters:
Scots in Science and Industry

Don't think, try.

—*John Hunter*

I

James Watt was instrument maker for the University of Glasgow when someone told him about a strange machine created by a Derbyshire man named Thomas Newcomen: a device that used steam to operate a water pump. The university even had a model of it, he was told, which was in London for repairs. Watt was interested in steam. He and his friend and teacher, Professor Joseph Black, had been arguing about its properties for years. Now, in the winter of 1763, he arranged for the model to be shipped back to Glasgow, and had a look at it.

It consisted of a boiler that sent steam into a vertical brass cylinder attached to a close-fitting piston, which in turn was attached to a metal rod. As steam went in, it pushed up the piston, depressing the rod. As it condensed back to water, the vacuum it created brought the piston down, raising the rod. Newcomen's "fire-engine," as some called it, was a clever device; miners in Wales had been using its up-and-down motion to pump water out of their coal pits. But as Watt fired it up and set it in motion, he saw the problem at once. The piston turned only two or three strokes at a time, because although the boiler attached was relatively large, most of the steam it generated escaped into the air.

Twenty-seven years old, Watt was largely a self-taught man, but what he knew impressed everyone who came into his shop. Even the university professors were impressed. "I saw a workman, and expected no more," recalled one, "but was surprised to find a philosopher." Watt also had an enormous supply of self-confidence. He believed he could fix, or make, anything. Once the Masonic Lodge in Glasgow needed a pipe organ and asked him to provide one. Watt, who knew nothing about music, mastered the subject over a few weeks, learned everything he could about organs, chose the necessary materials, laid out the design, and built the organ himself. These sorts of projects happily absorbed all his attention. Now figuring out how steam worked, and how to keep Newcomen's machine moving, became his daily obsession.

Watt labored over the "fire engine" for more than a year. Then, on a particularly fine afternoon (always rare in Glasgow) early in 1765, Watt set out for a walk. He opened the gate at the foot of Charlotte Street and walked past the old washing house. "I was thinking upon the engine at the time," he wrote later, "when the idea came into my mind that as steam was an elastic body it would rush into a vacuum, and if a communication were made between the cylinder and an exhausted vessel it would rush into it, and might be there condensed without cooling the cylinder. . . . I had not walked farther than the golf-house when the whole thing was arranged in my mind."

Contrary to myth, James Watt did not invent the steam engine. Two Englishmen, Newcomen and Thomas Savery, did that. What Watt did was typically Scottish: he perfected something created by someone else, and gave it a higher and wider application than its original inventor had imagined. Watt applied to the steam engine the idea of separate condensation, which allowed it to generate a constant motion, which, in 1781, Watt turned into a rotary motion. He had created the work engine of the Industrial Revolution. Commercial society was about to turn into industrial society, with technology as its driving force. He gave capitalism its modern face, which has persisted down to today.

The Scots did not invent technology, any more than they invented science—or capitalism or the ideas of progress and liberty. But just as in these other cases, the version of technology we live with most closely resembles the one that Scots such as James Watt organized and perfected. It rests on certain basic principles that the Scottish

Enlightenment enshrined: common sense, experience as our best source of knowledge, and arriving at scientific laws by testing general hypotheses through individual experiment and trial and error. Science and technology give civilization its dynamic movement, like the ceaselessly moving pistons of Watt's steam engine. To the Scots, they were the key to modern life, just as they are for us. A rapid succession of Scottish inventors, engineers, doctors, and scientists proved their point to the rest of the world.

James Watt, for example, grew up in Greenock, with no formal education, but surrounded by the paraphernalia of seagoing Glasgow, since his father supplied nautical equipment to local shipbuilders. Out of this environment of ships' stores, ropes, pulleys, sextants, quadrants, and compasses, he developed an interest in mathematical and mechanical devices. He failed to find adequate work in London or Glasgow, but when the university found itself heir to a collection of sophisticated astronomical instruments assembled by a local West Indies merchant, it hired him to recalibrate them. Then he met Joseph Black, and began learning chemistry. "No man I know," Adam Smith said, "has less nonsense in his head than Doctor Black." Black discovered the same was true of Watt, and the two began exploring the problem that perplexed Black most, the question of what happens to the heat after objects are heated and cooled, or what he called "latent heat."

Watt's work on the steam engine led him to conduct a series of experiments on precisely this problem. Those experiments demonstrated that heat was not a substance but a property of matter, just as his description of the principles of the steam engine laid the foundation of modern mechanical engineering. The issue for Watt, though, was always not just how a thing worked, but what to do with it afterwards. Through Joseph Black, he teamed up with a pair of ironmasters named Roebuck and Cadell, who offered to pay for his development of the new engine and arrange for a patent, if he would build them a prototype for their foundry at Kinneil on the river Carron.

The real breakthrough came, however, when he met the English ironmaster Matthew Boulton of Birmingham. Their partnership, formed in 1775, gave them a complete monopoly over steam engine construction for the next quarter-century. Together they transformed Britain's economic life. They turned the steam engine from primarily a water pump into a way to supply power for every conceivable industry, from John Wilkinson's ironworks and Josiah Wedgewood's pottery kilns to feeding the Birmingham Canal and dredging Glasgow's port. Their engines (they produced more than five hundred in those twenty-five years) operated looms in cotton and textile mills from Paisley and Deanston to Manchester and Liverpool, allowing that business to expand its output almost exponentially. They made the modern factory, and the factory system, possible. They also altered the way people saw the world. That became clear when James Boswell visited their Soho works outside Birmingham, and Boulton showed him around, uttering the famous phrase: "I sell here, sir, what all the world desires to have: *power.*"

A new concept had entered the modern consciousness. The idea of power not in a political sense, the ability to command people, but the ability to command nature: the power to alter and use it to create something new, and produce it in greater and larger quantities than ever before. At almost the same moment as Watt and Boulton were setting up their factory and producing their first steam engine, Adam Smith was writing that the division of labor was the key to creating wealth. Watt's invention revealed that the future of the division of labor was technological change. By unleashing the dynamic power hidden in nature itself, one could make it work to human advantage.

"Nature has its weak side," Watt liked to say, "if only we can find it." Finding that weakness was the job of science. Exploiting the opening that science provided was the job of the engineer—and his business sidekick, the entrepreneur.

Watt was perfectly comfortable with the idea that his scientific expertise, like his machine, should be used to make a profit. So was his mentor, Joseph Black. As Professor of Chemistry, Black devoted much of his attention to improving the system of bleaching used by Glasgow's linen manufacturers, just as Robert Foulis had conceived his school of design as a support center for textile printing. This was, again, very typical of the Glasgow Enlightenment's fusion of the practical and the theoretical. Black's own teacher, William Cullen, had launched the bleach-ing agent project when he was Professor of Anatomy at Glasgow. When he moved to Edinburgh in 1755, he was a distinguished figure not only in the field of medicine, but also in what might be called industrial science.

Cullen was a practicing doctor (he became Adam Smith's personal physician). So was Joseph Black. Other key figures in the early develop-ment of Scotland's industrial revolution were also trained as doctors, including Watt's first business partner, John Roebuck. The two fields resembled each other. The hallmarks of Scottish medicine were close clinical observation, hands-on diagnosis, and thinking of objects such as the human body as a system—not so different from the practical approach of engineers such as James Watt. In fact, science and medicine were probably more closely linked in Scotland than any other European country. Together with mathematics, they formed the triangular base of the Scottish practical mind.

Even before the formal creation of Edinburgh's medical school in 1726, Scotland was famous for its physicians. The field was dominated by two great dynasties of teachers, the Gregorys at Glasgow and the Munros at Edinburgh, who taught class after class of aspiring doctors in anatomy for nearly 130 years.* The dynasty's founder, Alexander Munro, Sr., made the study of anatomy central to the training of physi-cians. He was a student of the great Hermann Boerhaave at the University of Leyden, who broke away from the old medieval medical traditions and encouraged his students to use their eyes and ears to diag-nose disease at the patient's bedside. Boerhaave believed that progress in medicine depended on open-minded inquiry, a search for general laws based on observation—the key idea behind modern scientific method, in fact (Boerhaave was also a great admirer of Isaac Newton).

The first staff of Edinburgh's new medical faculty were all Leyden students, including Munro. The school was the brainchild of the same

---

*Charles Darwin sat in on the last of the Munros' classes in the 1820s, however, and remembered, "Dr. Munro made his lectures on human anatomy as dull as he was himself."

man who conceived the New Town, Provost George Drummond, and for the same reason: to give Edinburgh a distinctly modern and "civilized" identity, as a leading center for British medicine as well as British urban life. It succeeded beyond Drummond's dreams. Students flocked in from across the country—since in medicine as in everything else, Oxford and Cambridge were closed off to non-Anglicans. Edinburgh became the preeminent place in Europe for the study of anatomy. The school used human cadavers for dissection in such record numbers that supplying new ones became a problem.*

The Munros were the anchor of the school. Alex senior founded the Royal Infirmary, developed its celebrated lectures on anatomy and the central nervous system, and made the study of surgery a fundamental part of medical training. However, the pace changed dramatically when William Cullen, already Edinburgh's Professor of Chemistry, stepped in as Professor of the Theory of Physic in 1766. Cullen was an iconoclast. He created the same revolution in medicine that Francis Hutcheson had in philosophy, by lecturing in English rather than Latin. He encouraged students to challenge him in class and to think on their own, based on what they saw rather than what they had been taught to expect. He vehemently rejected academic speculation; his motto was, in effect, no facts, no theory. But as the first professor of chemistry in Britain, he also insisted his students equip themselves with the most up-to-date knowledge of the basic sciences.

The typical product of the Edinburgh school in those years was a new kind of modern doctor: the general practitioner, who was physician, surgeon, and apothecary rolled into one (Cullen published the first

---

*That led two enterprising Irish scoundrels, William Burke and William Hare, to offer a steady supply of dead bodies to anatomy professor Robert Knox with no questions asked—steady because they began murdering the victims themselves. When their hideous enterprise was revealed in 1829, the trial of Burke and Hare caused a major scandal. The grisly story inspired, among others, Robert Louis Stevenson's short story "The Body Snatcher." Knox himself was never charged, while Hare turned king's evidence. William Burke went to the gallows—and ended up as a cadaver for dissection at the medical school. His skeleton is still there, preserved in its museum.

modern pharmacopoeia in 1776). Other medical schools, especially Oxford and Cambridge, discouraged their students from any kind of physical contact with the patient. Probing a tender spot, or cleaning and dressing a wound—let alone cutting someone open to see what was going on—was left to menial servants, such as the barber-surgeon. Edinburgh taught its doctors to be hands-on generalists, who could spot a problem, make a diagnosis, and apply treatment themselves. Professor John Rutherford created the first system of clinical rounds for training medical students in 1750. More than just spouters of medical theory, Scottish doctors were in effect scientific missionaries, ready to push forward the frontiers of knowledge and progress wherever they went, and equipped to do battle against ignorance and apathy, as well as against disease.

Two brothers, William and John Hunter, best exemplified this Scottish approach. William studied with Francis Hutcheson and William Cullen at Glasgow, took Munro's anatomy classes at Edinburgh, and taught the subject to his brother John when he joined him in London in 1748. William turned the field of obstetrics into a scientifically precise discipline under the supervision of doctors. Critics even derided him as "the man mid-wife," as he broke down the barrier that made delivering babies the exclusive preserve of women. Feminist critics still deplore Hunter's efforts to turn childbearing, and the female body, into an object of medical knowledge. But Hunter was motivated not by male chauvinism but by the desire to make infant delivery more organized, more systematic, and safer than traditional methods— including banning the use of forceps. John Hunter worked to achieve a similar transformation of the fields of dentistry (he first coined the terms *incisor, bicuspid,* and *molar* for describing teeth) and surgery.

Despite incessant criticism and vast professional jealousy, both became spectacularly successful. William Hunter was personal physician to the rich and powerful, including Physician Extraordinary to Queen Charlotte. His brother held the same position to the King himself (still another Scottish medical man, John Arbuthnot, had been physician to Queen Anne). More than any other person, John Hunter turned surgery from a quick-and-dirty art, practiced part-time by barbers, into a scientific discipline resting on a solid foundation of both anatomy and biology. The Hunters were bona fide figures of the Scottish Enlightenment. Edward Gibbon and Adam Smith both attended William's lectures in the 1770s; John diagnosed David Hume's fatal illness, and treated Smith for hemorrhoids. He passed on his great motto, "Don't think, try," to his most famous English student, Edward Jenner. It probably helped to inspire Jenner's experiments with using cowpox inoculations to fight off its far deadlier relative, smallpox. Jenner gets the credit for inventing medical inoculation—although it was in fact another distinguished Scottish London physician, Charles Maitland, who first borrowed the technique from the Middle East and used it to protect his patients from smallpox outbreaks in the 1720s.

Scottish doctors were more popular with patients than English ones, since, as the historian Anand Chitnis has suggested, "their useful knowledge contrasted with the ornamental learning of the London physicians who were Anglican and Oxbridge-trained." Between 1800 and 1825, 258 of the Royal College of Physicians's 371 fellows and licentiates were Scottish-educated. Guy's Hospital in London offered a host of distinguished Edinburgh-trained doctors, including Richard Bright, Thomas Addison, and Thomas Hodgkin, each of whom gave his name to the disease he was the first to diagnose.

Scottish physicians also pioneered another aspect of modern medicine: the field of public health, which largely meant trying to halt dangerous epidemic diseases. John Pringle, another Boerhaave student, served as Physician-General of the British Army in Flanders. Appalled at the needless loss of thousands of soldiers to disease and neglect, he insisted on sweeping changes in the way the army treated its sick and wounded, including ventilation of field hospitals and barracks to prevent the spread of disease. He made sure that every soldier was issued a blanket, and that campsites included proper latrines and sanitation.

On one occasion, just before the army was about to engage the French in battle, Pringle suggested that the army's commander deploy his field hospitals in a clearly neutral area, away from the actual fighting, so that the wounded and those tending them would be out of harm's way. The commander was a fellow Scot, none other than the fourth Earl of Stair—grandson of the man who saved the Treaty of Union. Stair agreed. During the battle, the French saw what was happening and avoided shelling or attacking the British hospitals. They then adopted Pringle's idea, and other European nations followed suit. Pringle had established the fundamental principle of army medics and their patients as noncombatants, which would not only make European warfare more humane, but would also inspire organizations such as the Red Cross.

James Lind was the Scottish physician who discovered that scurvy, the scourge of common British seamen serving on long voyages in the South Atlantic and Pacific, could be cured by the use of citrus fruits. On May 20, 1747, Lind took on twelve patients with scurvy, who "all in general had putrid gums," he wrote, "the spots and lassitude, with weakness of their knees." He divided them into six pairs, treating some with a rich diet of mutton broth and pudding, others with a quart of cider a day, others with "twenty five gutts of elixir vitriol"—and the last pair with two oranges and a lemon a day. It may have been the first controlled experiment in medical history. The pair on the citrus diet recovered first; within six days they were fit for duty. "I am apt to think oranges preferable to lemons," Lind said, and suggested that British naval vessels carry a regular supply. Ignorance and obstinacy blocked his proposed reform. He did persuade Captain James Cook, who was a Scot by blood, to use citrus fruits on his voyage to the South Seas in 1769, but it took yet another Scot, Sir James Blane, finally to persuade the Admiralty in 1795 to require lime juice as standard issue on His Majesty's ships. It was a crucial contribution to Britain's recovery as a world power—and its acquisition of empire. The term *limey* stuck as a sobriquet for the British sailor, and later for Britons overseas. Scottish medicine was emerging as a bulwark of the new Great Britain.

James Hutton studied medicine at Edinburgh and Leyden in the late 1740s, but chose not to become a doctor. He took up farming instead, at the family estate in Berwickshire. Hutton was part of Edinburgh's enlightened intellectual elite. He would convene the Oyster Club with Adam Smith and Joseph Black and shared Black's passion for chemistry. Hutton was also an amateur geologist. One day in a farm field he picked up a peculiar stone that was clearly made up of layers of distinct minerals. It led Hutton on a fantastic journey to a completely new under-standing of the earth's geology. "In interpreting nature," he wrote, "no powers are to be employed that are not natural in the globe . . . and no extraordinary events to be alleged in order to explain a common appearance." Hutton concluded that the earth's crust was not only made up of debris from past geological upheavals, but was also far older than the six thousand years the Bible had allowed. In 1795, the same year James Blane finally moved the Admiralty to accept Lind's recommended cure for scurvy, Hutton published his revolutionary *Theory of the Earth*. In it he proposed that the earth had its own history of great and ancient changes, which, like diseases of the body, left their visible mark on its surface through fossil remains and sedimentary rock deposits. Planet Earth was the bedrock of *all* history, in fact. It long predated the appear-ance of man and would, Hutton assured readers, endure long after he had gone.

Hutton died just two years later. But the stage was set for a new view of nature—as well as of man. The natural and physical world turned out to be as dynamic, and progressive, as human society had been for the Scottish school. At least one scientist took Hutton's idea to heart, an English-born but Edinburgh-trained physician named Erasmus Darwin. Darwin expanded and inflated it into a full-blown theory of nature as a history of progress, in his *Zoonomia, or the Laws of Organic Life*. "Would it be too bold to imagine that . . . all warm-blooded animals have arisen from one living filament," he wrote, "with the power of acquiring new parts, attended with new propensities . . . and thus pos-sessing the faculty of continuing to improve by its own inherent activ-ity, and of delivering down those improvements by generation to its posterity, world without end?"

It was an insight that his grandson, also trained at the Edinburgh medical school, would refine even further. Charles Darwin developed his own theory of biological evolution with the help of Scottish geolo-gist Sir Charles Lyell, who did more to advance the field of theoretical geology, Darwin later stated, than "any other man who ever lived." Darwin created a vision of the history of nature that matched the one that the Scots had crafted for the history of man—a history of progress, a steady rise from the primitive and the simple to the more complex, which culminates, of course, in man himself. *On the Origin of Species* revealed that the assumptions of the Scottish school were becoming indispensable not only to the social sciences, but to the natural and physical sciences as well. In the English-speaking world, a "scientific outlook" on the world was coming to mean almost the same thing as a Scottish outlook.

II

Scots became experts in another technical aspect of modernization: transport and communication. More than anyone else, they understood how essential the free flow of goods, services, people, and information was to the creation of modern society.

As early as the 1740s Duncan Forbes had foreseen that effective roads were the key to advancing the forces of civilization in Scotland's Highlands; Dr. Johnson's injunction about Scotsmen finding "the high road to London" made the same point. Adam Smith realized early on that England had developed faster as a commercial society, and then as an industrial power, in part because it enjoyed a network of roads, canals, bridges, riverways, and harbors that permitted goods in one part of the country to reach the other parts with relative ease. Nothing like it existed in Scotland: the Highlands were as effectively sealed off from economic and social progress as if they had been surrounded by a stone wall.

General Wade and his army construction gangs had strung a thin network of roads through the Highlands years before, which were still used by civilian as well as military traffic. But they were crude and unreliable in poor weather, and they were far too few. Local roads were even worse, as one traveler found out during a trip through Forfarshire: "Many of these roads," he wrote in 1813, "were merely formed, by digging a ditch on each side of them, and throwing the spongy clay, here called mortar, upon the top of the road. Of course they are almost impassable. . . . In wet weather, horses sink to their bellies, and carts to their axles. . . ."

This began to change in the 1790s, thanks to two Scottish engineers. One was John McAdam, who devised a cheap and efficient way to build a sturdy roadbed by using crushed stones and gravel. This he did with typical Scottish thoroughness, first traveling nearly thirty thousand miles across Britain and examining nearly every major road and highway. McAdam discovered that as long as the roadbed remained dry, it could handle any amount of traffic in any kind of weather—while wagon wheels and horses' hooves constantly pressing crushed gravel into the road actually made it firmer and stronger. The macadamized road, as it became known, soon crisscrossed most of England and parts of southern Scotland, as it allowed wagons and carriages to travel as fast as horses could pull them. It is the ancestor of our modern asphalt or tarmacadam roadway (tarmac for short). On such roads the Independent Tallyho coach could carry a letter or passenger from London to Watt and Boulton's factory in Birmingham at the breathtaking speed of fifteen miles an hour. Travel time from London to Edinburgh shrank from ten days to less than two. By 1830 the journey from Edinburgh to Glasgow, which used to take Adam Smith a day and a half, now took only four and a half hours.

McAdam's method worked best for repairing old roads and highways. While it proved immensely useful in England, it could not solve the real difficulty Scotland faced, which was a lack of roads. The man who really opened up Scotland, and in so doing transformed the nature of modern communication, was Thomas Telford. No other builder or engineer looms as large in the nineteenth century as Telford: he in effect created the shape of our modern landscape.

Telford was cut from a heroic mold, which was also typically Scottish. He was born in 1757 at Glendenning, the son of a local shepherd. His father died soon after he was born, and he was raised in poverty by a single mother. Still, he managed to go to the local parish school, and learned to read, write (he wrote poetry, and good poetry, the rest of his life), and do mathematics. To earn his bread, he apprenticed with a local stonemason. When he had learned all he could, he went to Edinburgh and then London, where he worked for Robert Adam and William Chambers. Long after he made his fortune as a builder and engineer, Telford was crossing Waterloo Bridge (built by another Scottish engineer, John Rennie) with a friend, and he pointed to Somerset House across the water, saying "You see those stones there: forty years since I hewed and laid them, when working on that building as a common mason."

Like any young, ambitious Scot working in London, Telford sought out a well-placed fellow Scot to act as his patron. Sir William Johnstone had married the niece of the Earl of Bath, and was supposed to be the richest commoner in Britain. Telford had met Johnstone's brother on his trip down to London, and Sir William was sufficiently impressed to put Telford in charge of building the commissioner's house at Portsmouth Dockyard. Telford taught himself the basic principles of architecture, and went on to build churches, castles, and jails until 1793, when Sir William got him appointed surveyor and engineer of the Ellesmere Canal in Wales.

South Wales, like Scotland, suffered from an appalling lack of roads and navigable waterways. It was, in its own way, as remote and inaccessible as the Scottish Highlands. But it also produced many of the raw materials needed for industrialization, particularly iron ore and coal. The problem was how to get it out of Wales. The answer was canals, since water was still the cheapest form of transport of bulk goods across Britain. However, with Ellesmere Telford surpassed the work of all his predecessors. At two crucial points in the canal he built massive aqueducts on a scale and size not seen since Roman times. The second, Pontcysyllte (which simply means "great crossing"), rose 127 feet above the Dee River, on a one-hundred-foot raised bank, with an iron trough carrying boats and barges along a nearly quarter-mile span. Two hundred years later it is still there and still in use, its meticulously made metal joints as perfect and trouble-free as the day they were laid.

Pontcysyllte revealed Telford as something new in the emerging industrial world: a visionary, an artist in cast iron and stone who grasped the potentially titanic scale and power of the new technologies. Telford humbly saw himself as the servant of progress and capitalism. "I admire commercial enterprise," he wrote, "it is the vigorous outgrowth of our industrial life. I admire everything that gives it free scope, as wherever it goes, activity, energy, intelligence—all that we call civilization—goes with it." But money was not everything, either for civilization or for Telford. "I hold that the aim and end of all ought not to be a mere bag of money, but something far higher and better"—perhaps even, through his bridges and canals, a kind of immortality.

Striving for something higher and better infused all of Telford's projects, including the ones he never built. In 1800 he offered to put across the Thames a single-span bridge of more than six hundred feet—the longest bridge ever attempted. It never saw the light of day, but his project for a bridge across the Menai Strait into Anglesey did, with a span of 579 feet suspended from towers rising 153 feet into the sky. Each of the bridge's sixteen suspension chains, made of links almost a yard long, required two and half hours of exhausting and dangerous work to raise into position, which Telford oversaw himself. When it opened in 1826, it was the biggest bridge in the world, tall enough to allow Britain's largest warships to pass underneath—and for more than a hundred years it never needed the slightest repair.

Telford's record of building in Scotland was even greater, and with a more decisive impact. In 1801 he toured the Highlands at the request of the Pitt government and a group of landowners calling themselves the Highland Fisheries Society, who were desperate to find some way to promote economic growth on their lands—and keep their tenants from being permanently driven away by the spread of sheep and cattle. Telford proposed building roads, bridges, harbors, and docks to open up coastal areas to commercial fishing, and canals—including a canal to link all the inland lochs of the Great Glen to Inverness and the sea. It was a development scheme on a heroic, almost foolhardy scale; yet, surprisingly, the government agreed and offered to split the costs with the local lairds. Together they spent over twenty thousand pounds putting in a new harbor at Peterhead, and over seventy thousand pounds at Dundee, all under Telford's supervision. He also built a thousand miles of strong and secure roads crisscrossing the Highlands, more durable even than McAdam's; they made Highland tourism, the new industry Sir Walter Scott had set in motion, possible. He also built bridges across remote glens and gorges—more than 120 of them.

All of this unending labor and travel, which took Telford back and forth across Britain—"you know I am tossed about like a rubber ball," he told a friend, "the other day I was in London and since then I have been in Liverpool and in a few days I expect to be in Bristol"—had to be fitted around the greatest project of his life, building the Caledonian Canal.

The Caledonian Canal is a massive sea-to-sea navigable waterway, connecting the Atlantic Ocean to Inverness and the North Sea. Running sixty miles through the Great Glen, with more than twenty miles of canals and locks, it is one and a half times the length of the Panama Canal, and nearly two-thirds as long as the Suez (for which it was the model). Its construction is one of the great epics of modern engineering history. It took Telford almost fifteen years to build, using tens of thousands of workers, at an unheard-of cost of nearly a billion pounds—the equivalent of perhaps two trillion dollars in today's money. Almost all of the money came from the British government, for what was the first public inland waterway project in the nation's history. It opened up the central Highlands to commercial traffic for the first time, marking a new era in the history of that remote and aloof region.

At each stage Telford had to find a solution to a new engineering problem. There was dredging out the entrance to an existing loch, or cutting a new channel, or finding a secure bottom for his massive stone canal locks (at one point the bottom was so soft "that it was pierced with an iron rod to the depth of sixty feet"), or simply moving the enormous quantities of earth the construction of each lock required. He designed a huge dredging machine, powered by one of Watt's steam engines, that could bring up eight hundred tons of mud a day. His friend and fellow poet Robert Southey saw it in operation when he came to visit in 1819. Southey also watched the building of the series of locks connecting Loch Lochy and Loch Oich, or "Neptune's Staircase," which could raise a ship nearly one hundred feet above sea level—"the greatest work of its kind which has been ever undertaken in ancient or modern times." Southey was a romantic reactionary. Like Sir Walter Scott, he was more inspired by the beauty of mountains and lakes than by industrial machinery. But even Southey could appreciate the breathtaking sight of

Telford's soaring suspension bridges, such as the one at Bonar: "Oh! It is the finest thing that ever was made by God or man!" And Scott said much the same when he saw Menai Bridge, calling it "the most impressive work of art I have ever seen."

But what most impressed Southey was Telford himself. "There is so much intelligence in his countenance, so much frankness, kindness, and hilarity about him. . . ." He concluded, "Telford's is a happy life: everywhere making roads, building bridges, forming canals, and creating harbours—works of sure, solid, permanent utility. . . ." Permanent was right. More than 75 percent of Telford's projects are still in operation to this day. It was a life's work that flowed from a bottomless reservoir of creativity and self-confident energy. It continued to flow right down to his last years, when Telford began to work on a plan to build a canal in South America to connect the Atlantic and Pacific Oceans. The place he chose for it was the narrowest point on the North-South American land bridge, at Darien—the same place where William Paterson had launched his ill-fated colony 136 years earlier, when Scotland was starting its first tentative steps into the modern world.

Telford never got started on his new canal. He died in 1834, and was buried in Westminster Abbey, joining the growing contingent of Scottish geniuses laid to rest in that hallowed shrine to British achievement. Others recognized Darien's potential, however. The world would have to wait another fifty years before work would finally get under way. William Paterson's vision of the isthmus of Panama as "the door of the seas" would finally be realized—by Americans this time, not by the British, athough the first chief engineer on the Panama Canal would happen to be a Scot by descent, John Findlay Wallace.

Canals, roads, bridges, and renovated harbors were all crucial to the network of self-interested exchange that held together modern commercial society, and now industrial society. The next logical step was to improve the means of transport on those thoroughfares, with the help of Watt's steam engine. Strangely, Watt himself was reluctant to do this. He seems to have believed the tremendous power generated by his invention would make any ship or vehicle too dangerous to handle.

Instead, it fell to a series of other visionary Scots, and inventors of Scottish extraction, to turn the energy of steam into the new transportation of the industrial age.

Henry Bell put his steam-powered boat Comet on the river Clyde in 1812. It was an idea borrowed, as usual, from someone else (a Scot named William Symington, who sailed the first working steam-powered boat, Charlotte Dundas, back in 1788 on Loch Dalswinton); but Bell showed that it could power genuine seagoing vessels, not just light rivercraft or demonstration toys. By 1823 there were more than seventy-two steamships operating up and down the Clyde, almost 60 percent of Britain's total steam-powered shipping. An American of Scottish descent, Robert Fulton, made the idea functional in North American waters, as well. Fulton usually gets the credit for inventing the steamboat, but it was Bell who first made it commercially and nautically feasible, while Glasgow's dockyards became home to generations of increasingly advanced and powerful oceangoing steamships.

George Stephenson's background was very much like Thomas Telford's. His paternal grandfather was a Scot who settled in northern England near Newcastle, a region similar to Lowland Scotland across the border, with a history of religious dissent and austere poverty, but high levels of literacy and a tendency to turn out ambitious, self-made men. George fell in love with steam engines while working as a teenager in the West Moor Mines. Stephenson took up a Cornishman's invention, a locomotive engine powered by steam, and used it to build the first modern railway. Not surprisingly, Thomas Telford was thinking along the same lines, except he envisioned steam-powered cars moving along his sturdy and well-built roads, not on rigid iron rails. The lobby for rails won out, however, and by the end of the 1820s Stephenson and his team of engineers were building an intricate network of iron railways and bridges for their steam-powered locomotives.

A new chapter in the industrial age was about to begin, as hundreds of miles of rails reached out to connect the major cities and industrial centers of Britain, north and south. It was the most massive national construction project in history. Telford's dream of a national network of highways with motorized vehicles and passenger cars would have to wait for another century, and another form of power—gasoline rather than steam.*

<h1 style="text-align:center">III</h1>

There was one other unforeseen consequence of Watt's steam engine, which many contemporaries missed, but which a perceptive German observer named Karl Marx did not. Steam power allowed a factory or mill owner to build his place of business where it suited him, rather than having to rely on geographical accident, such as a swift-running river or access to cheap fuel such as coal, to dictate his choice of location. Where it suited him usually meant close to routes where he could transport his products and supplies cheaply, and where he could find a cheap and ready supply of labor—which in turn usually meant a city. In other words, Watt made industrial production an essentially urban activity. The classical industrial city was the result: Manchester, Liverpool, Birmingham, Essen, Lyons—and Glasgow.

Glasgow epitomized nearly every aspect of this development, and foreshadowed many of the rest. By 1801 it was Scotland's largest city. The era of the great tobacco lords and merchant capitalists was finally and decisively over. Instead, textiles, ironworking, and modern shipbuilding were the driving forces of economic and demographic growth. Smokestacks, brick factories, and fiery, glowing foundries ringed the city, as the austere old warehouses along Gallowgate were submerged by workers' tenements. The city's population expanded from 77,000 in 1801 to nearly 275,000 forty years later: almost a fourfold increase. In the earliest boom years, between 1801 and 1811, the population grew by 30 percent a year.

Archibald Buchanan built the very first "integrated" cotton mill in Britain at Glasgow in 1807, combining all its component processes under one roof. The manager of the Glasgow Gasworks, James Neilson,

---

*Here again, oddly enough, a Scot proved to be the pioneer: James "Paraffin" Young, who developed a technique for extracting kerosene from oil shale from the Lothian mountains in the 1840s, and created the foundations of the petroleum industry.

transformed the iron industry by developing the modern blast furnace in 1827, which likewise helped to integrate ironworking and the production of pig iron. Glasgow soon outstripped both England and Wales in its iron output, rising over twentyfold to half a million tons. Glasgow managers and manufacturers were famous for their technical skill, their efficiency, and their willingness to innovate and develop new materials or techniques. By the early 1830s, Glasgow was making much of the machinery used by the rest of Britain's industrial plant: "In these works," wrote one observer, "everything belonging to, or connected with, the Millwright or Engineer department of the [British] manufacture is fabricated."

Glasgow's emergence as a major industrial city made fortunes for business dynasties such as the Finlays, the Dunlops, who successfully made the transition from importing tobacco to making pig iron, and the Bairds of Gartsherrie, who eventually became the world's leading producers of pig iron. At the end of the century, William Baird was counted among the forty wealthiest men in Britain.

However, all this growth soared far beyond the city's capacity to offer safe and affordable housing, or even adequate sewage and sanitation. The tens of thousands of rural immigrants who flocked in looking for work had to cram themselves into the old decaying inner city of Glasgow, abandoned long ago by Glasgow's middle class. Just in the narrow area where Gallowgate intersects High Street and the Saltmarket, more than twenty thousand people were jammed together, dumping their refuse into the streets and behind their tenements, where, as one official put it, "sanitary evils existed to perfection."

Who were they? Contrary to myth, few were Highlanders fleeing the Clearances—perhaps no more than 5 percent at the beginning. The vast majority were Irish, who abandoned the abject poverty of their homeland for the low but real wages they could earn in Glasgow's cotton mills, iron foundries, and linen dye works. It beat starving for nothing. Clydeside's Irish were the precursors of the armies of unskilled but hardworking "guest workers" of modern industrial Europe, and of the flood of cheap Irish labor that would emigrate to the United States in the 1840s and 1850s. By the time of the First Reform Bill, in fact, one out of five Glaswegians had been born in Ireland. Locals resented them because they were Catholics. Most were stuck in "casual" or part-time employment at the lowest possible wage. Most were also women. Women, married and unmarried, made up fully 60 percent of workers in the Glasgow mills. Their children found jobs as chimney sweeps as young as five or six. When wages fell and the mills closed, as they did in 1815 and later in the 1820s, life became as horrible as anything portrayed in a Dickens novel—certainly worse than what Friedrich Engels saw in Manchester in the early 1840s, which moved him to write his *Conditions of the Working Class in England.*

Squeezed between squalid living conditions and falling wages, Glasgow's workers fought back. The violent confrontations between employers and employees in those years surpassed anything happening in any other British or European city of the time. Labor unrest culminated in the general strike and massive uprising of the so-called Radical War of 1820, which Glasgow activists hoped would spark workers' revolts across the rest of Britain. Instead, it ended in a battle with local cavalry at Bonnymuir, and the hanging of three rebel ringleaders: James Wilson, Andrew Hardie, and John Baird—all this little more than two years before the royal visit.

These battles foreshadowed the future of relations between labor and capital for the next hundred years, the "class struggle" that would embroil Europe's major industrial cities and perplex politicians and intellectuals right down to our own day. It also foreshadowed its end. Glasgow's workers did not set off a revolution of the proletariat because that was not what they wanted. In the end, early Scottish unions such as the Operative Turners Association and the Glasgow Cotton Spinners Association simply wanted a decent living, with a higher wage but also a sense of individual dignity and independence. In other words, like Scots everywhere, they wanted to be part of progress, not head it off at the pass.

This working-class challenge required a middle-class response. It came in two forms.

David Dale was a self-taught industrial entrepreneur who rose from weaver's apprentice to branch manager of the Royal Bank of Glasgow and founding member of Glasgow's Chamber of Commerce. In 1786 he set up a cotton mill at New Lanark, in partnership with the English inventor of the spinning jenny, Richard Arkwright. Deeply religious and personally scrupulous, Dale wanted the factory to be a model of its kind. His employees put in an "easy" schedule of only eleven hours a day, with a two-hour break for dinner, and had free housing. By 1800, New Lanark employed more hands than any factory in the world, two-thirds of whom were women and children recruited from local orphanages. Dale gave them clothes, including a Sunday suit, schooling, and a wholesome diet of porridge and milk, potatoes and barley bread, with beef and cheese. A visitor said, "[I]f I was tempted to envy any of my fellow creatures it would be men such as . . . Mr. Dale for the good they have done to mankind."

Dale's son-in-law, an English industrialist named Robert Owen, took over that same year. Owen was determined not just to maintain Dale's magnanimity, but to expand it. He wanted to turn New Lanark into *A New Kind of Society,* as he titled his first book, in which the character of man, debased by the greed of commercial society, would be elevated and transformed by Owen's orderly but benevolent regime. It became the first secular utopian community, and a new political system—socialism—was born.

In 1824 Owen moved his utopian dreams to America. In New Harmony, Indiana, he eventually found a home for his experiment in abolishing private property. It never worked out quite as well as Owen had imagined; the residents quarreled over who got what and refused to work, and after only three years New Harmony had to be abandoned. It turned out Lord Kames's basic law of human motivations—"Man is designed by nature to appropriate"—was more durable than Owen's belief, or that of subsequent generations of socialists, that man should be made to share.

The other type of response proved more long-lasting. Scottish middle-class liberalism learned to extend the benefits of civilization to those it had left behind. Liberal lawyers such as Francis Jeffrey and Henry Cockburn volunteered to defend labor leaders and radicals in the great sedition trials of 1817. The Scottish Reform Act of 1832 broke the back of the old Dundas patronage system by extending the franchise and giving the vote to Scottish cities. It set in motion events and trends that would ultimately bring the vote to working-class Scots and heal old wounds. Political change did not come as quickly or with as wide a reach as in England, but by 1868, fully two-thirds of Glasgow's electorate was working class. They and their middle-class employers cast their votes together for a Liberal Party that totally dominated Scottish politics for the next fifty years. During the second half of the nineteenth century, historian Thomas Devine has stated, "Liberal values represented Scottish values."

More immediately and perhaps more crucially, middle-class Scots took on the formidable job of cleaning up the mess that headlong industrialization had left behind. Scottish doctors took the lead as champions of municipal public health and hygiene as early as the 1780s, first in England, then in their own country. Manchester, the heart of the English Industrial Revolution, was totally transformed by Scots. Charles White, an Edinburgh M.D., founded the Manchester Infirmary and Lying-in Hospital. Another Edinburgh-trained doctor, Thomas Percival, browbeat Manchester hospitals into keeping statistics of births and deaths in order to allow doctors and officials to trace the progress of epidemic diseases in the city. John Farrier created the Manchester Board of Health, the first in England, set up special hospital wards for fever patients, and required the disinfecting of wards and private homes where fever was found. All these measures helped to limit the spread of infectious diseases such as typhus, and served as the model for other cities and public health officials.

In 1796, Farrier also established the link between unhealthy working conditions in the Manchester mills and the spread of disease and high mortality. He proposed that the mills "be subject to a general system of laws, for wise, humane, and equal treatment of all such works." The notion of government regulation of workplace safety and health was born, which took another forty years for Parliament to finally address.

What Farrier and others did for Manchester (the founders of the city's medical school in the early 1820s took Edinburgh as their direct model), John Heysham did for Carlisle in the 1780s, including introducing inoculation against smallpox. A similar group of unsung Scottish heroes took on Sheffield. Glasgow and Edinburgh had to wait until much later. William Alison, dean of the medical faculty at Edinburgh, took up public health issues only in the 1840s, and reform and slum clearances reached Glasgow still later.

By then the reforms of middle-class medicine were almost complete. James Simpson had introduced chloroform as an anesthetic for surgery in 1847, and then for childbirth. At the Glasgow medical school, William McEwen took up Joseph Lister's idea of sterilizing surgical instruments and bandages, and together with Edinburgh's Lister, made the use of antiseptics standard practice in British medicine. Over the long run, these changes, along with the gas streetlighting invented by one of Watt's assistants, William Murdoch, may have done as much to save lives and raise living standards as many of the large-scale public hygiene projects of the same years.

Scottish public health efforts also differed from their English counterparts in two crucial respects. They tended to look more to the private sector to supply the necessary support and capital, and were unwilling to involve the state if private resources were available. They also laid heavy stress on the need for education and moral uplift, as well as cleanliness and sanitation. Some of this sprang from religious motives: the Glasgow Sunday School Union, for example, was very active in the troubled early decades of the nineteenth century, and by 1819 had enrolled nearly 7 percent of the city's population. Thomas Chalmers preached voluntary relief as the solution to poverty, as part of the Kirk's traditional parochial responsibilities. But part of it, too, was the classical liberal faith in the power of the individual to do good, both for himself and for others. No one exemplified this more than Dr. Samuel Smiles, the author of that classic tract on the Victorian faith in the individual, *Self-Help.*

The book, and its famous motto, "God helps those who help themselves," used to be derided as self-delusional propaganda, or Victorian hypocrisy at its worst. It is a more complex book than that, and its author a more complex man. Smiles was born in Haddington, and was an knowledgeable fan of the emerging scientific industrial culture his fellow Scots had done so much to create. He wrote an admiring biography of Thomas Telford; his great heroes were James Watt and James Nasmyth, inventor of the industrial steam hammer. He was also a doctor, trained at Edinburgh medical school. In Smiles, in fact, all the strands of Scottish faith in science, industry, and technology come together, along with its enlightened liberal belief in individual freedom and responsibility. The second edition of *Self-Help,* published in 1869, opened with a quotation from the Scottish-descended philosopher John Stuart Mill: "The worth of a state, in the long run, is the worth of the individuals composing it."

Smiles wanted to inspire in his readers a sense of their own self-worth, both as individuals and as part of the rise of Britain as a great nation. *Self-Help* is the ancestor of all self-help and motivational books and audio tapes, the indispensable *vade mecums* of the person who feels overwhelmed by the tide and tempo of modern life. The emotional anchor Smiles offered his readers was the example of the great inventors, scientists, and businessmen who had risen above humble beginnings and conquered adversity to become useful and productive human beings. His examples were not exclusively Scottish or even British; they included Germans, French, and Italians (they were, however, all men). Each revealed the power of the individual to remake his life and his environment through hard work, perseverance (most of his examples are haunted by early failures), moral discipline, ceaseless optimism, and the energy to seize opportunities when they present themselves—Scottish virtues presented as a "personal power" to match the new mechanized power unleashed by the Industrial Revolution. You can be who you want to be, so choose carefully and learn to live with the result.

Smiles also stressed, like Telford, that success should not be measured just in material terms, or even personal, selfish ones. "National progress is the sum of individual industry, energy, and uprightness," he admonished, "as national decay is of individual idleness, selfishness, and vice."

Self-Help was published on the heels of Britain's embarrassing performance in the Crimean War, and its humiliation in the Indian Mutiny.

It was a time when the future of the British Empire seemed once again very dim. There is a distinct note of patriotic pleading to aspects of the book, especially in this striking passage: "The spirit of self-help, as exhibited in the energetic action of individuals, has in all times been a marked feature in the English character, and furnishes the true measure of our power as a nation."

The *English* character? If the eighteenth-century Scot had subordinated himself to a larger whole as a "North Briton," Smiles was now willing to carry things a step further. Scottish scientists and inventors such as Watt and Telford and Nasmyth, he was suggesting, were displaying a creative national character that turned out not to be Scottish at all, but English! It was an extraordinary piece of national self-effacement, especially since Britain was becoming more reliant on its Scots than ever. If England's claim to greatness in the second half of the nineteenth century rested on its laurels of empire, it was an empire largely built and organized by Scots.

CHAPTER THIRTEEN

The Sun Never Sets:
Scots and the British Empire

> Success, like war and like charity in religion,
> covers a multitude of sins.
>
> —*Sir Charles Napier*

One afternoon Robert Louis Stevenson noted a story in an Edinburgh newspaper about an apartment house in the Old Town that had suddenly collapsed, burying the residents in plaster and rubble. "All over the world," he mused to himself, "in London, in Canada, in New Zealand, fancy what a multitude of people could exclaim with truth, 'The house that I was born in fell down last night!'"

The Scottish mass migration of the eighteenth and nineteenth centuries (Stevenson himself was born in Edinburgh and died in Samoa) was as momentous as any in history. In sheer numbers, it hardly stands out: perhaps 3 million all told, compared to the 8 million Italians who left their native land between 1820 and World War I. Yet its impact was far-reaching in more ways than one.

Scots blanketed the British dominions in North America from Georgia and Nova Scotia to Vancouver. They ranged across the Pacific to Australia and New Zealand. Scots found employment in the teeming cities of India and on the South African veldt. Some set off for China, while others, like Stevenson himself, wandered the islands of the South Pacific and remote corners of Latin America. Nor should one forget the more than a half-million Scots who, like Henry Brougham and James

Watt and Thomas Telford, packed their bags and headed for new horizons and new careers in London or Birmingham or Liverpool.

The great Scottish diaspora followed, and in some cases led, the development of what historians sometimes call the "second" British Empire. The first, organized around England's monopoly of the Atlantic trade, effectively perished in the American Revolution. The new empire was a far more extensive and complex amalgam of far-flung dominions, territories, colonies, naval bases, and assorted dependencies, which eventually covered nearly one-fifth of the earth's land surface and one-quarter of the world's population. It was the first global community, an empire "on which the sun never sets," in the phrase John Wilson of *Blackwood's Magazine* first made famous. And without the Scots it might never have existed—let alone reached the status of legend it still holds today.

In fact, a Scot created the idea of the British Empire. Charles Pasley came from Eskdalemuir in Dumfriesshire, not far from where Thomas Telford had grown up. Like Telford, he had prodigious intellectual gifts (he translated the New Testament from Greek at age eight) that found their main outlet in solving technical problems. He served in the Royal Engineers in the Napoleonic Wars, and became Europe's leading demolitions expert and siege warfare specialist. In 1810 he published *An Essay on the Military Policy and Institutions of the British Empire*. It completely changed the way Britons thought about their empire in relation to the rest of the world. In fact, Pasley had created modern geopolitics.

Pasley warned his fellow Britons that they could no longer rely on their "splendid isolation," or the British navy, to keep them safe in the future. In the modern world, true national security rested on policy and power—especially military power. That included large overseas colonies, which could supply sailors for its navies and soldiers for Britain's armies. "War we cannot avoid," he warned. But if Britain thought offensively and acted vigorously, "what nation upon earth can resist us?"

Between the Battle of Waterloo and the end of the American Civil War in 1865, the British Empire grew by an average of 100,000 square miles per year. At each turn, a coterie of Scots or men and women of

Scottish descent took the lead. They operated sheep farms in New South Wales, grew rye and barley in Lower Ontario, worked in lumber camps in British Columbia, trapped beaver and otter along the Mackenzie River, managed coffee plantations in Ceylon, sold ships' stores in the Falkland Islands, guarded the Officers' Club in Mysore—and traded opium in Hong Kong and Canton. Their ubiquity and universal success inspired the frequently quoted maxim of Prime Minister Benjamin Disraeli: "It has been my lot to have found myself in many distant lands. I have never been in one without finding a Scotchman, and I never found a Scotchman who was not at the head of the poll."

I

Part of their success was due to the fact that most Scottish emigrants, even the poorest, had more skills and education than their other European counterparts. This broad-based "brain drain" was bad news for Scotland over the long haul, but good news for the rest of the world. People wanted Scottish immigrants in their country, as temporary or permanent "guest workers," whether in Australia or Argentina or the United States.

Also, this Scottish restlessness was nothing new. Scots had crisscrossed Scotland and Europe for centuries, looking for work and opportunity. They supplied the crucial manpower for England's first overseas empire, as well: first as settlers in Northern Ireland during the reign of James I, and then as soldiers in His Majesty's army.

The very first Highland "Watch," or armed patrol, was raised in 1667 under Charles II. However, the Jacobite wars led the Crown to lose faith in the loyalty of its Scottish contingents, and they were disbanded. After the Fifteen clans loyal to the Stuarts raised a levy of troops to prowl the glens to suppress the remaining rebels. General Wade issued a dark-blue-and-green tartan for these companies of Highlanders, which gave them their name, the "Black Watch."

The 42nd Highland Regiment, as the Black Watch was officially known, inspired imitators. Between 1740 and 1815, eighty-six Highland regiments were officially raised, many drawing their recruits and officers from a single clan. Some, like Munro's regiment and the Royal Scots Fusiliers, fought at Culloden against the Jacobite clans; others, like Fraser's Highlanders (the old 78th and 71st Regiments) and Keith's and Campbell's Highlanders, served with distinction in George II's wars in North America and Europe. Later they fought loyally against the American colonists and Napoleon. By 1800 they were the backbone of the British army.

Recruiting volunteers was fairly easy. In the early years the official ban against all weapons and wearing of the tartan at home induced even chiefs' sons and tacksmen to sign up as common soldiers. Chieftains ordered their clansmen to enlist in exchange for bounty, or as a matter of pride. The Duchess of Gordon raised her clansmen for the Gordon Highlanders in 1794 by touring the Huntly lands in regimental jacket and bonnet, and offering every new recruit a golden guinea and a kiss.* Of the 2,200 men in Lord MacLeod's Highlanders (the 73rd Regiment), almost three-quarters came from MacLeod's own clan area. Many of their fathers had fought for Bonnie Prince Charlie—just as MacLeod himself had done, until George III issued him a pardon and brought him home to raise his regiment.

Sadly, the Highland Clearances solved any remaining difficulties about finding recruits. A national tragedy became the individual's opportunity, as young men driven off their land found a new life and a future for themselves in His Majesty's pay. Besides, by serving in a Highland regiment, they managed to preserve a lifestyle, with kilts, swords, bonnets, and bagpipes, that was quickly dying out in their native land: a world of martial valor, loyalty, and personal honor. Scottish soldiers were famous for their bravery under fire, as well as for their excellent discipline. But they were more than just cannon fodder. They did not hesitate to mutiny at what they considered slights against their honor—entire regiments did so in the 1790s.

In 1804, when the British government contemplated doing away with the kilt and issuing standard uniforms to their Scottish troops,

---

*Legend has it the volunteers took the kiss and gave the guinea away to their neighbors.

there was a massive uproar. An exasperated Colonel Alan Cameron of the 79th Camerons passionately defended the *féileadh-beag* and its

> free congenial circulation of pure wholesome air (as an exhila-rating native bracer) which has hitherto so peculiarly benefitted the Highlander for *activity,* and all the other necessary qualities of a soldier, whether for hardship upon scanty fare, *readiness in accoutring,* or making *forced marches* & *c.,* beside the exclusive advantage, when halted, of drenching his kilt & c., in the *next brook,* as well as washing his limbs, and drying *both,* as it were, by constant *fanning,* without injury to either, but on the contrary feeling clean and comfortable. . . .

Cameron summed up the feelings of all the Highland regiments when he concluded: "I sincerely hope His Royal Highness will never acquiesce in so painful and degrading an idea (come from whatever quarter it may) as to strip us of our native garb . . . and *stuff* us in breeches." Whitehall dropped the idea.

A private in the Camerons or the Black Watch usually sent part of his pay to his destitute family. He also kept friends and relatives in a remote glen or Hebridean isle informed about the world outside. Walter Scott's friend David Stewart of Garth served with the 78th Highlanders (the Ross-shire Buffs) in the West Indies, Minorca and Gibraltar, Egypt, Sicily and Italy, as well as in Kent, and his soldiers with him. Army service opened a window on the world most Englishmen, let alone Highland Gaels, never knew existed. The Highland regiments were in many ways the advance parties for the later Scottish diaspora, as soldiers told their families where they could go when the sheep came and they had to choose between starvation and finding a new home.

That is, if they lived to tell about it. Like all soldiers of that era, they suffered horribly from diseases such as typhus, smallpox, cholera, scurvy, and yellow fever, especially in tropical climates. The five-month trip to India in 1782 cost the Seaforth Highlanders 230 out of 1,100 men from scurvy—thanks largely to the obstinacy of Whitehall, since James Lind had discovered the cure almost sixty years earlier. The

Gordon Highlanders reached Jamaica in June of 1819. Over the next six months, without a shot being fired, they lost ten officers, thirteen sergeants, eight drummers, and 254 other ranks. This was more than all the men the regiment had lost in battle since its formation twenty-five years earlier. It was a high price to pay for the Duchess of Gordon's kiss.

The Seaforths and the 74th Highland Regiment were the only regular British troops in the Duke of Wellington's army in India in 1803, when he confronted a Maratha army ten times his size at Assaye. The 74th met the initial Indian cavalry charge head-on, and lost an incredible 459 men out of 495 effectives, a casualty rate of 92 percent. The regiment lost every officer except Quartermaster James Grant, who joined the ranks and fought on until the battle was won and the Marathas were routed. For their sacrifice, the 74th received the almost unique honor of carrying a third flag on parade, in addition to the Union Jack and the regimental colors. It would bear the Assaye Color until it ceased to be a regiment in 1881.

Wellington's Highland troops in India, like those that fought for him at Waterloo, faced an enemy with cannon, muskets, and ammunition much like their own. Then a series of technological changes made the British soldier a much deadlier opponent, again thanks to a pair of Scottish inventors.

In 1776 Major Patrick Ferguson of the 71st Highlanders patented a rifle that loaded from the breech rather than the muzzle. It could fire four shots a minute, twice the rate of a muzzle-loader under the best conditions, at a target two hundred yards away—in other words, more than twice the distance. Ferguson gave it to his troops, who used it with telling effect against the Americans at the Battle of Brandywine in September 1777. However, the English general Howe was furious that Ferguson had acted on his own without permission, and ordered the guns confiscated. What might have happened to the American cause if the British had realized what a secret weapon they had, or if Ferguson had not been killed at King's Mountain in October of 1780, is anyone's guess.

Instead, the breech-loader would have to wait another eighty years before it came into general use. But by then another Scottish invention, almost as crucial, had enhanced the firepower of military arms. This was the percussion lock, invented in 1807 by a clergyman and chemist named Alexander Forsyth. Instead of igniting the bullet's powder with a flint, Forsyth's gun hammer used a minute portion of potassium chlorate to fire the weapon. The result was a gun that could shoot in any kind of weather and under any kind of conditions. A standard army flintlock usually misfired three out of ten rounds; Forsyth cut that rate to 4.5 misfires per thousand rounds. When a Scot from Philadelphia named Joshua Shaw then found a way to fit the potassium chlorate into a tiny metal button, the percussion cap was born. A new kind of infantry warfare was born with it, in which the individual soldier could kill at twice the range almost with impunity, and massed fire meant certain death to anyone caught in it.

Some found the prospect daunting. In 1817, a letter signed "An English Gentleman" appeared in a London magazine deploring Forsyth's new invention:

> If, moreover, this new system were applied to the military, war would shortly become so frightful as to exceed all bounds of imagination, and future wars would threaten, within a few years, to destroy not only armies, but civilization itself. It is to be hoped, therefore, that many men of conscience, and with a reflective turn, will militate most vehemently for the suppression of this new invention.

In fact, the percussion-lock rifle did move warfare onto a bloodier plane. Even before the advent of high explosives, or the rapid-fire breech-loader, or the brass cartridge bullet (another invention from Britain's Woolwich Arsenal), contests between European-style armies in the Crimea and the American Civil War were already foreshadowing the slaughter of Verdun and the Somme in the next century. But the percussion lock, and its successor the breech-loader, particularly stacked the odds in colonial warfare, as relative handfuls of soldiers could now take on large numbers of Pathans or Ashantis or Zulus, and butcher them almost at will. A dangerous technological gap was opening up between Europeans and the rest of the world, which would threaten even wealthy and advanced non-Western cultures such as those of China, Persia, and India.

India, of course, was the centerpiece of the British Empire of the nineteenth century, the imperial "crown jewel." But it had not always been so highly regarded. In the eighteenth century the British had triumphed there, then languished. They controlled only three enclaves of territory, which had grown up around the East India Company's trading sites at Bombay, Madras, and Calcutta. The company itself enjoyed a trade monopoly of the sort Adam Smith had analyzed and despised. Its greed and incompetence had helped to spark a revolution in America, provoked angry scenes in Parliament, and nearly pushed the British government into bankruptcy. In 1773 it lost the power to run India as it saw fit, but not its political clout or its economic monopoly. A half-century of official corruption and neglect of the indigenous population—which later anti-imperialists applauded as benign but which in fact sprang from a callous indifference toward the people they ruled—left the subcontinent, and British interests, in a shambles.

Then, in 1806, the East India Company commissioned a thirty-three-year-old Scotsman named James Mill to write a history of the British presence in India. They had no idea what they were about to get for their money. Mill was a mediocre writer and something of a crank. His father had been a minister, and he was trained as one. He had been a pupil of Dugald Stewart, but left no trace at the University of Edinburgh. He had moved to London in hopes of becoming a distinguished man of letters, as so many other Scots of his generation had. Instead he constantly found himself on the brink of bankruptcy.

Mill had never been to India, nor had he any great interest in it. He accepted the India Company's money because he needed to support his wife and his son, John. However, driven by necessity, and haunted by the intellectual tradition he had encountered in Edinburgh, Mill produced his masterpiece, *The History of British India*.

It was the first systematic attempt to apply the Scottish school's four-stage theory to a non-European culture. Mill thought it would take him three years; in fact it took him eleven. Weighing the Hindu and

Muslim cultures of India in the scale of civilization's progress over barbarism, Mill found them woefully wanting. He dismissed India's ancient religious traditions as "superstition"; he attacked its emperors and rajahs as small-minded tyrants who abused their subjects and grew fat and lazy on the backs of the poor. He reserved a special contempt for its laws, which he compared to those of Europe in the Dark Ages, and its caste system, which "stands a more effective barrier against the welfare of human nature than any other institution which the workings of caprice and of selfishness have ever produced."

Mill's attack on India's culture and civilization makes hard reading in today's multiculturalist age. But his anger sprang from his liberal, even radical, sympathies (he was the friend and disciple of the founder of English radicalism, Jeremy Bentham). He wanted European-style progress to raise up the lives of the Indian peasant and urban artisan, who found themselves overtaxed and powerless, as well as denied a basic human dignity by Hinduism's relentlessly rigid rules of caste. If India's rulers were incapable of changing this, Mill declared, then the British had to. "A simple form of arbitrary government," Mill wrote, "tempered by European honour and European intelligence, is the only form which is now fit for Hindustan." He wanted the British to take command—not in order to enhance their own power and profits (the East India Company already had plenty of both), but to make India into a modern, "civilized" society.

It was the issue of bringing progress to the Highlands all over again, but in a tropical climate. Mill had given birth to the idea of what Rudyard Kipling would call "the white man's burden," and the impact on British policy was swift. Mill was appointed to a post at East India House, and the book itself went into four editions. The president of the Board of Control took Mill's arguments to heart, as did a future president, Thomas Babington Macaulay. Macaulay detested Mill's left-wing politics and wrote a famous essay ridiculing them in the *Edinburgh Review*. But Mill's radical ideas on legal reform, which Macaulay thought unsuitable for England, he saw as perfect for India. Macaulay called *The History of British India* "the greatest historical work which has appeared in our language since Gibbon." He pressed hard to implement its proposed reforms, along with a national English-language school system for India—shades of Scotland's own common parish schools.

But a new British policy was already taking shape in India, thanks to another coterie of Scots. They were the brilliant and dedicated protégés of Lord Minto, the Edinburgh-educated governor-general who arrived in India in 1806 after the Duke of Wellington had pacified the Maratha princes. Minto himself oversaw the end of the East India Company's monopoly over British trade in 1813. In southern India, Thomas Munro, later governor of Madras, fought to reduce the tax burden on ordinary farmers and pushed for a system of honest tax collectors (which Parliament approved in 1812) and for independent village courts (which it did not). John Campbell spent sixteen years in the remote hill country between Madras and Calcutta rescuing potential victims of ritual human sacrifice, or *meriah*. By the time he finished, he had saved more than fifteen hundred lives and prevented the kidnaping of thousands more.

John Malcolm, an Eskdale native, negotiated a groundbreaking treaty with Persia, which brought peace along India's northwestern border. Mountstuart Elphinstone became Lord Minto's most trusted aide, and broke the power of the last Maratha robber barons. A skilled diplomat and a tough soldier, he was also a devoted classical scholar who rose every morning in the summer at four to read Sophocles before his predawn gallop across the landscape. Like all the best Scottish imperialists, Elphinstone saw Britain's rule in India as basically temporary. He wrote to James Mackintosh, who was then Recorder in Bombay, that the Empire's "most desirable death" would be "the improvement of the natives reaching such a pitch as would render it impossible for a foreign government," including Britain, to retain power. Which is, in fact, what did happen, 140 years later.

This was a new kind of imperialism, a liberal imperialism, which came to characterize British rule elsewhere in the world. It involved taking over and running another society for its own good—not by saving its soul through Christianity, as other European imperialisms had claimed to do, but in material terms. One could even say, in Scottish terms: better schools, better roads, more just laws, more prosperous towns and cities, more money in ordinary people's pockets and more food on their tables. Governor-General George Bentinck even framed it with a nod to Francis Hutcheson: "England's greatness is founded on Indian happiness." And for all its faults and shortcomings and hypocrisies, this liberal imperialism did manage to transform India into a more humane, orderly, and modern society. One could even say a freer society, except, of course, in the "narrow" political sense.

Or at least James Mill and others saw it as narrow. Mill's teacher Dugald Stewart had repeatedly emphasized to students that *how* a government came into being—whether by democratic or representative means, or by hereditary rule or even by conquest—mattered less than *what* the government did when it got there. As long as it promoted progress and protected the rights of the individual and property; as long as it kept pace with social and economic change and expanded opportunities for everyone, then it was good government, no matter who was in charge. If it did not, then it was a failure, no matter how many people voted for it.

In 1707 Scotland had surrendered her political sovereignty and allowed herself to be run by a government five hundred miles away. The results had been spectacularly successful, particularly for Scotland's urban middle class. Why not the Indians? Why not other peoples waiting to be brought up from barbarism and superstition into the bright glare of modernity?

James Mill made this quasi-paternalist view the cornerstone of British colonial policy. Eventually it affected politics in Britain as well. The later Scottish school of Dugald Stewart had reached a startling conclusion, which also contained a paradox: politics as an expression of "the will of the people" mattered less than previous thinkers had imagined. On the one hand, self-government was the fruit of civilized advancement and a worthy goal for any people—including Indians. On the other, the general welfare of a modern, complex society profited most from applying "the science of legislation," in Dugald Stewart's phrase, which increasingly meant rule by experts and bureaucrats.

A fundamental rift was beginning to surface in the modern political imagination, with intelligent Scots aligned on both sides. The last generation of the Scottish Enlightenment became convinced that the only politics a modern society requires is strong effective government. The growth of the civil service and bureaucracy in nineteenth-century Britain, the beginnings of the welfare state in the twentieth—all were confident expressions of government's ability to manage and anticipate the massive social changes modern society creates, so that people can get on with their lives. But this confidence also blinded liberals to the emotional force and appeal of nationalism, which, by contrast, old-fashioned Tories such as Sir Walter Scott clearly understood. It blinded William Gladstone, son of the middle-class Scottish diaspora, who destroyed the Liberal Party when his plan for Home Rule for Ireland provoked massive resistance not only from the British and Ulster Protestants, but from the Irish themselves. It blinded future British governments when the passion for independence struck other parts of the empire: in Afrikaaner South Africa in the 1890s; in India in the 1920s; and eventually, at the tail end of the twentieth century, in Scotland herself.

Of course, all this lay far in the future when Charles James Napier arrived in 1841 to take over as governor of Sind. That part of India, in what is now Pakistan, was still a dangerous and disorderly frontier, with constant wars between the local rulers and Sikh warrior bands, and between Muslims and Hindus. Napier was there to straighten it out. His father, George Napier, had been born in Edinburgh and tutored by David Hume; some of Hume's cool, cynical view of human nature, and that of his mentor, Lord Kames, seems to have rubbed off on Charles as well. The family lived in Ireland, where his father was quartermaster of a British regiment when the Irish Revolt of 1798 broke out. Major Napier barricaded his house, armed his five sons with muskets, and held the place as a virtual fort until help arrived.

Soldiering was in Charles Napier's blood. As Jan Morris has said, "his cousins, forebears, and descendants commanded armies, ships, garrisons, or colonies from one end of the empire to the other." He joined the army at age twelve, and saw action in Spain under Wellington. At the battle of La Coruña he was wounded five times, including a saber cut across the head and a bayonet in the back; at Busaco he took a bullet through the face. All this did nothing to quell Napier's thirst for excitement, but did build in him a contempt for inessentials, such as keeping up appearances, or what we call Victorian hypocrisy. His formula for empire-building was "a good thrashing first and great kindness afterwards." This is what he proceeded to do in Sind.

Napier was a political radical like James Mill, with an intense sympathy for oppressed people, whether in Britain (he supported the working-class Chartists) or in India. "How feeble is a system of iniquity!" he wrote as he watched the local rulers at work. "How weak is injustice!" The remark reminds us of the sober truth that many of the traditional regimes the British toppled, both in India and elsewhere, had spent centuries making their subjects wretchedly unhappy. When their fate hung in the balance, most of their populations would refuse to lift a finger to save them. For native peoples, the British might not be their first choice. But, in many cases, thanks to Scots like Napier, they were better than what they had.

Napier was still trying to protect the territory from marauding Sikhs when the governor-general decided to annex the entire province. It was the single biggest expansion of British rule in India in a generation, and it was hugely unpopular in Britain. Napier knew the annexation of Sind had no legal rationale, but approved of it anyway. It was, he wrote, "a very advantageous, useful, humane piece of rascality." As governor, Napier instituted all the reforms the old rulers never did or could. He lowered taxes, created the port of Karachi, encouraged steam navigation on the Indus River, created a police force to keep order, and proposed irrigation schemes to allow local farmers to expand their fields and crops. He changed life in Sind in other ways, as well. When he banned the Hindu practice of *suttee,* of burning a widow on her husband's funeral pyre, the local Brahmin priests protested that this was interfering with an important national custom. "My nation also has a custom," Napier replied. "When men burn women alive, we hang them. Let us all act according to national custom."

Napier foretold the best of the later British Raj, with his stern but generous paternalism, which combined the rule of law with humanitarian principles—when it was feasible. The Raj system itself came into being under a Scottish governor—General James Dalhousie, Lord

Ramsey. In his eight years as de facto ruler of India, from 1848 to 1856, he gave the subcontinent the trappings of a modern society. He built its first railroads, strung thousands of miles of telegraph wire, and created a national postal service. Schools, roads, and irrigation projects flourished under his tenure, while he also expanded British control over lower Burma, Oudh, and several smaller principalities. In each he abolished *suttee* and *thuggee,* or the ritual murder cult, as well as the last remains of human sacrifice.

Dalhousie also pushed for what he called a "social revolution" in the Indian attitude toward women. This marked a new departure for Scots. Scottish society had always been highly patriarchal; the Scottish Enlightenment was an almost exclusively male enterprise. But the degraded status of Indian women, like that of Chinese women, shocked everyone who had contact with it. "The degradation of their women has been adhered to by Hindus and Mohammadans more tenaciously than other customs," Dalhousie wrote, "and the change will do more towards civilising the body of society than anything else could effect." He wrote laws banning child marriage, polygamy, and the practice of killing unwanted female children. He created the first schools for girls, arguing that nothing was "likely to lead to more important and beneficial consequences than the introduction of education for their female children." By the time he left India in 1856, Dalhousie had made more changes in Indian society than it had seen in centuries—more, in fact, than it could stomach.

Native resentment against Dalhousie's self-confident paternalism and the sweeping changes he implemented exploded in the Indian Mutiny of 1857. A Scot's progressive reforms had ignited the revolt; two Scottish soldiers, Generals Colin Campbell and Hugh Rose, stamped it out. The mutiny, which convulsed the entire subcontinent for two years, marked a watershed in Anglo-Indian relations and destroyed whatever independence was left to its native rulers. But it also demonstrated the dual nature of the new British Empire: when its high-minded reforms were blocked or threatened, it would not hesitate to use brute military force to get its way. And Scots were the mainstays of both.

India's role within the Empire had changed also. It was now crucial to British policy because of one crop: opium. Opium was the single commodity the British could trade in bulk to the other great empire to the east, China. There was only one problem: opium was illegal in China.

No European who had any dealings with imperial China had the slightest sympathy or respect for its anti-opium policy. European and British merchants knew many of the imperial officials were opium addicts themselves, who turned a blind eye to the illegal trade in exchange for a cut of the profits. They knew, too, that the same officials also unmercifully squeezed the Chinese *hongs* or merchants, who were officially licensed to trade with "the round-eyed devils." This kept profits low on all legal exports from China, such as porcelain, silk, and, most important of all, tea. Most British traders saw smuggling Indian opium as a fitting revenge on a government that made doing business in China a misery. But two men, and two only, saw the true potential of the opium market in China, and had the skill and determination to do something about it.

James Matheson came from the Sutherland branch of the Matheson clan, which dominated the lands in the western Highlands around Loch Alsh. He was working for a Scottish trading firm in Calcutta when he met William Jardine, a shrewd, hardheaded* Lowlander and former Royal Navy surgeon who had become involved in trade as well. Together they realized the place to make money was in opium; they became partners in 1827, and within a decade Jardine Matheson and Company was the dominant force in the illegal China trade.

Their skill and ingenuity in exploiting the immense Chinese drug market reflected the hard side of the Scottish character. Matheson and Jardine knew Britain had no drug problem, except for a few eccentric English intellectuals such as Samuel Coleridge and Thomas De Quincey; neither did India, which had been growing the stuff for thou-

---

*Literally hardheaded: one day Jardine was walking on the street in Canton when an iron bar fell from a construction site and hit him on the head. Jardine simply walked on. The Chinese gave him the nickname of Iron Head Rat—which was meant as a compliment.

sands of years. If the Chinese government could not control their own people and their seemingly insatiable appetite for it (one estimate put the number of Chinese opium addicts at nearly 1 percent of the total population, perhaps as many as two million persons), Jardine and Matheson believed, that was their lookout. They also grasped that the imperial system was on its last legs. Once China had been a model of civilized commercial society to Scottish scholars such as David Hume and Adam Smith. Now, to Britons trained to look with James Mill's disdainful eye, it looked corrupt, decadent, and barbaric. The Chinese Empire was dying. Jardine and Matheson intended to be in on the kill.

Besides, smuggling was a long-standing Scottish tradition. The Jardine-Matheson cartel simply raised it to a new sophisticated level. They sailed their fast clipper ships into Whampoa harbor under the eyes of the Chinese authorities and smaller boats up the rivers to China's principal cities. Jardine also brought in a 115-ton steamer, which he named—naturally—the *Jardine,* to sail the Pearl River between Canton and Macao. On its first voyage the Chinese opened fire on it and forced it to reverse course. Jardine was furious. Earlier he had warned the British government that the conflicts over the opium trade could lead to full-scale war unless it persuaded the Chinese to give way. "Nor indeed should our valuable commerce and revenue both in India and Great Britain be permitted to remain subject to a caprice. . . ." The outcome of such a war, he wrote, "could not be doubted." In other words, total defeat of the imperial government and the final opening of China to the West.

The First Opium War, as it was called, was the premeditated project of three men: William Jardine, British foreign minister Lord Palmerston, and the second Lord Minto, First Lord of the Admiralty.* Together they

---

*Ironically, Minto and Palmerston also happened to be Dugald Stewart's pupils. Palmerston later wrote that studying with Stewart was where "I laid the foundations of whatever useful knowledge and habits of mind I possess." A curious compliment, since it is hard to think of a man more immune to Stewart's principled high-mindedness than Palmerston.

cooked up the war to save the opium trade and make Britain the arbiter of political fortunes in China. Once again the technological gap between West and non-West came to the rescue, this time in the form of a steam-powered iron gunboat called the *Nemesis*.

The Scottish shipbuilder John Laird constructed her in his yards at Liverpool. She was 184 feet long and powered by two sixty-horsepower engines. She carried two large thirty-two-pound cannon and five six-pounders, and a Congreve rocket launcher. Laird had also divided her hull into watertight compartments, to prevent any waterline damage from sinking her. The *Nemesis* was a formidable fighting machine, the ancestor not only of ironclads such as the *Monitor,* but of the later modern cruisers and battleships of the Royal Navy.

The *Nemesis* left Portsmouth on March 28, 1840. It was the first iron ship to sail around the Cape of Good Hope. When it reached Macao in November, it was the most powerful warship in the China Sea. Twice the size of ordinary Chinese war junks, it turned their wooden hulls and masts to matchsticks when it turned its guns on them. In addition, the gunboat had a draft of only six feet, so that it could sail up any navigable river to wreak havoc on the hapless Chinese. In a single afternoon's battle up the Whampoa, the *Nemesis* took out nine war junks, five forts, one artillery battery, and two military supply posts. Its captain wrote exultingly to John Laird: "It is with great pleasure I inform you that your vessel is as much admired by our own countrymen as she is dreaded by the Chinese." The British commander in charge of the operation wrote that it proved "that the British flag can be displayed throughout their inner waters wherever and whenever it is thought proper by us, against any defence or mode [the Chinese] may adopt to prevent it."

By the next year the *Nemesis* had been joined by other steamships and gunboats, including her sister, the 510-ton *Phlegethon.* Together they pounded the imperial Chinese forces into submission. The Chinese government signed a peace treaty at Nanking in August 1842, finally opening up the opium trade and other commercial exchanges with Britain. Jardine became the *tai-pan* of the new colony he had founded, called Hong Kong. Britain had fought the first major colonial war in East Asia and won. Other European powers would follow, but Great Britain was now the dominant political power in the region—thanks to John Laird and the Scottish drug lords.*

II

Some territories came under British rule through conquest, others through settlement. Canada and Australia began as integral and supportive parts of the empire; they also remained the most loyal after they gained their independence as dominions. Not coincidentially, they were also where Scots were the dominant influence.

Scotsmen had been involved in the making of Canada from its very beginnings. They had settled Nova Scotia for Scotland; later, they spread to the other Maritime Provinces as well, whose wild and desolate rocky shores reminded them of home (which, geologically speaking, made sense). Newfoundland served as a way station for tobacco merchant smugglers operating between Virginia and Scotland in the days before the Union. At that time Canada belonged to the French. Then, in 1759, General Wolfe and the Fraser Highlanders took the Heights of Abraham overlooking the city of Quebec, and Quebec Province, and with it the key to French Canada, fell to Great Britain.† Wolfe's second-in-

---

*However, the ironies do not end there. In 1820 the Scotland-born commissioner for Assam in India, Robert Scott, found a strange species of camellia he had never seen before. He sent it to London for analysis: it turned out to be a wild tea plant. Within a generation, Indian-grown tea would shoulder the Chinese product out of the British market. If Palmerston and Minto had only waited, the demand for China tea would have faded and, with it, the need to smuggle opium. But then Hong Kong, Asia's premier commercial city and modern China's window onto the capitalist West, would not exist.

†Even here, ironies abounded. As an English officer at the battle of Culloden, Wolfe had tried to save the life of young Fraser of Inverlochy, colonel of the Fraser regiment in Prince Charles's army. Now, Wolfe commanded the Frasers as a British regiment, dying just as Fraser had, at the end of the battle. Prince Charles's Scottish aide, the Chevalier Johnstone, also took part in the battle of Quebec—as an aide to Wolfe's French opponent, General Montcalm.

command, General James Murray, was a Scot who became its first British governor.

Canada's main value to Europeans was its fur trade, and within a few years the Scots dominated that as well. The best traders and trappers tended to come from Scotland's northern islands the Orkneys. The Orcadians, as they were called, enjoyed many advantages over their English counterparts. Canada's bitterly frigid climate, the deep isolation of months in icebound inlets and rivers, and the ceaseless work in cold and wet posed no hardship for them. The standard joke was that the Orkneymen joined the Hudson's Bay Company in order to get warm. One of the company's factors admitted, "The Orkneymen are the quietest servants and the best adapted for this country than can be procured." Another, on a trip in 1779, said, "A set of the best men I ever saw together, as they are obliging, hardy, good canoe men." They earned the respect of the Native Americans as well. Yet Orcadians were also notorious for their secretiveness, their reluctance to betray emotion, and their keenness to enrich themselves. One English officer asked that he be recalled to England "if any person from the Orkney Isles be placed over me." Their finest tribute comes from the American historian Bernard de Voto, who said the Canada Orkneymen "pulled the wilderness round them like a cloak, and wore its beauty like a crest."

They and their Highland cousins virtually took over the Hudson's Bay Company, so that by the turn of the eighteenth century four out of five employees were Scots. "The country is overrun with Scotchmen," an English trader complained.

Then, in 1782, another Scot, Simon MacTavish, created the Northwest Company, operating out of Montreal. MacTavish's employees trapped beaver, otter, and seal, or hired those who did, up and down Quebec and Ontario, and built settlements west into the Red River valley. One of them, a twenty-five-year-old trapper from the Isle of Lewis named Alexander MacKenzie, set up a fur-trading post with his cousin on Lake Athabasca, in what is now Alberta. A large river flowed out of Athabasca to the north at Fort Chipewyan, near their log-cabin post. MacKenzie decided to see where it went. In 1789, the year Parisians besieged the Bastille and George Washington was sworn in as the first President of the United States, the trapper set out on a three-thousand-mile trek up what is now the Mackenzie River, all the way to the Arctic Ocean. Four years later MacKenzie found a passage through the Canadian Rockies and, on July 22, 1793, crossed what is now British Columbia to find himself facing the Pacific Ocean. Meriwether Lewis and William Clark usually get the credit for first crossing the North American continent to the Pacific. In fact, that honor belongs to Alexander MacKenzie, who did it ten years earlier.

In 1821 the Hudson's Bay Company and the Northwest Company merged, forming the largest corporate landholder in the world—more than 3 million square miles, from the American border to the Arctic Circle. Its Scottish president, George Simpson, governed ten times more territory than had the Roman emperors. Simpson was a West Highlander, with a strong sense of his own dignity and command. An eyewitness remembered watching him on the move:

> When he went out of doors he wore a black beaver hat worth forty shillings. When traveling in a canoe or boat . . . he still wore his beaver hat, but it was protected by an oiled silk cover and over his black frock coat he wore a long cloak made of Royal Stuart tartan lined with scarlet or blue bath coating.

Simpson also traveled with his own bagpiper, who would play long pibrochs for his master as they canoed across an icy transparent lake to the next trading post or Indian village.

Simpson was also a master of handling men, and the company's Native American allies. He stopped the rum trade with local Indian tribes, and resorted to legitimate exchange to get his beaver pelts. By contrast to the American frontier, the Canadian version involved no violent confrontations with native peoples, no massacres or reprisals. Instead it witnessed one hundred years of virtually unbroken peace and order. Simpson's active and evenhanded stewardship of the Hudson Bay lands formed the basic core of what would become modern Canada.

Scots arrived as settlers, as well. Hundreds of Loyalist refugees from the Mohawk Valley in New York moved into eastern Ontario, in what is now Glengarry. They were soon joined by hundreds of Highland cousins, fleeing the Clearances. Today the land is flat, a checkerboard of fertile cornfields and grain silos. Then it was almost entirely forest, which the hardy Highlanders cut down and shipped to Quebec. Many stayed with the lumber business and followed it into northern Ontario, down to Michigan and Minnesota, and across to British Columbia. They became the Glengarry "shantymen," the most skilled lumberjacks in North America, artists with the ax and saw.

The rest stayed to farm, making Glengarry County, Ontario, the largest Gaelic-speaking community in the world outside Scotland. "Go not to Glengarry if you be not a Highlandman," warned one publication for prospective Scottish emigrants in 1829. Twenty years later the census revealed that one of every six of the county's 17,500 residents was surnamed either MacDonnell or MacDonald.

Other Highlanders settled the north shore of Lake Erie in Elgin County, named after Canada's most famous Scottish governor-general. John Kenneth Galbraith, the Harvard economist, was born and grew up on one of these farms. The Galbraiths had come over from Argyllshire, like many of their neighbors, and years later Galbraith remembered the intense concentration of Scots in Dunwich Township: "Beginning at the Currie Road were first the McPhails, and Grahams, then more Grahams, the MacFarlanes, the McKellar property, Camerons, Morrisons, Gows, Galbraiths, McCallums, more McPhails, more Morrisons, Pattersons, and among others the MacLeods."

Life in Dunwich Township followed very much the pattern of life in Highland clan *bailtean*. The people were frugal, hot-tempered, prone to fight and drink heavily, but scrupulously honest. "No houses were ever locked," Galbraith remembered, "perhaps partly because there was little in them to steal." They paid little attention to ordinary rules about personal hygiene or polite conduct. The only important distinction was who made the most money—but that conveyed respect rather than social status. In keeping with the Scottish stereotype, no one parted with their money very easily; as Galbraith puts it, "they believed a man could love his money without being a miser." Those who truly were misers, and left their houses in disrepair and their families in rags, were generally despised: but when their names came up, locals would refer to them as being "very Scotch."

The opening of the interior of Canada was also a largely Scottish enterprise. In 1834 John MacLeod reached the headwaters of the Sitkine River, and in 1847 Alexander Murray built Fort Yukon on the Yukon River. Two Scottish employees of the Hudson's Bay Company did the first complete survey of the Arctic coastline between 1837 and 1854. However, the greatest transformation of Canada came when John MacDonald launched the construction of the Canadian Pacific Railway, connecting the country from Atlantic to Pacific. It was one of the largest public-private joint ventures in history. Scots dominated the syndicate to promote its construction, from Donald Smith and his cousin George Stephen of the Bank of Montreal to London banker John Rose. Its principal engineer was also a Scot, Sandford Fleming.

The building of the 3,700 mile Canadian Pacific was an epic achievement worthy of Thomas Telford. It defied obstacles and challenges as forbidding as anything the Americans faced with their transcontinental railroad. Fleming and his surveyors, engineers, and road crews had to lay track along nine hundred miles of bottomless muskeg, across the empty prairies of Manitoba and Alberta, and into the steep foothills of the Canadian Rockies. The place where Fleming decided to cross the Rockies was at Kicking Horse Pass. He and his men had to battle temperatures that plunged to thirty and forty degrees below zero, in addition to treacherous snowslides and hurricane-force winds.

When the last spike went in at Craigellachie, British Columbia, on November 7, 1885, Prime Minister John MacDonald arrived by train for the ceremony. The Canadian Pacific was his proudest achievement. It united the country geographically much as MacDonald had united it politically.

It was a Scottish governor-general, Lord Elgin,* who first opened

---

*Elgin was the son of the Scottish diplomat who brought the Parthenon's famous marble friezes from Athens to London, where they would remain as the Elgin Marbles.

the door to the independence of British North America, as Canada was then called. Governor-General Elgin carried out reforms similar to those of other Scottish colonial administrators. He abolished the remnants of feudal land tenure left over from the French and built up Canada's education system. He signed a reciprocity agreement with the United States in 1854, putting an end to the enmity and tension between the two halves of North America, which extended back to the American Revolution.

He also warned his superiors that if London did not consider granting Canadians some form of self-government, they might throw in their lot with the Americans. If London gave them independence, however, Elgin believed, Canadians might actually want to strengthen their ties to Britain. He proved right. And without knowing it, Elgin had enunciated the principle on which the future British Commonwealth was based: that if a former colony was given the choice, it would prefer to remain associated with Great Britain than try to go it alone.*

The man who guided Canada through the crucial steps to independence was John MacDonald. Born in Glasgow of Highland parents, he had emigrated with them to Kingston, Ontario, in 1820. "I had no boyhood," he wrote later. He had to make his own living at age fifteen, but eventually scraped together enough money to get himself a law degree. Lawyering led to politics, which in Canada meant rough-and-tumble provincial politics, with bitter enmities pitting liberals against Tories, Presbyterians against Episcopalians, French Canadians against English-speakers, and everybody against the Americans. Tough, hard-tempered, addicted to cigars and whisky, MacDonald was deeply contemptuous of the English. "There is no place in Canadian government," he wrote, "for overwashed Englishmen, who are utterly ignorant of the country and full of crochets as all Englishmen are." But he also knew his dream of a united, independent Canada would never come true unless someone brought the French Catholics and English-speaking Protestants together. So his Liberal-Conservative Party, which spearheaded the

---

*Later, William Gladstone tried the same thing with Ireland that Elgin had done in Canada—unfortunately, with disastrous results.

independence movement, included a strong wing in French Quebec. MacDonald's cultivation of his French-speaking allies, and respect for their grievances, helped to heal ancient wounds. It also set the governing style of Canadian prime ministers all the way down to today.

MacDonald drew up almost every one of the Quebec Resolutions, which set forth the principles for the British North America Act that the British Parliament passed in 1867, giving Canada independence. He presided over the 1866 Confederation conference (of the ten "Founding Fathers" of the Canadian Confederation, in fact, eight, including MacDonald, were Scots) and served as Canada's first prime minister. In that post he created the most distinctive symbol of modern Canada, the Royal Canadian Mounted Police. He brought British Columbia into the confederation (completion of the Canadian Pacific was the price of admission), along with Manitoba and Prince Edward Island—and kept unhappy Nova Scotia from leaving.

MacDonald's successor was also a native-born Scot, Alexander Mackenzie. By the turn of the century, Scots and persons of Scottish descent were virtually running the country. One-third of Canada's business elite was of Scottish origin, and Scots single-handedly ran entire industries, such as papermaking (as usual), iron and steel, oil and gas, and the fur trade. They also enjoyed a lock on Canadian higher education. An author wrote in 1896, "There is not a college or university in Canada, where at least one 'son of the heather' is not to be found in some high capacity." Schools such as Dalhousie University (founded in 1818), McGill University (1821), and the University of Toronto (founded in 1827 by another Scot, James Strachan) enshrined the basic principles of Scottish education and the two great exponents of commonsense philosophy, Thomas Reid and Dugald Stewart.

The Canadian who best exhibited the key virtues of the Scottish mind and what it could do, however was the Canadian Pacific's hard-driving, Scottish-born chief engineer, Sandford Fleming. As the final leg of the railroad neared completion, Fleming realized one great obstacle to the cross-continental railway's success remained: Canada's clocks. Like clocks everywhere in the world, they were set according to local sunrise and sunset; where the sun was in the sky at any given moment determined what time it was.

This meant that everyone's local time was different from everyone else's. When it was noon in Toronto, it was 12:25 in Montreal, and 11:58 in Hamilton. In the United States alone, there were more than one hundred different standard times. People had learned to live with this constant disparity since they first began telling time. Even the advent of mechanical clocks in the fourteenth century, which increasingly made counting the hours and minutes more accurate, did nothing to help. In a horse-drawn age, when distances to be traveled were small and trips infrequent, a variation of ten or fifteen minutes, even an hour or two, did not matter much. But now it caused mass confusion for railway schedules, since no one could say exactly when a train was due in at a given station: there were simply too many different answers to the same question.* Travel was beginning to demand a level of chronological precision the world's clocks could no longer provide.

So Sandford Fleming decided to solve the problem. He took out a map of the world and divided it into twenty-four different time zones, each measuring fifteen degrees of longitude. The Americans had adopted a similar scheme for organizing their railroad timetables: now Fleming gave it a wider application than anyone had imagined. Then, for the next half-decade, he launched a one-man crusade to get first the Canadian government and then other world governments to adopt the new time zones and set their clocks according to the new single standard. Fleming was so tenacious and persuasive, and his idea so immediately sensible and useful, that he succeeded. An international conference held in Washington in 1882 confirmed the final arrangements. Finally, on November 17, 1883, clocks and watches around the world were for the first time in history synchronized according to one standard time. It laid

---

*British railways had overcome this difficulty by adopting Greenwich Mean Time, long familiar to mariners and sailors. But an English traveler soon learned that clocks in Paris or Berne or Lisbon or even Calcutta kept a local time totally unrelated to what he considered the true hour of the day.

the essential foundation for the globalization of travel, communications, and economies. When we are able to fly from New York and arrive in Rome or Singapore in time to meet a loved one, or phone a customer in San Francisco or Karachi to see if they received our shipment, we must thank Sandford Fleming.

III

Scots made it possible for Canada to be the first British colony to receive recognition as an independent nation. They did the same for Australia, but in a different way. There they turned a brutal and disorganized colony of doomed men and women into a civilized community.

After Captain James Cook (who was born in Yorkshire of Scottish parents) first landed there in 1770, Australia sat virtually forgotten until Prime Minister William Pitt established it as the site for a British penal colony. The first fleet of convict ships, carrying one thousand prisoners, arrived at Botany Bay, just south of the future Sydney Harbour, in 1788. More than 160,000 others followed, both men and women. Some were convicted of murder and other violent crimes, and accepted transportation to New South Wales, as the colony was called, in lieu of a death sentence. But many others went there for simple cases of theft or lesser offenses. One woman had stolen her employer's dress and was sentenced to seven years' transportation. One male prisoner, aged seventeen, stole food on board his convict ship. He was tried, convicted, sentenced, and hanged within an hour.

Most convicts saw transportation, and the eight-month journey to Australia, as preferable to languishing in an English prison. But conditions were harsh and the work brutal. Prisoners were assigned to whatever kind of work their keepers wished, and contracted out, like slaves, to free settlers, who grew rich on the cheap labor. Beatings were common, sometimes to the point of death, as were hangings. One warder remembered a prisoner who had been flogged so often his back "appeared quite bare of flesh," while his collarbones were exposed "like two Ivory polished horns." It was, the warden said, "with some difficulty we could find another place to flog him."

What sustained convicts through all this sadistic brutality was the possibility that after working four years of a seven-year sentence, or six of a fourteen-year one, you could earn your release. New South Wales offered lots of cheap, arable land, a healthy climate, and a future—if you got your certificate of emancipation. Even then, the free settlers still treated freed prisoners with suspicion and disdain. The slightest complaint might mean rearrest and more hard labor.

At the turn of the eighteenth century Australia was a hard, vicious, ugly place. Two Scots came to change that, in two contrasting ways: one by altering Australia's economy, the other by reforming its way of life.

John MacArthur arrived at Botany Bay with the second fleet of transported prisoners, to serve as lieutenant in the local army garrison. He was tough and violent-tempered, with an animal magnetism and a shrewd nose for a business deal. He might have given *tai-pans* William Jardine and James Matheson a run for their money. MacArthur bought a farm for himself of 250 acres and began raising wheat and sheep. He also organized an illicit rum-running ring with other officers in the garrison. One day he fought a duel with his own colonel and wounded him in the shoulder. Sent back to England for court-martial, MacArthur turned the tables on his enemies. He won an acquittal, and brought back a brace of long-haired merino sheep he somehow secured from King George III's private stock, and a special royal grant of two thousand acres of land to set up a sheep farm, which he called Camden.

MacArthur began experimenting, crossing the valuable but finicky merino with the Bengal sheep and the so-called Fat-Tail breed from South Africa. The hybrid he produced became the foundation of the Australian wool industry. Within a decade he and his wife and son had set up the first Australian sheep run or ranch, which became so successful that it grew to almost sixty thousand acres. To this day, the essential bloodlines of Australian sheep-breeding trace their origins to Camden Farm.*

MacArthur was also a compulsive meddler in New South Wales pol-

---

*Those that do not trace their lines to Scotch-Irish immigrant Alexander Riley, who followed MacArthur in importing Saxon merino at his sheep station at Cavan.

itics. When the new English military governor, William Bligh of *Bounty* mutiny fame, arrived in 1805, he found MacArthur's high-handed ways intolerable, and ordered him arrested. From his prison cell MacArthur plotted Bligh's downfall. His accomplice in the rum-running cartel and fellow Scot George Johnstone kidnapped Bligh at gunpoint and set him on a ship to England. For two years MacArthur, Johnstone, and a military junta ran New South Wales, rewarding cronies and terrorizing enemies. The colony had clearly reached a crisis. At last the British government recognized the need for serious reform, and dispatched the man who could set Australia straight.

Lachlan Macquarie had served nearly twenty years in the 73rd Highlanders in India and the Middle East, when he learned that the post of governor of Australia had fallen vacant. He lobbied hard for it, and in the summer of 1809 he set out on the journey to Sydney. He arrived in January, to find the colony "in most ruinous decay." The houses and government buildings were a shambles; the Government Advocate's house was, as he put it, "a perfect pigstye." Sydney's three churches were tents pitched on vacant lots. The main street was a dirt road, rutted and filled with animal excrement. Morale among prisoners and warders alike was at an all-time low, and drunkenness at an all-time high.

Macquarie was a hardheaded, clear-eyed workhorse, with a military man's sense of order, a martinet's sense of discipline, and a Scotsman's sense of fairness and justice. In Robert Hughes's words, "In guts, moral vigor, and paternal even-handedness, as well as in his bouts of self-righteousness and bull-headed vanity," Macquarie had few equals, even among other Scottish colonial officials. He banned the trade in rum, and ordered Sydney's bars closed during religious services on Sunday. He made church attendance compulsory for all convicts, and set up Sunday schools for the local children.

Even more important, Macquarie realized the key to keeping order in the colony was to treat the convicts as men and women, rather than as beasts of burden. He argued to his superiors in London that "emancipation" was "the greatest inducement that can be held out to the Reformation of Manners of the Inhabitants." He met every arriving convict ship personally and reminded the prisoners that while they had an obligation to obey their warders and employers, they also had rights. He would tell them "what a fine fruitful country they are come to," remembered one convict who first saw Macquarie standing on the dock with the medical examiner and garrison commander, "and what he will do for them if their conduct merits it."

Macquarie set most of the convicts, almost two-thirds of the skilled ones, to sprucing up Sydney. They cleared away the garbage, put a proper road through the center of town, rebuilt the government buildings, and built permanent churches as well as schools, houses, hospitals, and squares. One of Macquarie's prisoners turned out to be a former student of the celebrated Regency architect John Nash. Macquarie's wife had brought with her a book of buildings and town designs. Like James Craig laying out Edinburgh's New Town, the trio not only redesigned Sydney, but also constructed a series of townships in the surrounding territory, all in the metropolitan neoclassical style Robert Adam had established and Nash had embellished.

Macquarie also expanded the colony from its now-overcrowded enclave. He encouraged his team of cartographers and explorers to push north of Sydney, where they found the great fertile Liverpool Plains in 1818, and southwest into what is now Victoria. He contracted sixty convicts to build a road across the Blue Mountains, which locals and aborigines said were impassable. If they could do it in six months, he told them, they would be free. The convicts built the entire route, all 126 miles of it, in the time allotted, and Macquarie was as good as his word. It was proof, he told his superiors, of what could be accomplished by using incentives instead of coercion, through the work of free men rather than slave labor—the same point Adam Smith had made in the *Wealth of Nations* nearly forty years earlier.

Macquarie raised the quality of life in Sydney even as he cut costs. He even tried to find ways to assimilate Australia's aborigines into the new community he was creating. However, his fair-minded treatment of the convicts, and his insistence that "emancipated" workers receive the same rights and benefits as other citizens of Sydney, grated on locals who were used to having their own way with convict labor (among them, it must be admitted, John MacArthur). Eventually they turned his superiors against him, and Macquarie, worn out and disappointed, returned to England in 1821. He had served longer than any other governor in Australia's short history, almost eleven years. His successor, yet another Scot named Thomas Brisbane, was sent to reimpose the harsh discipline of the pre-Macquarie days. But he soon discovered this was impossible. Change had caught up with the penal colony, and the Emancipants, as freed convicts were called, were now embedded in the fabric of New South Wales society.

So instead Brisbane expanded many of Macquarie's reforms, permitted freedom of the press, encouraged the planting of tobacco and sugar cane, and expanded voluntary emigration into Australia. Then he, too, ran afoul of the local landowners and was recalled. A series of English governors temporarily brought back the floggings and brutal discipline. But when, in 1840, the Edinburgh-born naval officer and former professor of geography Alexander Maconochie took over Norfolk Island, the penal colony's own penal colony where the most recalcitrant prisoners were sent, it signaled the beginning of the end of the old system. Liberals in Parliament had already recommended abolishing transportation. Maconochie's humane and farsighted reforms, which included setting up a prison library (with a complete set of Scott's Waverly novels) and forming an orchestra, proved that prisons could go beyond a harsh system of punishment and discipline, even with the hardest cases. Genuine penal reform in Britain was still a generation away. But finally London stopped the convict ships in 1867—the same year Canada became the first British Dominion.

By the 1880s Australia had the fastest-growing economy and the highest per capita income in the world. Scots were as active in every major aspect of Australian life, including business, education, religion, and farming—almost 40 percent of Australia's borrowed capital came from Scottish banks—as they were in New Zealand.* MacArthur's

---

*New Zealand's origins were far less sinister than those of its sister colony to the west. It was founded by pious and business-minded Scotsmen, who first arrived in 1807 and never stopped coming. Scots set up the first permanent settlement at Petone, near Wellington, in 1840. John Logan Campbell owned the first ship to sail

sheep produced its principal export, wool. Queensland and South Australia now hosted large-scale settlements (including Brisbane, named after Macquarie's successor), with emigrants flooding into the country, among them a quarter of a million Scots. One of them, ironically enough, was the son of Alistair McDonnell of Glengarry. Despite the old man's brutal clearances, the burden of debt still fell heavily on his son and heir, Anaeas. Finally, in 1840, Anaeas MacDonnell had had enough. He sold his remaining estates except a tiny section of Knoydart, and emigrated to New South Wales with his family, his servants, several bolts of tartan, a couple of prefabricated timber houses, and his piper. He set out for the South Land to start a new life—as a sheep farmer.*

III

Africa was the last populated continent to be explored and penetrated by the British or any Europeans. It was called "the Dark Continent" because it was shrouded in mystery. No one knew what its vast interior held, or what people or riches might be found there. All trade and contact was through African middlemen. The mosquito-infested coast and disease-ridden swamps and jungles barred any European from probing farther. Working for the Royal African Company, or serving in a British garrison in Sierra Leone or the Cape Coast Command, which monitored Britain's ban on the slave trade, was for a European the equivalent of a death sentence. When Scottish missionary Mungo Park tried to lead an expedition up the Niger in 1805, every European on the trip died.

---

directly from England to New Zealand; he founded the city of Auckland and shipped the first cargo of New Zealand produce back to Britain in 1844. Otago was New Zealand's first planned community, founded by Scotsman George Rennie. One of its leaders was Robert Burns's nephew Reverend Thomas Burns. By 1861 almost a third of New Zealand's population were Scots.

*Unfortunately, the story does not end well. Having failed in the sheep business, Anaeas MacDonnell returned to Glengarry and died there in 1852. His widow was left with the same old debts and a young son. She settled the debts the only way she could, by clearing the last inhabitants from Knoydart.

Two-thirds of the British soldiers who landed on the Gold Coast between 1823 and 1827 died of diseases ranging from malaria and dysentery to sleeping sickness and yellow fever. In 1824 alone, 221 out of 224 perished. Africa truly was "the white man's graveyard," a permanent enigma sealed off from curious or prying European eyes.

The first person to challenge this accepted view was the shipbuilder's son MacGregor Laird. He believed the steam-powered boats his family firm was starting to build could be used to explore West Africa's great Niger River, from its mouth at the Bight of Benin up the channel and deep into the interior. Europeans, he believed, could then trade directly for raw materials with the natives, bring them manufactured goods in exchange—and spread the word of Christianity to Africa's heathen masses. Steam, he wrote to Lord Grey, "will convert a most uncertain and precarious trade into a regular and steady one, diminish the risk of life, and free a large portion of capital at present engaged in it." In 1832 Laird set up his company for commercial development of the Niger and took two steamboats to Africa. The venture failed. Of forty-eight Europeans who started out on his first voyage up the Niger, only nine returned. Laird himself nearly died, and returned to England in January 1834 in a feeble state—indeed, his health never recovered. But he persevered in pushing for steam power as the key to unlocking the dark secrets of Africa, and expanding the British Empire. The voyage of the *Nemesis* to China six years later was the result.

In the end, however, it was not the desire for empire or profits that finally opened up Africa, but another powerful force in the Scottish cultural repertoire—religion. A single man did it, not in order to enrich himself or to plant the Union Jack on another distant shore, but for the Africans themselves, to bring them education, medicine, freedom from the threat of slavery—in other words, "civilization" in enlightened Scottish terms—as well as Christianity. His name was David Livingstone, and in many ways his life epitomizes much of what made Scots so respected and influential around the world.

He was born in Blantyre in 1818, eight miles from Glasgow, to a family of mill workers. His grandfather Neil, a crofter on the tiny island of Ulva in the Inner Hebrides, had been driven from the family farm during the Clearances, and had found work in Blantyre's cotton mill. The son learned to read and write and became a clerk in the same factory, and then made a precarious living as a traveling tea salesman. David Livingstone grew up in a one-room tenement house on Shuttle Row, as it was called. Since the family needed every penny it could scrape together, David started work himself in the factory at age ten, climbing under the huge steam-driven looms to repair broken threads. According to an early biographer, a Blantyre neighbor remembered the Livingstone boys, David and Charles, coming from work. "If they was walkin' along the road and cam' tae a puddle, Charlie wud walk roon, but Dauvid—he'd stamp right through."

After fourteen hours of hard labor in the factory, David Livingstone attended night classes to get the education he craved. He spent his first paycheck on a Latin grammar. By the time he was fourteen he had learned Latin and Greek, and mastered stacks of theological literature. His father was a Calvinist Congregationalist who distributed religious tracts as he sold tea, so it is not surprising that religion was a powerful force in the son's life. But it had also become a resurgent force in Scotland.

For fifty years after the Moderates had defeated the Evangelical party for control of the Scottish Kirk in 1757, Scottish culture had secularized itself and become "enlightened" on matters of religion. Dugald Stewart, Henry Brougham, James Mill, even Sir Walter Scott, all treated most of the history of organized Christianity, particularly in Scotland, as one of superstition and intolerance. Then, with the new century, Protestant evangelism experienced a powerful rebound. Part of it was a reaction against the atheism of the French Revolution. Part of it, too, was the rebellion against an established Church of Scotland that had become so refined and aloof from everyday life that it offered nothing to people who needed a strong emotional outlet. Just as American Presbyterians had caught religious fire from Scottish Evangelicals in the eighteenth century, setting off the Great Revival, so Scottish and English Calvinists now turned to American revivalism for a new kind of "religion of the people."

The country went through an unabashed phase of being "born

again." Protestant sects such as the Congregationalists, Baptists, and Methodists found eager converts among Scotland's rural and urban workers. Shops, taverns, even most city services, strictly observed the Sabbath—a custom that persisted until very recently. Church leaders such as Thomas Chalmers became civic leaders in the fight against poverty and slum conditions. Eventually the revivalist tide swept over the Kirk itself. In 1843 nearly 450 ministers resigned their offices and joined with Chalmers in forming the new "Free Protesting Church of Scotland," or the Free Kirk, an evangelical alternative to Scotland's government-subsidized church.

However, this resolute, churchgoing, Sabbath-keeping, psalm-singing Scotland stayed in line with this modernizing predecessor. No one wanted to turn back the clock or reverse the accomplishments of the past hundred years. Instead, the new evangelism sought to provide a steadily improving inner spiritual life, to match the progress of society and "civilization." As the young David Livingstone discovered when he read the works of the Scottish astronomer and theologian Thomas Dick, science and religion were parallel paths to revealing God's truth. In other words, the thirst for knowledge of the world and the desire to be one with Jesus Christ were not at odds with each other. The God of nature and the God of Revelation were one. "In the glow of love which Christianity inspires," Livingstone remembered years later, "I resolved to devote my life to the alleviation of misery"—both as a missionary and as a doctor.

Livingstone took up studies in chemistry and theology at Anderson College at the University of Glasgow. At twenty-three he was older than most of the students, but he was as keen and alert as the best—who were very, very good. One of his classmates in Thomas Graham's chemistry class was William Thomson, later Lord Kelvin, who would become the most influential chemist of the nineteenth century. Another was Lloyd (later Lord) Playfair, grandson of the brilliant mathematician.

In 1838 he had his medical degree, and he hoped to go to China to open a mission there. However, the outbreak of "that abominable Opium War" forced him change his plans. Then he met Englishman Robert Moffat, who gave a lecture in Glasgow on the mission he had just opened in southern Africa. As Moffat told his audience of the vast-ness of the African continent and its unexplored beauty, of rising in the morning to see "the smoke of a thousand villages where no missionary had been before," the image stuck in Livingstone's mind. Here was a chance not only to do the Lord's work but to embark on a great adven-ture, an opportunity to journey to places where no white man, not even Moffat, had gone before.

David Livingstone set sail from Liverpool on December 8, 1840, hardly dreaming he would not see home again for sixteen years. He grew restless on the three-month trip, and decided to learn the art of navigation from the ship's captain, which would come in handy when he began his treks across Africa, and later sailed his own boat across the Indian Ocean. After reaching the British colony of Cape Town, Livingstone set off for Moffat's station at Kuruman, six hundred miles north, on the edge of the great Kalahari Desert. It turned out to be a bitter disappointment. Moffat had found fewer than forty converts, and although he and his daughter Mary tried to create an oasis of civilization and security in their tiny mission, they drew no takers. So Livingstone decided to take a different tack. Instead of waiting for the natives to come to him, he would go to them, wherever they happened to be—even if that meant penetrating hundreds of miles into trackless jungle and mountains.

He set off on his first journey to the African interior in October 1841, traveling nearly five hundred miles northeast through a series of remote villages, where he learned what he could about African life and language.* The risks Livingstone was willing to run for the sake of his mission were staggering. Quite apart from the physical dangers of trav-eling across wild and often hostile country—at one point Livingstone was attacked by a lion and severely mauled, which cost him the use of his right arm—there was also the hidden menace of diseases and fever. He caught malaria early on, and its recurrent bouts never left him. But

---

*Livingstone published the first dictionary of Setsowma in 1852, and was the first European to realize that the various Bantu tongues belonged to the same linguistic family.

he managed to limit its effects, and to protect other members of his party from its ravages, by taking doses of a new drug developed by French chemists, called quinine, which he usually dissolved in a glass of sherry. Livingstone was the first person to use quinine in Africa. Although he was never entirely convinced it was completely effective in preventing malaria—he preferred a home remedy he developed of quinine, calomel, rhubarb, and resin of julep—it changed the odds in Europeans' favor for the first time. Like James Lind's discovery of citrus against scurvy, quinine opened a pathway for long-distance travel in the tropics, in this case overland—and in doing so it would save the lives of hundreds of thousands, both black and white.

For all the risks he ran, Livingstone enjoyed the strenuous effort his itinerant mission involved. "The mere animal pleasure of traveling in a wild unexplored country is very great," he wrote. "Great exercise imparts elasticity to the muscles, fresh and healthy blood circulates through the brain, the mind works well, the eye is clear, the step is firm." He also discovered he got on well with Africans—better, in fact, than he did with white Europeans, who sometimes found him too abrupt and unafraid to say what was on his mind. There was also the thrill of finding one new vista and discovery after another.

The first was Lake Ngami, which unexpectedly greeted him when he arrived at the upper reaches of the Kalahari. The most famous, however, was Victoria Falls—"so lovely," he wrote, "it must have been gazed upon by angels in their flight"—and the Zambezi River, one of the great rivers of the world, which flows from northwestern Zambia across the heart of Africa to the Indian Ocean. As he gazed for the first time over its broad expanse, more than five hundred yards across in places, with foothills and mountains rising up in the distance, Livingstone said it awakened memories of "the long-lost scenes of the Firths of Clyde and Forth, which came back so vividly, I might have cried."

That trip in 1853–56 took him across Africa from ocean to ocean, as the first European to do so. It revealed that the interior of Africa was not desert or barren savannah, as some had guessed, but a world of lush vegetation and millions of human beings. Livingstone decided that rivers such as the Zambezi were the key to opening Africa up to the rest of the world. He believed they constituted a great "water highway" that could bring goods, services, and the Gospel to even the most remote parts, and trigger the continent's economic and social advance—much as Telford's roads and canals had opened up the Highlands. Later, he hoped the Zambezi could be declared an open waterway for the use of all nations, but the Portuguese, who occupied crucial parts of its head-waters in Angola, refused to permit it.

The one service he could bring to Africa's heartland himself was his medical practice. Livingstone became truly the first "doctor without borders," traveling thirty or forty miles out of his way to visit whatever village or people needed his assistance. Livingstone brought the sharp analysis and technical knowledge of Scottish medicine to some of the remotest places in the world. His efforts won him the respect of local tribesmen and their leaders—and, as he expected, a steady stream of conversions to Christianity.

As Livingstone saw it, there were two great barriers to Africa's eventual road to Christianity, commerce, and "civilization." One was white racial prejudice. Like most Scots, Livingstone was largely immune to racial theories of white supremacy (belief in white *cultural* supremacy itself was another matter). In one colonial setting after another, Scots proved themselves far better able to get along with people of another culture and color than their English counterparts. In addition, the whole weight of Scottish Enlightenment tradition was on the side of belief in a universal human nature, which all human beings shared, but which was shaped according to environment and a society's developmental stage—"nurture," in other words, rather than "nature."

Livingstone despised the sort of race prejudice and brutality he found in the Cape Colony. He had become fast friends with missionary John Philip, another Scot, who fought for the rights of aboriginal peoples in South Africa. Livingstone clashed repeatedly with the local Boers, especially when he supported a local native revolt against their rule. "Every nation on earth worthy of freedom," he wrote, "is ready to shed its blood in its defence. We sympathize with the Caffres [sic]; we side with the weak against the strong." Rebellion, he said, was prima facie evidence of bad government to begin with. His forthright stance so infuriated the South Africans that they practically herded him out of the country.

He spoke even more forthrightly on race when he published *The Zambesi and Its Tributaries,* and included a sharp riposte to race theorists who believed Livingstone's travels showed that the black Africans were savages and incapable of understanding the values of civilization. "We must smile at the heaps of nonsense which have been written about the negro intellect. . . . I do not believe in any incapacity of the African in either mind or heart." Black Africans merely exhibited the kind of cultural backwardness one would expect from anyone cut off from mainstream civilization, Livingstone said. "A couple of centuries back the ancestors of common people in England were as unenlightened as the Africans are now." And how unenlightened was a matter of opinion. "Africans are not by any means unreasonable," he wrote. "I think unreasonableness is more a hereditary disease in Europe."

When Livingstone returned to England in 1856, he discovered he was famous. His lectures on his exploits and adventures drew huge crowds and gained an audience with Queen Victoria. So did his impassioned attacks on the African slave trade.

This was the second great barrier to Africa's development. Britain had abolished the buying and selling of slaves in 1807, and virtually shut it down all across the Atlantic. It had freed its own slaves in 1833. However, Arab traders continued the ugly business of seizing, buying, and selling human captives for export. The wars that African kingdoms waged with one another in order to find captives to sell to the slave traders, and the incessant deportation of thousands of victims to the great slave-trading port of Zanzibar, had devastated entire sections of central and southern Africa. On Livingstone's travels overland, he would come across parties of people linked together by wooden yokes on their march to the Arab slave markets, a journey that could be even more horrific and lethal than the Atlantic "middle passage." Livingstone wrote in his diary, "We passed a slave woman shot or stabbed through the body and lying on the path. . . . An Arab who had passed early that morning had done it in anger at losing the price he had given for her, because she was unable to walk."

Livingstone did what he could to hinder the slave traders—he did not hesitate to give modern firearms to African communities to fight them off. But in the end he believed the final remedy had to be the spread of legitimate trade and commerce with European nations across Africa. When local chiefs realized they could make more money selling palm oil or ivory, instead of their own people, Africa's ways would change. And rivers for commerce and communication were the key to making it happen. It drove him to launch more and more exploratory expeditions into the interior, and to insist that Britain had to take the lead in making Africa safe, for white and nonwhite alike.

After two years of speeches and celebrity, Livingstone was eager to return to Africa. On February 8, 1858, he was appointed Her Majesty's Consul and "commander of an expedition for exploring Eastern and Central Africa, for the promotion of commerce and civilization with a view to the extinction of the slave trade." Livingstone and his companions, including his wife, Mary Moffat Livingstone, his son Robert, and his brother Charles, reached the mouth of the Zambezi on May 14. They traveled up the river as far as Quebrabasa Rapids in the world's first steel-hulled steamboat, *Ma Robert* (or "mother of Robert," which locals called Mary Livingstone), which handled the rocks and inevitable beachings without a mishap.

Then things began to go wrong. Livingstone quarreled with the English members of the missionary society over the goals of the journey: he wanted to combat the slave trade, while they wanted to convert the natives. Then disease descended on the party. On the hard journey up the Zambezi rapids, Mary died, as did their infant child. When Livingstone and the other survivors reached Lake Nyasa (now Lake Malawi), the second-largest body of water in Africa, a war between local tribes broke out. The British government, discouraged by reports of death, disaffection, and a local drought, ordered Livingstone home.

Livingstone's third and final African expedition was sponsored by the Royal Geographical Society. He planned to discover the source of the Nile in eastern Africa, but Livingstone's hopes went further than that. He intended to show that the culture of ancient Egypt derived its remote origins from black Africa—a thesis that in many ways anticipates those of modern afrocentrist scholars. "One of my walking dreams," he told friends, "is that the legendary tales about Moses coming up into Inner Ethiopia with Merr, his foster-mother, and founding a city which he called in her honor 'Meroe,' may have a substratum of fact."

He never had the chance. He set out into the bush in 1866 with no white companions, only thirty porters, a band of Indian sepoy soldiers, students from a government school for freed African slaves, and a few local recruits. Like the extras in a Tarzan movie, the porters and the rest bolted the expedition at the first sign of trouble. When they made their way to the coast, they spread the rumor that Livingstone had been murdered. No one knew the truth of what had happened to the man who had made Africa a part of everyday conversation. Nothing but silence came from the endless expanse of jungle and savannahs.

For two years no one knew anything about Livingstone's fate. Some speculated that he really was dead; others that he was in hiding; still others that he had discovered the fabled ancient cities of Christian Ethiopia and their mythical king, Prester John. The story of Dr. Livingstone became an international sensation. Finally the Scottish-descended owner of an American newspaper sent a reporter, Henry Stanley, to find him as a way to generate publicity and sell newspapers. It was no pleasure junket. Stanley's two-year trip across the heart of east central Africa proved as uncertain and dangerous as any of Livingstone's expeditions. At last, in 1872, Stanley found him in the village of Ujiji, with a handful of loyal followers. Livingstone's health had finally given way. For months he had lain on a cot, too ill to move or lift a pen. But he refused to leave Africa. Instead, he said farewell to Stanley and set off on his final journey into the interior, still hoping to hit on the Nile's source.

On May 1, 1873, Livingstone died. His two constant companions, Chuma and Susi, former freed slaves, found his body kneeling at the foot of his cot, as he was about to say his prayers. They buried his heart under an *mpundu* tree seventy miles from Lake Bangweulu. Then, having wrapped his body in calico to try to preserve it, they set off on an incredible eleven-month, fifteen-hundred-mile journey to the coast to have his body buried in a European cemetery. It was a labor of love and a tribute to Livingstone from the people he had tried to protect and serve.

A similar tribute poured out when Livingstone's body returned home. Britain went into mourning. His body was buried at Westminster Abbey, with the epitaph

DAVID LIVINGSTONE:
MISSIONARY, TRAVELLER, PHILANTHROPIST

They forgot to mention: Scottish doctor.

CHAPTER FOURTEEN

Self-Made Men:
Scots in the United States

America would have been a poor show
had it not been for the Scotch.
—*Andrew Carnegie*

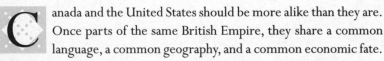anada and the United States should be more alike than they are. Once parts of the same British Empire, they share a common language, a common geography, and a common economic fate. Both are, in their own way, nations of immigrants—including, in both cases, sizable and influential numbers of Scots.

Yet their histories run in very different directions. The development of Canada was largely a public enterprise, controlled and in many cases financed from the top down. The Hudson's Bay Company started that tradition; the building of the Canadian Pacific epitomized it. Americans built their world around the principles of Adam Smith and Thomas Reid, of individual self-interest governed by common sense and a limited need for government. The U.S. Constitution of 1787 enumerated the powers of the federal government, and left the rest to the individual states. The Canadian Confederation of 1867 explicitly gave the provinces certain powers, and kept the rest for itself. It reflected the political vision of Dugald Stewart: government as a resource for society's progress, rather than a hindrance to it.

Despite these differences, the Scots themselves were almost as important to the development of the United States as to that of Canada. In Bernard Aspinwall's phrase, they were "the shock troops of modernization," the first echelon of skilled immigrant labor to reach America's shores and make it a productive nation. They transformed the new republic from an agricultural community of "agrarian yeoman" into an industrial powerhouse, the quintessential modern nation.

The Scots who came to the United States in the nineteenth century reveal once again why the Scottish diaspora was so different from other mass immigrations in history. Despite their relatively small numbers (less than three-quarters of a million, compared with 5 million Irish), the vast majority of Scottish immigrants could read and write English. Most knew some trade other than farming. Almost half of the Scottish males who came to America between 1815 and 1914 qualified as either skilled or semiskilled workers. In fact, while Canada tended to draw Scotsmen who wanted to own a farm and lead a rural life, the United States attracted those who were determined to succeed in a trade or in a factory job. Their work ethic and moral discipline were bywords. "Of all immigrants to our country, the Scotch are always the most welcome," wrote the entrepreneur and prohibitionist Neil Dow in 1880. "They bring us muscle and brain and tried skill and trustworthiness in many of our great industries, of which," he added pointedly, "they are managers of the most successful."

Of all American immigrant groups, probably only the Jews had more or comparable skills. But unlike the Jews, or the Irish for that matter, Protestant Scottish immigrants were not held back by religious discrimination. And unlike the English, they did not expect special or preferential treatment. They lived by Sir Walter Scott's famous maxim, "I am a Scot and therefore I had to fight my way into the world." They anticipated hard work as a matter of course.

Nor were they intimidated by their new environment. On the contrary, it had a certain familiar feel: an Anglo-Saxon privileged elite who dominated politics and government; an Anglicized urban middle class divided into competing Protestant sects; Irish immigrant workers crowded into growing industrial cities; an inaccessible interior governed by tribal warrior societies about to be displaced by the forces of progress—here was Scotland all over again.

It is not surprising that so many Scots came to identify with America. They saw it as the fulfillment of their own hopes and desires, and Scottish men and women as indispensable to its forward progress. Andrew Carnegie's famous declaration quoted above echoed the sentiment of many others, that "the United States was Scotland realized beyond the seas." It was a place where the Scotsman could create a new life for himself out of the opportunities the continent offered, and a new identity. After all, being an American was above all an idea, just as being a "North Briton" had been, or civilization itself. All it required was a goal and a desire to succeed—and a person could become anything, or anyone, he wanted.

This was a self-confident individualism as old as the Renaissance: "Man can do all things if he will." But then it had been an ideal for an elite. It presupposed a fixed social structure, a hierarchy of status groups in which individual talent, like water, would eventually find its own level. No such thing existed, or seemed to exist, in America. The field was wide open, just as the country itself was wide open—"an empire of liberty," as Thomas Jefferson phrased it, which the Louisiana Purchase in 1803 had more than doubled in size. It was the Scots who would show the rest of the Americans how to operate in that kind of social and cultural void—where nothing seems impossible, where a man can take his skills and his willpower and turn it into gold.

A new social ethos was born, which the rest of the world would come to see as quintessentially American—and quintessentially modern. In fact, it is quintessentially Scottish, and the Scots in America would also demonstrate that the endless possibilities of this inventive self-fashioning and the pursuit of individual success do not have to end in chaos. They can spawn a new kind of civic community, which respects the right of all people to pursue their own ends as long as they respect that right for others. It is an enlightened community, with echoes of David Hume's secular Golden Rule. But it is reinforced, like concrete with steel rods, by a traditional moral discipline, the legacy of Presbyterianism.

Scots had helped to create the new American nation. Now they would show how it could work.

I

In 1788 Benjamin Rush wrote to John Adams, "America has ever appeared to me to be the theater on which human nature will reach its greatest civic, literary, and religious honours. Now is the time to sow the seeds of each of them."

Rush had come back from his sojourn to Scotland in 1774, where he had recruited John Witherspoon to Princeton and studied medicine with William Cullen, energized and enthused. With an almost missionary zeal, he had thrown himself into the revolutionary cause and then into shaping the newly born republic into a modern nation. Rush founded the first antislavery society in America, recognizing in that "peculiar institution" precisely the kind of tyranny that had prompted Americans to break with Britain. He became a pioneer in the temperance movement, and he led a crusade for humane treatment of the mentally ill, making him America's first clinical psychologist. He helped to found the American Philosophical Society, based on the Edinburgh original, and supplied its operative motto: "Knowledge is of little use, when confined to mere speculation." This captured perfectly the practical side of the Scottish Enlightenment, and Rush's own desire to see an America take shape in conformity to that model.

The basis of this new enlightened American identity, Rush believed, was going to be its system of education, and above all its universities. Here his influence was enormous and long-lasting. He completely remade the College of Philadelphia's medical school, where he was a popular and influential teacher, recasting the teaching of medicine according to the Edinburgh model. He founded Dickinson College in western Pennsylvania, with a Scottish president, which became the vehicle for Rush's vision of a new kind of nondenominational educational institution. He argued for moving Latin and Greek out of the center of the curriculum (although he still believed in the importance of classical languages), and ushering science in. The university should be a place that pushed forward the frontiers of knowledge in all areas, Rush believed, through research and innovation, as well as a center of instruction.

His own College of Philadelphia had already taken up reforms along related lines under its Scottish president, William Small, which were based on the University of Aberdeen. So Rush and Small's college (later the University of Pennsylvania) became one important conduit for the Scottish remaking of American education; John Witherspoon's Princeton was another.

Even after his death in 1794, Witherspoon's influence on the new republic continued to be enormous. He had made Princeton into a training ground for a leadership elite. During his tenure Princeton had produced a future United States president (James Madison), a vice president (Aaron Burr), six members of the Continental Congress, nine cabinet officers, twenty-one senators, thirty-nine congressmen, three Supreme Court justices, twelve governors, thirty-three state and federal court judges, and thirteen college presidents. He had made science an integral part of the college curriculum, along with history, English, and moral philosophy.

After 1825 Harvard, Yale, Brown, and Columbia began moving in the same direction as Princeton and Philadelphia. Later, Harvard and a new addition to the academic constellation, the Johns Hopkins University, would deviate slightly from the Scottish norm, and look to the Germans. But on the whole, American higher education remained resolutely Scottish all the way down to World War I.

This was helped by two Scots in Scotland who made their mark on American education by remote control, as it were. One was Dugald Stewart. He had always stressed the importance of moral philosophy as the matrix discipline, the place where all the other disciplines, arts and sciences alike, met. His lectures on philosophy and ethics became the standard guides for nearly twelve academic generations of American scholars and educators. They offered a blueprint for building a curriculum based on the Scottish school, as did the writings of another influential Scot, George Jardine.

Jardine taught at the University of Glasgow for fifty years, from 1774 until his retirement in 1824. His heroes were Hutcheson and Adam Smith. His ideas on what a university education was supposed to offer, and how it was supposed to be taught, changed the face of higher education not only in America but in Scotland as well. Jardine was professor of logic and rhetoric; he became convinced early on "that something was wrong in the system of instruction; that the subjects on which I lectured were not adapted to the age, the capacity, and the previous attainment of pupils." So Jardine created the introductory college course, which presented new or difficult material in small and digestible pieces rather than as a single imposing system that students had to either understand or fail. Jardine also insisted that lectures be interspersed with regular examinations, in order to gauge the students' progress, and on which students had to write themes or original essays. Jardine's famous example was "There was fine linen in Egypt in the time of Moses," which would lead students to do research about the government, society, and political economy of ancient Egypt, as well as about the Bible.

Jardine's *Outlines of Philosophical Education, Illustrated by the Method of Teaching the Logic Class at the University of Glasgow* became one of the most popular textbooks in American higher education. It explained how to create a stimulating intellectual atmosphere in the classroom and lecture hall. It created a system of "writing across the curriculum," as it would later be called, with compositions, essays, and research papers assigned in every class and at every level, which taught students how to think for themselves, but also how to write clear, incisive, original English prose. The typical Edinburgh Reviewer became the ideal American college graduate—a person of strong moral sense and independent judgment, with a knowledge of history, philosophy, literature, and science at his fingertips, in whom "all the faculties of the mind are exerted, and powers unused before, are awakened into life and activity."

All these trends came together in 1868, when Princeton University needed a new college president and turned to the reigning figure at Queen's College in Belfast, the philosopher James McCosh. It was exactly one hundred years since Princeton had turned to another Scot, John Witherspoon, to revive its fortunes. The arrival of McCosh caused almost as much of a stir. One undergraduate remembered it being "like an electric shock." McCosh brought Princeton physically and intellectually into the modern age: he put together a distinguished faculty in both the arts and the sciences; he founded the first graduate school, as well as schools of science, philosophy, and art; he erected a series of new buildings on campus,* including a gymnasium and a seventy-thousand-volume library. "Some critics found fault with me," McCosh remembered later, "for laying out too much money on stone and lime; but I proceeded on system, and knew what I was doing. I viewed the edifices not as an end, at best as outward expressions and symbols of an internal life."

In McCosh's case, that internal life had multiple components and involved complex elements. Like Witherspoon, McCosh was a Presbyterian minister as well as a philosopher. He had helped to lead the Great Disruption in 1843, when he and Thomas Chalmers had inspired other clergymen to walk out of the General Assembly and create a new independent evangelical church, the Free Kirk. But he was also the direct heir to the mainstream tradition of the Scottish Enlightenment, a century and a half of intellectual achievement that McCosh synthesized and summarized under a single title: "the Scottish philosophy."

The Scottish philosophy, he said, "is different from nearly all the philosophies which went before, from many of those which were contemporary, and from some of those which still linger among us." It stressed observation and experience as the primary source of knowledge. It saw human consciousness as our window on reality, and onto the self. And it stressed that as human beings, we come equipped to grasp the truth about ourselves and about the world around us, including a sense of right and wrong.

This was the legacy that the Scottish school had left for the generations that came after them. It was the friend of science and moral confidence, and the enemy of moral relativism, pessimism, and doubt. "We have the express testimony of a succession of illustrious men for more than a century, to the effect that it was Hutcheson, or Smith, or Reid, or Beattie, or Stewart, or Jardine . . . who first made them feel they had

---

*In fact, Princeton was the very first college to which the word *campus* applied. John Witherspoon had used the Latin word, meaning an open field, to describe the college's site.

a mind, and stimulated them to independent thought." They may not have been the most startling or original thinkers in history, McCosh concluded. "But the great merit of the Scottish philosophy is in the large body of truth which it has if not discovered, at least settled on a foundation which can never be moved."

A foundation which can never be moved. Yet even as McCosh was writing his tribute to the Scottish school, he knew that the assumptions on which it was based were being steadily whittled away. A new force was stirring in the Western educational world, that of the German university ideal, which stressed rigorous research and professional specialization rather than the generalist approach that McCosh and the Scots favored. And then there was the threat from the other direction, the newfangled system of course electives. In 1885 McCosh traveled to New York to debate Harvard president Charles W. Eliot on the ideal college curriculum. McCosh condemned Eliot's plan to allow students to select their classes from a list of more than two hundred offerings. It encouraged dilettantism, he argued, and, more important, destroyed the notion of a fundamental unity of knowledge, leaving everything "scattered like the star dust out of which worlds are said to have been made."

Many thought McCosh, who was then seventy-three years old, had won the debate. But in the coming years elective courses would grow in their numbers and popularity, along with new academic subjects from agricultural science and business administration to anthropology, economics, psychology, and political science—disciplines that, ironically, often owed their origins to the great figures of "the Scottish philosophy." But they also sounded the death knell of that older ideal of an education which, as David Hume had put it, "softens and humanizes the temper and cherishes those fine emotions, in which true virtue and honour consists," and which Witherspoon had said promoted "the order and perfection of humanity."

Like Witherspoon, McCosh had seen the goal of education as producing a strong Christian as well as an educated man. That ideal, too, was fading, in an intellectual climate that had become more secular and skeptical. The Scottish school's faith in a universal common sense, and in the solid reality of the world around us, began to sound naive—especially when scientists, including the Scottish physicist James Maxwell, were showing that that reality might not be so predictable and knowable after all. American philosophers were starting to turn to French and German thinkers such as Kant, Hegel, and Auguste Comte—and still later and even more disturbingly, Karl Marx.

When McCosh retired in 1888, the Scottish tradition, to which he had dedicated so much of his life, was already on the retreat in the intellectual frontiers across America and Europe. Before it faded, however, it had created the American liberal arts college and the American university. Its offspring would increase with the years, often without acknowledging their patrimony. But the Princeton Class of 1889 made up for all of them, when it unanimously asked that former President McCosh's name be inscribed on their diplomas, along with his successor's. When he met their delegation in the front hall of his house, McCosh listened to their request, quickly dabbed at his eyes, and called to his wife. She listened, took her husband's handkerchief from the pocket of his clerical frock coat for her own eyes, and said tenderly, "Jamie, yer lads are nae for forgettin' ye."

II

The Scottish influence in nineteenth-century America was a matter of muscle as well as mind. Scots and Ulster Scots immigrants had created the first American frontier along the eastern slopes of the Appalachians and Alleghenies. After the American Revolution, their descendants helped to extend and govern the result—Andrew Jackson, John C. Calhoun, James K. Polk, Jim Bowie, Daniel Boone, William Clark (of the Lewis and Clark expedition), Sam Houston, and General Winfield Scott, whose grandfather fought at Culloden.

Then, in the first decades of the nineteenth century, a second, much larger wave of emigration left Scotland for the United States, this time including numbers of skilled workers from the Lowlands, as well as impoverished Highlanders fleeing the clearances and the great cholera epidemic. By the early 1840s Scotland was in the grip of "Amerimania," as Glasgow-based ship companies such as the Cunard line established regular routes to New York, Baltimore, Philadelphia, and even, for a time, New Orleans. A popular Scottish song captured the mood of those setting out from Glasgow or Greenock for a new future:

To the West, to the West, to the land of the free;
Where the mighty Missouri rolls down to the sea;
Where the man is a man even though he must toil,
And the poorest may gather the fruits of his toil.

Not everyone headed west to the mighty Missouri. Thousands found employment in eastern seaboard cities, where their job skills, along with their frugal work habits, made them popular with employers. As early as the 1790s the incipient American industrial base came to rely on Scottish engineers, mechanics, and workers to set up its cotton mills, maintain and repair its steam-engine pumps, and operate its power looms. A textile worker from Paisley quickly discovered that he or she could work the same hours in a factory in Massachusetts and earn far more money, with a lower cost of living. This is what emigration guidebooks meant when they said North America was "the best poor man's country" because "the price of grain is very low and the price of labor very high." In addition, factory owners often employed their Scottish immigrant workers to teach the Americans proper work skills and habits—which meant a Scottish worker soon found himself managing the factory floor.

The confidence in Scottish workers extended to women workers. In 1853 an agent for Hadley Falls Mills in Massachusetts recruited eighty-two unmarried women mill workers from Glasgow, while one in Holyoke Mills hired sixty-seven. In a couple of months they had earned enough to pay off their entire transatlantic fare and buy themselves some new clothes and shoes. For a Scot in the United States, a factory job was always a stepping-stone to something else, to something better.

Scots poured into shipbuilding yards in Philadelphia, iron foundries in Pittsburgh, stonecutting quarries in New England and Ohio, and papermaking factories in New York. The entire typemaking industry in

New York City was said to be largely a Scottish monopoly. Others became pioneers in the new dry-goods industry, where by the Civil War a new technique of merging all the different aspects of the trade under one roof emerged. The department store was essentially a French invention, but Scots, both in Britain and the United States, made it profitable on a new scale. David Nicholson in Philadelphia, Dugald Crawford in St. Louis, Robert Borthwick in Buffalo, Robert Dey in Syracuse, John Forbes in Kansas City, Carson Scott in Chicago, William Donaldson in Minneapolis, and Alexander Stewart in New York City all founded department stores that helped to revolutionize the retail business in the United States. They were not only businessmen but civic leaders: pillars of the local chamber of commerce, members of the Masonic Lodge, presidents of the local chapter of the St. Andrew's Society, serving on the boards of hospitals and universities, rebuilding the city's Presbyterian churches, and providing funds for a new city hall or school. They were essential links between business enterprise and the rest of the community. They truly represented the "human face" of American capitalism.

Other immigrants settled in Illinois (two of the original founders of Chicago were Scots, John Kinzie and Alexander White), Ohio, and the upper Midwest. But large numbers were drawn farther out, to the Pacific Northwest (Scottish-born Robert Stuart blazed the original Oregon Trail), Utah (the earliest Mormon missionaries were Scottish-born Presbyterian converts), and above all California. In 1814 California's very first non-Hispanic, non-Indian resident was a Scottish sailor named John Gilroy. By 1830 there were fifty Scottish families living in California, and as early as 1839 Alexander Forbes, a Scottish merchant in Tepic in Mexico, was urging colonization of California—by *Britain*. George Simpson, top-hatted executive of the Hudson's Bay Company, agreed. "English it must become," he said of California. "Either Great Britain will introduce her well-regulated freedom of all classes and colours, or the people of the United States will inundate the country with their own peculiar mixture of helpless bondage and lawless insubordination."

In the end, the "lawless insubordination" did win out, but not the forces for slavery. California's multicultural mix, with whites, Spanish Creoles, Hawaiians, and Native Americans posed no problem for Scots. Scottish-descended mountain men such as Kit Carson and Isaac Graham came from Kentucky and Tennessee to live, trade, play, and quarrel with Spaniard, Indian, and Englishman alike. Hugh Reid was the sandy-haired, blue-eyed son of a Cardross shopkeeper who emigrated to Los Angeles in 1834 and became partners with James McKinley. Reid married the daughter of a local chief, opened a school for boys, and dubbed himself Don Perfecto Hugo Reid. He soon owned one of the largest haciendas in California, the Rancho Santa Anita, which covered most of present-day Pasadena. He sat in California's constitutional convention when it became a state, and led the fight to bring it into the union as a free state. He also called the white settlers' treatment of the Indians "the shame of this country and a disgrace" and became a leading defender of Indian rights and interests until his death in 1852.

Then, in January 1848, a Scottish immigrant named James Wilson Marshall was inspecting the mill race of John Sutter's mill not far from San Francisco, when "my eye was caught by something shining in the bottom of the ditch. . . . I reached my hand down and picked it up. It made my heart thump, for I was certain it was gold. The piece was about half the size and shape of a pea. Then I saw another. . . ." Marshall raced back to the mill, shouting, "Boys, I believe I have found a gold mine."

So he had. The California Gold Rush not only brought thousands of new residents, including Scots, but also changed the very nature of success in America. It offered instant wealth for the asking—by 1857, total production of gold reached over $500 million, almost all of it going to private individuals. Riches, for those who were quick or cunning or lucky enough to find them, became the promise of California and the West.

For example, the Donahoe brothers were actually of Irish ancestry, but born and raised in Glasgow. Michael was the first to come to America in 1831, to work with his uncle in New York. All three brothers, Michael, Peter, and James, then went to work for a locomotive builder in Paterson, New Jersey, until the Gold Rush drew them to

California. All three became millionaires but, as is appropriate for hardworking Scots, not as gold prospectors. Peter opened a steamship line carrying prospectors and other immigrants between San Francisco and Sacramento. He built the first steam engine for a U.S. Navy vessel on the West Coast, and the first steam locomotive in California. James and Michael became partners in the Union Iron Foundry, and while James retired, rich and satisfied, Michael opened another major foundry in Davenport, Iowa, with a sideline in steam engines and agricultural machinery. Meanwhile, Scottish engineer Andrew Hallidie designed and built San Francisco's cable car network in 1873, a symbol of the city to this day—but also of the Scottish aptitude for engineering, transportation, and communication.

As early as the 1850s Scottish clerical missionaries such as William Ander-son of San Francisco's First Presbyterian Church and William Scott of the Calvary Presbyterian were prophesying that the new California would become the American Utopia. Scott, who had been born in Tennessee in a log cabin and had been Andrew Jackson's personal spiritual adviser, even saw San Francisco as the new Athens—a kind of Edinburgh on the Pacific. But the most influential of these Scottish-descended California clerics was the Methodist William Taylor, whom one historian has dubbed the John the Baptist of the Gold Rush. In addition to preaching, "California" Taylor visited the San Francisco hospital daily where men from the gold fields had been abandoned by their friends to die. He organized revival meetings along the Long Wharf every Sunday, where hundreds would gather to sing hymns and hear him preach on a passage from Scripture particularly appropriate for Californians: "For what is a man profited, if he shall gain the whole world, and lose his own soul?"

In 1854 San Francisco became famous for another reason. The *Flying Cloud* arrived in harbor from New York, having made the trip in eighty-nine days and eight hours—a world record. The *Flying Cloud* was built by Donald McKay, born in Canada of Scottish parents, whose shipyards in East Boston were the nursery of the great clipper ships of the age. "If great length, sharpness of ends, with proportionate breadth and depth conduce to speed," wrote Duncan Maclean of the *Boston Daily Atlas,* "the

Flying Cloud must be uncommonly swift." She certainly was. Running 225 feet long and 41 feet wide, with iron straps stretched over her hull's planks for more durability, the *Flying Cloud* set the Cape Horn world speed record not once but twice.

In the decades before steam "annihilated distance" in transoceanic travel, the McKay clippers could sail more than four hundred miles a day. They opened up the oceans to a new pattern of world trade, as did those of his Scottish competitors. Scottish-built China clippers became legends, such as the *Thermopylae* of William Thompson's White Star Line from Aberdeen, and the *Cutty Sark,* built in Dumbarton in 1869, which started in the tea trade but then broke into the Australian wool trade as the fastest ship in the world, steam or no steam. Meanwhile, McKay's nautical masterpieces, such as the *Lightning* and the *Great Republic,* the biggest clipper ship ever built, connected the United States from east to west, from Boston and New York to San Francisco, before the railroads drew the coasts together with rails of iron.

Even before the railroads, however, the American continent became connected in another, perhaps more important way.

Samuel Finley Breese Morse was an accomplished portrait painter living in New York City. Like other Americans of Scottish origins or ancestry,* such as Charles Willson Peale and Gilbert Stuart, he found portrait painting the perfect combination of artistic expression and good business. He painted the rich and famous, including President James Monroe; Morse also helped to found the National Academy of Design. To make even more money, he began experimenting with a new science the English and French had pioneered, the field of telegraphy. In 1834 Morse devised a system for transmitting messages electrically by wire, using a series of dots and dashes to represent each letter. The Morse telegraph, and Morse code, made a system of long-distance communication possible; a message could travel, without danger of being lost or destroyed, over thousands of miles in a matter of hours rather

---

*His mother's father was Ulster-born Princeton president Samuel Finley, who had inspired Benjamin Rush and the last pre-Witherspoon generation of Princeton graduates.

than months. He laid out a line between Baltimore and Washington in 1844, and sent the first true long-distance message. Ten years later America was covered with over 23,000 miles of telegraph wire. Laden with money and honors, Morse became a pillar of the New York community. He even ran for mayor twice. He had developed the ancestor of all forms of modern electronic communication, from satellites and television to radio and the telephone.

Alexander Graham Bell grew up in Edinburgh and was educated in Edinburgh High School and Edinburgh University. His family had built a reputation as experts on communication with the human voice; the old Scottish obsession with correct English pronunciation had spawned an entire industry devoted to elocution, phonetics, and speech. His father Alexander Melville Bell had developed a "visible speech system," which he hoped would be the prototype of a universal phonetic alphabet. His son, in turn, invented a method for teaching the hearing-impaired to speak (Bell's mother was deaf, as was his future wife), before the family emigrated to Canada in 1870.

In 1865, as telegraph wires connected the American continent from California to the east coast, and the transcontinental railroad was nearing completion, the eighteen-year-old Alex had conceived the possibility of the electrical transmission of actual human speech, not just dots and dashes on a keyed device. In the summer of 1874 he laid out his theory to his father at their house in Brantford, Ontario. "If I could make a current of electricity vary in intensity precisely as the air varies in intensity during the production of sound," he concluded, "I should be able to transmit speech telegraphically."

Others were working on similar devices, and some aspects of Bell's original design were already in experimental use. As usual, however, with Scottish scientists and engineers, it was his ability to organize and systematize the ideas of others, and beat them to the punch, that ultimately paid off. In 1875 Bell was teaching at the Boston School for the Deaf—among his students was Helen Keller—when he and his friend Thomas Watson devised a telephone, or "harmonic telegraph," which transmitted sounds over a wire. His patent application went on file at the United States Patent Office on February 14, 1876—just two hours before his leading competitor took the first step in filing his own. On March 10, Bell and Watson spoke to each other for the first time from different rooms. Bell showed his device at the Philadelphia Centennial Exposition, and the following year he was talking from Boston to New York, using the Western Union Company's telegraph wires. In 1878 President Rutherford B. Hayes (the third U.S. president of Scottish descent) installed the first telephone in the White House. By the 1880s it was becoming a familiar instrument to residents in New York, Boston, and Chicago.

What appealed to Bell about the telephone was that it permitted direct, personal, long-distance communication, not just station-to-station messaging, as the telegraph did. He was determined to make telephones available to everyone who could afford them, and set up his National Bell Telephone Company in 1877 to manufacture them. By then his rivals had gotten into the act. Bell had to contend with more than six hundred lawsuits from individuals and corporations such as Western Union, whose employees Elisha Gray and Thomas Edison were working on a similar device. Eventually Bell won out, securing his monopoly of patents for telephone technology.

Bell was now a rich man. By 1883, just seven years after he had unveiled his invention to the rest of the world, his net worth was nearly a million dollars. He moved his family to Washington, D.C., where, on Winfield Scott Circle, he built a magnificent home that filled an entire block, complete with electric lighting and heating. He built himself an estate in Nova Scotia, where the ocean and the mountains reminded him of his native Scotland. He continued his work with the deaf, spending over $450,000 of his own money on new research, and became president of the National Geographic Society. Bell never became as rich as a Morgan or a Rockefeller or a Carnegie. But thanks to the telephone, he was at least as well known and powerful. Bell had become one of the new breed of American businessmen: the industrial magnate.

The rise of industrial corporations such as Bell Telephone and its long-distance subsidiary, American Telephone and Telegraph (AT&T), signaled a radical change in the way capitalism organized itself. Big business was replacing the merchant-entrepreneur as the driving wheel of commerce: technology had spawned mass production, which in turn gave birth to a new system for meeting the demands of consumers and suppliers. That system, however, did not spring out of nowhere. It was the brainchild of another Scot, the creator of the prototype of modern corporate enterprise and the most famous self-made man of all: Andrew Carnegie.

III

He was born in 1835 in Dunfermline, a linen-weaving town that was also the final resting place of Robert the Bruce. The first distinct sound he could remember hearing as a child was the sound of his father's hand loom working in the living room below his crib. Machinery would play various roles in Carnegie's life, just as the whole range of Scotland's past and present seems to come together in the education of this poor hand-loom weaver's son.

From his maternal uncle he learned about traditional Scottish history, and acquired a lifelong love for the novels of Sir Walter Scott and the poetry of Robert Burns. His grandfather Andrew Carnegie, Sr., was the self-appointed discussion leader of the workingman's "college" in nearby Pattiemuir, a working-class representative of the Scottish Enlightenment. "The participants," the grandson recalled, "well fortified with malt whisky, were equal to any topic—philosophical, political, or economic, that might be presented." His other grandfather, Thomas Morrison, came from a wealthy Edinburgh merchant family who had lost their fortune and position. Undeterred, Thomas had learned to be a shoemaker and made a snug life for himself in Dunfermline. He was also a committed Radical and a correspondent with the English reformer William Cobbett, and published numerous articles in Cobbett's *Political Register*. From the one grandfather Carnegie learned his own egalitarian politics, summed up in the Scottish Radicals' motto, "Death to privilege." From the other he got his sense of optimism and intellectual energy, as well as a belief in education as the foundation of democracy.

In 1848 new power looms driven by Watt's steam engine were

replacing the old hand looms, so the Carnegie family left for America. Andrew was twelve when they settled in the former Fort Pitt at the confluence of the Allegheny and Monongahela Rivers, which had been renamed Pittsburgh. The town was a magnet for Scots looking for work in the coal mines, iron foundries, and lumber mills that were transforming Pittsburgh into the industrial workshop of the upper Mid-Atlantic. The Carnegies found a place to live with an aunt, who rented them two backrooms in a grim, overcrowded alley in the working-class suburb of Allegheny City. While his father took work in a textile factory, Andrew became a bobbin boy in the same factory for a dollar twenty a week. He was just a few months shy of thirteen.

Yet, like the "lad o' parts" of popular Scottish novels of the day, Andrew Carnegie was grimly determined to better himself. That meant education. He read everything he could get his hands on, and learned Morse code. Within a year he landed a job as a messenger boy at the Atlantic and Ohio telegraph office in Pittsburgh. Most of the other young boys were also Scots or Ulster Scots, who all became successful in later life, as did their supervisor, James Douglas Reid. But Andrew outdid them all. He memorized the locations of all the office's main customers, so he lost no time in delivering messages. He could translate the clicks of the telegraph even before they appeared on the printed tape. It was a skill bound to attract attention; and when Thomas Scott of the Western Division of the Pennsylvania Railroad learned about it, he hired Carnegie on the spot as his personal telegraph operator and secretary. The job paid thirty-five dollars a month, almost three times what his father earned after a lifetime's experience of manual labor. When Scott asked him, "Are you native born?" Carnegie answered, "No, sir, I am a Scotchman"—a reply that, he wrote later, made him "feel as proud as ever Roman did when it was their boast to say, 'I am a Roman citizen.'"

Carnegie's first fortune came not in the iron or steel business, but in the railroads. He was only twenty-two when his boss moved to Philadelphia, leaving the post as supervisor of the Western Division to his young assistant. When the Civil War broke out, Carnegie moved to Washington, where he helped to create the system of military supply by rail that helped to guarantee a Union victory. At war's end the rising young executive sank his personal savings into a new company that was manufacturing sleeping cars for passenger trains. The company owner was George Pullman. In less than a year Pullman made a fortune, as did his investor. Andrew Carnegie could count his personal worth at more than $400,000. The only question was what to invest in next.

The answer seemed obvious: steel. It was essential to railroad construction, which was clearly the key to America's next stage in economic development, and to the military. But it was also becoming the primary material of a rising industrial civilization, for buildings, bridges, machine tools, and even household items such as cooking utensils and sewing machines. The British had dominated the steel industry for more than a century, thanks in large part to James Watt's steam engine and J. B. Neilson's blast furnace. Now an English scientist named Henry Bessemer had developed a new way of forging steel directly out of molten pig iron, which drastically cut the labor involved and dramatically increased the production.

Carnegie met Henry Bessemer on a trip to England in 1873, and decided his new method held the key to the future of steel. He began inspecting a neighbor's land for a site on which to build the first Bessemer plant in North America. He bought the land and started building the plant, naming it after Edgar Thomson, the president of the Pennsylvania Railroad, who he assumed would be his largest customer. A collection of fellow Scots joined the Carnegie "clan" as partners in the business: his brother Tom, his cousin "Dod" Lauders, John Scott, and Gardner McCandless, as well as non-Scots such as Henry Phipps and Charles M. Schwab. Together they bought out other steelmakers and converted their businesses into Bessemer plants, all the while relentlessly finding ways to make the process simpler, quicker, and cheaper. The Scottish thoroughness and attention to cutting business costs, and willingness to take risks, paid off. In less than twenty years, by 1892, the Carnegie Steel Company was producing steel equal to one-half of the entire production of Great Britain.

This was Adam Smith's capitalism on a truly gigantic scale. In fact, Carnegie Steel Corporation, later United States Steel, is the ancestor of the modern industrial corporation. Carnegie created a perfectly "verti-cally integrated" business, controlling every aspect of production from extraction of the raw iron ore and coal to the distribution of the final product, much as John Rockefeller did with Standard Oil. But Carnegie also changed the nature of division of labor, which for a hundred years Adam Smith and his disciples had understood to be the source of all productive wealth. He did this by effectively standing the relationship between business and technology on its head. Before Carnegie, business had to wait for technological advances by scientists such as Charles Macintosh (the inventor of vulcanized rubber) and engineers such as James Watt to create new products or increase production. Now the demands of production themselves would force technological change. The manager, not the engineer or the foreman or the quick-witted employee, decided by looking at his flow charts where processes could be made more efficient or pennies could be saved. The engineer and the employee followed the manager's lead. If they did not, they were fired. It was a principle all of Carnegie's managers and supervisors followed, such as William Jones and Charles Schwab and Henry Clay Frick. Industrial capitalism had become as simple, and as ruthless, as that.

And all the time, Carnegie and his subordinates were constantly probing, checking, and rechecking for ways to save money. It became the key to Carnegie's way of doing business. Once he asked his friend the New York publisher Frank Doubleday how much money he made in the course of a month. Doubleday could not say; he pointed out that publishers generally drew up their balance sheet at the end of the year. "Do you know what I would do if I were in that kind of business?" Carnegie asked. "No, what?" said Doubleday. "I would get out of it," Carnegie replied.

And by examining his records so minutely, Carnegie discovered a new principle: that the best way to cut the cost of making a product was to make *more* of it. He stated it clearly and simply: "Cheapness is in proportion to the scale of production. To make ten tons of steel a day would cost many times as much per ton as to make one hundred tons. . . . Thus the larger the scale of production the cheaper the prod-uct." Carnegie had discovered "economies of scale," an indispensable idea for modern industrial production, and for corporate capitalism generally.

Yet this hardheaded, relentless business sense was balanced by his keen, buoyant optimism. Carnegie believed not just in his own corporate future, but in the possibilities for America and the world generally. He was a keen disciple of Adam Smith, but also of Robert Burns. Burns's refrain "a man's a man for a' that" constantly rang through his public pronouncements, which tended toward the radically progressive. He wrote a book called *Triumphant Democracy* in which he prophesied that industrial capitalism would become the great vehicle for the expansion of democratic opportunity. "The Republic may not give wealth or happiness," he wrote, "she has not promised these. It is the freedom to pursue these, not their realization, we can claim. But if she does not make the emigrant happy or prosperous, this she can do and does do for everyone, she makes him a citizen, a *man*."

He often visited Scotland, where he lectured his former countrymen on the need to make Britain more democratic. He spoke to large crowds in a voice that was "occasionally marred by an American accent," as a Scottish journalist noted, "but his feeling is always Scotch and his Americanisms soon relapse into his mother tongue." Carnegie extolled the virtues of the American system, telling Britons, "The great error in your country is that things are just upside down. You look to your officials to govern you instead of you governing them." He became an enthusiastic admirer of the English libertarian philosopher Herbert Spencer, who expanded Adam Smith's belief in the virtue of free markets into an entire social philosophy. Carnegie foresaw "a new industrial world" taking shape, a world "without war or physical violence, in which through the genius of invention and the miracle of mass production, the fruits of industry would become so abundant that they could be made available to all." The title of Carnegie's next book summed it all up: *The Gospel of Wealth*. Capitalism had become a form of secular redemption; it was the final permutation of the Scottish school's celebration of commercial society, civilization, and progress.

Unfortunately, Carnegie had to pass through a personal purgatory first. His hopes for "an industrial world without war or physical violence" were shattered by the bloody Homestead Strike in 1892. Nine people died at his steel works at Homestead, Pennsylvania, in the worst labor violence in American history, and he was vilified across the country. Carnegie recognized his responsibility and bitterly regretted that he had allowed the response to the strike to fly out of control. "The pain I suffer increases daily," he wrote to a friend. "[T]he Works are not worth one drop of human blood. I wish they had sunk." But the memory of Homestead marred his public image and ruined his love affair with the steel business. In 1901 he approached the financier J. P. Morgan to ask what he would pay in order to own U.S. Steel. Morgan told him to name his price. Carnegie took a pencil and on the back of an envelope wrote the number: "$480 million." He passed it to Morgan, who looked at it and said without hesitation, "I accept."

Carnegie's share came to over $300 million—in the era before income taxes, an almost unimaginable sum. In keeping with his egalitarian principles, he said, "the man who dies rich dies disgraced," and for the next decade he set about translating that sentiment into action. Like Bell, he came to think of his fortune as public property. More than $180 million of his money went to a variety of very Scottish projects. One was building public libraries. Soon there were more than 2,800 Carnegie libraries around the world, including nearly two thousand in the United States. By the time of Carnegie's death, the total number of readers in the United States using his free public libraries every day was estimated at 35 million. He also built 7,689 pipe organs for churches, as well as parks, swimming pools, auditoriums (such as Carnegie Hall in New York), and medical research laboratories (such as the one at New York's Bellevue Hospital).

A very large chunk went to education, albeit only of a certain kind. Carnegie took to a new extreme Benjamin Rush's principle that "knowledge is of little use, when confined to mere speculation." He saw science, engineering, and vocational training as the future of American education, and refused to fund anything that strayed outside those practical bounds. "The flavor and philosophy of Poets and wise men is the sweetest of all foods," he used to say, "but for others, not so and these the majority who must earn a living." To Carnegie, offering a new school for petrochemical research or hydraulic engineering promised more for the future of democracy than the same old courses in Roman drama—or even philosophy, the traditional mainstay of Scottish higher education. The new president of Princeton University, Woodrow Wilson, discovered that when he approached Carnegie in the summer of 1902.

It was an important moment. The two strands of the Scottish legacy for America, already closely related, were about to briefly cross paths. One traced its origins to the Scottish Enlightenment's vision of intellectual effort as the benchmark of progress, which Princeton University embodied and Wilson touched through his predecessors McCosh and Witherspoon. The other represented the raw human power of the Scottish diaspora, which understood progress in terms of technical know-how and good business sense. In his letter to Carnegie, Wilson leaned heavily on Princeton's Scottish heritage: "She has been largely made by Scotsmen, being myself of pure Scots blood, it heartens me to emphasize the fact." He saw Princeton raising a great School of Jurisprudence and Government with Carnegie's largesse, for the training of future statesmen and jurists. However, he was willing to add this proviso: "[N]o doubt it would be wise . . . to expand the part which commerce and industry have played, and increasingly must play, in making for international as well as national peace and for the promotion of all the common interests of mankind."

Carnegie visited Princeton, and did give generously to the school. But it was not a school of government, or a library, or even a laboratory. Instead, it was a lake. Carnegie told Wilson he wanted Princeton to have a rowing team like Harvard and Yale, in order "to take young men's minds off football." The fifty-acre body of water known as Lake Carnegie was the result. That, and nothing else. The two strands of Scotland's legacy had met, and retreated in mutual incomprehension.

IV

The intellectual legacy of the Scottish Enlightenment in America was nearly spent. But its practical scientific side seemed to be just getting started. While Carnegie and Woodrow Wilson were parting company, two other men were organizing a momentous experiment in Washington, D.C., along the banks of the Potomac. They were Alexander Graham Bell and Samuel Langley. They had met at the Smithsonian Institution, where Langley was executive secretary, and which had been turned from an antiquarian curiosity shop into an important center for scientific and engineering research by another son of Scottish immigrants, Joseph Henry.* Langley had told Bell about his new idea of creating a heavier-than-air machine that could fly. Bell was enthusiastic, and gave Langley five thousand dollars for more research. On May 6, 1896, Langley made his attempt at unmanned flight, with his steam-powered *Aerodrome V.* It flew for nearly half a mile before it settled into the waters of the Potomac. Langley and his team winched it out of the river and set it off on another successful trip, the first airplane flight ever recorded on film. The man handling the camera was none other than Bell himself. Afterward he wrote, "No one who was present on this interesting occasion could have failed to recognize that the practicability of mechanical flight had been demonstrated."

Manned flight was next. On October 7, 1903, Bell and Langley assembled their team for a test flight with a pilot, once again along the Potomac River. This time, however, it failed. A second attempt on December 8 failed also. Then, on December 18, they read in the newspaper that the day before, at Kitty Hawk, North Carolina, brothers Orville and Wilbur Wright had flown a machine 120 feet with Orville on board. The Wright brothers had taken the laurels for the first successful manned flight. But in 1914 a pilot did manage to fly Bell and Langley's airplane, and Bell himself went on to make new discoveries and devise new inventions (including, in 1918, a speed-record-breaking hydrofoil). A new era of modern technological progress had opened up, along with a whole new way to realize the Scottish dream of creating communication and exchange between human beings. The Wright brothers deserve the credit for the first manned, powered flight. But it

---

*As secretary of the Smithsonian from 1846 until his death in 1878, Henry also created the National Weather Service.

is significant that when the Smithsonian Institution decided to build a display for the first airplane, it hung up Bell and Langley's prototype instead.

When Samuel Morse had sent his first telegraphic message from Baltimore to Washington in 1844, the words he chose came from the Bible: "What hath God wrought?" The words have since seemed prophetic, expressing the sense of astonishment, almost foreboding, at how the world would change over the next century and a half, thanks to technology and the industrial age. From that point of view, he could have sent a slightly different message:

"What have Scotsmen wrought?"

Conclusion

Breathes there a man with soul so dead,
Who never to himself has said,
This is my own, my native land!

—*Sir Walter Scott*

I

As the nineteenth century waned, the intellectual capital of the Scottish Enlightenment waned with it. James McCosh was probably that tradition's last survivor in the field where it all started, moral philosophy. Other isolated giants remained. Alexander Bain, virtually self-educated and the son of a weaver, rose to become professor of logic at Marischal College, Aberdeen, and founder of *Mind,* Britain's most important philosophical journal. The University of Glasgow laid claim to one of the two most important physicists in Britain, William Thomson, Lord Kelvin. Aberdeen had the other, James Clerk Maxwell, the father of modern electrodynamics, whose work cleared the way for Einstein's theory of relativity. In 1890 Sir James Frazer published *The Golden Bough,* which revolutionized modern anthropology. However, Maxwell had left Aberdeen early in his career for the University of London and then Cambridge. Frazer looked as much to German and French thinkers as he did to the "System of the North," or Scottish school.

Scotland's days as the generator of Europe's most innovative ideas were over. However, she had done her work: the future direction of the modern world, which Scotland had done so much to chart and establish, was now set. What still hung in the balance was the fate of Scotland herself.

In one sense, Scotland had finally arrived—at least as far as Great Britain was concerned. Glasgow was now the industrial workshop of the empire. Its thriving banking and business center boasted an imposing neoclassical architecture of marble, granite, and sandstone to rival that of Edinburgh. Its iron and steel foundries and shipbuilding yards turned out close to one-third of the nation's total output in each industry. It supplied locomotives and boxcars to Canada, South America, and the rest of Europe, as well as India and Asia. Shipbuilding firms along the Clyde, such as Napier's, John Brown's, and Fairfield's, turned out one-fifth of the world's total shipping tonnage. They made the British navy the most modern afloat and built the revolutionary new battleship *Dreadnought* in 1902.

As Glasgow's population neared the one-million mark, seven out of ten men and women living in the city worked for some kind of industrial manufacturer—including twelve thousand at the new Singer Sewing Machine factory in Clydebank, one of the largest in the world. Other cities, such as Dundee and Paisley, flourished as well. Paisley was home to the largest cotton-thread-making company on earth, Coates-Paton, which dominated nearly 80 percent of the world market. Scotland had become a dominant player in the "global economy" long before the phrase was invented.

Scots dominated British politics, just as they pretty much ran the empire. Westminster saw five prime ministers hold office between Gladstone's resignation in 1894 and the battle of the Somme in 1916. Three were Scots: Lord Rosebery, Arthur James Balfour, and Henry Campbell-Bannerman; a fourth, Herbert Asquith, was married to a Scotswoman, and sat for Scottish constituencies for his entire thirty-five-year political career.

The election in 1906 was a landslide for the Liberal Party, which owed its existence and credo to Scots. The Liberals took fifty-eight out of seventy-two Scottish seats. Balfour, the defeated Conservative prime minister, who claimed descent from Robert the Bruce, had also had a Scottish chancellor of the Exchequer and a Scottish home secretary. Another future prime minister, Ramsay MacDonald, sat in the new

Parliament as a member of the rising new Labour Party, which had also been founded by a Scot, Keir Hardie.

Scotland's landed families were now pillars of Britain's social and political elite. They sent their sons to England's finest schools, Eton and Harrow, Oxford and Cambridge. Worrying about "scotticisms" in speech and behavior was a thing of the past; Scotland's ruling class was now indistinguishable from its English counterpart. Archibald Primrose, the fifth Earl of Rosebery, was educated at Eton and Oxford, and married a Rothschild. In addition to being prime minister, he was also a prominent figure in English horseracing and the Turf Club.

The Duke of Buccleuch hunted foxes on his 433,000-acre estates, just like any English squire. Others regularly invited English guests to their Highland castles or Lowland shooting-boxes to join in the annual slaughter of deer, grouse, pheasant, snipe, woodcock, trout, and salmon, which consumed so much of the leisure time of Edwardian upper-class males. The Clearances had left the Highlands devoid of people, but they did leave it a playground for the rich, and a vacation spot for tourists from London and Manchester and Glasgow and Edinburgh.

Yet, by the same token, Scotland's upper and middle classes were losing that hard-driving entrepreneurial edge which had been a part of their cultural heritage. They increasingly settled into the ideal of the English gentleman. The values of Eton, Cambridge, and Oxford, of the Reform and Athenaeum clubs, and of Lord's Cricket Grounds steadily replaced those of a grittier homegrown variety. Balfour, who was a founding member of the super-elitist Cambridge Apostles as well as the darling of English upper-crust society, once described a member of his cabinet as "that rare bird, a successful manufacturer who is fit for something besides manufacturing." Lord Rosebery admitted, "There is no thought of pride associated in my mind with the idea of London" or Britain's great urban industrial wealth. When Andrew Carnegie proposed giving Scotland's four universities more than two million pounds for sponsoring new science and engineering programs, he received a stern rebuke from *Blackwood's Magazine,* now the voice of genteel British conservatism. "Success for him is the accumulation of dollars. . . . Maybe

Mr. Carnegie has never heard the fable of Midas. . . . To get money you must strangle joy and murder peace." If Carnegie had his way, *Blackwood's* warned, "presently the American ideal will be our own."

The sad truth was that, to many educated Scots, their own culture now seemed more provincial than ever. Scotland's success had brought with it a sense of disquiet, an increasing feeling that the rewards were not everything that had been promised. Part of it was due to being the "good child" of the United Kingdom, while the "bad child," Ireland, stole the headlines with the issue of Home Rule. Also, in the two decades before the start of World War I, Scotland learned some unpleasant truths about the costs and consequences of becoming a modern nation in such a rapid and headlong way.

For one thing, for all of Scotland's industrial growth, poverty remained as intractable a problem as ever. Wages in Glasgow always lagged behind those in the rest of Britain; that was partly what made it so attractive to manufacturers. Quality of life suffered, however. Infant mortality remained higher than in other British cities. Disease and malnutrition haunted the crumbling tenements of Glasgow's inner city. Scotland's other industrial cities told similar stories. In Dundee in 1904, for example, one-fifth of the city's six thousand houses had no toilets or sanitary accommodations. Belatedly, Glasgow's city authorities began to push large-scale slum clearances and new housing. But the damage had already been done. At the start of the Boer War in 1898, two out of three Glasgow recruits for the British army had be turned away because they could not meet the minimum health requirements. As one writer has put it, "Scotland in the Edwardian era was no place to be poor, sick, aged, or unemployed."

Farther north, the nightmare of the Highland Clearances was over, although fierce confrontations between crofters and landlords had continued down to the 1880s. Poverty remained the fate of most of those who stayed. Their diet had changed little from almost two centuries earlier—oatmeal porridge, bread and oatcakes, a little beef or mutton. No wonder emigrants continued to stream out of the country in record numbers. In the first decade of the twentieth century, almost a quarter of a million people left Scotland—and not only from the Highlands.

Town and rural laborers in the Lowlands realized a much brighter future awaited them in Canada or America; in the fifty years before 1920, in fact, more than half of Scotland's emigrants headed for the United States.

Scotland had been the first fully literate nation. Its education system, particularly its universities, had once inspired the rest of the English-speaking world. Now it seemed to lag far behind. In 1882 the rector of Edinburgh's hallowed High School, James Donaldson, bitterly complained that the curricula of Scottish universities were still pretty much what they had been three hundred years earlier. In terms of modern research facilities and laboratories, Donaldson suggested, the Scottish university was "the handloom weaver of the intellectual world." Edinburgh, Glasgow, and Aberdeen no longer attracted Scotland's best and brightest: anyone in pursuit of an advanced degree in the humanities or sciences went to Cambridge, Oxford, or London instead.*

Ten years later the universities tried to update themselves by instituting entrance exams, creating the bachelor of science and honors degrees, and finally admitting women. University students of thirteen or fourteen years old were now a thing of the past; the academic body more closely resembled that of other Western universities. It was not clear, however, whether all this was really for the better. Poorer and less qualified students, who once could have sneaked into Edinburgh and St. Andrews and gotten their university training, now got caught in the mesh of entrance exams. Overall, the Scottish university became more elitist in its orientation, all in the name of higher standards and professional excellence. And still the best and brightest traveled south for their degrees.

Other parts of the education system struggled to keep the old egalitarian ideal intact. In 1872 Parliament created for Scotland the first system of compulsory primary education in Britain, and transferred control of the traditional burgh schools to a new public board, which

---

*Here, as always, ironies abounded. The University of Edinburgh had been the conscious model for University College, London, when it was founded in 1810: the bulk of its first faculty were Scots or Scottish-trained.

also provided money so that schools could now abolish students' fees. One out of seven Scottish children went to secondary school in 1914, compared with one in twenty in England. But the problem of drawing into school those who most needed it, the poorest and most disadvantaged, remained as intractable as ever. Something like 15 percent of Glasgow's children never saw the inside of a classroom. Increasingly it was government that was called in to help; as with urban renewal and social reform, reform in education steadily passed out of private hands or church-based organizations and into the arms of the state, which meant London.

Scottish businessmen had once led innovations in the printing industry and the book trade. The *Edinburgh Review* had set the standard for the English-speaking world of serious intellectual culture. The last issue of the *Review* appeared in 1929. (*Blackwood's* managed to hang on until 1980.) Now Scots were pioneers in a new field: the tabloid press. Alfred Harmsworth set up the half-penny-a-copy *Daily Mail* in 1896, which spawned a host of imitators, such as the *Daily Mirror* and *Daily Express*. The best-known Scottish writers were no longer philosophers or political economists or essayists or historians, but masters of the field of fantasy and escapist literature. Robert Louis Stevenson's *Treasure Island* delighted children and adults alike, while *Kidnapped* and *The Master of Ballantrae* put the final touches on the Highland myth Sir Walter Scott had started. Arthur Conan Doyle not only authored the most famous detective of the age, Sherlock Holmes, but a series of science-fiction novels, including *The Lost World*. A Roman Catholic, Doyle was a champion of spiritualism and seances—a far cry from the hard-headed realism of Hume and Reid. James Barrie led a pack of authors writing sentimental stories about rural Scotland, which critics dubbed "the Kailyard school." But his most famous work, *Peter Pan,* with its tale of a talented boy who refuses to grow up, reflected a Scottish intellectual tradition that now seemed to be running in reverse.

Traditional Scottish culture had likewise retreated into self-caricature. Music-hall comedian Harry Lauder had come up from nothing. He had worked at a flax mill in Arbroath at age twelve, and then as a miner. He went on to become the most popular entertainer of the age.

But his stories and songs, such as "The Lass o' Killiecrankie" and "Roamin' in the Gloamin'," created a Scottish persona of the "ower thrifty wee mannie" with a thick brogue, battered bonnet and kilt and beard, which dominated the outside world's view of the typical Scot for nearly half a century. Sentimental ballads such as "The Blue Bells of Scotland" and "Loch Lomond" conveyed the impression that Scotland was a land of bekilted lads and lassies who wandered wistfully o'er the glen and sighed for the return of Bonnie Prince Charlie. Charlie himself, or at least his smooth, youthful visage, graced tins of Walker's Butter Buscuits. Robert the Bruce helped to sell tartans and scarves.

The commercialization of traditional Highland culture played a crucial role in the formation of the Scotch whisky industry, as well. For centuries Scottish families had distilled their own spirits or *uisge beatha,* "water of life." In the eighteenth century it had been the drink of choice of the lower classes, as it continued to be, despite tax excises and temperance campaigns, in the nineteenth. Then Parliament in 1823 lifted the onerous taxes and made owning a distillery legally and financially possible. By 1870 Scottish distillers discovered there was a huge market for whisky south of the border. Two in particular, John Walker and Tommy Dewar, skillfully tapped into it.

John Dewar had worked in a wine shop in Perth before he started his own business, offering whisky in glass bottles instead of the traditional jars or wooden casks. His sons Jimmy and Tommy opened a branch in London in 1885, and exploited the associations between whisky and the romantic land of tartans and bagpipes in their advertising. The symbol of Dewar's was a Highland drum major with a bearskin bonnet and kilt: in fact, Highland costumes, bagpipes, and kilts became de rigueur for all Scotch whisky advertising for nearly a century. But their "Scotch," like that of their counterpart John Walker of Kilmarnock, was geared to English tastes. Blended whisky took the husky, peaty edge off the traditional Scottish malts. It made it smoother and more appealing to the southern palate. By the 1890s whisky-and-soda became the preferred drink of the English gentlemen. The Dewars became multimillionaires. Tommy Dewar entered the House of Lords—the first Whisky Lord to do so—and was the third man in Britain to own a motorcar. (The first was the Scottish tea magnate Thomas Lipton; the second was the Prince of Wales.)

The Scottish character did continue to be recognized and admired: its moral discipline, its integrity and honesty, its capacity for hard work and ambition for advancement. But it, too, found itself on the verge of a cultural distortion as the new century dawned. The Scottish Enlightenment had always dubbed man a "social animal," meaning that interaction with others was indispensable for his or her intellectual and moral development. Adam Smith had even insisted that the opinions of others acted as a kind of moral mirror, without whose reflection we never form a sense of right and wrong. But when carried to extremes, such a view bred in the middle-class Scot of the late Victorian and Edwardian era an acute need to conform to social norms. The emphasis on conformity blocked innovation and creativity in ways that could be stifling, even dangerous. James Barrie put it best with a bitter irony: "The grandest moral attribute of a Scot is that he'll do nothing which might damage his career."

As all of Europe mobilized for war in August 1914, believing its soldiers would be home "before the leaves fall," three of the most important soldiers in the British army were Scots: Field Marshal Lord Robertson, Sir Ian Hamilton of the General Staff, who had been Lord Kitchener's chief of staff, and General Douglas Haig, later Field Marshal Earl Haig. For more than a century, Scots had been the backbone of the British army. One out of every four officers had been of Scottish birth as early as the 1750s. But what had made them so useful, besides their physical courage and sense of honor, was their daredevil attitude, their willingness to defy the rules as well as the odds. One looked high and low for such qualities in these three men. Hamilton was largely responsible for the disastrous Gallipoli campaign in Turkey; Lord Haig presided over the ceaseless slaughter at the Somme, Ypres, and Passchendaele, which sent more than half a million Britons to their deaths. Robertson, despite his own misgivings, refused, out of professional courtesy, to stop him.

Intelligent and conscientious soldiers, Haig, Robertson, and Hamilton had mislaid the habit of independent judgment, the ability to think outside the box. Trained to concentrate on the means, they had lost sight of the ends. They were vivid examples of what Adam Smith and Adam Ferguson had warned might happen in an overspecialized modern society, where "the minds of men are contracted and rendered incapable of elevation"—but now at the top of society rather than the bottom. Thousands of English, Welsh, Canadian, Scottish, Irish, Australian, and Indian soldiers paid the price.

The end of World War I ushered in a period of acute hardship and unemployment for Scotland. World War II revised the picture somewhat, when Scottish factories turned out the Spitfires and Rolls-Royce Merlin engines that won the Battle of Britain. In the 1950s, the great shipyards along Clydeside continued to produce nearly 15 percent of the world's shipping. Coal, iron, steel, and engineering were as essential to Scotland's economy as ever, although they were almost all nationalized. The average workingman's income in 1958 was almost three times what it had been in 1938.

But Scotland's relish for its ties to a fading empire had begun to sour. As the 1960s dawned, it had no clear sense of direction or inspiration. Scottish doctors were giving way to Indians and Asians as the hardworking footsoldiers of the National Health Service. Whisky, golf, football, and auto racing seemed to sum up its cultural achievements. Then Scotland turned up an unlikely cultural hero: James Bond.

Few people realize that Ian Fleming's fictional spy was supposed to be a Scot (he even goes to school in Edinburgh), even though his best-known screen interpreter, Sean Connery, is probably the best-known Scot in the world. Fleming himself was of Scottish descent; he certainly modeled Bond after a Scot, Commander Fitzroy Maclean, a leading commando during World War II.

Bond remains in many ways an allegory of how the relations between the Scottish spirit and the contemporary world had evolved in the postwar world. He is born half Scot and half French Swiss. "The one element explains both his puritanical streak," writes critic Kingsley Amis, "and the granite gift of endurance, while the other makes him fluent in French and German, at home on skis, and a wine lover and gourmet." Bond is a soldier and servant of empire, like so many generations of Scots, in this case "in Her Majesty's secret service." He lives in London and identifies himself with gentlemanly English values: he is deeply patriotic while others see him as impeccably and irremediably British.

But Bond is also stuck in a cultural vacuum. He is made rootless by his profession, and wanders through a world debased and hardened by the Cold War. He sees the world in purely utilitarian terms. In the novels, every detail of scene, food, weaponry, and personal appearance is described with meticulous accuracy. Bond even assesses the physiognomy of his opponents with the cool detachment of his predecessor Sherlock Holmes (who was modeled on one of Conan Doyle's professors at Edinburgh medical school, the brilliant diagnostician Joseph Bell), as in this passage from *Moonraker*:

> [Hugo] Drax had grown a bushy reddish moustache that covered half his face, and allowed the whiskers to grow down to the level of the lobes of his ears. He also had patches of hair on his cheek-bones. The heavy moustache served another purpose. It helped to hide a naturally prognathous upper jaw and a marked protrusion of the upper row of teeth. Bond reflected that this was probably due to sucking his thumb as a child and it had resulted in an ugly splaying, or diastema, of what Bond had heard his dentist call "the centrals."

Bond arrives at decisions quickly; we never see him hesitate or agonize over a choice of action. He always manages to keep his cool—even in the most horrific and violent circumstances. He is the embodiment of the Scottish commonsense mind: sure of his judgments, confident of his skills, certain that even if he makes a mistake, he did the best that he could with the available information. Above all, Bond always knows what he wants. His goals are never fuzzy or ambiguous. He views everything, even pleasurable activities such as seducing a woman, beating Drax at cards or Goldfinger at golf, as available means to necessary ends: victory over the Russians, the Chinese, or SPECTRE and SMERSH.

Yet those ends are no longer his own. Despite his courage and physical prowess, he is, to put it bluntly, a hireling. Bond is a professional killer employed by a British spy establishment that was in reality heavily populated by Scots (including the head of the Secret Service, "C," or Stewart Graham Menzies, on whom Bond's own boss, "M," is based). Personal happiness plays no part in the shrunken Bond worldview: in his one attempt at it, his bride, Tracy di Vincenzo, is murdered by his enemies within hours of their wedding. He has become like Adam Ferguson's vision of commercial society's soldier or bureaucrat, "made, like the parts of an engine, to concur to a purpose, without any concert of their own," like ants in an anthill.

James Bond reveals a modernizing spirit that has finally run its course. The Sean Connery films make us think of James Bond as a character from the 1960s, or even '70s. It is a shock to realize that the first novel, *Casino Royale,* appeared in 1953, when Winston Churchill was still prime minister and three years after an incident that suggested that an entirely new spirit was beginning to take root in Scotland.

II

This book began with college students. It now ends with them.

On Christmas Eve of 1950, three Scottish collegians—Glasgow law student Ian Hamilton, Gavin Vernon, and Alan Stuart—broke into Westminster Abbey near Poets' Corner, not far from the tomb of James McPherson. Passing quietly through the cold, darkened church, they made their way to the Coronation Chair, which for more than six hundred years rested on the Stone of Scone, the ancient symbol of Scottish monarchy. With a grunt and a shove, the young men wrestled the 336-pound chunk of sandstone out of the church and into the trunk of their car driven by a fourth student: teacher trainee Kay Matheson. They then headed north for the border and home.

If the police and press believed at first that the theft was just a college prank, they soon realized their mistake. The four students were Scottish nationalists, and with one stroke they had (symbolically at least) reversed the direction of British history. A new force had entered on the postwar Scottish scene, inspired in part by the success of Irish nationalism and its militant arm, the IRA. It would provide a powerful rallying point for resentment about what had happened to Scotland over the previous century. It also offered a new challenge to the ideals of the Scottish Enlightenment and the kind of future it had envisioned.

The story of the Stone of Scone, or Stone of Destiny—*Lia Fail* in Gaelic—is in large part the history of Great Britain itself. Steeped in history and legend, it stood for four hundred years as the symbol of the ancient Scottish monarchy. Tradition has it that it was originally the stone on which the Bible's Jacob laid his head when he dreamed his vision of a ladder to heaven. It then made its miraculous way from Egypt to Ireland, where Saint Patrick supposedly blessed it for Irish chieftains to use for their coronations. According to legend, one chunk of it became the Blarney Stone. In 503, it seems, St. Columba brought another to the monastery at Iona, where it may or may not have been used for crowning local kings. In 843, Vikings swept over Iona. Kenneth McAlpin brought the chunk to the mainland, and eventually to Scone Castle, where he was crowned and where every Scottish king would be crowned until 1292.

England's King Edward I robbed it from its resting place in 1296, as the triumphant spoils from his victory over the Scots. Since 1306 every English king and queen has been crowned while sitting above the stone; in the words of Dean Stanley, in his *Memorials of Westminster Abbey,* it is the "one primeval monument that binds together the whole Empire . . . a link to the traditions of Tara and Iona." And, the tradition says, "empire abides where the stone stays."

Legends, myths, miracles, and symbols: a far cry from the practical and precise hardheaded world Scotland and the Scots had inhabited since the Act of Union. These are, however, the farther but familiar shores of nationalism, which had convulsed the rest of Europe in the previous century, and which inevitably found its way to Scotland as well.

Scottish nationalism found its roots in a classic British political issue: Home Rule. Inspired by the example of Canada's successful move to Dominion status, Prime Minister William Ewart Gladstone decided it was time to give the non-English peoples who actually lived in the British Isles more say over their own destiny. He did not want to break up the United Kingdom any more than the first members of the Scottish Home Rule Association did; the goal was a classic Scottish ideal, of making government more responsive to those who lived under it. Gladstone himself was a son of the Scottish diaspora. His father had moved to Liverpool from Scotland and become a successful businessman and member of Parliament. William Gladstone was, typically for the age, educated at Eton and Oxford rather than Edinburgh. All the same, he retained the Lowland Scot's faith in free-market capitalism, in a strong evangelical religion, in a high moral tone in public as well as private matters, in the power of education, and in improving the lot and dignity of the common man, whether in Britain or abroad.

"By 1885," writes historian Keith Webb, "Gladstone was fully converted to Home Rule for both Ireland and Scotland." Ireland was the more urgent case: unfortunately, Gladstone's hopes for a peaceful transition to self-government for Ireland ran aground on the rocks of religious and ethnic conflict, and even split the Liberal Party itself. Scottish Home Rule became a back-burner issue, with the failure of Ireland as a warning to anyone trying to undo Westminster's control over other parts of the United Kingdom.

Home Rule was originally a Liberal Party issue, just as the Liberal Party was Scotland's principal political party. As the Liberals withered and died after World War I, so did Scotland's hopes that it might reverse the trend of two centuries and bring some control over its own affairs away from London and back to Edinburgh. Tories were inalterably opposed to any devolution, so Home Rulers turned to the Labour Party—after all, many of its key founders, such as Keir Hardie, were also Scotsmen. But Labour had come to see Scotland's working class as an essential part of their own political base: they saw Scottish self-rule as political suicide. So in 1928 disgruntled Scots broke from Labour and formed their own Scottish Nationalist Party, or SNP.

The amazing story of the SNP's rise and eventual triumph in the face of tremendous official hostility and bitter factional infighting closely follows the decline of traditional British politics. The SNP came to fill the void created by the demise of the Liberals and classical liberalism: as the other political parties made class struggle and whether to extend or demolish the welfare state their principal issues, Scottish voters began to turn to a party that, if nothing else, offered a way out of Scotland's malaise. Whether it was devolution, or autonomy, or outright independence (the SNP leadership often quarreled bitterly over which they wanted), it was at least something different—and something that struck a chord that most Scots deeply felt but had been afraid to acknowledge: a sense of national pride.

The struggle to gain respectability was long and arduous. Hard times and the Great Depression raised the SNP's appeal, particularly in working-class Glasgow and Edinburgh, while recovery undermined it. By 1939 the SNP was nearly bankrupt. Then, in 1942 John MacCormick broke from the party and set up his own Scottish Union, and then the Scottish Convention. His goal was a separate sovereign party for Scotland, although still within the framework of a union. But MacCormick's people were also inspired by a cultural Anglophobia: already in the 1930s there were complaints about the "Englishing of Scotland." Folklorist Ronald MacDonald Douglas went even further and tried to organize an IRA-style military insurrection in 1935 (it ended up a farce and Douglas was exiled to the Irish Free State). In 1949, just a year before Hamilton and his fellow students struck, MacCormick published his Covenant on Scottish self-determination, which looked to the seventeenth-century Presbyterian Covenanters as its inspiration.

Scottish history was starting to come full circle. MacCormick then filed a lawsuit complaining that Britain's new queen could not call herself Elizabeth II since Scotland had never had a queen named Elizabeth—under the literal terms of the Act of Union of 1707, MacCormick insisted, she should be Queen Elizabeth I of Britain (the case was eventually thrown out). It was news of the theft of the *Lia Fail,* however, that moved the Scottish nationalist movement from the shadows to center stage. It ignited a major sensation in Scotland as the public cheered the thieves on. After an exhaustive and slightly hysterical four-month hunt, the authorities finally found the stone at Arbroath Abbey. It came back to Westminster in time for Elizabeth II's coronation (or was it Elizabeth I?), although the Crown declined to prosecute

Hamilton and his colleagues—in part, it was rumored, because the English could not offer any proof of ownership in the first place.

Why Hamilton chose Arbroath as the stone's final resting place was itself significant. It was there in 1320 that a gathering of Scottish bishops and barons declared defiance of the English king and their commitment to the independence of Scotland after the death of Robert the Bruce. The declaration is the Scottish equivalent of the Magna Carta and reads in part:

> for as long as a hundred [of us] remain alive we are minded never
> a whit to bow beneath the yoke of English dominion. It is not for
> glory, riches or honours that we fight: it is for liberty alone, the
> liberty which no good man relinquishes but with his life.

The Declaration of Arbroath, like the *Lia Fail* itself, was now a symbol of a Scotland tired of subordinating its identity to an abstract political ideal, that of Great Britain. Scots, Hamilton and other nationalists were saying, will be North Britons no longer.

In any case, the spell had been broken. Although the SNP continued to languish as a political party in the postwar boom of the 1950s, when Prime Minister Harold Macmillan (scion of the great Scottish publishing firm) announced to the British public that, "you have never had it so good," few Scots believed it. The next two decades confirmed their worst fears. The great Clydeside shipyards began to close, as did the Lanarkshire coal pits and the blast furnaces. Between 1979 and 1981, Scotland lost close to 11 percent of its industrial output and 20 percent of all its jobs. Even the discovery of oil off Scotland's North Sea coast in 1975 only served to push the British pound higher and ruin Scotland's exports. Textile production in the Border country fell by 65 percent. Active Scottish coal pits declined from fifteen to just two. "Today ours is a fearful, anxious nail-biting nation," wrote SNP activist Jim Sillars in 1985.

In the midst of national crisis and decline, the SNP stepped into the breach. Contrary to myth, it was not the promise of nationalizing North

Sea oil that propelled the SNP into prominence. It emerged as a mass political party in the late 1960s and early 1970s—long before engineers had any idea of the vast oil reserves located just off the continental shelf from Aberdeen. Instead, it was the failure of either British Labour or Tory conservatism to offer a solution to Scotland's sense of decline that made the SNP a political powerhouse. "There is no alternative," Margaret Thatcher would say as she announced the closing of yet another government-run shipbuilding yard or coalfield; yet to millions of Scottish voters there seemed an alternative: Scottish independence and the promise of devolution.

In 1996 a beleaguered government in London tried to appease this sentiment by a symbolic gesture—symbols having become, in this post-modern age, suddenly very powerful. On November 15, two Army Landrovers and a transit van carried the Stone of Scone across the bridge at Coldstream, from England to Scotland and eventually Edinburgh, to great fanfare and the sound of bagpipes and politicians' speeches. England had renounced its claim to the *Lia Fail*. Ian Hamilton, the stone's original thief, had defied authority and tradition as Thomas Aikenhead had. Unlike Aikenhead, however, he had won. Yet now, at age seventy-three and rector of Aberdeen University, Hamilton refused to attend the installation ceremony at Holyrood Palace. His getaway driver, Kay Matheson, did, as did Gavin Vernon, who flew in from Canada. But Hamilton denounced the ceremony as a "charade" and warned "Betty Windsor" not to show her face north of the border. He declared, in tones reminiscent of Knox and James Buchanan: "We are no longer ruled by sovereigns. Sovereignty now rests with the Scottish people."

Today, in 2001, Hamilton nearly has his wish. Scotland finds itself with a separate Scottish Parliament for the first time in nearly three hundred years, a new Parliament House, a growing computer technology industry, and a burgeoning service sector economy. Some are finding that the hopes they pinned on devolution may go unfulfilled: politicians in a Scottish Parliament turn out to be not much better than the ones in a British Parliament, while Scotland's larger economic problems, such as unemployment, remain unsolved. Just as becoming a modern industrial nation created as many problems for late nineteenth-century Scotland as it solved, so devolution turns out to be less won-derful than everyone had anticipated.

Of course, any of the figures of the Scottish Enlightenment could have told them that. No one can blame Scots for wanting to wrest some control over their lives back from London. In one sense, it fulfills the vision of modern liberty of the great Scots of the eighteenth century: that of increasing the independence and freedom of individuals in as many aspects of their lives as possible. Yet the great insight of the Scottish school was that politics offers only limited solutions to life's intractable problems; by surrendering her sovereignty the first time in 1707, Scotland gained more than she lost. She has to be careful that, in trying to reclaim that sovereignty, she does not reverse that process.

Scotland, like much of the modern West, has seen the results of too much modernization. It is easy to forget, therefore, the penalties that accrue from having too little. One of the disturbing trends in Scottish intellectual life in the past two decades has been an increasing hostility to the great legacy of the Scottish Enlightenment. Scholars decry the Act of Union as a betrayal of "true" Scottish culture, while others con-demn the founders of the Scottish school as sexists and elitists. "Whatever did not square with their philosophy was not knowledge and they loftily dismissed anything they could not understand," is the way William Ferguson loftily dismisses Hume and Robertson in *The Identity of the Scottish Nation*.

In 1975 Michael Hechter even published a book that suggested that Scotland shared a common identity with Ireland, India, and the Third World as the exploited victims of English colonialism and "underdevel-opment." Andrew Fletcher has emerged as the new hero of radical Scottish nationalism (forgetting, perhaps, his call for mandatory slavery as the solution for Scotland's ills), while the Declaration of Arbroath and William Wallace occupy center stage in a Scottish nationalist history that smacks more and more of acute Anglophobia. Some have even ven-tured onto the further fringes of pan-Celtic nationalism, calling for a Celtic League to draw Scotland into union not only with Ireland and Wales, but also Brittany, Cornwall, and the Isle of Man.

Like the legends surrounding the Stone of Scone, these are appeals to myths and historical fantasies. Scotland was never an exclusively Celtic nation: it included Anglo-Saxons, Normans, and Scandinavians from its first medieval beginnings. Likewise, the notion that its history as part of the British Empire is one of systematic abuse and exploitation is absurd: if anything, Scots have been *overrepresented* as part of its ruling establishment for more than two hundred years. The effort to turn Scots into Irishmen—trying to make them bitter and resentful about their links to Britain—does a disservice not only to historical truth, but to Scotland herself.

The great insight of the Scottish Enlightenment was to insist that human beings need to free themselves from myths and to see the world as it really is. This kind of intellectual liberation, they said, is required for living a free and active life. William Robertson, like Adam Smith and David Hume, cared deeply about human freedom and his homeland. Yet he does not even mention the Declaration of Arbroath in his *History of Scotland*—not because he was a brainwashed Anglophile, but because he saw it in historical context, as a well-worded defense of the old Scottish feudal regime by its oligarchic beneficiaries. Robertson and his generation of Scottish Whigs welcomed union because they were all too familiar with the Scotland that preceded it; their successors remained grateful for what union had accomplished. From Robertson and Reid to Dugald Stewart and Walter Scott, the Scottish mind understood that genuine human liberty was the by-product of a historical process that ground men like the Arbroath signers into dust—and would also have saved Thomas Aikenhead from the gallows.

That process was the making of the modern world—a process, for all its faults and failures, blind spots and injustices, in which Scotland and Scots have played a crucial part. As Scotland moves toward its new and uncertain future, it must not forget that achievement, any more than it should forget its earlier, premodern past.

As the first modern nation and culture, the Scots have by and large made the world a better place. They taught the world that true liberty requires a sense of personal obligation as well as individual rights. They showed how modern life can be spiritually as well as materially fulfilling. They showed how a respect for science and technology can combine with a love for the arts; how private affluence can enhance a sense of civic responsibility; how political and economic democracy can flourish side by side; and how a confidence in the future depends on a reverence for the past. The Scottish mind grasped how, in Hume's words, "liberty is the perfection of civil society," but "authority must be acknowledged essential to its very existence"; and how a strong faith in progress also requires a keen appreciation of its limitations.

Sources and Guide for
Further Reading

Scottish history suffers from a profusion of very general surveys, a multitude of specialized studies and monographs, and not enough good books in between. Historians who write for a general audience tend to be drawn to the more romantic episodes in Scottish history, such as the life of Mary Queen of Scots and the Jacobite uprising of 1745. Go to any public library and these are the books you find on the Scottish shelf, along with a life or two of Robert the Bruce or William Wallace, and perhaps an older volume on Scotland during the English Civil War (such as John Buchan's life of the Earl of Montrose, who raised the clans for Charles I in 1645).

In recent decades a trio of scholars have set out to correct this problem. Thomas Devine's *The Scottish Nation: A History, 1700–2000* (New York, 1999) is an invaluable guide to the economic and social history of modern Scotland. But Devine has also published useful books on topics as diverse as the Glasgow Tobacco Lords (in 1975), clan life in the Highlands after Culloden, and *The Transformation of Rural Scotland* (Edinburgh, 1994), and edited several more. Another model of scholarly industry is Professor Bruce Lenman at St. Andrews University, whose books such as *The Jacobite Risings in Britain, 1689–1746* (London, 1980), *The Jacobite Clans of the Great Glen* (London, 1984), and *Integration and Enlightenment: Scotland, 1746–1832* (London, 1981) offer an insightful and level-headed look at the evolution of eighteenth-century Scotland, on which I have relied for this book.

The late John Prebble spent a lifetime trying to uncover the forgotten tragic episodes of modern Scottish history and make them come alive for the modern reader. It is not going too far to say that his trilogy on the defeat of Highland Scotland—*Culloden* (London, 1961), *The Highland Clearances* (1963), and *Glencoe: The Story of the Massacre* (1966)—altered the face of Scottish historical writing and helped to fuel the flames of modern Scottish nationalism.

Prebble did nothing to disguise his populist anti-English bias in his triology or his other books, such as *The Darien Disaster* (London, 1968) and his last book, *The King's Jaunt* (London, 1999). The intelligent reader sets that bias aside when it gets to be too much, and simply enjoys the absorbing story and the wealth of vivid detail. Prebble also published a personal survey of Scottish history, *The Lion in the North* (New York, 1971). Every scholar working in the field owes Prebble, who was a journalist and not a professional historian, a debt of gratitude.

Three other general works, all out of print, also deserve mention. Wallace Notestein's very dated but still interesting *The Scot in History* (New Haven, 1947) touches some of my themes, but concentrates on the impact of the Scottish Reformation. Neil McCallum's *A Small Country: Scotland, 1700–1830* (Edinburgh, 1983) presents a series of vignettes and anecdotes relating to the rise of eighteenth-century Scotland, some of which found their way into this book. Iain Finlayson's *The Scots* (London, 1987) tried to summarize the "Scottish national character" in broad and vivid strokes, and sometimes succeeded, although his chapters on Scotland as part of modern Britain no longer have much relevance in the age of devolution.

PROLOGUE

Details of the Thomas Aikenhead case can be found in *A Complete Collection of State Trials and Proceedings,* edited in thirty-three volumes by T. B. Howell in London in 1812, of which volume 13 contains information relating to the trial, including affadavits from the witnesses, Aikenhead's petition to the Privy Council, and the letter from Lord Anstruther from which I drew the relevant quotations. The John Locke connection is found in volume 6 of *The Correspondence of John Locke,* E.S. de Beer, ed. (Oxford, 1981). The anecdote concerning Baron Polwarth in the family burial vault is from the second volume of Samuel Cowan's *The Lord Chancellors of England* (Edinburgh, 1911). The Edinburgh town council's resolutions are in *Extracts from the Records of the Burgh of Edinburgh—1689 to 1701,* H. Armet, ed. (Edinburgh, 1962). The full quotation from Henry Gray Graham on the famine of 1695 can be found in David Daiches's biography of Andrew Fletcher (see Chapter Two, below).

CHAPTER ONE: THE NEW JERUSALEM

Rosalind K. Marshall is supposed to publish a new biography of John Knox, which is badly needed. Until then the reader must turn to Jasper Ridley's *John*

Knox (New York, 1968) and Stanford Reid's 1974 biography of the same name. Roger Mason has also edited a brand-new edition of Knox's political writings for the Cambridge History of Political Thought series, which is available in paperback along with George Buchanan in the same series. For a discussion of their revolutionary endorsement of popular sovereignty, see Quentin Skinner's *The Foundations of Modern Political Thought, Volume 2: The Age of Reformation* (Cambridge, 1978).

A highly readable account of the Scottish uprising against King Charles is in C. V. Wedgewood's *The King's Peace, 1637–1641* (London, 1955; paperback edition 1969). A more scholarly one is David Stevenson's *The Scottish Revolution, 1637–1644: The Triumph of the Covenanters* (New York, 1973). The expert on the post-Reformation "parish state" in Scotland is Rosiland Murchison, especially her essay on the Poor Law in *People and Society in Scotland,* volume 1 (Edinburgh, 1988), edited by Murchison and Thomas Devine.

The place of literacy in post-Reformation Scotland has prompted a great deal of debate and revision recently. The standard view takes statistical form in Professor Lawrence Stone's classic article, "Literacy and Education in England, 1640–1900," published in *Past & Present* in 1969. The revisionist view is found in R. A. Huston's *Scottish Literacy and Scottish Identity 1600–1800* (Cambridge, 1985), which argues that the supposed Scottish bias toward literacy is a myth—an argument which for various reasons I find unconvincing. Another provocative thesis is found in Alexander Broadie's *The Tradition of Scottish Philosophy* (Savage, MD, 1990), which argues for a deep continuity of Scottish thought from the Middle Ages all the way to the Enlightenment. See also George Davie's *The Democratic Intellect: Scotland and Her Universities in the Nineteenth Century* (Edinburgh, 1961) for the lasting impact of the Scottish educational ideal. The evidence for the public library in Innerpeffay comes from Anand Chitnis's *The Scottish Enlightenment* (London, 1976).

G. Whittington and I. D. White, *An Historical Geography of Scotland* (London, 1983), give a valuable overview of the changes in the Scottish economy from the sixteenth century to the eve of union, as do the relevant chapters in Thomas Devine's *The Scottish Nation,* mentioned above. John Prebble's *The Darien Disaster* provides all the relevant material on William Paterson's ill-fated scheme, although a much older work, *The Darien Venture* (New York, 1926), still provides some interesting details—including the quotation from William Paterson on Panama as "the key of the universe."

CHAPTER TWO: A TRAP OF THEIR OWN MAKING

There are several books on the relations between England and Scotland before the Act of Union: the best is probably William Ferguson's *Scotland's Relations with England: A Survey to 1707* (Edinburgh, 1977). The best book on the debate over union is by Charles Dand, *The Mighty Affair* (Edinburgh, 1972), which can be supplemented by information on the financial details in John Shaw's *The Political History of 18th Century Scotland* (London, 1999) and P.W.J. Riley's *The Union of England and Scotland: A Study in Anglo-Scottish Politics of the Eighteenth Century* (Manchester, 1979). The description of the opening ceremonies for the opening of the Scottish Parliament is from Frederick Watkeys's *Old Edinburgh,* volume 1 (Boston, 1907).

David Daiches wrote a brilliant and vivid introduction for his *Andrew Fletcher of Saltoun: Selected Political Writings* (Edinburgh, 1979), which is not only a condensed biography of Fletcher but a fine summary of Scottish political history between the Glorious Revolution of 1688 to the Act of Union in 1707. However, Daiches must now be supplemented with Paul H. Scott's full-length biography, *Andrew Fletcher and the Treaty of Union* (Edinburgh, 1992) and John Robertson's edition of *Andrew Fletcher: Political Works* (Cambridge, 1997).

I made two slight modifications in the historical sequence in this chapter. Besides including the rituals of "the riding of Parliament," which took place in 1703, my quotations for Fletcher's arguments against the economic consequences of Union actually come from Fletcher's *An Account of a Conversation Concerning a Right Regulation of Government,* published in 1704.

CHAPTER THREE: THE PROPER STUDY OF MANKIND I

Probably no figure in the history of the Enlightenment is more discussed *in passing* than Francis Hutcheson. Everyone acknowledges his enormous influence on both sides of the Atlantic, and on both sides of the English Channel; everyone admits his role as the founding father of the Scottish Enlightenment. But precisely because Hutcheson is such a useful foil for scholars who really want to talk about two even greater figures, Adam Smith and David Hume, and because his works now make (to be honest) tedious reading, the list of books dedicated to Hutcheson, and Hutcheson alone, is woefully short. We have to make due with W. R. Scott's venerable biography, which first appeared more than one hundred years ago, and some excellent scholarly articles published in learned books and journals. The one that most influenced my approach to Hutcheson is by James Moore, "The Two Systems of Francis Hutcheson," in *Studies in the Philosophy of the Scottish Enlightenment,* M. A. Stewart, ed. (Oxford,

1990). Chapters on Hutcheson by Donald Winch and Ian Ross in their books on Adam Smith are particularly useful as well (see Chapter Nine, below).

Hutcheson's milieu in Dublin can be reconstructed from Scott, *Francis Hutcheson,* and M.A. Stewart's illuminating article, "John Smith and the Molesworth Circle," which appeared in 1987 in *Eighteenth Century Ireland.* Lord Islay's role in the hiring of Hutcheson at Glasgow, and in Scottish academic politics generally, is covered in Roger Emerson's "Politics and the Glasgow Professors, 1690–1800," in *The Glasgow Enlightenment,* Andrew Hook and Richard Sher, eds. (East Linton, 1995).

Hutcheson's writings suffer from the same neglect as the story of his life. Bernhard Fabian put together a facsimile reprint of the 1755 edition of Francis Hutcheson's *Collected Works,* published in Hildesheim, Germany, in 1969. Excerpts of his writings are available in an inexpensive Everyman Classics paperback edition, and in Alexander Broadie's selections of various authors in *The Scottish Enlightenment* (Edinburgh, 1999). *A System of Moral Philosophy* and *An Inquiry into the Original of our Ideas of Beauty and Virtue,* from which I quote extensively in this chapter, both exist in modern editions but are out of print. On the other hand, one of Hutcheson's earliest and shortest treatises, his *Remarks on* [Bernard Mandeville's] *"Fable of the Bees,"* which denounced Mandeville's idea that private vices yield public benefits, does circulate in numerous versions, and can even be found on the Internet—again, since it serves as a foil for the economic theories of Adam Smith.

CHAPTER FOUR: THE PROPER STUDY OF MANKIND II

From a biographical point of view, Lord Kames fares much better. Two modern biographies exist, William Lehmann's *Henry Home, Lord Kames and the Scottish Enlightenment* (The Hague, 1971) and Ian Ross's *Lord Kames and the Scotland of His Day* (Oxford, 1972), which is the better of the two. Even the 1814 biography by Alexander Fraser Tytler of Woodhouselee bears rereading, especially for its discussion of his fellow judges on the Court of Session. There is also invaluable information in Ernest Mossner's *The Life of David Hume* (see Chapter Eight, below).

Kames's writings, unfortunately, have fared even worse than Hutcheson's. A modern edition of *Essays on the Principles of Morality and Natural Religion* appeared some years ago. Otherwise, if you want to read *Historical Law Tracts* or *Sketches on the History of Man,* you will need to visit a large university library.

The main theme of these chapters is the origins of the Scottish Enlightenment. The old classic on the subject is Gladys Bryson's *Man and*

Society: The Scottish Enquiry of the Eighteenth Century (Princeton, 1945) but the illustrated volume edited by David Daiches, Peter Jones, and Jean Jones, *Hotbed of Genius: The Scottish Enlightenment, 1730–1790* (Edinburgh, 1986), might be a better place to begin, while Anand Chitnis's *The Scottish Enlightenment* (mentioned above, Chapter One) still offers the best account of the social background to this amazing episode in the history of European culture. The now-famous collection of essays in *Wealth and Virtue: The Shaping of Political Economy in the Scottish Enlightenment,* I. Hont and M. Ignatieff, eds. (Cambridge, 1983), have shaped my own approach: David Lieberman's essay in that collection, "The Legal Needs of a Commercial Society: The Jurisprudence of Lord Kames," was important to this chapter, as well. Robert Wokler, "Apes and Races in the Scottish Enlightenment: Monboddo and Kames on the Nature of Man," in Peter Jones's edited volume, *Philosophy and Science in the Scottish Enlightenment* (Edinburgh, 1988), covers Kames's views on race and history. The Joseph Knight case deserves more attention than it gets: my description is from Ross's biography of Kames.

CHAPTER FIVE: A LAND DIVIDED

Neil Macallum's *A Small Country* offers interesting details on Edinburgh in the early eighteenth century, as does A. J. Youngson's *The Making of Classical Edinburgh* (Edinburgh, 1966). *The Works of Adam Petrie, The Scottish Chesterfield* (Edinburgh, 1877) offers up the rich material of Petrie's guides to civilized comportment.

The standard work on the Scottish-English "culture wars" of the eighteenth century is David Daiches's *The Paradox of Scottish Culture* (Oxford, 1964). The journals and correspondence of James Boswell, however, provide plenty of material for analyzing this problem; the volumes edited by Frederick Pottle and William Wimsatt, especially *Boswell's London Journal, 1762–1763* (New York, 1950), *Boswell For the Defence, 1769–1774* (New York, 1959), and *James Boswell: The Earlier Years, 1740–1769* (New York, 1966), are very useful—as well as fun reading. Boswell's fantasy of upbraiding Rousseau in broad Scots comes out of *The Earlier Years.* A fascinating article on Scots, "A Corrupt Dialect of English?" by Brian Osborne, appeared in *Highlander* magazine in May/June 1998. The quotation from Robertson that starts this discussion is from the second volume of the 1811 edition of his *History of Scotland.*

My interpretation of Highland society and culture has been decisively shaped by two works by Bruce Lenman, *The Jacobite Clans of the Great Glen, 1650–1784* (London, 1984) and *The Jacobite Risings in Britain,* supplemented by

Thomas Devine's *Clanship to Crofter's War: The Social Transformation of the Scottish Highlands* (Manchester, 1994), R. A. Dodgson, "The Nature of Scottish Clans," in R.A. Huston and I. D. White's *Scottish Society, 1500–1800* (Cambridge, 1989), and I. F. Grant and Hugh Cheape's *Periods in Highland History* (London, 1987). The account of Coll MacDonnell of Barrisdale is from Frank McLynn's *The Jacobites* (London, 1985), as is the quotation from Cassius Dio that opens the chapter. The story of Big Archie MacPhail comes out of John Prebble's *Glencoe,* which like its companion volume, *Culloden,* gives an especially vivid picture of Highland life.

Prebble also discusses Duncan Forbes of Culloden and his quizzical view of his Highland neighbors; so does Robert Clyde in *From Rebel to Hero: The Image of the Highlander 1745–1830* (East Lothian, 1995), and both can be supplemented with George Menary's vintage biography, *The Life and Letters of Duncan Forbes of Culloden* (London, 1936).

CHAPTER SIX: LAST STAND

I found the Jacobite song that opens the chapter in Robert Chambers's *History of the Rebellion of 1745–6* (1840; Edinburgh, 1869). The new scholarship that clarifies the importance of Jacobitism, both in England and in Scotland, is too extensive, and probably too scholarly, to cite at length for the general reader. But any works by Evelyn Cruickshank (such as *Political Untouchables: The Tories and the '45*) and Paul Monod's *Jacobitism and the English People, 1688–1788* (Cambridge, 1989) will give the reader some idea of how historians are coming to appreciate the crucial role of Jacobitism as a political ideology in the Age of Reason.

Oddly enough, no such scholarly work exists on Jacobite ideology and sentiment in Scotland, although there are literally shelves of books on the Jacobite risings in Scotland, both in 1715 and in 1745. The usual starting place for learning about the Forty-five is a biography of Bonnie Prince Charles. Almost every writer of British history for a popular audience eventually tries his or her hand at recounting the prince's story. Everyone has his candidate for the best version: David Daiches's *Charles Edward Stuart: The Life and Times of Bonnie Prince Charlie* (London, 1973) seems to me to have the right balance between readability and scholarly accuracy. I have not hesitated to use it in shaping this chapter, although I also relied on Frank McLynn's more detailed *Charles Edward Stuart* (London, 1988) and Chambers's *History of the Rebellion* and his *Jacobite Memoirs of the Rebellion of 1745,* published in Edinburgh in 1834.

The stories about the Edinburgh volunteers come from John Home's *The*

History of the Rebellion in the Year 1745 (London, 1802) and Alexander Carlyle's *Anecdotes and Characters of Our Times,* which is available in various editions. For the battle of Culloden itself, John Prebble's *Culloden* cannot be surpassed, just as Prebble offers the definitive account of the battle's bloody aftermath. However, I have also relied on Katherine Tomasson and Francis Buist's *Battles of the '45* (London, 1962) for its lucid discussion of the military aspects of the campaign as a whole.

Eric Linklater's *The Prince in the Heather* (London, 1965) is a vivid account of Prince Charles's escape and time in hiding in the remotest corners of Scotland, although there is a more recent version in Hugh Douglas and Michael J. Stead's *The Flight of Bonnie Prince Charlie* (Edinburgh, 2000). The final remarks by Samuel Johnson come out of *A Journey to the Western Islands of Scotland,* which exists in several editions, although I chose to use the Yale University Press version, edited by Mary Lascelles and published in 1971.

CHAPTER SEVEN: PROFITABLE VENTURES

The invaluable book on the Glasgow tobacco trade and its participants is Thomas Devine, *The Tobacco Lords* (1975; Edinburgh, 1990), and what it sometimes lacks in discussion of personalities I more than made up for by turning to George Stewart's *Curiosities of Glasgow Citizenship, as Exhibited Chiefly in the Business Career of Its Old Commercial Aristocracy* (Glasgow, 1881), C. A. Oakley's *Our Illustrious Forbears* (Glasgow, 1980), and Margaret Lindsay's *Portrait of Glasgow* (London, 1972). Adam Smith's relations with commercial Glasgow are covered in Ian Ross's biography (see Chapter Three, above), as are his relations with Robert Foulis. For the Foulis brothers themselves, I relied on David Murray's *Robert and Andrew Foulis and the Glasgow Press* (Glasgow, 1913), and *Some Letters of Robert Foulis* (Glasgow, 1917), and Richard Sher's "Commerce, Religion, and the Enlightenment in Eighteenth Century Glasgow," in *Glasgow, Volume I: Beginnings to 1830,* edited by T. M. Devine and Gordon Jackson (Manchester, 1995).

The book I found most helpful for understanding the physical evolution of Glasgow was Andrew Gibb's *Glasgow: The Making of the City* (London, 1983). For Edinburgh, A. J. Youngson's classic study, *The Making of Classical Edinburgh* (Edinburgh, 1966), is still indispensable; Charles MacKean's *Edinburgh: An Illustrated Architectural Guide* (Edinburgh, 1992) is a handy street-by-street, almost house-by-house guide to the evolution of this fascinating city. On James Craig, see Kitty Croft and Andrew Fraser's *James Craig, 1744–1795* (Edinburgh, 1995).

The Adam family, father and sons, still have not received the kind of systematic scholarly attention they deserve. It is possible to find editions of *Works in Architecture,* whose preface gives the best idea of their political and social agenda, as well as their aesthetic creed. Otherwise, the scholar still relies on a wonderful little book by John Fleming, *Robert Adam and His Circle in Edinburgh and Rome* (Cambridge, MA, 1962), which is a model of what professional historical scholarship should be: careful, detailed, but also gracefully written. Also useful for this chapter were Joseph and Anne Rykwert's *Robert and James Adam: The Men and the Style* (London, 1985), Steve Parissien's *Adam Style* (London, 1992), and Sterling Boyd's *The Adam Style in America, 1770–1820* (New York, 1985). Those curious about Charles Cameron can check Dimitri Shvidkovsky's *The Empress and the Architect* (New Haven, 1996).

CHAPTER EIGHT: A SELECT SOCIETY— ADAM SMITH AND HIS FRIENDS

The bibliography on Adam Smith is, of course, vast—especially since those who write about him come at their subject from three, or even four, different directions. Historians conjure up an Adam Smith who is slightly different from the one philosophers discuss, while economists manage to come up with yet another version, and sociologists still another—compare, for example, the Adam Smith described in Donald Winch's *Adam Smith's Politics* (Cambridge, 1978) with the one in Robert Heilbronner's *The Worldly Philosophers* (1953; seventh edition, 1999). However, the best place to start for understanding Adam Smith in his own time and place might be in a book in which he appears only as a minor character: Richard Sher's *Church and University in the Scottish Enlightenment: The Moderate Literati of Edinburgh* (Princeton, 1985). It is the indispensable guide to the intellectual milieu of Edinburgh in the second half of the eighteenth century, and offers the proper context for understanding the reception and impact of Smith's ideas. The two best introductions to Smith himself are Donald Winch's book mentioned above, and Jerry Z. Muller's *Adam Smith in His Time—And Ours* (New York, 1993).

Ian Ross's biography of Smith (see Chapter Three, above), was of course crucial for writing this chapter, as was Dugald Stewart's *Biographical Memoir of Adam Smith,* which first appeared in 1793 but which was reprinted from the collected works of Dugald Stewart in 1966. Adam Smith's two major works, *An Inquiry Into the Nature and Causes of the Wealth of Nations* and *The Theory of Moral Sentiments,* are generally available, while even his lectures on jurisprudence and *Lectures on Rhetoric and Belles Lettres,* both of which are based on notes by former students, can be found in modern editions. The edition of *Wealth of Nations* I found most useful for this chapter is the University of Chicago Press edition, edited by Edwin Canaan.

William Robertson's celebrity as historian and author is all but forgotten now: but Stewart Brown's edited volume, *William Robertson and the Expansion of Empire* (London, 1997), helps to set the record straight, especially Richard Sher's brilliant little article, "'Charles V' and the Book Trade."

The amount of scholarship on David Hume is almost as staggering as that on Adam Smith—although in this case it is the philosophers who enjoy the main right of way (an excellent overall guide is David Norton's *The Cambridge Companion to Hume,* which became available in paperback in 1993). A key advantage of all this attention is that, as in Smith's case, almost all of Hume's works are in print in one form or another, even his *Essays Moral, Political, and Literary,* of which the best edition is the one edited by Eugene Miller for the Liberty Press in 1985. Even Hume's *History of England* can be found in abridged form for the general reader—although no one should take on Hume as historian without first reading Duncan Forbes's *Hume's Philosophical Politics* (Cambridge, 1975) and the relevant section on Hume in J.G.A. Pocock's *The Machiavellian Moment* (Princeton, 1975), which has decisively shaped my approach to Adam Smith, as well.

My interpretation of Hume is bound to strike some as controversial; not surprising, since Hume is always controversial, even two hundred years later. A different approach to mine, and in some ways a compelling one, can be found in Donald Livingston's *Hume's Philosophy of Common Life* (Chicago, 1981). In any case, the basis for any serious treatment of Hume as a historical figure is Ernest Mossner's unsurpassed biography, *The Life of David Hume* (Oxford, 1954), which is now available in paperback, and his collection of essays on Hume, *The Forgotten Hume,* first published in 1943. A biographical shortcut is Nicholas Phillipson's stimulating and intelligent *Hume,* published by Cambridge University Press in 1989 but now unfortunately out of print. The general reader will enjoy perusing Hume's short autobiography, which is reprinted in the Liberty Fund edition of the *Essays,* and even *The Letters of David Hume,* published in Oxford in 1932.

Thanks to his connections to Hume and Smith, who were also his harshest critics, Adam Ferguson is the recipient of a tidy little scholarly industry. There are two modern editions of his *Essay on the History of Civil Society;* there is a trail of excellent critical studies, of which the best might be Duncan Forbes's *Adam Ferguson and the Idea of Community* (Paisley, 1979); and even a fine study of

Ferguson's influence on European thought, in Fania Oz-Salzberger's *Translating the Enlightenment: Scottish Civic Dicourse in Eighteenth Century Germany* (Oxford, 1995), which clearly shows Ferguson's influence on German thinkers such as Fichte and Hegel—and by extension, on Karl Marx. Edward Gibbon's relations with the Scottish school are detailed in J.G.A. Pocock's magisterial study, *Barbarism and Religion: The Enlightenments of Edward Gibbon, 1737–1764* (Cambridge, 2000). The quotation about Gibbon's debt to Hume comes from *The Autobiography of Edward Gibbon,* edited by John Murray (London, 1896).

CHAPTER NINE: "THAT GREAT DESIGN"— SCOTS IN AMERICA

I must mention two invaluable guides to the Scottish diaspora at the outset. Duncan Bruce's *Mark of the Scots* (Seacaucus, 1996) is a comprehensive reference guide not only for tracing the Scottish impact on American life, but its effect around the world. Mr. Bruce's more genealogical approach is different from mine, and we disagree on certain details—such as whether the Scots actually discovered America before Columbus! But my work was made much easier by being able to turn to his comprehensive catalog of famous Scots in history, which he supplemented with *The Scottish One Hundred: Portraits of History's Most Influential Scots* (New York, 2000). There is an older prototype of Bruce's project, *Scotland's Mark on America* by George Fraser Black (New York, 1921), which is still useful.

The standard guide to the Ulster Scot influence in America is James Leyburn's *The Scotch-Irish: A Social History* (Chapel Hill, 1969). It is a dated work in many respects; Leyburn also refused to see the Scotch-Irish as Scots. It is a view which, as I hope the chapter makes clear, I reject. In fact, both groups had a great deal in common with settlers from the English Border region, a point David Hackett Fisher makes in his *Albion's Seed: Four British Folkways in America* (Oxford, 1989), a principal source for the first half of this chapter, especially my discussion of words and things, along with Layburn and Grady McWhiney's *Cracker Culture: Celtic Ways in the Old South* (Tuscaloosa, 1988).

Otherwise, two fine books cover the relationship between Scots and Americans in the eighteenth century: W. R. Brock's *Scotus Americanus* (Edinburgh, 1982) and Andrew Hook's *Scotland and America: A Study of Cultural Relations* (Glasgow, 1975). My source on the Scottish impact on the Great Awakening is Marilyn Westerkamp, *Triumph of the Laity: Scots-Irish Piety and the Great Awakening, 1625–1760* (Oxford, 1988). For Benjamin Rush, I looked to

Donald D'Elia, *Benjamin Rush: Philosopher of the American Revolution* (Philadelphia, 1979); the quotation from President Samuel Davies comes from John Kloos's *A Sense of Diety: The Republican Spirituality of Doctor Benjamin Rush* (Brooklyn, 1991).

Most Americans are totally unaware of John Witherspoon's role in the making of their revolution and the Declaration of Independence. Even scholars rarely include him among the charmed company of "Founding Fathers," perhaps because of his anomalous status as a clergyman. Nevertheless, an academic subculture of Witherspoon studies continues to thrive. Thomas Miller edited *The Selected Writings of John Witherspoon* (Carbondale, 1990), including the central text of *The Dominion of Providence;* L. Gordon Tait recently published a study of Witherspoon's thought, *The Piety of John Witherspoon: Pew, Pulpit, and Public Forum* (Geneva Press, 2000); Witherspoon plays a major role in several articles that appear in Richard Sher and Jeffrey Smitten, *Scotland and America in the Age of Enlightenment* (Edinburgh, 1990). However, the only detailed biography remains Varnum Collins's *President Witherspoon: A Biography,* two volumes (Princeton, 1925). The story of Witherspoon's recruitment to preside at Princeton is found in Lyman Butterfield's *John Witherspoon Comes to America* (Princeton, 1953).

Tracking the Scottish Enlightenment's impact on the Founding Fathers follows a more familiar path. Even general readers can enjoy Douglass Adair's brilliant and stimulating article "'That Politics May Be Reduced to a Science': David Hume, James Madison, and the Tenth Federalist," which is republished in *Essays by Douglass Adair,* edited by Trevor Colborn (New York, 1974). In it Adair states my central point definitively: "The young men who rode off to war in 1776 had been trained in the texts of Scottish social science." Garry Wills made the same point somewhat differently in his *Inventing America: Jefferson's Declaration of Independence* (New York, 1978). Wills was justly criticized for casting his net too wide in his search for Scottish influences, and for trying to make all the Scottish Enlightenment's disparate elements fit into a single communitarian mold. But he deserves great credit for forcing everyone to pay attention to the crucial role thinkers like Hutcheson, Reid, and Hume played in shaping the mental frame for the American Revolution.

For Thomas Reid himself, the bibliography is almost, but not quite, as extensive as it is for David Hume. Perhaps the best place to begin is Knud Haakonsen's stimulating introduction to his edition of *Practical Ethics* for Princeton University Press in 1990. D. D. Todd offers another good summary of Reid's philosophy in his introduction to *The Philosophical Orators of Thomas*

Reid (Carbondale, 1989). I also found quite useful Peter J. Diamond's *Common Sense and Improvement: Thomas Reid as Social Theorist,* which is now available in paperback, and George Davie's classic study, *The Social Significance of the Scottish Philosophy of Common Sense* (Dundee, 1973).

Finally, my discussion of James Wilson relies on Mark David Hall, *The Political and Legal Philosophy of James Wilson 1742-1798* (Columia MO, 1997), and Shannon Stimson's brilliant piece, "A Jury of the Country," in the Sher and Smitten volume on Scotland and America cited above.

CHAPTER TEN: LIGHT FROM THE NORTH— SCOTS, LIBERALS, AND REFORM

The best way to learn about Edinburgh's so-called Golden Age, roughly the years from Adam Smith's death in 1790 to the Royal Visit in 1822, might be to go direct to the source. This means Henry Cockburn's *Memorials of His Time,* of which the edition by Karl Miller for the University of Chicago Press in 1974 is the most accessible; even though it is out of print, it should be available at any good library. Otherwise, Youngson's *The Making of Classical Edinburgh* is still useful for this later period in Scottish architecture and city planning, including the construction of the new university and Charlotte Square. David Daiches's *Sir Walter Scott and His World* (New York, 1971) neatly summarizes the cultural life that era, as does the section on Scotland in Paul Johnson's *The Birth of the Modern, 1815–1830* (New York, 1991)—which, unfortunately, talks exclusively about Edinburgh and neglects the other two powerhouses of new ideas and new men, Glasgow and Aberdeen.

The full story of how Scotland emerged from the Enlightenment and took over the cultural controls of Britain in the early nineteenth century has not been told before. However, Anand Chitnis in *The Scottish Enlightenment and Early Victorian English Society* (London, 1986) points out the path and the principal features on the way. Chitnis fully grasps the importance of John Millar, just as John Burrow, Stefan Collini, and Donald Winch uncover the crucial role Dugald Stewart played in shaped the early Victorian mind, in their fascinating collection of essays, *That Noble Science of Politics* (Cambridge, 1983). We are still waiting for a single definitive study or biography of Stewart. So for understanding Stewart's relationship to Thomas Reid, I looked to John Veitch's "A Memoir of Dugald Stewart," reprinted in the 1966 edition of Stewart's *Biographical Memoir of Adam Smith, William Robertson, Thomas Reid* (see Chapter Eight, above). The quotation about Stewart's appeal to the English mind comes from James McCosh in his essay on Stewart in *Scottish Philosophy* (1875), which

can be found in various reprint editions and even online (www.utm.edu/
research/iep/text/mccosh/mccosh).

Dugald Stewart languishes in a scholarly limbo. No such fate has befallen
his gifted students who founded the *Edinburgh Review*. The classic study is by
John Clive: *Scotch Reviewers: The Edinburgh Review, 1802–1815* (London, 1957).
It can be supplemented with Joanne Shattock's *Politics and Reviews: The
Edinburgh Review and the Quarterly* (Leicester, 1989) and Biancamaria Fontana's
Rethinking the Politics of Commercial Society: The Edinbugh Review (Cambridge,
1985). Several biographies of Brougham and Jeffreys exist, including Henry
Cockburn's invaluable portrait of his friend Jeffreys. I found Robert Stewart's
Henry Brougham (London, 1985) particularly useful. The quotation about the
Lothian workers cheering "Henry Brougham forever!" when they learned the
Tories were out and the Whigs were in, comes from that work.

On Thomas Macaulay, one book does the job: John Clive's *Macaulay: The
Shaping of the Historian* (New York, 1973). Macaulay's two most important parliamentary orations can be found in various collections of his essays, since these
were once considered indispensable models of English prose. Today we have no
need of Macaulay, since we have Joan Didion, or perhaps P. J. O'Rourke, so
these collections are hard to find in print; but it is still possible to spring one
loose from a used bookstore or public library.

CHAPTER ELEVEN: THE LAST MINSTREL— SIR WALTER SCOTT AND THE HIGHLAND REVIVAL

Why is there is no full-length literary biography of Sir Walter Scott, apart from
Edgar Johnson's *Sir Walter Scott: The Great Unknown,* two volumes (London,
1970), which is now more than thirty years old? One reason, without a doubt,
is that Scott remains the most underrated major author in modern literature;
this is a sad fate for an author of whom William Hazlitt said, "his worst is better than anyone else's best," and whose novels, which have been ignored by
serious critics for generations, have been turned into popular movies (witness
Ivanhoe and *Rob Roy*). So the curious reader still needs to turn to *The Journal of
Sir Walter Scott,* published in one volume in Edinburgh in 1950, and his son-in-
law James G. Lockhart's biography, *The Life of Sir Walter Scott,* which appeared
in seven volumes in 1837–8—although Lockhart himself has been savagely
attacked in a curious little book by Eric Quayle, *The Ruin of Sir Walter Scott*
(New York, 1968), who puts the blame for Scott's financial disasters later in
life squarely on Scott himself, and accuses Lockhart of covering up the facts.

Scott has also suffered from the scorn of Scottish nationalist writers because of his associations with the Royal Visit in 1822. However, Paul H. Scott's *Walter Scott and Scotland* (Edinburgh, 1981) is actually a sympathetic and deeply perceptive treatment—the reader's only wish is that it were longer. The same is true of David Daiches's *Sir Walter Scott and His World,* mentioned under Chapter 10, above. Graham McMaster's *Scott and Society* (Cambridge, 1981) gives a good overview of Scott's reliance on the Scottish historical school, including John Millar. For Scott's relations with other folklorists and collectors of Scottish heritage, including Hogg and James Wilson, the scholar turns to Jane Millgate's *Walter Scott: The Making of the Novelist* (Toronto, 1984) and Donald Carswell, *Scott and His Circle* (Garden City, N.Y., 1930).

There are by one count over nine hundred biographies of Robert Burns— just about one for every possible taste. I turned to the study by the editor of Burns's letters, James MacKay: *RB: A Biography of Robert Burns* (Edinburgh, 1992). But any biography by David Daiches is worth reading, including his *Robert Burns* (New York, 1966), and Hugh Douglas offers a new version of Burns's life in *Robert Burns: The Tinder Heart* (1999). Anything else relating to Burns studies can be found in *The Burns Encyclopedia,* edited by Maurice Lindsay in 1959, but reissued in paperback more recently in 1996. Burns's poems, of course, are available nearly everywhere, including in the heads of most literary-minded Scotsmen.

The best book on James McPherson is by Fiona Stafford, *The Sublime Savage: A Study of James McPherson and the Poems of Ossian* (Edinburgh, 1988), who also wrote the introduction to the best modern edition of *The Poems of Ossian,* edited by Howard Gaskill for the Edinburgh University Press and available since 1996 in paperback.

John Prebble told the harrowing story of the Highland Clearances in his book of that title in 1963, but it needs to be balanced with Thomas Devine's *Clanship to Crofters' War* (Manchester, 1994). Also useful is Alexander MacKenzie's *History of the Highland Clearances,* which first appeared in 1883 but which has been reissued by Mercat Press in Edinburgh; it contains Donald MacLeod's description of the clearing of Strathnaver in Sutherland quoted in this chapter. James Robertson's biography of David Stewart, *The First Highlander: Major-General David Stewart of Garth* (Edinburgh, 1998), is not only informative about his career and writings, but also has a detailed description of his role in the Royal Visit—which the reader can supplement with John Prebble's *The King's Jaunt.* Books on the "invention" of Highland traditions and Scottish identity abound, and even on the "invention" of the Highlands them-selves (meaning the construction of an ideological myth surrounding them)—

anyone curious on the subject can find a author to match his own opinions and feelings, which usually range from mild amusement to outrage. I think Robert Clyde's *From Rebel to Hero: The Image of the Highlander* (see Chapter Five, above) does as well as any other, but it is safe to say that no one has had the last word on this tendentious and volatile issue.

CHAPTER TWELVE: PRACTICAL MATTERS— SCOTS IN SCIENCE AND INDUSTRY

My sources for this and the next two chapters are so many and various as to defy adequate summary. So I will limit myself to pointing out where certain quotations and facts came from, and what books are particularly useful for the discriminating reader.

I have relied on two sturdy classics on James Watt: John Lord's *Capital and Steam Power,* first published in 1923 and reprinted in a second edition in 1965, and Thomas Marshall's 1925 biography. The discussion about the relations between Glasgow professors and local industrial entrepreneurs is from David Daiches's essay in *Hotbed of Genius,* which also has a valuable article on James Hutton. The starting point for any discussion of the roots and impact of Scottish medicine is David Hamilton's *The Healers: A History of Medicine in Scotland* (Edinburgh, 1981). For Boerhaave and his students, the standard work is G. A. Lindeboom's *Hermann Boerhaave: The Man and His Work* (London, 1968). The background to the relationship between medicine and science is carefully delineated in A. L. Donovan's *Philosophical Chemistry in the Scottish Enlightenment* (Edinburgh, 1975).

The Hunter brothers are the subjects of several, not always accessible, biographies. I found Charles Ilingworth's *The Story of William Hunter* (Edinburgh, 1967) still useful, along with George Quist's *John Hunter, 1728–1793* (London, 1981); the best most recent piece is Roy Porter's lovely essay on William Hunter in Richard Sher's edited volume, *The Glasgow Enlightenment* (Edinburgh, 1995). The role of Scottish doctors in the development of public health policy in Manchester and elsewhere is set out in Anand Chitnis's *Scottish Enlightenment and Early Victorian English Society.*

For a good overview of the transportation revolution in Scotland and Britain, see A.R.B. Haldane's *New Ways Through the Glens: Highland Road, Bridge, and Canal Makers in the Early Nineteenth Century* (London, 1962). Of the biographies of James Macadam, I like W. J. Reader's *Macadam: The Macadam Family and the Turnpike Roads* (London, 1980) best. Thomas Telford is the subject of a very recent biography by Anthony Burton (London, 2000), but I have relied more on Derrick Beckett's *Telford's Britain* (Newton Abbot, 1987). There is also a stimulating account of Telford at work in Paul Johnson's *Birth of the Modern* (mentioned under Chapter Ten, above). On Henry Bell and the steamship, see Brian Osborne's *The Ingenious Mr. Bell* (Argyll, 1995). Samuel Smiles's *Self-Help* can be found in various editions, but his *Lives of the Engineers* deserves almost as much attention and was helpful for writing this chapter. Smiles should have his own biographical treatment; unfortunately, most authors who deal with him are so dismissive or condescending that their books have only passing value.

Finally, another study of Scottish engineers should not be missed: that of Robert Louis Stevenson's family and their construction of lighthouses, described in delightful detail by Bella Bathurst in *The Lighthouse Stevensons* (New York, 1999).

CHAPTER THIRTEEN: THE SUN NEVER SETS— SCOTS AND THE BRITISH EMPIRE

I first saw the quotation from Robert Louis Stevenson in Ian MacLeod's *The Scots* and have not hesitated to borrow it here. The overseas Scots diaspora is a large and complex subject. The best place to start might be Thomas Devine's chapter on emigration in *The Scottish Nation* and the collection of essays in R.A. Cage's edited volume, *The Scots Abroad, 1750–1914* (London, 1985). Also worth reading is Gordon Donaldson's *The Scots Overseas* (Westport, CT, 1976).

Duncan Bruce's *The Mark of the Scots* has a section on Scots and the British Empire; James Morris's *Heaven's Command: An Imperial Progress* (London, 1973) is an entertaining survey of the British Empire at its height, even though it says nothing particularly about Scots—except for a wry and witty essay on Charles Napier, which I have quoted in this chapter.

Paul Johnson discusses Charles Pasley in *The Birth of the Nation;* Pasley's *Military Policy and Institutions of the British Empire* went into successive editions: I used the fourth, published in London toward the end of the Napoleonic wars in 1813. There is an abridged edition of Mill's *History of British India* from the University of Chicago Press, edited by William Thomas in 1975, which can be found in some used bookstores. More accessible is the Cambridge University Press selection of *Political Works* by James Mill. Suresh Chandra Gosh's *Dalhousie in India: 1848–56* (New Delhi, 1973) gives a fascinating summary of Dalhousie's attempts to raise the quality of life for India's women.

The story of the *Nemesis* and its role in the First Opium War comes from Daniel Headrick's *Tools of Empire: Technology and European Imperialism in the Nineteenth Century* (Oxford, 1981), which also summarizes the impact of the breech-loading rifle and its percussion cap. On the Jardine-Matheson partnership, see Robert Blake's entertaining *Jardine Matheson: A History* (London, 1999). For Scots in Canada, there is Stanford Reid, *The Scottish Tradition in Canada* (Guelph, 1976). The account of the Orcadians' role in the Hudson's Bay Company is from Peter Newman's *Company of Adventurers* (New York, 1985); the description of George Simpson is from Bartlett Brebner's *Canada: A Modern History* (Anne Arbor, 1960). John Kenneth Galbraith's *The Scotch* (second edition, Boston, 1985) is a charming and astute portrait of the Scottish legacy in Canada. The quotations about Glengarry come from James Hunter's *A Dance Called America: The Scottish Highlands in the United States and Canada* (Edinburgh, 1994), which was helpful for this chapter and the one that follows. There is a new biography of Sandford Fleming by Clark Blaise, *Time Lord: Sandford Fleming and the Creation of Standard Time* (New York, 2001).

For Lachlan Macquarie, see Robert Hughes's fascinating *The Fatal Shore* (New York, 1987). I relied heavily on George Seaver's *David Livingstone: His Life and Letters* (New York, 1957) for my portrait of Dr. Livingstone. In this multicultural age, some biographers try to debunk the Livingstone legend, but even Judith Listowel in *The Other Livingstone* (1974) can only criticize him for claiming to find some places when others deserve some of the credit. Dorothy Helly's *Livingstone's Legacy* (Athens, OH, 1987) ends up vindicating Livingstone's progressive racial views.

CHAPTER FOURTEEN: SELF-MADE MEN— SCOTS IN THE UNITED STATES

In addition to the works by Duncan Bruce and George Black already mentioned (for Chapter Nine, above), I think the best guide to understanding the Scottish contribution to the United States is Bernard Aspinwall's *Portable Utopia: Glasgow and the United States, 1820–1920* (Aberdeen, 1984) and his tightly packed article "The Scots in the United States" in R.E. Cage's volume mentioned for the previous chapter. The numbers for immigration to the United States come from Gordon Donaldson's *The Scots Overseas,* also mentioned above.

Douglas Sloan gives a solid account of the Scottish contributions to American education in *The Scottish Enlightenment and the American College Ideal* (New York, 1971), which can be supplemented with David Hoeveler's *James McCosh and the Scottish Intellectual Tradition* (Princeton, 1981). George Jardine deserves his own biography: nineteenth-century copies of *Outlines of*

Philosophical Education abound, which is itself significant, but Jardine himself remains largely ignored, even in Sloan's otherwise fine work.

My account of Scots in California owes a large debt to Kevin Starr's *America and the California Dream* (Oxford, 1973) and Susanna Bryant Dakin's *A Scotch Paisano: Hugo Reid's Life in California, 1832–1852* (Berkeley, CA, 1939). On William Taylor, see John Paul's *The Soul Digger or The Life and Times of William Taylor* (1928). I used S. I. Prinne's *The Life of Samuel F.B. Morse, LL.D.* (New York, 1875) to trace Morse's Scottish and Scotch-Irish lineage, and Robert Bruce's *Bell: Alexander Graham Bell and the Conquest of Solitude* (Boston, 1973) for the life of the inventor of the telephone. Bell's role in the making of Langley's airplane is summarized in Duncan Bruce's notice on Bell in *The Scottish One Hundred;* other details can still be gleaned from the exhibit at the Smithsonian's Air and Space Museum.

Unlike his colleagues John D. Rockefeller and J. P. Morgan, Andrew Carnegie still has not found an author able to turn his life into a bestseller. So I have relied on an older biographer, Joseph Frazier Wall, and his *Andrew Carnegie* (New York, 1970) and Harold Livesay's concise and brilliant *Andrew Carnegie and the Rise of Big Business,* both of which can be found in paperback. But the reader curious about Carnegie does not need to stop there; his *Autobiography,* available in many modern editions, is not only a mine of information, it is charmingly written, especially the sections on Scotland.

CONCLUSION

The scholar I quote on the grim conditions of everyday life in late nineteenth-century Scotland is C.W. Hill in his *Edwardian Scotland* (1976). However, better and more detailed accounts of Scotland in those years exist, including the later chapters of Thomas Devine's *The Scottish Nation* and I.G.C. Hutchison's *Scottish Politics in the Nineteenth Century* (London, 2001). David Daiches's *Scotch Whisky: Its Past and Present* (Glasgow, 1976) is the perfect guide to understanding the swift rise and then decline of the Scottish distilling industry in the nineteenth century. For trying to understand James Bond, I always turn to Kingsley Amis's *The James Bond Dossier* (London, 1967), which is sadly out of print.

Pat Gerber gives the best most recent account of the *Lia Fail* in her *Stone of Destiny* (Edinburgh, 1997), which bravely attempts to sort out the fact from the fiction surrounding the many versions of the stone's origins and travels. Kay Matheson's eyewitness account of the 1950 heist comes from that book, as does the quotation from Ian Hamilton when the stone was returned to

Scotland. Books on Scottish nationalism and the future of Scotland under devolution grow thick on the bookshelves with each passing month: however, I think Keith Webb in *The Growth of Nationalism in Scotland* (Glasgow, 1977) gives the best and most balanced account of the movement's origins and links to mainstream politics. The fact that in 1977 neither Webb nor anyone else knew where the Scottish Nationalist Party would finally end up gives the book, oddly enough, a kind of detached perspective more recent and more enthusiastic accounts do not. Colin Kidd's *Subverting Scotland's Past: Scottish Whig Historians and the Creation of an Anglo-British Identity* (Cambridge, 1993) is actually a more balanced book than the title implies: it reveals the tension between the Enlightenment's desire to establish a modern identity for Scots as well as Britons, and the traditionalists' pride in Scotland's past, including the Declaration of Arbroath. For those who want a more nationalist-driven view of these matters, there is always William Ferguson's *The Identity of the Scottish Nation* (Edinburgh, 1988). One can only hope this debate will finally end on a less angry note.

Acknowledgments

S pace will not permit me to give proper thanks to every person and institution who helped me, through wise words or generous gesture, to complete the book. But here they are: the Mitchell Library in Glasgow, the National Library of Scotland in Edinburgh, the Folger Shakespeare Library, the Library of Congress, the Lauinger Library at Georgetown University, the Fenwick Library at George Mason University, the Evergreen Society at the Johns Hopkins University; Adam Bellow, John Billings, Daniel Boorstin, Jennifer Bradshaw, Lillian Brown, Faye Dale Browning, John Barclay Burns, Jack Censer, Jan Cleaver, Deborah Gomez, Ian Hazlett, Lynn Hopffgarten, Peter Klepper, Nick Lyons, Angus MacDonald, Robert Matheson, Jerry Z. Muller, Marvin Murray, Nick Phillipson, J.G.A. Pocock, Richard Sher, Mark Seiler, Caroline Sincerbeaux, Robert Vey, David Wooton, and Fred Warshofsky.

Paul Koda listened patiently to my original plans for this project, offered his usual sensible advice, and has remained an enthusiastic ally right up to the end. My learned friend Charles T. Matheson read an early version of the entire manuscript. My parents Arthur and Barbara Herman cast their expert critical eyes over the final manuscript and the galleys. Special thanks also go to Peter J. Diamond of New York University, Bruce Lenman of St. Andrews University, and Will Hay of the Foreign Policy Research Institute. They read versions of separate chapters and, bringing all their skill and erudition to bear, agreed with some points, argued with others, and corrected errors throughout. Any errors left are entirely my own doing.

In addition, there are six people without whom this book would not exist. Lloyd John Ogilvie, Chaplain of the United States Senate, offered counsel and inspiration from start to finish. Lynn Chu and Glen Hartley proved, as always, that they are intellectual partners as well as literary agents. The enthusiastic support of my original editor at Crown, Bob Mecoy, made writing the book both a pleasure and a personal journey. Emily Loose took over in mid-race, and with her brilliant and efficient editing, guided the book across the finish line.

My wife, Beth, gave me her advice and insight over the five years this project was in gestation. The final result is lovingly dedicated to her.

Index